Criminal Law

Criminal Law
Fifth edition

Tony Storey
and
Alan Lidbury

WILLAN
PUBLISHING

Published by:

Willan Publishing
Culmcott House
Mill Street, Uffculme
Cullompton, Devon
EX15 3AT, UK
Tel: +44(0)1884 840337
Fax: +44(0)184 840251
e-mail: info@willanpublishing.co.uk
website: www.willanpublishing.co.uk

Published simultaneously in the USA and Canada by:

Willan Publishing
c/o ISBS, 920 NE 58th Ave, Suite 300,
Portland, Oregon 97213-3786, USA
Tel: +001(0)503 287 3093
Fax: +001(0)503 280 8832
e-mail: info@isbs.com
website: www.isbs.com

First edition published 2001
Second edition 2002
Third edition 2004
Fourth edition 2007
Fifth edition 2009

ISBN 978-1-84392-696-2

British Library Cataloguing-in-Publication Data
A catalogue record for this book is available from the British Library

FSC
Mixed Sources
Product group from well-managed
forests and other controlled sources

Cert no. SGS-COC-2482
www.fsc.org
© 1996 Forest Stewardship Council

Project managed by Deer Park Productions, Tavistock, Devon
Typeset by TW Typesetting, Plymouth, Devon
Printed and bound by T.J. International Ltd, Padstow, Cornwall

Contents

Part 4 Offences against property

Part 5 Defences

Part 7 Studying criminal law

Publisher's acknowledgements

We are indebted to OCR (Oxford, Cambridge and RSA Examinations) for permission to reproduce questions and other material from past examination papers and specimen papers.

Advice on possible answers to questions reproduced in this book are provided by the author, and have not been provided or approved by the boards.

Crown copyright material is reproduced with the permission of the Controller of Her Majesty's Stationery Office.

Table of cases

Table of statutes

Introduction

The purpose of this book is to provide a comprehensive review of the general principles of criminal law. It also examines some of the more common offences and the defences that may be available to the accused. It is written mainly for A-level students but will also be a valuable resource for others taking professional examinations at this level, or for undergraduates who are looking for a clear and detailed introduction to criminal law.

For those embarking upon a college or sixth form course, a new approach was adopted to studies at A-level from 2000. This new approach was designed to encourage flexibility and breadth at 16–18 and offers the student the opportunity to take four or more AS (Advanced Subsidiary) level subjects during their first year and to then choose at least three A2 (full A-level) subjects during their second year. The detailed study of criminal law normally forms part of the second year of these studies (A2) and follows an initial study of the general principles of English law which will have introduced the student to the personnel and structures of the English legal system. The Qualifications and Curriculum Authority (QCA) has required all the examination Boards to revise the current six-unit structure of the GCE A-level in order to replace it with a new suite of four units. The intention is to reduce some of the assessment burden and to make it logistically and administratively simpler. The standard remains unaltered. Oxford, Cambridge and RSA Examinations (OCR) has been the first of the national exam boards that offer law to implement these changes, and teaching on the new AS qualification began in September 2008. Teaching on the A2 criminal law option begins in September 2009.

Chapters at the end of the book deal with some of the key features that were introduced under Curriculum 2000 (and which have been retained in the new four-unit objectives) including advice and guidance on synoptic assessment and key skills, as well as a chapter that reminds the student that the principles of criminal law must be studied in context and not in isolation. In addition, the source materials intended for use by OCR as the basis for the synoptic assessment Paper G154 in the examinations for January and June 2010 are fully reproduced. Students are strongly recommended to familiarise themselves with these requirements from the start of their course.

One welcome change has been the reintegration of the subject matter of the specification into one unit G153. This enables a more coherent study of criminal law to be undertaken and creates the possibility of combining problem questions with offences and defences from any part of the specification. Another key development much welcomed by QCA has been the introduction of a new Section C into the Criminal Law Paper. This consists of two short scenarios. Candidates may choose to answer either one of them. The scenarios are followed by a series of four statements or propositions to which the candidate is asked to respond by evaluating the truth or accuracy of each statement. This is essentially a skills-based task requiring identification and application of legal rules rather than the recall of detailed knowledge. Examples of these types of questions are given at the end of the book following the 'Answers Guide'.

As you encounter the various Acts of Parliament and cases that have shaped the rules and principles of law they may at first seem rather like random pieces of a jigsaw. The clear picture is revealed only after some time when the pieces fall into place. This is natural and you should not be put off at the outset by the occasional Latin expression or unfamiliar word.

Indeed, one of the first things the aspiring law student has to grasp is a precise command of words. This is nothing new. Every new student for generations has had to do the same. The sooner you are prepared to open your mind to some new terminology, and to understand how and why it has become an important element in the peculiar vocabulary of law, the quicker you will be prepared to address the more important issues which make the study of criminal law so fascinating and attractive. It will become apparent that this special terminology represents the distilled wisdom of Parliament, the courts and academics over a long period. All have played their part in developing the principles of criminal law.

In turn, anyone who studies criminal law will also become familiar with the particular elements that must be established if a successful conviction is to be obtained in an English court of law. They will learn that these elements are no whimsical factors dreamt up on the spur of the moment in the courtroom, but have instead been evolved after careful consideration by judges in previous cases. These are rules and principles of common law, forged and tested over time. The offence of murder is the prime example of a crime which has developed in this way.

Alternatively, the criminal lawyer may encounter, in a new Act, the challenge of fresh concepts and offences devised by Parliament after proper debate and consultation. These may sweep away old rules and replace them with new ones overnight. Such is the authority of the sovereignty of Parliament in our democracy.

However, the beauty and frustration of law is that very often there may be no certain agreement about what the law on a particular topic actually says. Even when an Act of Parliament may appear to be clear and unambiguous, it will require further interpretation by judges before it can be applied with certainty and confidence. This may help to explain why there are so many legal disputes and appeals. If the law were always crystal clear there would be rather less opportunity for professional and academic lawyers to make a living by arguing about it.

For the student this uncertainty need not be a source of worry since very often extremely learned judges in the same court do not agree with each other. From the examiner's point of view it enables questions to be set which allow the student to demonstrate their awareness of these rather 'grey' areas of uncertainty.

Equally, it must be remembered that the adversarial nature of criminal trials typify the essence of the English legal system. Under our system a person accused of a crime is presumed innocent until proven guilty by the prosecution, and the burden of proving that guilt rests upon the Crown Prosecution Service which acts on behalf of the state. An accused still has a right to remain silent but normally chooses, through his or her legal representatives, to put forward a defence. Therefore, the student of criminal law must be able to see the possibilities that may exist for both sides of the argument. What offences may a person have committed and what defences may be available to them?

In recent times, the introduction of the Human Rights Act 1998 was widely predicted to have significant consequences for some aspects of criminal law. At the time of writing, however, the major impact of the Act has been seen in procedural and evidential matters associated with the Right to a Fair Trial under Article 6 of the European Convention on Human Rights or, for example, the recent declaration that it is unlawful for the Home Secretary to determine the length of time for which those sentenced to life imprisonment for murder may be detained in prison.

Article 6: right to a fair trial

In *Bianco* (2001), the Court of Appeal held that denial of the defence of duress (see Chapter 18) through lack of evidence was not in breach of Article 6. D had been charged with importing heroin. His defence was that threats had been made to him some three months prior to the smuggling trip. The trial judge decided – rightly in the opinion of the appeal court – that there was insufficient evidence to justify putting the defence to the jury, who convicted. This case is extremely important – it shows that the Court of Appeal is not going to be easily persuaded to allow unmeritorious appeals just because of the Human Rights Act 1998.

In *L v DPP* (2002), the High Court was asked whether a 'reversed' onus of proof was contrary to Article 6. A reversed onus of proof requires the defence to actually prove something, usually a defence, as opposed to just raising evidence of it and then requiring the prosecution to disprove it. D appeared before a district judge charged with possession of an offensive weapon (a lock-knife) contrary to s.139 of the Criminal Justice Act 1988 (CJA). The Act allows a defence, that D had the weapon with him for 'good reason' or with 'lawful authority', but the onus of proof is on the defendant, albeit on the balance of probabilities. D was convicted and appealed that the reversed onus of proof was contrary to Article 6. However, the High Court dismissed his appeal. Parliament was entitled to introduce legislation such as the CJA placing the onus on the defence, in order to deter persons from carrying bladed or sharply pointed articles, without infringing the European Convention. Another justification was that D was proving something (his 'good reason' for having the lock-knife) that was within his own knowledge.

In the context of this book, a reversed onus of proof appears twice: in the defence of diminished responsibility (Chapter 6) and the defence of insanity (Chapter 15). The decision in *L v DPP* strongly suggests that the reversed onus of proof in those defences will survive any attack made upon them based on Article 6, because they also involve D proving something (the condition of his own mind) that is within his own knowledge.

In *Misra v Srivastava* (2004), a case involving gross negligence manslaughter, the Court of Appeal ruled that the law relating to the controversial offence of gross negligence manslaughter was sufficiently well defined in English law. It did not therefore offend against Article 7 of the European Convention on Human Rights in terms of the circularity involved in requiring a jury to consider whether conduct is so 'gross' as to amount to a crime.

It remains to be seen whether there will eventually be any notable influence on substantive criminal law, for example, the debate over euthanasia. Nevertheless, students are encouraged to keep themselves abreast of developments that may emerge under the Act.

Having read the book you should not only have gained an appreciation and understanding of the principles of criminal law but also have acquired the necessary knowledge and skills to succeed in your examination. The authors hope that you will also have been encouraged to take your studies further following this introduction to a fascinating and challenging branch of English law.

How to use this book

This book is written primarily for A-level students who are studying Criminal Law as an option choice during their A2 studies. It can be used by students studying alone or under the guidance of a teacher or tutor. It aims to be both clear and concise with regard to the relevant law as well as providing useful information, advice and examples of examination questions and suggested answers to them, thus enabling the self-study student the opportunity to assess and correct their own work.

The main layout of the book is described in the opening Contents section and there is an alphabetical index of key words at the end of the book. It is important for law students to familiarise themselves with the particular features of a legal text as well as using these obvious ones.

The special features of any worthwhile law textbook include a Table of Cases and a Table of Statutes. The Table of Cases is set out in alphabetical order according to the names of the parties involved. As time goes by and you become aware of the names of cases it is a useful tool in order to quickly find the page or pages which discuss or refer to the case. Only major cases which have gone to appeal are officially reported although the growth of the internet and the increase in the number of databases mean that nowadays it is possible to gain access to many 'unreported' cases as well. Each case has an official citation giving details of the original source where the case has been reported, for example *Jones* [1990] 3 All ER 886. It is usually the name of the defendant on its own that is cited in a criminal case even though the full citation would be either *R v Jones or Jones v R* depending upon which party had made the appeal that is being reported. 'R' is short for *Regina* or *Rex*, the Latin for Queen or King on the throne at the time of the prosecution. Prosecutors often use the phrase 'the Crown against Jones'. The citation is then followed in italicised numerals by the page number or numbers showing where the case is mentioned in the text so, in our example, *Jones* [1990] 3 All ER *320, 322, 323*. This makes it easier to cross reference a case that has significance in different parts of the book and you should always check this. The year inside the square brackets refers to the year in which the case report was published and not necessarily the year in which the original trial was held. Indeed it could be some years after the incident giving rise to the facts of the case.

In addition, significant cases are explained in detail in the text by detailed summaries of their facts and usually, but not exclusively, appear within grey shaded boxes. It is appreciated that it is not practical for students at Advanced level to spend a great deal of money on an additional casebook which many would find daunting and inaccessible because of the precise and often convoluted language used by judges in delivering their judgments. Nevertheless, knowledge of the facts nearly always aids a truer understanding of the principles developed in any given case, hence their inclusion. Students would not normally be required to recite the facts of cases in the examination room but a brief sentence or two may be appropriate in the context of a question or answer.

Statutes or Acts of Parliament are listed alphabetically under the Table of Statutes section at the front of the book. Detailed knowledge is required of only a few sections of some statutes e.g. ss.1–9 Theft Act 1968, ss.47, 20 and 18 Offences Against the Person Act 1861, ss.2 and 3 Homicide Act 1957 and s.1 Criminal Attempts Act 1981. Others are important, however; for example, in connection with strict liability where the modern law is almost entirely derived from statute.

Two further features of the book are as follows:

- Within the text there are boxed questions asking students to consider a variety of moral, ethical and social issues associated with the operation of the criminal law. These provide reminders to think about these kinds of issues, and to consider the way in which justice is achieved within the broad context of the society within which we live. These are designed to encourage consideration of evaluation or the development of problem-solving skills which are central to the attainment of AO2 marks. AO2 refers to evaluation, discussion, criticism, consideration or analysis in essay questions and to identifying the relevant law and applying it in problem questions. This may become an increasingly important expectation in the near future when all A level specifications must be capable of offering candidates the opportunity to demonstrate 'stretch and challenge' in their work.
- Examination questions are set at the end of each Part. These relate predominantly to the subject matter of that particular Part and are taken from recent OCR papers. Answer guidelines to questions are provided at the end of the book so that students and teachers have the opportunity to test their knowledge against the expectations of the authors, who are both experienced examiners.

The fifth edition is fully updated and reflects the changes to the specification to be examined for the first time in January 2010. The law is stated as the authors believe it to be on 1 May 2009.

Part 1

General principles 1

1 *Actus reus* and *mens rea*

Introduction

The convicted criminal is the object of loathing and fascination in almost equal measure – an outcast, a person with few friends. The hardened, dangerous criminal is liable to be punished by imprisonment or fine. His or her prospects of obtaining or retaining employment and returning to a normal life in society are, in many cases, severely damaged.

So what is it that leads to a criminal conviction? A great deal of detection work? Often, yes. The careful unravelling of clues and evidence that will stand up to careful scrutiny and cross-examination in court? Normally, yes.

Yet it is more than this. It is up to the prosecution (the State, represented by the Crown Prosecution Service) to prove that an accused is guilty (the burden of proof). It involves a court being satisfied that the accused is guilty beyond a reasonable doubt (the standard of proof) following a due process of law. An accused is entitled to a fair trial upon consideration of the relevant facts and the law that relate to their case. A person cannot be convicted upon suspicion alone. Generations of criminal law students have become familiar with the Latin maxim, '*actus non facit reum nisi mens sit rea*'. Do not be afraid of the fact that you 'haven't got the Latin'! Loosely translated, this phrase means that in English law a person cannot be convicted merely upon proof of the fact that they have committed the crime in question (the *actus reus*). It must be established by the prosecution that they also had an accompanying guilty mind (the *mens rea*). The significance of this phrase or maxim is that great importance is attached to the mind of the accused at the time of the offence when determining his or her liability. Therefore, in theory at least, the innocent person is protected from false conviction. Throughout this book a shorthand is used in order to describe the accused person, or defendant, as 'D', while the victim of the defendant's crime is referred to as 'V'.

Actus reus

As stated above, the 'doing part' of any crime is referred to as the *actus reus*. *Actus reus* means the physical elements of the crime. It includes some or all of the following:

- Conduct

- Consequences

- Circumstances

In murder, for example, the *actus reus* could be described as causing the death of another human being under the Queen's Peace. Thus, to be guilty of murder, the defendant (D) must:

- Cause death (this is a consequence)

- Of another human being (this is a circumstance)

- Under the Queen's Peace (this is another circumstance)

In theft, to take another example, the *actus reus* is to appropriate property belonging to another. Thus, to be guilty of theft, D must:

- Appropriate (this is conduct)

- Property (this is a circumstance)

- Belonging to another (this is another circumstance)

You will note that in murder (see Chapter 5) there is no specific conduct requirement, merely that death is caused by the accused. This means that D could (though it is unusual) commit murder by *doing nothing.* Liability for doing nothing will be considered in Chapter 2. In theft, on the other hand, there is no specific consequence required. That is, D does not have to escape with property in order to be guilty; he simply has to 'appropriate' it (this means to assume a right of ownership).

If any one of the *actus reus* elements of a crime are not proven against D, then he cannot be guilty of that offence. D may well cause the death of another human being – but if it was committed during wartime, it would not be 'under the Queen's Peace' and one of the elements of the *actus reus* of murder would be missing. Therefore, D would not be liable. This does not necessarily mean that D will escape liability altogether. There may be other crimes that he has committed. Suppose D administers a slow-acting poison to V, and V drinks it, but V – coincidentally – drops dead of a heart attack before the poison can take effect. D has tried to commit murder, but he has not done so – he did not 'cause death'. In this case, D is not guilty of murder, but he would be convicted of attempted murder instead. This is, in fact, exactly what happened in *White* (1910).

Causation

As indicated above, to be guilty of murder, D must 'cause death'. This is an example of one aspect of the *actus reus*, 'causation'. Causation must be established for nearly all offences but it so happens that the crime of murder provides the best illustrations of the operation of the principles involved. Whether D's acts or omissions actually caused V's death is always for the jury to decide. The judge should direct them as to the elements of causation, but it is for them to decide if the causal link between D's act and the prohibited consequence has been established. Usually it will be sufficient to direct the jury 'simply that in law the accused's act need not be the sole cause, or even the main cause, of the victim's death, it being enough that his act contributed significantly to that result' (*Pagett* [1983]).

When a problem arises, as occasionally happens, then it is for the judge to direct the jury in accordance with the legal principles which they have to apply. There are two main principles. D may be convicted of murder, for example, only if the jury is satisfied that D's conduct was both:

- a factual cause; and

- a legal cause

of V's death.

Factual causation

D's conduct must be a *factual cause* of the prohibited consequence. This is commonly applied using the *'but for'* test. In other words it must be established that the consequence would not have occurred as and when it did but for D's conduct. If the consequence would have happened anyway, there is no liability (*White* [1910]).

White (1910)
White put potassium cyanide into his mother's drink with intent to kill her, in order to gain under her Will. Later his mother was found dead, sitting on the sofa at her home in Coventry, with the glass full of the poisoned drink beside her. However, medical evidence established that she had died of a heart attack, not poisoning. In any event, White had not used enough cyanide for a fatal dose. White was acquitted of murder: he had not, in fact, caused her death. (But he was convicted of attempt.)

The mere establishment of a factual connection between D's act and V's death is insufficient. Suppose D invites V to his house for a party. On the way V is run over and killed. Clearly if D had not invited V he would not have died in those circumstances, but (quite apart from lack of *mens rea*) there is no *actus reus*. The missing element is legal causation.

Legal causation

This is closely associated with moral responsibility. The question is whether the result can fairly be said to be the fault of D. In *Dalloway* (1847), D was driving a horse and cart without holding the reins when a child ran in front of the cart, and was run over and killed. D was charged with manslaughter, but was acquitted as the jury believed that D could have done nothing even if holding the reins. Thus, although the child was killed by D's cart, which was being driven negligently, the death would have happened in exactly the same way if he had been driving with all due care.

Application of this principle was recently seen in *Marchant and Muntz* (2004), a case of causing death by dangerous driving.

> *Marchant and Muntz* (2004)
> Edward Muntz, a Warwickshire farmer, owned a *Matbro TR250* loading machine, an agricultural vehicle with a grab attached at the front for lifting and moving large hay bales. The grab consisted of nine spikes (called tynes), each 1 metre in length. Muntz gave instructions to an employee, Tom Marchant, to take the vehicle onto a public road to deliver some hay bales. Marchant stopped, waiting to make a turn onto a farm track when Richard Fletcher, a motorcyclist, approached at high speed (estimated at 80mph) from the opposite direction, collided with the vehicle and was impaled on one of the tynes. He suffered 'catastrophic' injuries and died. Muntz and Marchant were convicted, respectively, of causing death by dangerous driving and procuring the offence, but the Court of Appeal quashed their convictions. Expert evidence at trial indicated that the tyne could have been 'covered by some sort of guard' but Grigson J concluded that 'even had such a guard been in place, it would not have prevented the collision. The consequences to anyone striking a tyne *or the guard* at speed would have been very severe, if not fatal' (emphasis added). In other words, Marchant had not caused V's death (and Muntz had not procured it).

It is often said that D's act must be a 'substantial' cause of death; this probably states the case too favourably for D. It is sufficient that D's act makes a *more than minimal contribution*. In *Kimsey* (1996), D and a female friend had been involved in a high-speed car chase. Tragically, she lost control of her car at high speed and was killed. It was not absolutely clear what had happened prior to the car going out of control. The Crown case was that it was D's driving which had led her to lose control. The trial judge told the jury that they did not have to be sure that D's driving 'was the principal, or a substantial cause of the death, as long as you are sure that it was a cause and that there was something more than a slight or trifling link'. On appeal, it was argued that it was wrong to say that his driving did not have to be a 'substantial cause'. The Court of Appeal dismissed the appeal; reference to 'substantial cause' was not necessary. Reference to 'more than a slight or trifling link' was perfectly acceptable.

The acceleration principle

D's act will be considered a cause if it has accelerated V's death. It is no defence to say that V was dying of a fatal disease anyway. In *Adams* (1957), D was a doctor charged with the murder of one of his patients, who was terminally ill, by means of an overdose of pain-killers. Devlin J directed the jury that it did not matter that V's days were numbered: 'If her life were cut short by weeks or months it was just as much murder as if it was cut short by years.'

Contributory causes

It is therefore clear that D's act need neither be the sole, nor even the main cause of death. It is sufficient if it is a cause. Other causes may be:

- the actions of third parties, or

- actions of V herself.

Actions of third parties

Suppose D poisons V with a fatal dose but, before she dies E, an escaped lunatic, comes along and stabs her through the heart – then D will not be liable for her death (though he would certainly be liable for an attempt (as in *White*, above). Here, E's act was the sole cause of death. But what is the case where the third party's actions are not quite so unpredictable? The courts tend to take the view that it is only in extreme circumstances that D can avoid liability for causing someone's death by trying to blame someone else. The following case illustrates this:

Pagett (1983)
In this case, several police officers were trying to arrest D for various serious offences. He was hiding in his first-floor flat with his pregnant girlfriend, Gail Kinchen. D armed himself with a shotgun and, against her will, used Gail's body to shield himself as he tried to escape. He fired at two officers, who returned fire; three bullets

fired by the officers hit and killed Gail. D was convicted of manslaughter; the Court of Appeal dismissed his appeal. In this case it was said that it was reasonably foreseeable that the police would return fire either in self-defence or in the lawful exercise of their duty.

1. What was the immediate factual cause of death in *Pagett*?
2. Why did the Court of Appeal uphold Pagett's conviction?

Medical treatment

The majority of cases in the area of legal causation involve medical treatment. Where D inflicts an injury on V, typically with a knife or a bullet, which requires medical treatment, will D be held liable for murder or manslaughter if that treatment is improper, or even negligent, such that V eventually dies? The answer, generally speaking, is yes. In *Smith* (1959), Lord Parker CJ said:

> If at the time of death the original wound is still an operating cause and a substantial cause, then the death can properly be said to be the result of the wound, albeit that some other cause of death is also operating. Only if it can be said that the original wounding is merely the setting in which another cause operates can it be said that the death did not result from the wound. Putting it another way, only if the second cause is so overwhelming as to make the original wound merely part of the history can it be said that the death does not flow from the wound.

Smith (1959)

Thomas Smith was a soldier stationed in Germany. He stabbed David Creed, a soldier in another regiment, twice with a bayonet during the course of a barrack-room fight. Another soldier carrying C to the medical station twice dropped him. The medical staff were under pressure as two others had been injured in the fight, and did not treat him for 45 minutes. As C had been stabbed in the back, they did not immediately realise that one of the wounds had pierced a lung, causing a haemorrhage. Consequently, they gave C treatment which, in the light of this, was described in court as 'thoroughly bad and might well have affected his chances of recovery'. C died, and S was convicted of murder at a court martial in Germany. The Courts Martial Appeal Court dismissed the appeal – the original stab wound was still 'operating' and 'substantial' at the time of death.

A more recent case has shifted the focus slightly, away from the question of whether the wound was still 'operating' to a broader question of whether the death can be attributed to the acts of D. In *Cheshire* (1991), Beldam LJ said that, 'Treatment which falls short of the standard expected of the competent medical practitioner is unfortunately only too frequent in human experience'. Beldam LJ went on to provide a direction that juries should be given in cases involving alleged medical negligence:

It is sufficient for the judge to tell the jury that they must be satisfied that the Crown have proved that the acts of [D] need not be the sole cause or even the main cause of death, it being sufficient that his acts contributed significantly to that result. Even though negligence in the treatment of [V] was the immediate cause of his death, the jury should not regard it as excluding the responsibility of [D] unless the negligent treatment was so independent of his acts, and in itself so potent in causing death, that they regard the contribution made by his acts as insignificant.

Cheshire (1991)
On 9 December, David Cheshire and Trevor Jeffrey were in a fish and chip shop. They got into an argument, and Cheshire produced a handgun. Jeffrey was shot in the stomach. In hospital, he underwent major bowel surgery. This was successful but respiratory problems then ensued, necessitating a tracheotomy (the insertion of a breathing tube into the neck). By 8 February, J was still recovering in hospital, when he began to complain of breathing difficulties. Doctors thought that his respiratory problems were caused by 'anxiety'. In fact his condition deteriorated rapidly on the night of 14 February and he died of a heart attack, as a result of his windpipe becoming obstructed; a side-effect of the tracheotomy. By this time, the gunshot injuries had almost healed and were no longer life-threatening. D's murder conviction was upheld by the Court of Appeal. The court held that it was only in the most extraordinary and unusual case that medical treatment would break the chain of causation.

> Using the Smith test of 'operating' cause would the jury have been able to convict David Cheshire of murder?

The status of *Cheshire* as the appropriate test to use was confirmed by the Court of Appeal in *Mellor* (1996).

Mellor (1996)
V, a 71-year-old man, was attacked by a gang of hooligans, including D, late one winter's evening. He was taken to hospital suffering facial bruising and complaining of chest pain. He died in hospital two days later. D tried to avoid liability by claiming that the hospital had failed to give V sufficient oxygen in time, as a result of which he had developed pneumonia, which was the medical cause of death. But D was convicted of manslaughter and the Court of Appeal upheld the conviction.

In *Warburton and Hubbersty* (2006), the Court of Appeal confirmed that the law as stated in *Cheshire* and *Mellor* was correct, namely 'did the acts for which D is responsible significantly contribute to the victim's death?'

Of course, *Smith* has never been overruled, so presumably a judge has the choice when directing the jury. If the wounds are still operating, use *Smith*; if they have healed, fall back on *Cheshire*. Thus, D will be liable of murder or manslaughter if:

- his acts are a more than minimal cause of death; and *either*

- the injuries that he inflicted were still an 'operating' cause at the time of death; *or*

- the injuries inflicted were a 'significant' cause of death.

However, there is one case that supports the proposition that sometimes medical negligence will be so extreme that D will be relieved from liability for his victim's death. In *Jordan* (1956), Hallett J said:

We are disposed to accept it as the law that death resulting from any normal treatment employed to deal with a felonious injury may be regarded as caused by the felonious injury . . . It is sufficient to point out here that this was not normal treatment.

Jordan (1956)

The victim of a stabbing had been taken to hospital and given a drug called terramycin to prevent infection, when he had shown intolerance to a previous injection. Medical experts for the defence described this treatment as 'palpably wrong'. Furthermore, large quantities of liquid had been administered intravenously, which had caused V's lungs to become waterlogged. This was also described as 'wrong' by the defence doctors. As a result of the waterlogging, V developed pneumonia, the medical cause of death. By the time of death, the stab wounds had mainly healed. The Court of Criminal Appeal quashed the conviction: if the jury had heard this evidence, they 'would have felt precluded from saying that they were satisfied that death was caused by the stab wound'.

In *Blaue* (1975), the Court of Appeal described *Jordan* as 'a case decided on its own special facts'. In *Malcharek, Steel* (1981), the Court of Appeal said that *Jordan* was 'very exceptional'. Nevertheless, *Jordan* has never been overruled and, presumably, in a future case where medical treatment is found to be 'palpably wrong', a jury will be entitled to find that the chain of causation has been broken. Indeed, in *Blaue*, the Court of Appeal added that *Jordan* was 'probably rightly decided'.

Life-support machines

A particular problem concerns victims who are placed on life-support machines. If there is no prospect of recovery, the doctors may decide to switch the machinery off. Does this affect D's responsibility? In *Malcharek, Steel* (1981), where two virtually identical cases coincidentally committed at opposite ends of the country were brought before the Court of Appeal together, it was argued that in such cases it was the doctors who had caused death. The Court of Appeal rejected the argument, describing the notion that Malcharek and Steel had not caused death as 'bizarre'.

Malcharek, Steel (1981)

Richard Malcharek had stabbed his wife nine times at her flat in Poole, Dorset. She was admitted to hospital and seemed to be recovering, but then suffered a pulmonary embolism, which stopped her heart. During open-heart surgery, a massive blood clot was removed but severe brain damage had been caused, from which she never recovered. The doctors carried out various tests recommended by the Royal College for establishing 'brain death' and switched off the life support.

> Anthony Steel had randomly attacked a woman in a Bradford street. He battered her about the head with a large stone, causing severe head injuries, and left her for dead. She was rushed to hospital and placed on life support immediately. However, she never recovered consciousness, and the support was withdrawn two days later after brain stem tests proved negative.
>
> M and S were both convicted of murder and the Court of Appeal rejected both appeals.

The same principles apply if V is not 'brain dead' but is in a 'persistent vegetative state' (PVS). In *Airedale NHS Trust v Bland* (1993), Lord Goff said that a doctor in discontinuing treatment was 'simply allowing the patient to die in the sense that he [is] desisting from taking a step which might prevent his patient from dying as a result of his pre-existing condition'.

It is clear from the above cases that the courts are extremely reluctant to allow an accused to escape liability by claiming that better medical treatment would have saved the victim's life or reduced the seriousness of their injury. This is sensible public policy. The medical profession and hospital emergency rooms are all too often stretched to the limit at present. In many a town the effects of Saturday night drinking in particular result in violence and a consequent influx of casualties. In such circumstances medical staff do their best to cope, often being verbally or even physically abused in the process. Very rarely mistakes are made or the treatment given is negligent. As far as criminal liability is concerned it would be invidious to hear the attacker, who put that person at risk in hospital, claim, 'So why wasn't the best Harley Street consultant called to attend to my victim?' In all but the most exceptional circumstances the primary liability rests legally, as well as morally, with the original perpetrator.

Actions of the victim

Fright or flight

Where D caused V to apprehend violence, and death occurred while she was trying to escape or otherwise protect herself, then, generally speaking, D remains a legal cause of V's death . . . There are limits to this principle, however. Incredibly, the courts have introduced what can only be termed the 'daftness test'! In *Roberts* (1972), Stephenson LJ said that if V does something 'so daft or so unexpected that no reasonable person could be expected to foresee it', then it would break the chain of causation.

In *Williams and Davis* (1992), the Court of Appeal confirmed the 'daftness test'. Stuart-Smith LJ highlighted the key question: whether V's conduct was 'proportionate to the threat, that is to say that it was within the ambit of reasonableness and not so daft as to make it his own voluntary act'.

Williams and Davis (1992)

Barry Williams and Frank Davis had given a lift to a hitchhiker, John Shepherd, who was on his way to the Glastonbury festival. Shortly afterwards, S opened a rear door and jumped out of the moving car. He did not survive the impact. It was the Crown's case that S had jumped clear trying to escape being robbed. Williams and Davis were both convicted of robbery and manslaughter. The Court of Appeal, in quashing their convictions, referred to a lack of any direction by the judge on the question of causation. The jury should have been asked whether S's reaction in jumping from the moving car was 'within the range of responses' which might be expected from a victim placed in such a situation.

In *Corbett* (1996), D head-butted and punched V before the latter ran off with D in pursuit. V fell into the gutter, and was run over and killed by a passing car. The Court of Appeal followed *Roberts*, noted that V's reactions to the attack were not 'daft' but came within a foreseeable range, and upheld D's manslaughter conviction.

The most recent example of the *Roberts* principle is *Marjoram* (2000).

Marjoram (2000)

A gang of people including D had been shouting abuse and kicking V's hostel room door. They forced open the door and burst into the room, at which point V fell, or possibly jumped, from the window. V sustained serious injury in the fall and D was convicted of inflicting grievous bodily harm (see Chapter 8). On appeal, D claimed that V's response was unreasonable but the Court of Appeal upheld the conviction. The reasonable person could have foreseen V's reaction in attempting to escape as a possible consequence of D's actions.

The decision, then, rests with the jury to assess whether the victim's responses to the perceived threat were reasonable and foreseeable in the circumstances, taking into account that V may well have been frightened at the time. This is probably the best compromise that can be achieved since it relies upon jury equity to apply a common-sense conclusion. If they think that the victim's response is 'daft' they will acquit. Otherwise they will convict.

Self-neglect

If V mistreats, or neglects to treat, his own injuries, this will not break the chain of causation. In *Holland* (1841), D cut V on the finger with an iron instrument. The wound became infected, but he ignored medical advice that he should have the finger amputated. The wound caused lockjaw and, although the finger was then amputated, he died. The judge directed the jury that the question was simply whether the wound inflicted by D was the cause of death. The jury convicted. Despite enormous advances in life-saving medical technology, it is still no answer that V refuses medical treatment (*Blaue* [1975], where the Court of Appeal followed *Holland*). In *Dear* (1996), D slashed V with a Stanley knife, severing an artery. V (for reasons that are not entirely clear) failed to do anything to staunch the blood flow. It appears he took the opportunity to commit suicide! The jury convicted of murder and D's appeal was dismissed. The cause of V's death was blood loss which, in turn, was caused by stab wounds inflicted by D. Hence, D caused V's death.

Voluntary acts

In *Kennedy* (2007), the House of Lords ruled that a voluntary act by V also breaks the chain of causation. D supplied V with heroin, which V self-injected. V overdosed and later died. The Law Lords unanimously agreed that D's manslaughter conviction had to be quashed. Lord Bingham stated:

> The criminal law generally assumes the existence of free will . . . Thus D is not to be treated as causing V to act in a certain way if V makes a voluntary and informed decision to act in that way rather than another . . . The finding that [V] freely and voluntarily administered the injection to himself, knowing what it was, is fatal to any contention that [D] caused the heroin to be administered to [V] or taken by him.

Kennedy (2007)

D was a drug dealer and V was a heroin addict. One night, at V's request, D prepared a dose of heroin and gave V a syringe ready for injection. V injected himself but later died. D was convicted of manslaughter, but appealed on the basis that he had not actually caused V's death. The Court of Appeal rejected his appeal but certified a question for the opinion of the House of Lords: 'When is it appropriate to find someone guilty of manslaughter where that person has been involved in the supply of a class A controlled drug, which is then freely and voluntarily self-administered by the person to whom it was supplied, and the administration of the drug then causes his death?' The Law Lords allowed the appeal and quashed D's conviction. Lord Bingham said that the answer to the certified question was: 'In the case of a fully-informed and responsible adult, never.'

Intriguingly, the High Court of Justiciary in Edinburgh has recently decided, on very similar facts to *Kennedy*, that V's self-ingestion of drugs supplied by D does not necessarily break the chain of causation. In *MacAngus & Kane v HM Advocate* (2009), the Court held that:

The adult status and the deliberate conduct of a person to whom a controlled drug is . . . supplied by another will be important, in some cases crucial, factors in determining whether that other's act was or was not, for the purposes of criminal responsibility, a cause of any death which follows upon ingestion of the drug. But a deliberate decision by the victim of the reckless conduct to ingest the drug will not necessarily break the chain of causation.

Thus, the criminal law in England and Wales (*Kennedy*) and that in Scotland (*MacAngus & Kane*) differs on whether self-ingestion of drugs breaks the causal chain. In fact, it appears that the law on this point differs across much of the common law world, with at least one court in Canada agreeing with *Kennedy* (chain of causation always broken) but several courts in the USA reaching similar decisions to that in *MacAngus & Kane* (chain of causation may or may not be broken depending on the circumstances).

The accused must take the victim as he finds them

D cannot complain if his victim is particularly susceptible to physical injury, for example haemophilia (a condition where the blood does not clot in the normal way). In *Martin* (1832), Parke J said that it was 'perfectly immaterial' that V 'was in a bad state of health'. If D 'was so unfortunate as to accelerate her death, he must answer for it'. In a more modern example, *Mamote-Kulang* (1964), the High Court of Australia upheld D's manslaughter conviction, dismissing his appeal that it was his wife's physical condition that was the real cause of her death. D had punched his wife, with considerable force, but on her side. Such a blow would not normally be fatal, but she died soon afterwards. The post-mortem revealed that the blow had ruptured her spleen, which was at the time 'large, soft and mushy'. However, this was no defence. Being punched by D was the sole cause of her death.

The principle that D must take his victim as he finds them is not confined to pre-existing physical or physiological conditions. It has been extended to religious beliefs. In *Blaue* (1975), Lawton LJ said:

> It has long been the policy of the law that those who use violence on other people must take their victim as they find them. This in our judgment means the whole man, not just the physical man. It does not lie in the mouth of the assailant to say that [V's] religious beliefs which inhibited her from accepting certain kinds of treatment were unreasonable. The question for decision is what caused her death. The answer is the stab wound. The fact that [V] refused to stop this end coming about did not break the causal connection between the act and death.

Blaue (1975)
Robert Blaue stabbed Jacolyn Woodhead after she refused to have sex with him. One wound penetrated a lung. She was admitted to hospital and told that surgery – and a blood transfusion – were necessary to save her life. Being a Jehovah's Witness, she refused and died soon after. Medical evidence indicated she would have survived had she accepted the transfusion. B was convicted of manslaughter. On appeal, he argued that her refusal was unreasonable and broke the chain of causation. This was rejected (NB B avoided murder liability by pleading diminished responsibility – see Chapter 6).

1. Professor Williams, an academic expert on criminal law, has argued that justice might have been better served by convicting Blaue of the offence of wounding with intent contrary to s.18 of the Offences Against the Person Act 1861. The sentence would probably have been the same. What do you think?

2. Suppose Blaue had stabbed V in a remote place and she died before medical assistance could reach her. His liability would certainly be manslaughter (because of the diminished responsibility). So why should he be allowed to escape a manslaughter conviction on the ground that V was stabbed in a built-up area near to a hospital but refused treatment?

Mens rea

Mens rea refers to the mental elements of a crime. *Mens rea* means the mental element, or state of mind, that D must possess at the time of performing whatever conduct requirements are stated in the *actus reus*. Typical examples include:

- Intention

- Recklessness

- Knowledge

- Dishonesty

So, in *murder*, the *mens rea* requirement is called 'malice aforethought' and this, in turn, means intention (either to kill V or to cause really serious injury). In *theft*, the *mens rea* is the dishonest intention to permanently deprive the owner of their property. Again, if one of these elements is missing, D cannot be guilty of the crime. D may well kill another human being – but he is not guilty of murder unless he intended death or really serious injury. D may well appropriate someone else's property, but this is not theft unless he was dishonest and intended never to return it.

With a number of different offences, the *actus reus* is identical, only the *mens rea* is different. For example, the *actus reus* is the same in murder and manslaughter. The *mens rea* of manslaughter is very different from 'malice aforethought', however. Another example is provided by the offences of 'wounding' and 'wounding with intent'. Obviously the *actus reus* of these crimes is identical – the wounding. However, the *mens rea* is different. One crime clearly requires intent. The other does not – it requires recklessness.

Finally, with some crimes the *mens rea* is identical but the *actus reus* is different. The offences of 'battery' and 'assault occasioning actual bodily harm' have different *actus reus* elements. The former can be committed literally by just touching someone. The latter requires 'actual bodily harm' (a consequence), and requires proof of something like a broken nose. But the *mens rea* is the same – intention or recklessness. The meaning of the term 'recklessness' will be explained in Chapter 3; while the meaning of the terms 'intention' and 'malice aforethought' will be explained in Chapter 5.

Coincidence of *actus reus* and *mens rea*

It is not enough that D has the *actus reus* for a crime if he does not have the *mens rea*, or guilty mind, that goes with it. The following case illustrates this.

Taaffe (1983)

In this case, as D arrived in the UK he told a customs officer that he had nothing to declare. The officer was suspicious and a search revealed several packages containing cannabis resin hidden in D's car. When D was asked what he thought was in the packages he replied, 'Money'. He was convicted of being knowingly concerned in the fraudulent evasion of the prohibition on the importation of cannabis. However, the Court of Appeal quashed his conviction and the House of Lords dismissed the prosecution appeal. As D did not 'know' that the packages contained cannabis, he had no *mens rea.*

D actually thought that he was committing an offence. However, importing currency is not illegal. Thus, D's *mens rea*, such as it was, related to a non-existent crime. In the Court of Appeal, Lord Lane CJ described D's actions as 'morally reprehensible', but this did not turn the import-ation of currency into a criminal offence. D's views on the law as to the importation of currency were irrelevant.

The *mens rea* must coincide in point of time with the act that causes the *actus reus.* Accidentally running over your neighbour, then jumping for joy at the result, does not make you a murderer. Similarly, *mens rea* implies an intention to do a present act, not a future one. Suppose that D is driving to V's house, intent on shooting him. A person runs out in front of D's car, giving D no chance of avoiding the accident. By sheer chance, it is V. D is not guilty of murder.

However, if D does an act with intent thereby to cause the *actus reus*, and does so, it is immaterial that he has repented before the *actus reus* occurs. Thus, in *Jakeman* (1983), D dispatched suitcases which she knew to contain cannabis from Ghana to London. Before they arrived she repented, but was convicted.

A similar principle applies if the very final act is involuntary or accidental. In the Australian case of *Ryan* (1967), D was in the process of tying up a petrol station attendant, whom he had robbed, when she suddenly moved, startling him so that he pulled the trigger of the shotgun he was carrying. His conviction of manslaughter was upheld by the High Court of Australia, despite his argument that the pulling of the trigger was a 'reflex action'.

The continuing act theory

Where the *actus reus* takes the form of a continuing act, it has been held that it is sufficient if D forms *mens rea* at some point during its course. In *Fagan v Metropolitan Police Commissioner* (1969), James J said:

We think that the crucial question is whether, in this case, the act of the appellant can be said to be complete and spent at the moment of time when the car wheel came to rest on the foot, or whether his act is to be regarded as a continuing act operating until the wheel was removed. In our judgment, a distinction is to be drawn between acts which are complete, though results may continue to flow, and those acts which are continuing... There was an act constituting a battery which at its inception was not criminal because there was no element of intention, but which became criminal from the moment the intention was formed to produce the apprehension which was flowing from the continuing act.

Fagan v Metropolitan Police Commissioner (1969)
Fagan was being directed to park his car by PC David Morris in Fortunegate Road, north London. He drove his car onto the constable's foot. PC Morris said 'Get off, you are on my foot', but Fagan responded, 'F*** you, you can wait', and switched off the engine. PC Morris repeated several times his request for F to move and, eventually, F switched the engine back on and reversed slowly off the officer's foot. F was charged with assault. The magistrates were unsure whether F had deliberately or accidentally driven onto PC Morris's foot; however, they were satisfied that he had 'knowingly, provocatively and unnecessarily allowed the wheel to remain on the foot' afterwards and convicted. The Divisional Court upheld the conviction.

The transaction theory

Where the *actus reus* is itself part of some larger transaction or series of events, it may be sufficient that D forms *mens rea* at some point during that transaction. In a number of cases, D has assaulted or inflicted a wound on V with intent to kill. V has been knocked unconscious, but D, believing him to be dead, disposes of the 'body'. V dies not from the original injuries but from the consequences of being 'disposed of' – typically from drowning or exposure. At the time of the *actus reus* (the disposal) D did not have *mens rea*; at the time of the *mens rea* (the assault or wounding) there was no *actus reus*.

The leading case is the Privy Council decision in *Thabo Meli and Others* (1954). Lord Reid stated:

There is no doubt that the accused set out to do all these acts in order to achieve their plan, and as part of their plan: and it is much too refined a ground of judgment to say that, because they were at a misapprehension at one stage and thought that their guilty purpose was achieved before it was achieved, therefore they are to escape the penalties of the law.

Thabo Meli and Others (1954)
The appellants, in accordance with a pre-arranged plan, took V to a hut where they plied him with beer so that he was partially intoxicated, then struck him over the head. Believing him to be dead, they rolled his body over a low cliff, making it look like an accident. In fact, V was still alive and eventually died from exposure. They were convicted of murder in South Africa and the conviction was upheld. The Privy Council, which used to hear appeals from South Africa and whose decisions are highly persuasive in English law, said it was 'impossible to divide up what was really one series of acts in this way'.

The above quote suggests that the answer might be different if the acts were not part of a pre-arranged plan. However, the Court of Appeal has followed *Thabo Meli*, in several cases where there was no previously arranged plan. The first of these was *Church* (1965).

Church (1965)
In this case the defendant, Cyril Church, had dumped what he *thought* was the body of a dead woman, Sylvia Nott, into the River Ouse. In fact she was only unconscious – he had punched her during a violent argument concerning his failure to satisfy her sexually and knocked her out – but drowned in the river. The jury convicted him of manslaughter, after a direction that they could do so if they regarded his behaviour 'from the moment he first struck her to the moment when he threw her into the river as a series of acts'. The Court of Criminal Appeal upheld the conviction.

In *Le Brun* (1991), the Court of Appeal again applied the transaction principle. Lord Lane CJ said that:

Where the unlawful application of force and the eventual act causing death are parts of the same sequence of events, the same transaction, the fact that there is an appreciable interval of time between the two does not serve to exonerate the defendant from liability. That is certainly so where the appellant's subsequent actions which caused death, after the initial unlawful blow, are designed to conceal his commission of the original unlawful assault.

> *Le Brun* (1991)
> Le Brun, in a quarrel with his wife on the way home late at night, punched her on the chin and knocked her unconscious. While attempting to drag the 'body' away, probably to avoid detection, he dropped her, so that she hit her head on the kerb and died. The jury was told that they could convict of murder or manslaughter (depending on the intent with which the punch was thrown), if D accidentally dropped V while (i) attempting to move her against her wishes and/or (ii) attempting to dispose of her 'body' or otherwise cover up the assault. He was convicted of manslaughter. The Court of Appeal upheld the conviction.

Mens rea is not the same as motive

Mens rea is the state of mind that D must have had at the moment of committing the *actus reus*. The typical *mens rea* states given above (intention, recklessness, etc.), are all different from D's motivation. For example:

- In murder, D's 'motive' in killing V could be to claim an inheritance, to be rid of an abusive husband, or to earn £20,000 (if D is a professional hired killer). But none of these states has anything to do with *mens rea* (malice aforethought), apart from strengthening a prosecution case.

- In theft, D's 'motive' in stealing food from a shop may be hunger, greed, kleptomania, boredom, or to satisfy a dare. But to be guilty of theft, D must have had the *mens rea* (the dishonest intention to permanently deprive the owner of their property).

Exception: racially aggravated crime

The Crime and Disorder Act 1998 introduced motive into the criminal law, or at least certain aspects of it, for the first time. There are four areas that are affected:

- assaults (including actual bodily harm, grievous bodily harm and wounding) – considered in Chapter 8

- criminal damage – considered in Chapter 13

- public order offences

- harassment.

The definition of 'racially aggravated' appears in s.28 of the 1998 Act. The section provides that an offence is racially aggravated if:

- at the time of committing the offence, or immediately before or after doing so, the offender demonstrates towards the victim of the offence hostility based on the victim's membership (or presumed membership) of a racial group; or

- the offence is motivated (wholly or partly) by hostility towards members of a racial group based on their membership of that group.

Prior to the 1998 Act, if D had assaulted V, causing a broken nose, and the offence was 'motivated' by racial hostility, then D would have been convicted of assault occasioning actual bodily harm contrary to s.47 of the Offences Against the Person Act 1861. The *same* liability would have followed even if the offence had *not* been racially motivated. That is, D's motivation would not have affected his liability. Now, however, D commits a different offence: the offence of racially aggravated assault, contrary to s.29 of the Crime and Disorder Act 1998. His motivation means that he is *guilty of a different offence* and he will be sentenced accordingly.

Transferred malice

If D, with the *mens rea* of one crime, performs the *actus reus* of that crime, then he is guilty. It does not matter if D accidentally performs the *actus reus* in a different way from the one he intended. For example, if D intends to kill someone, but accidentally kills the wrong victim, he is still guilty of murder. Suppose D intends to shoot P, and shoots at a person he believes is P; he hits the person and kills him. The person is, in fact, Q. D is, nevertheless, guilty of murder.

Similarly if D, intending to shoot P, fires at a person who is P, but misses, hits and kills Q who is standing nearby, D is guilty of murder. This second situation is an example of the doctrine of transferred malice. Consider the facts of *Attorney-General's Reference (No. 3 of 1994) (1997).*

Attorney-General's Reference (No. 3 of 1994) (1997)
D had stabbed his girlfriend, P, who was about 23 weeks pregnant. She subsequently made a good recovery from the wound but, some seven weeks later, gave birth prematurely. It was clear the stab

wound had penetrated the foetus. D was charged with wounding P with intent, and pleaded guilty. Subsequently, the child, Q, died some four months after birth. D was charged with Q's murder, but was acquitted after the judge held that the facts did not allow for a homicide (murder or manslaughter) conviction against the child. The Court of Appeal, however, held that the trial judge was wrong – a murder conviction was possible because it was unnecessary that the person to whom the malice was transferred, the 'transferee', be in existence at the time of the act causing death. On further reference, however, the Lords decided that, *at most*, manslaughter was possible. The Lords took exception to the Court of Appeal's use of the doctrine. Lord Mustill said that he would not 'overstrain the idea of transferred malice by trying to make it fit the present case'.

Giving judgment in this case, Lord Mustill said:

> The effect of transferred malice . . . is that the intended victim and the actual victim are treated as if they were one, so that what was intended to happen to the first person (but did not happen) is added to what actually did happen (but was not intended to happen), with the result that what was intended and what happened are married to make a notionally intended and actually consummated crime.

In such a situation, however, it is critical that the (unintentionally killed) human being was in existence at the time of the *actus reus.*

In *Latimer* (1886), Latimer had a quarrel in a public house with P. He took off his belt and swung it at P. The belt glanced off P and struck Q with full force, severely wounding her. The jury found that the injuries to Q were 'purely accidental' and 'not such a consequence of the blow as [Latimer] ought to have expected'. Nevertheless, he was convicted of wounding her.

In *Mitchell* (1983), D was waiting impatiently in a busy post office in Tottenham. He tried to force himself into a queue but he was admonished by a 72-year-old man. D punched the man, causing him to stagger backwards into an 89-year-old woman, who was knocked over; she subsequently died of her injuries. The Court of Appeal used *Latimer* in order to uphold D's manslaughter conviction.

However, if D, with the *mens rea* of one crime, performs the *actus reus* of *another*, *different* crime, he cannot, generally speaking, be convicted of either crime. The *actus reus* and *mens rea* do not coincide. The leading case is *Pembliton* (1874). Here, D committed the *actus reus* of malicious damage (an offence which no longer exists) with the *mens rea* of assault. He was guilty of neither crime.

23

> *Pembliton* (1874)
> Pembliton was involved in a fight outside a pub in Wolverhampton. At about 11pm a crowd of about 40–50 had been turned out of the pub for being disorderly. They began fighting. After a time P separated himself from the group, picked up a large stone and threw it in the direction of the others. The stone missed them and smashed a large window. P was convicted of malicious damage but his conviction was quashed. The jury had found that he intended to throw the stone at the people but did not intend to break the window.

The transferred malice principle is expressly preserved in the Government's draft Offences Against the Person Bill (1998). This draft Bill is considered in more detail in Chapter 9, but for present purposes Clause 17(2) provides that:

> A person's intention, or awareness of a risk, that his act will cause a result in relation to a person capable of being the victim of the offence must be treated as an intention or (as the case may be) awareness of a risk that his act will cause that result in relation to any other person affected by his act.

Summary

- *Actus reus* means the physical elements of a crime, things like conduct, consequences, and circumstances.

- *Mens rea* means the mental element that D must possess at the time of performing whatever conduct requirements are stated in the *actus reus*. Different *mens rea* states are intention, recklessness, dishonesty.

- The *actus reus* and *mens rea* elements must all be present. If any are missing, D cannot be guilty of that crime, although they may be guilty of a different offence.

- The *actus reus* and *mens rea* must coincide at the same point in time. If they do not, D cannot be guilty of that offence, although they may be guilty of a different offence.

- Causation is a question of fact and law. Factual causation is tested using the 'but for' test (*White*). Legal causation involves looking at whether there is any break in the chain of causation.

- The chain of causation is not broken if the injuries inflicted by D remain 'operating' and 'substantial' at the time of death (*Smith*).

- Alternatively, D remains liable if the injuries he inflicted 'contributed significantly' to the death (*Cheshire*).

- Medical negligence will very rarely break the chain of causation (*Cheshire*), although it might do if the treatment was 'palpably wrong' (*Jordan*). Doctors switching off life-support machines after brain-death has been diagnosed definitely do not break the chain of causation (*Malcharek, Steel*).

- If D attacks or threatens V who tries to escape and dies in the process, D remains liable unless V's reaction was 'daft' (*Roberts*; *Williams and Davis*; *Corbett*).

- A voluntary act by V is capable of breaking the chain of causation (*Kennedy*).

- D must take his victim as he finds her (*Blaue*).

- Motive is not the same thing as *mens rea.* Normally, motive is irrelevant. However, it does now feature in the crimes of racially motivated assault, racially motivated criminal damage, etc.

- If D, with the *mens rea* of one crime, performs the *actus reus* of that crime, then he is guilty. The fact that he accidentally performs the same *actus reus* but in a different way (e.g. by aiming a gun at P but missing and shooting Q) is irrelevant. This is transferred malice.

- But if D, with the *mens rea* of one crime, performs the *actus reus* of a different crime, then they are not guilty of either crime. They would not have the *actus reus* and *mens rea* of the same crime, as required by the rule that all the elements of the crime must be present and coincide at the same point in time.

2   Liability for omissions

Introduction

Generally speaking, English law punishes only those who caused a prohibited result by a positive act. There is no general duty to act in order to do good deeds. There may well be a moral obligation on someone to be a 'Good Samaritan', but there is not a legal one. Consider this scenario. A stabs B with a knife, causing serious injuries. If C is standing beside B, he is under no duty to do anything – either to try to stop A, or even to assist B – so, legally, he can simply walk away.

The whole approach to the imposition of criminal liability for failing to act in given situations is influenced by general public policy issues that affect most aspects of criminal law. In particular the balance to be struck between the individual's freedom to do and think as he or she wishes and the individual's responsibility to the rest of society. As with all such issues in criminal law it is up to the courts or Parliament to set the appropriate minimum standards of behaviour that are felt to be acceptable in a civilised society. Since society is a loose affiliation of many disparate groups this is not an easy task. It has become accepted that parents are under duties to care for their children. It is not yet accepted that individuals should be criminally liable for failing to go to the assistance of friends or neighbours who find themselves in distress. Whether there is a moral duty to do so is generally left to the conscience of the individual, and Parliament and the courts have been reluctant to intervene.

This is not true in all countries. In France and the Netherlands, for example, there is a so-called 'Good Samaritan' law which makes it an offence in some circumstances not to help somebody in an 'emergency situation' even though they may be a stranger.

Nevertheless, English law does punish those who fail to act, in two situations.

- First, there are a large number of crimes that may be committed *only* simply because you do not do something.

- Second, it is possible to be found guilty of crimes that normally require a positive act – such as murder or manslaughter – because you failed to act. However, for this to happen, you must have been under a 'duty of care' at the time. Thus, in the above scenario, if C was related to B – her father or husband, perhaps – or if C was a police officer, then they would be under a duty to act. Any failure to intervene could now lead to criminal liability. Their liability would be for the same offence as if they had used the knife themselves.

Why do you think there is no general duty to act in order to do good deeds?

Consider for example:

● How far it is desirable to encourage 'neighbourliness' in society?
● Could the well-meaning but ignorant 'busybody' do more harm than good, at the scene of an accident, for example?
● Whether the criminal law should ever interfere with questions of morality?
● When to distinguish between allowing a person to die rather than to keep them alive by continuing life preserving medical treatment?
● Is it proper to impose a criminal duty of care upon a person who may not have the social awareness to appreciate the existence or extent of the duty?
● Is it up to a judge or a jury to decide that an accused is under a duty of care?

Crimes that can be committed only by failing to act

The vast majority of these crimes are statutory and are usually strict liability offences (see Chapter 4). For instance, a motorist who *fails to provide* a police officer with a specimen of breath when required to do so, under s.6 of the Road Traffic Act 1988, commits an offence. Similarly, *failing to stop and provide your name and address* to any person reasonably requiring it when your vehicle has been involved in an accident where there has been injury to another person or damage to another vehicle is an offence under s.170 of the same Act. More seriously, the offence of *failing to disclose information* is an offence under s.19 of the Terrorism Act 2000.

S.5(1) of the Domestic Violence, Crime and Victims Act 2004 creates an offence of allowing the death of a child or vulnerable adult. The accused (D) must have been 'a member of the same household' as the victim (V) and 'had frequent contact with him'. If the prosecution can prove either that D caused V's death or that D was, or ought to have been, aware that there was a 'significant risk of serious physical harm being caused to V' but 'failed to take such steps as he could reasonably have been expected to take to protect V from the risk', with the result that V died 'in circumstances of the kind that D foresaw or ought to have foreseen', then D faces liability.

The first reported conviction under s.5 occurred in *Mujuru* (2007). Sandra Mujuru had gone to work leaving her live-in partner, Jerry Stephens, alone with her four-month-old daughter, Ayesha, despite knowledge of his history of violence against Ayesha. On a previous occasion, Stephens had broken Ayesha's arm. On the fateful day, Stephens killed Ayesha either by striking her head with an instrument or by slamming her head into a hard surface. Stephens was convicted of murder and Mujuru was convicted under s.5 of the 2004 Act. The Court of Appeal upheld her conviction. The jury was entitled to conclude that by going to work and leaving Ayesha in Stephens's care, Mujuru had failed to take such steps as she could reasonably have been expected to take to protect her daughter.

In a more recent case, *Khan* (2009), which involved the death of a 'vulnerable adult', Lord Judge CJ said that 'the 2004 Act created a new offence based on a positive duty on members of the same household to protect children or vulnerable adults from serious physical harm'.

However, at least one such offence – misconduct whilst acting as an officer of justice – is a common law offence (*Dytham* [1979]).

Dytham (1979)

PC Dytham, a police officer, was on duty near Cindy's nightclub in St Helens at about 1am. He was standing near a hot dog stand about 30 yards away when a man called Stubbs was ejected from the club by a bouncer. A fight ensued in which a large number of men joined. There was a great deal of shouting and screaming. Three men eventually kicked Stubbs to death in the gutter. All of this was clearly audible and visible to the officer. However, PC Dytham took no steps to intervene, and when the incident was over adjusted his helmet and drove off, telling the owner of the hot dog stand and a bystander that he was going off duty. PC Dytham was convicted. He had wilfully omitted to take any steps to carry out his duty to protect Stubbs or to arrest or otherwise bring to justice his assailants. The Court of Appeal upheld his conviction.

Committing crime by failing to act when under a duty to act

There are two elements that need to be established before liability can be imposed for a failure to act:

- The crime has to be one that is capable of being committed by a failure to act;

- D must have been under a duty to act.

Was the offence capable of 'commission by omission'?

Not all offences are capable of 'commission by omission'. Whether a crime is so capable is a question for the courts. Murder and manslaughter are good examples of crimes that may be committed by omission (see, respectively, *Gibbins and Proctor* [1918] and *Pittwood* [1902], below). Indeed most of the cases concern these two crimes. Other crimes capable of being committed by omission are arson (*Miller* [1983]) and assault and battery. This point was decided in *DPP v Bermudez* (2003).

> *DPP v Bermudez* (2003)
>
> V, a female police officer, wished to search D. She asked him to turn out all his pockets, which he did. V asked him if he had removed everything; he replied 'Yes'. She then asked, 'Are you sure that you do not have any needles or sharps on you?' D said, 'No'. V commenced her search but when she put her hand into one pocket she pricked her finger on a hypodermic needle. V noticed that D was smirking (which suggested that he realised that there was at least one needle in his pocket all along). Magistrates convicted D of assault and this conviction was upheld by the Divisional Court.

Some crimes, however, cannot be committed by omission; for example, burglary and robbery. Sometimes the definition of the crime makes it clear a positive act is required. In *Ahmad* (1986), D, a landlord, was charged with 'doing acts calculated to interfere with the peace and comfort of a residential occupier with intent to cause him to give up occupation of the premises', contrary to s.1 of the Protection from Eviction Act 1977. The Court of Appeal decided that he could not be guilty of this crime by failing to act, as the offence clearly required 'acts'.

One further problem with imposing liability when D fails to act is the requirement of causation (this issue was examined in Chapter 1). Suppose a man sees his young son fall into a canal, but simply stands and watches. There is no doubt that the father is under a duty to save the boy, and deliberate failure to do so could well be regarded as murder. But did the father cause the boy to die? The boy would almost certainly have died in exactly the same way if no-one had been there.

Was the defendant under a duty to act?

The second factor is that D must be under a duty – recognised by the law – to act in the circumstances. In *Khan and Khan* (1998), the Court of Appeal quashed the manslaughter convictions of two drug dealers. They had failed to summon medical assistance after V, a 15-year-old girl, to whom they had supplied heroin, overdosed and died. The men could have helped her; instead they left her to die alone. The court said that, before they could convict, the jury had to be sure that the men stood in such a relationship to V that they were under a duty to act. In the case, the trial judge had not directed the jury in relation to that crucial issue.

The Court of Appeal in *Khan and Khan* did not decide that no duty was owed on the facts, rather that it must be left to the jury to decide whether a duty of care was owed. Specifically, the Court of Appeal said that it was for the trial judge to decide whether, on the facts, a duty of care was *capable* of arising and it was for the jury to decide whether it did, in fact, arise (criminal convictions are sometimes quashed by the Court of Appeal where the judge has misdirected the jury at the original trial. This does not necessarily mean that the Court of Appeal thinks that the accused is entirely innocent, merely that the trial decision is unsafe). This point was recently confirmed in *Evans* (2009), discussed below.

A duty to act may be owed in a variety of situations. Such a duty has been held to exist in the following circumstances.

Duty arising out of contract

Where failure to fulfil a contract is likely to endanger lives, the criminal law will impose a duty to act. This duty will typically be held by the following (this is not an exhaustive list):

• Doctors

• Members of the emergency services

• Lifeguards

In *Adomako* (1994), an anaesthetist was convicted of manslaughter on the basis that he had failed to notice that a vital breathing tube had become disconnected during an eye operation, with the result that the patient suffered loss of oxygen to the brain, massive brain damage and eventual death. This sort of conviction is quite easy to justify – the anaesthetist's (well-paid) job is to ensure that the equipment works because, if it does not, people will be very likely to die or to be injured.

Cases such as *Adomako* and *Pittwood* (1902) demonstrate that the duty is owed to anyone who may be affected by D's breaches of contract, not just the other parties to the contract (that is, D's employers).

> *Pittwood* (1902)
> Pittwood was convicted of manslaughter. He was a signalman employed by the railway company to look after a level crossing and ensure the gate was shut when a train was due. He left the gate open

and was away from his post, with the result that someone crossing the line was hit and killed. The court rejected his argument that his duty was owed simply to the railway company: he was paid to look after the gate and protect the public.

Why do you think that PC Dytham (above) was charged with misconduct whilst acting as an officer of justice, and not manslaughter based on his duty of care as a police officer?

Duty arising out of a relationship
Though there is little direct authority, it is accepted that:

- parents are under a duty to their children (*Gibbins and Proctor* [1918]);

- spouses (husbands and wives) owe a duty to each other (*Smith* [1979]).

Duty arising from the assumption of care for another
A duty will be owed by anyone who voluntarily undertakes to care for another, whether through age, infirmity, illness, etc. The duty may be express or implied. In *Instan* (1893), D went to live with her elderly aunt, who became ill and, for the last 12 days of her life, was unable to care for herself or summon help. D did not give her any food or seek medical assistance, but continued to live in the house and eat the aunt's food. D was convicted of manslaughter and this was upheld on appeal.

The leading case now is *Stone and Dobinson* (1977).

Stone and Dobinson (1977)
John Stone lived with his mistress, Gwen Dobinson, in South Yorkshire. In 1972, Stone's sister, Fanny, 61, came to live with them. Fanny was suffering from anorexia nervosa and, although initially capable of looking after herself, her condition deteriorated. Eventually she was confined to bed in the small front room. Stone was then 67, partly deaf, nearly blind and of low intelligence. Dobinson was 43 but was described as 'ineffectual' and 'somewhat inadequate'. Both were unable to use a telephone. They tried to find Fanny's doctor but failed. (Fanny refused to tell them, as she believed she would be taken away.) Fanny refused to eat anything other than biscuits, although she used to sneak downstairs to make meals when

the others went to the pub (which they did every night). One day, Dobinson and a neighbour tried to give Fanny a bedbath. Shortly afterwards, Fanny died, weighing less than 5 stone. She had two huge, maggot-infested ulcers on her right hip and left knee, with bone clearly visible. The two defendants were convicted of manslaughter, and the Court of Appeal upheld this. They had assumed a duty of care to Fanny, and their pathetically feeble efforts to look after her amounted to gross negligence (which is sufficient for a manslaughter conviction – see Chapter 7).

Stone and Dobinson did their best but their best was simply not good enough. Did they deserve to be convicted of manslaughter? Would they have been better off simply ignoring Fanny after she became bedbound?

All of the cases above involved manslaughter. This is because D has assumed a duty of care to someone but has then, for reasons of incompetence or forgetfulness, allowed that person to die. However, a murder conviction is possible if D deliberately fails to assist someone in their care – intending to kill or seriously injure them. This was the case in *Gibbins and Proctor* (1918).

Gibbins and Proctor (1918)
Gibbins was the father of several children including a 7-year-old daughter, Nelly. His wife had left him and he was living with a lover, Proctor. They kept Nelly separate from the other children and deliberately starved her to death. Afterwards they concocted a story about how Nelly had 'gone away'; in fact, Gibbins had buried her in a brickyard. There was evidence that Proctor hated Nelly and had hit her. They were both convicted of murder and the Court of Criminal Appeal upheld the convictions. Gibbins owed Nelly a duty as her father; Proctor was held to have undertaken a duty to her.

Parliament subsequently incorporated parental responsibilities into legislation in the Children and Young Persons Act 1933. In addition, other adult carers such as teachers and guardians now stand '*in loco parentis*' with regard to children in their care.

Duty arising from the creation of a dangerous situation

Where a person inadvertently starts a chain of events – which, if uninterrupted, will result in harm or damage – that person, on becoming aware that they were the cause, is under a duty to take all such steps as lie within their power to prevent or minimise the harm. If they fail to take such steps then they may well be criminally liable for the consequences. In *Miller* (1983), a vagrant who was squatting in a house in Sparkbrook, Birmingham, awoke to find that a cigarette he had been smoking had set fire to the mattress. He did nothing to extinguish the fire but moved to another room and went back to sleep. The fire spread and caused £800 damage. Miller was convicted of arson (see Chapter 13) and the Court of Appeal and House of Lords upheld his conviction.

What do you think James Miller should have done, instead of simply going to sleep in another room?

Should he have tried to extinguish the fire himself?

What if it would be dangerous to tackle the fire personally?

Three recent cases have seen the *Miller* principle being discussed.

In *Matthews and Alleyne* (2003) (the full facts of which appear in Chapter 5 in the context of intention), D and E pushed V (who was unable to swim) from a bridge into a river where he drowned. The trial judge suggested that D and E could have been convicted of murder if they subsequently realised that he was unable to swim and (with intent that he should die or suffer serious injury) took no steps to rescue him. The appellants and V were strangers to each other prior to this event, so the basis on which D and E owed V a duty to act could be regarded as similar to that in *Miller*.

In *DPP v Bermudez* (2003), the facts of which were given above, the Divisional Court expressly applied *Miller* as the basis for finding D's duty of care to V. Kay J said that, when D gave V a dishonest assurance about the contents of his pockets, he exposed her to a reasonably foreseeable risk of injury. His subsequent failure to inform her of the presence of needles in his pockets constituted an evidential basis for a finding that the *actus reus* of assault occasioning actual bodily harm had occurred.

The latest case to apply the *Miller* principle is *Evans* (2009), a gross negligence manslaughter case. Lord Judge CJ summarised the law as follows:

When a person has created or contributed to the creation of a state of affairs which he knows, or ought reasonably to know, has become life threatening, a consequent duty on him to act by taking reasonable steps to save the other's life will normally arise.

Evans (2009)

Gemma Evans lived with her half-sister Carly Townsend, 16, a heroin addict, and their mother Andrea Townsend in Llanelli in south Wales. One day, Evans bought £20 of heroin and gave some to Carly, who self-injected. Later, it was obvious that Carly had overdosed but neither Andrea nor Evans contacted the emergency services as they were fearful that they and/or Carly might get into trouble. Instead they put her to bed hoping that she would recover. Instead, she died during the night. Both Andrea and Evans were convicted of gross negligence manslaughter. Evans appealed, but the Court of Appeal dismissed her appeal. Andrea owed Carly a parental duty, and Evans owed her a duty based on *Miller*.

Release from duty

One issue that is still unresolved is whether a duty – once undertaken – may be relinquished. In *Smith* (1979), D's wife had given birth to a still-born child at home. She hated doctors and would not allow D to call one. When she finally gave him permission it was too late and she died. The judge directed the jury to balance the wife's wish to avoid calling a doctor against her capacity to make rational decisions. The jury was unable to agree and D was discharged.

Thus, it would appear that, if V is rational, they may release a relative or carer from their duty of care. In *Airedale NHS Trust v Bland* (1993) – a civil case – the House of Lords provided further guidance on this difficult area. The Trust had applied to the Lords for a declaration that it was lawful for doctors to withdraw life-supporting medical treatment, including artificial feeding, from Tony Bland, a patient in one of its hospitals who was in a persistent vegetative state (PVS) with no prospect of improvement or recovery as a result of being badly crushed in the Hillsborough football stadium disaster in 1989. The House of Lords held that withdrawal of treatment would be lawful. Lord Goff, giving the leading judgment, stated several principles, which should also apply in the criminal law.

- There is no absolute rule that a patient's life has to be prolonged no matter what. The fundamental principle is the sanctity of life, but respect for human dignity demands that the quality of life be considered.

- The principle of self-determination requires that respect be given to the patient's expressed wishes. An adult patient of sound mind could refuse treatment; doctors must respect that. If a patient is incapable of communicating, an earlier expressed refusal of consent will probably be effective. Where there is no such refusal, that does not mean that life has to be prolonged.

- Treatment may be provided, in the absence of consent, by a patient incapable of giving it, where that treatment is *in the patient's best interests* (see '*Re F [Mental Patient: Sterilisation]*' [1990]); conversely, it may be discontinued if this is *in the patient's best interests.*

- Where treatment is futile, there is no obligation on a doctor to provide it – because it would no longer be in the patient's best interests. Any omission to provide treatment would not be unlawful, because there is no breach of duty to the patient. Similar principles apply to the decision to commence treatment in the first place.

Reform

Some academics have argued that, where rescue of the victim would not pose a danger to D, then liability should be imposed for failing to act, even where there was no pre-existing legal duty on D (see, for example, Professor A. Ashworth, '*The Scope of Criminal Liability for Omissions*' [1989] 105 LQR 424). Some countries, such as France and the Netherlands, do have legislation like this – usually referred to as 'Good Samaritan' laws. There are, however, serious difficulties created by such legislation:

- *Definitional problems*: When would the duty be imposed? When it was 'easy' for D to rescue V? But could you define what an 'easy' rescue attempt would involve? Should there be a minimum age limit before this liability would be imposed? If so, what would it be? What about a maximum age limit? Presumably, persons with certain physical and/or mental disabilitiess would be exempt – but which ones? Would pregnant women be exempt?

- *Moral objections*: For example, why should ordinary citizens be forced to watch out for and actually take steps to protect each other? After all, most citizens already pay (through taxes) for highly trained and well-equipped professionals (police, fire brigade officers, life boat crews, paramedics, etc.) to do that job on their behalf.

- *Practical problem (1)*: 'Good Samaritan' laws create a very real possibility that D may misjudge the situation and either fail to attempt a rescue when it was in fact 'easy' (D thinking it would be dangerous), or attempt a dangerous rescue (D thinking it was actually easy). In the former scenario, D faces potential liability for homicide if V is killed. In the latter scenario, D's own life is put at risk and genuine rescuers (police, etc.) now have two people to rescue (D and V) instead of just V.

- *Practical problem (2)*: 'Good Samaritan' laws also involve the possible imposition of liability on a large number of people. For example, would all the sunbathers on a crowded beach, who all choose to ignore V who was clearly drowning 20 yards from shore, be held liable for her manslaughter?

Summary

- There is no general duty to act.

- Some (mostly statutory) crimes may be committed only by failing to act (Road Traffic Act).

- Otherwise, the crime must be one that is capable of being committed by an omission (*Ahmad*).

- Murder and manslaughter are capable of commission by omission.

- D must be under a duty to act (*Khan and Khan*).

- A duty to act may be imposed by contract (*Pittwood*; *Adomako*).

- A duty to act may be imposed by a relationship with another person (*Gibbins*; *Smith*; *Evans*).

- A duty to act may be imposed by assuming a responsibility to care for another person (*Instan*; *Proctor*; *Stone and Dobinson*).

- A duty to act may be imposed in order to minimise the consequences of a dangerous situation that D created himself (*Miller*; *Evans*).

- A duty to act may be brought to an end, either because the other person requests it (*Smith*) or because it would not be in their best interests (*Bland*).

3   Recklessness

Introduction

Recklessness is a word in everyday use in the English language. When we use the word 'reckless' we probably do not analyse carefully what we mean by its use. For the most part it conveys something that we might also be happy to call dangerous, or very careless or even anti-social. We are not being that precise. We read of reckless tackles in football matches; of reckless statements in the press; of reckless drinking in Ibiza, etc. To the law student, however, the words 'reckless', 'recklessly' and 'recklessness' take on a new and special significance. To discover why this should be, one must begin by realising that the word 'reckless' to the lawyer is not a general description of someone or their behaviour. It is a word which refers to a very particular state of mind. It is, indeed, one of those *mens rea* words referred to in Chapter 1.

To a criminal lawyer recklessness involves two things:

- The taking of an unjustifiable risk; and

- An awareness of the risk.

Risk is part of life. Each time we take a car journey there is a risk that we might be injured in a road accident (a small risk of a serious consequence). Each time we place a stake on the National Lottery we risk losing that money (a high risk in return for a potentially high reward). Whether we consciously calculate whether such risks are 'reckless' is doubtful. They simply are part of life and we could probably justify them without serious argument were we asked to do so. Such behaviour by itself is hardly regarded as reckless. On the other hand, the car driver who travels at excessive speed or the single parent who gambles half of their weekly income on the Lottery is likely to be perceived as reckless, whether they themselves think so or not.

The taking of other risks is less easy to justify. Is it 'reckless' to smoke 40 cigarettes a day, for example? Is it 'reckless' to go mountaineering? What are the risks involved and how do we assess them? Does the individual alone decide? Alternatively, do the family of that individual or the taxpayers, for example, have a legitimate say about the potential medical treatment costs of a lung cancer patient or an injured climber? What about the emotional suffering the risk-taker might cause to others?

It is the question of who must be aware of the consequences of taking serious and unjustifiable risks that has caused all the problems in criminal law.

The taking of an unjustifiable risk

Whether a risk is unjustifiable involves a balancing of the social utility of D's act on one hand, against the seriousness of harm that will result if the risk manifests itself, on the other. Hence:

- Flying a plane with 500 passengers from London to New York. This carries a risk that the plane will crash, killing everyone on board. However, the probability is low and the social utility high, hence the risk is justifiable.

- Stealing a fire engine to go on a high speed joyride. This carries a dual risk (a) that the fire engine will be involved in a crash, causing injury or death and property damage; (b) that if a fire starts somewhere the engine will not be able to attend. The probability of the former risk is high, the latter less so; but the social utility of stealing fire engines is nil, so the risk is unjustifiable.

Awareness of risk

Recklessness generally involves D taking an unjustifiable risk of a particular consequence occurring, with awareness of that risk. Sometimes the question is whether D was reckless as to the existence of a particular set of circumstances.

Recklessness is the *mens rea* state sufficient for many crimes, some very serious, including:

- involuntary manslaughter (see Chapter 7)

- malicious wounding, contrary to s.20 of the Offences Against the Person Act (OAPA) 1861 (see Chapter 8)

- inflicting grievous bodily harm (GBH), also contrary to s.20 OAPA (see Chapter 8)

- assault occasioning actual bodily harm (ABH), contrary to s.47 OAPA (see Chapter 8).

The question that has troubled the appeal courts for 25 years is whether recklessness should be assessed 'subjectively' – that is, by looking at the case from the defendant's perspective, or 'objectively' – that is, looking at the case from the perspective of the reasonable man. It will be seen that the courts have gone on a long, circular journey. After deciding upon a subjective test in the 1950s, an objective test was introduced in the early 1980s. For a short time in the mid-1980s it seemed that the objective test would replace the subjective test, but the original test began a comeback in the mid-1980s and continued to reassert itself throughout the 1990s. Finally, in 2003, the objective test was banished to the pages of history.

The Cunningham test: 1957

The original case on the definition of recklessness is *Cunningham* (1957). Here the court gave us the classic, subjective test for recklessness. The question for the Court of Criminal Appeal was actually what was meant by the word 'maliciously' (in s.23 OAPA 1861). The judge had directed the jury that it meant 'wickedly'. The Court of Criminal Appeal did not agree. In quashing his conviction, the court approved a definition given by Professor Kenny in 1902:

> In any statutory definition of a crime, 'malice' must be taken not in the old vague sense of wickedness in general but as requiring either (i) an actual intention to do the particular kind of harm that in fact was done or (ii) recklessness as to whether such harm should occur or not (i.e. the accused has foreseen that the particular kind of harm might be done, and yet has gone on to take the risk of it).

Cunningham (1957)
Roy Cunningham ripped a gas-meter from the cellar wall of a house in Bradford, in order to steal the money inside. He left a ruptured pipe, leaking gas, which seeped through into the neighbouring house, where Sarah Wade (actually the mother of Cunningham's fiancée) inhaled it. Cunningham was convicted of maliciously administering a noxious substance so as to endanger life, contrary to s.23 OAPA 1861, but his conviction was quashed. The crux of the matter was whether Cunningham had foreseen the risk; that is, the risk of someone inhaling the gas.

This definition was subsequently applied throughout the OAPA 1861 (for example, *Venna* [1976], a case of ABH) and to other statutes, such as the Malicious Damage Act 1861 (MDA), whenever the word 'malicious' was used. In 1969, the Law Commission was working on proposals to reform the law of property damage. In their final Report on Criminal Damage, they recommended the replacement of the MDA with what became the

Criminal Damage Act 1971 (CDA). The Law Commission considered that the mental element, as stated in *Cunningham*, was properly defined, but that for simplicity and clarity the word 'maliciously' should be replaced with 'intentionally or recklessly'. Unfortunately, the Act does not define 'reckless' anywhere; it is left to the courts to interpret.

After 1971 the courts initially continued to apply subjective recklessness. In *Stephenson* (1979), D was a schizophrenic, homeless man. One November night he had decided to shelter in a hollowed-out haystack in a field on the North Yorkshire moors. He was still cold, and so lit a small fire of twigs and straw in order to keep warm. However, the stack caught fire and was damaged, along with various pieces of farming equipment. Some £3,500 worth of damage was caused. D was charged with causing criminal damage 'recklessly'. Evidence was given that schizophrenia could have deprived D of the normal ability to foresee risks. The judge told the jury that D was reckless if he closed his mind to the obvious risk of starting a fire in a haystack, and they convicted. The Court of Appeal quashed his conviction. What mattered was whether D himself had foreseen the risk. This seems to be fair as it is concerned with the state of mind of the accused person, his *mens rea*. Lane LJ said:

> A man is reckless when he carries out the deliberate act appreciating that there is a risk that damage to property may result from his act ... We wish to make it clear that the test remains subjective, that the knowledge or appreciation of risk of some damage must have entered the defendant's mind even though he may have suppressed it or driven it out.

The Caldwell test: 1981–2003

In 1981, the House of Lords in *Caldwell* [1982] AC 341, a criminal damage case, introduced an objective form of recklessness. That is, recklessness was to be determined according to what the 'ordinary, prudent individual' would have foreseen, as opposed to the *Cunningham* test of what the defendant actually did foresee. Lord Diplock, with whom Lords Keith and Roskill concurred, said:

> A person charged with an offence under s.1(1) of the Criminal Damage Act 1971, is 'reckless as to whether or not any such property be destroyed or damaged' if (1) he does an act which in fact creates an obvious risk that property will be destroyed or damaged and (2) when he does the act he either has not given any thought to the possibility of there being any such risk or has recognised that there was some risk involved and has nonetheless gone on to do it. That would be a proper direction to the jury.

Lord Diplock gave a number of justifications for this new test, which can be summarised as follows:

- Lord Diplock thought that recklessness was 'an ordinary English word', not some 'term of legal art with some more limited esoteric meaning than that which it bore in ordinary speech'. In other words, if in ordinary language we would describe someone who acted without thinking as 'reckless' then the legal language should be interpreted in the same way.

- He also thought that inadvertence (i.e. failing to think about) an obvious risk was just as blameworthy as advertence (i.e. thinking about) a risk and taking it. Under the *Cunningham* test, only the latter state of mind leads to criminal liability; under *Caldwell*, both states of mind attracted culpability.

- Lord Diplock also thought that his new test would be simpler for juries to understand and apply.

These justifications were described as 'pathetically inadequate' and the Caldwell decision itself 'profoundly regrettable' by Professors Sir John Smith and Glanville Williams, both leading academic authorities.

Because *Caldwell* was a criminal damage case it meant that, while *Stephenson* would be overruled, other areas of law were still subject to the *Cunningham* definition. However, in *Lawrence* (1982), the House of Lords gave an objective definition to recklessness in the context of the crime of causing death by reckless driving. A year later, in *Seymour* (1983), a reckless manslaughter case, the House of Lords applied the objective test here too. Their Lordships also indicated that the *Caldwell/Lawrence* definition of recklessness was 'comprehensive'. Lord Roskill said that, 'Reckless should today be given the same meaning in relation to all offences which involve "recklessness" as one of the elements unless Parliament has otherwise ordained.'

Obviously this comment was *obiter* (and thus of persuasive precedent only). Courts in future cases decided to reject Lord Roskill's opinion. In the early 1990s the courts began a gradual process of rejecting *Caldwell* and returning to the *Cunningham* subjective test. In *DPP v K* (1990), the Divisional Court had applied *Caldwell* to s.47 OAPA 1861, but almost immediately the Court of Appeal in *Spratt* (1991) declared that *DPP v K* was wrongly decided. In *Spratt*, D had been convicted of the s.47 offence after firing his air-pistol through the open window of his flat, apparently unaware that children were playing outside. One was hit and injured. At his trial, D pleaded guilty (on the basis that he had been reckless in that he had failed to give thought to the possibility of a risk that he might cause harm) and appealed. The Court of Appeal quashed his conviction. McCowan L pointed out that Lord Roskill's dictum in *Seymour* was clearly *obiter* and could not have been intended to overrule *Cunningham.* McCowan L added:

> The history of the interpretation of [the OAPA 1861] shows that, whether or not the word 'maliciously' appears in the section in question, the courts have consistently held that the *mens rea* of every type of offence against the person covers both intent and recklessness, in the sense of taking the risk of harm ensuing with foresight that it might happen.

Shortly afterwards the House of Lords dealt with a joint appeal involving both s.47 and s.20 OAPA 1861. In *Savage, DPP v Parmenter* (1992), Lord Ackner, giving the unanimous decision of the House of Lords, said that: 'in order to establish an offence under s.20 the prosecution must prove either that [D] intended or that he actually foresaw that his act would cause harm'. The reference to what D 'actually foresaw' clearly means *Cunningham* subjective recklessness. In 1995, the House of Lords effectively overruled *Seymour* in *Adomako* (1995). Lord Mackay LC decided that objective recklessness set too low a threshold of liability for such a serious crime as manslaughter and restored the test based on gross negligence (see Chapter 7). In 2000, the Court of Appeal in *Lidar* decided that, while *Adomako* had abolished objective reckless manslaughter, it was possible for D to be guilty of reckless manslaughter based on the subjective *Cunningham* test (see also Chapter 7).

Back to Cunningham: G and R (2003)

In October 2003, the House of Lords completed the circle begun 22 years earlier by overruling *Caldwell.* In *G and R* (2003), the House of Lords unanimously declared that the objective test for recklessness was wrong and restored the *Cunningham* subjective test for criminal damage. The case itself involved arson, as had *Caldwell.* The certified question from the Court of Appeal was:

> Can a defendant properly be convicted under s.1 of the CDA 1971 on the basis that he was reckless as to whether property would be destroyed or damaged when he gave no thought to the risk, but by reason of his age and/or personal characteristics the risk would not have been obvious to him, even if he had thought about it?

In a number of earlier cases, most notoriously *Elliott v C* (1983), this question had been answered 'Yes'. That case involved a teenage girl of subnormal intelligence committing arson and being convicted because, under the *Caldwell* test, it was irrelevant that she had failed to appreciate the risk of property damage created by starting a fire in a garden shed. Crucially, the risk would have been obvious to the ordinary prudent adult. However, in *G and R* (2003) the House of Lords held that the certified question should be answered 'No'. According to Lord Bingham, the question was simply one of statutory interpretation, namely, what did Parliament mean when it used the word 'reckless' in s.1 of the 1971 Act? He concluded that Parliament had not intended to change the meaning of the word from its *Cunningham* definition. The majority of the Law Lords in *Caldwell*, specifically Lord Diplock, had 'misconstrued' the 1971 Act. There were four reasons for restoring the subjective test:

1. As a matter of principle, conviction of a serious crime should depend on proof that D had a culpable state of mind. While it was 'clearly blameworthy' to take an obvious risk, it was not clearly blameworthy to do something involving a risk of injury (or property damage) if D genuinely did not perceive that risk. While such a person might 'fairly be accused of stupidity or a lack of imagination', that was insufficient for liability.
2. The *Caldwell* test was capable of leading to 'obvious unfairness', of which *Elliott v C* was the prime example. It was neither 'moral nor just' to convict any defendant, but least of all a child, on the strength of what someone else would have appreciated.
3. There was significant judicial and academic criticism of *Caldwell* and the cases that had followed it. In particular, Lords Wilberforce and Edmund Davies had dissented in *Caldwell* itself and Goff LJ in *Elliott v C* had followed *Caldwell* only because he felt compelled to do so because of the rules of judicial precedent.
4. The decision in *Caldwell* was a misinterpretation of Parliament's intention. Although the courts could leave it to Parliament to correct that misinterpretation, because it was one that was 'offensive to principle and was apt to cause injustice' the need for the courts to correct it was 'compelling'.

Lord Bingham also observed that there were no compelling public policy reasons for persisting with the *Caldwell* test. The law prior to 1981 revealed no miscarriages of justice with guilty defendants being acquitted.

G and R (2003)
One night in August 2000 the two defendants, G and R, then aged 11 and 12, entered the back yard of a Co-op shop in Newport Pagnell. There they found bundles of newspapers, some of which

they set alight using a lighter they had brought with them. They threw the burning paper under a large, plastic wheelie-bin and left the yard. Meanwhile, the fire had set alight the wheelie-bin. It then spread to another wheelie-bin, then to the shop and its adjoining buildings. Approximately £1 million damage was caused. G and R were charged with arson (that is, damaging or destroying property by fire, being reckless as to whether such property would be destroyed or damaged). At trial, they said that they genuinely thought the burning newspapers would extinguish themselves on the concrete floor of the yard. Hence, looking at the case *subjectively*, neither of them appreciated a risk of damage to the wheelie-bins, let alone that the shop and its adjoining buildings, would be destroyed or damaged by fire. The judge, however, directed the jury according to the *Caldwell* test. The jury, looking at the case *objectively*, was satisfied that the ordinary prudent adult would have appreciated that risk, and therefore convicted the two boys. The Court of Appeal dismissed their appeal but certified the question for appeal to the House of Lords.

The House of Lords did give consideration to arguments from the prosecution that the *Caldwell* definition could be retained in a modified form. Two possibilities were advanced for the Lordships' consideration, both of which were rejected.

1. That *Caldwell* be adapted for cases involving children and mentally disabled adults. Thus, according to the prosecution, a teenage defendant could be convicted if he had failed to give any thought to a risk which would have been obvious to a child of the same age. The House of Lords rejected this on the basis that it was just as offensive to the above principles. It would also 'open the door' to 'difficult and contentious arguments concerning the qualities and characteristics to be taken into account for the purposes of comparison'.
2. That *Caldwell* be adapted so that D would be reckless if he had failed to give thought to an obvious risk which, had he bothered to think about it at all, would have been equally obvious to him. This argument was rejected because it had the potential to over-complicate the jury's task. It was inherently speculative to ask a jury to consider whether D would have regarded a risk as obvious, had he thought about it. Lord Bingham thought that the simpler the jury's task, the more reliable its verdict would be.

Another very welcome result of *G and R* is that a theoretical legal loophole has finally been closed. In *Shimmen* (1986) it was pointed out that, under the *Caldwell* test of recklessness, if D considers whether his actions created a risk of property damage and concludes – honestly but incorrectly – that no such risk exists, then he is not reckless. This would be the outcome even if the ordinary prudent individual would have regarded the risk as obvious. In the *Shimmen* case itself, D was still convicted because he admitted that he had considered whether a risk existed and concluded that it was very small (but not that there was no risk at all). Now that *G and R* has overruled *Caldwell*, the loophole has disappeared. The question for juries and magistrates in future cases is simply this: when D acted, was he aware that his actions created a risk (or property damage, injury or death, depending on the offence with which D is charged)? If yes, he is reckless; if no, he is not guilty.

The first case to reach the Court of Appeal after *G and R* was *Cooper* (2004). At his trial in early 2003, D had been convicted of arson, being reckless as to whether life would be endangered, and sentenced to life imprisonment, after the judge directed the jury in accordance with *Caldwell* recklessness. Thus psychiatric evidence that D had mental health difficulties was regarded as irrelevant. After the decision in *G and R* in October 2003, D successfully appealed, arguing that it was no longer appropriate in criminal damage/arson cases to direct the jury to consider the perception of the ordinary bystander. Rather, the jury should have been asked to decide whether D had consciously taken a risk (that is, using *Cunningham* recklessness).

Cooper (2004)
Martin Cooper had lived in a North London hostel for those with mental health difficulties for about five years. One night in September 2002, he set fire to his mattress, using lighter fuel and matches. Fortunately the fire alarm sounded and the fire brigade arrived in time to prevent any damage other than scorching to the mattress. D admitted using the lighter fuel and matches but claimed that he had only intended to hurt himself. He said that 'it did cross my mind a bit' that someone else could be hurt but 'nobody would have got hurt anyway'. The Court of Appeal allowed his appeal.

A similar outcome occurred in *Castle* (2004), where D was convicted of aggravated arson after he broke into an office and then set fire to it. There were flats above the office although they were unoccupied. D claimed to have no knowledge of the flats but was convicted on the basis that, under the *Caldwell* test for recklessness, it was irrelevant whether or not D actually realised that there was a risk to life. The Court of Appeal quashed his conviction, relying on *G and R*. As D was not aware of the flats, he was not reckless as to whether life would be endangered.

Summary

- Recklessness involves two things: the taking of an unjustifiable risk and an awareness of the risk.

- Recklessness is tested 'subjectively', which means looking at events from the defendant's point of view (*Cunningham*). Thus, if D foresaw a risk of death, injury or damage (depending on the circumstances) and took that risk, he may be said to have been 'reckless'.

- Recklessness is not a crime in itself. But it is a *mens rea* element of the following crimes: reckless manslaughter, inflicting grievous bodily harm, malicious wounding, assault occasioning actual bodily harm, assault and battery, criminal damage and arson.

- The *Caldwell* test, which tested recklessness 'objectively', that is, by looking at events from the perspective of the ordinary, prudent individual, was introduced in 1981 but has now been abolished by the House of Lords (*G and R*). The *Caldwell* loophole identified in *Shimmen* has been closed.

4 Strict liability

Introduction

As we have seen, the prosecution will normally have to establish that an accused has carried out the prohibited criminal act (*actus reus*) with the accompanying 'guilty mind' (*mens rea*). This sounds fair enough. After all, it is essentially the state of mind of an accused that marks his behaviour out as 'criminal' and is reflected appropriately in the sentence. For example, intentionally causing serious harm is a far more serious offence than recklessly (maliciously) causing serious harm since the harm is actually intended rather than simply being risked. The convicted criminal is likely to be given a heavier sentence as a result and we can see that this can be justified. It will, however, come as little surprise to learn that there are one or two exceptions to this general rule.

Crimes which do not require proof of *mens rea* – intention, recklessness or even negligence – as to one or more elements of the *actus reus* are known as offences of *strict liability*. D will have no excuse, no matter how careful he has been. Simply causing the prohibited consequence will be sufficient to convict. This was demonstrated in the case of *Callow v Tillstone* (1900).

> *Callow v Tillstone* (1900)
> D, a butcher, asked a vet to examine a carcass to check that it was fit for human consumption. On receiving the vet's recommendation that it was fit, he offered it for sale. But the vet had been negligent, and the meat was not fit. D was convicted of exposing unsound meat for sale, even though he had exercised due care and taken reasonable steps to avoid committing the offence.

Short of not selling the meat, there was no way D could avoid liability. This, of course, scarcely seems fair to the individual. Similarly, D will be liable for driving while unfit through drink (s.4, Road Traffic Act 1988) or driving with a level of alcohol in their blood, breath or urine above prescribed limits (s.5 RTA) even if they were unaware of their condition and not responsible for it; for example, where their soft drink has been surreptitiously spiked with alcohol. So how can this be justified?

The answer is that Parliament, and in rare cases the courts, have been prepared to surrender the traditional insistence upon proof of a guilty mind where there is a greater benefit to be obtained to the public as a whole. Typically strict liability offences are the less serious, regulatory offences involving road safety, pollution or food hygiene. In cases of doubt the courts maintain a vigilant attitude wherever possible so as to protect an individual against unjust conviction. This they do by asserting that they will normally require the prosecution to prove *mens rea* unless convinced by the wording of a statute that Parliament has clearly intended otherwise. In any case of ambiguity the benefit of doubt goes to the accused.

While liability may be strict in respect of one element of the *actus reus*, other elements of the *actus reus* may require intention, recklessness or negligence. Consider the offence under s.55 of the Offences Against the Person Act 1861, taking an unmarried girl under the age of 16 out of the possession of her father against his will (now repealed). In *Prince* (1875), D was convicted – despite his defence that he reasonably believed the girl was 18 – because the court held that liability with respect to the age of the girl (who was in fact 15) was strict. However, in *Hibbert* (1869), D was acquitted – it was not proved that he knew the girl was in the possession of her father – because liability with respect to this aspect of the offence was not strict.

Contrast with absolute liability

Where an offence is one of *strict* liability, the prosecution must still prove that D committed the *actus reus*; if D acted involuntarily then there is no *actus reus* and so D cannot be held liable. Hence, D has a defence of automatism to driving offences if it is not proven that D was actually 'driving' (see Chapter 16). On the other hand, if an offence is one of absolute liability, even the lack of a voluntary act by D will not allow them to avoid liability (*Larsonneur* [1933], *Winzar v Chief Constable of Kent* [1983]).

Common law offences

There are few remaining common law offences of strict liability since the courts have always been opposed to the notion. One example is criminal contempt of court. When Parliament passed the Contempt of Court Act 1981, s.1 expressly affirmed 'the strict liability rule' for the offence of contempt, which continues to be a common law offence, albeit modified by the Act. Another such offence was blasphemous libel, but that has recently been abolished by s.79 of the Criminal Justice & Immigration Act 2008.

Statutory offences

The vast majority of strict liability offences are statutory. They have their origins in eighteenth- and nineteenth-century regulatory statutes relating to the adulteration of tobacco and foodstuffs, alongside legislation concerning liquor, factories, pollution and other public welfare matters. Faced with a welter of legislation, the courts abandoned the requirements of *mens rea* in many cases where there were no express words in the statute requiring proof of fault.

Strict liability has survived its Industrial Revolution origins and new offences may still be created (see *Harrow LBC v Shah & Shah* [1999], below, for a recent example). Indeed it is now accepted that the ordering of a complex modern society is simply not possible without the existence of such offences. The House of Lords has upheld the principle of strict liability on many occasions, the first being *Warner v MPC* (1969). In that case the Lords held that the offence of unauthorised possession of drugs, contrary to s.1 of the Drugs (Prevention of Misuse) Act 1964, amounted to a crime of strict liability.

Identifying offences of strict liability

The presumption of *mens rea*

There could, in theory, never be any doubt whether *mens rea* is required or not. It can be expressly stated in a statute that *mens rea* is required by using a word like 'intentionally', 'recklessly' or 'knowingly', or it can be stated that no *mens rea* is required (as in s.1 of the Contempt of Court Act 1981). However, many statutory offences remain silent, and the courts must resort to statutory interpretation.

The overriding principle is the presumption of *mens rea*. Judges have recognised that the starting point in interpreting a statutory offence is that Parliament intended the offence to be one of *mens rea*. In *Sherras v De Rutzen* (1895), Wright J said that there was 'a presumption that *mens rea*, or evil intention, or knowledge of the wrongfulness of the act, is an essential ingredient of every offence'. In *Sweet v Parsley* (1970), the Lords affirmed the presumption. Where Parliament expressly provided that an offence was strict, the courts must follow that. But, in other cases, the courts would assume that 'Parliament did not intend to make criminals of persons who were in no way blameworthy'. Thus, said Lord Reid, 'whenever a section is silent as to *mens rea* there is a presumption that . . . we must read in words appropriate to require *mens rea* . . .'

> *Sweet v Parsley* (1970)
> Stephanie Sweet, a school teacher, had rented a farmhouse near Oxford intending to live in it. However, this proved impracticable and instead she sub-let rooms to students. She did retain one room for her own use on the occasions when she visited the property to collect rent and see that everything was in order. Sometimes she

stayed overnight. Apart from those visits, the students had the property to themselves. The students were all using cannabis and LSD, though it appeared Ms Sweet had no knowledge whatsoever that this was going on. Nevertheless, she was convicted of being concerned in the management of premises, which were used for the purpose of smoking cannabis, contrary to s.5 of the Dangerous Drugs Act 1965. The Divisional Court upheld her conviction but the Lords allowed her appeal. Knowledge that the premises were being used for the prohibited purpose was required.

NB s.8 of the Misuse of Drugs Act 1971, which replaced s.5 of the 1965 Act, expressly provides that knowledge is required.

In 2000, the House of Lords delivered an important ruling on the use of strict liability in sex crimes where one of the elements of the *actus reus* is the age of the victim. In *B v DPP* (2000), B, aged 15, was convicted of inciting a child under the age of 14 to commit an act of gross indecency with him, contrary to s.1 of the Indecency with Children Act 1960. He had persistently, but unsuccessfully, asked a 13-year-old girl to perform oral sex on him. When charged, he claimed that he genuinely thought she was older, at least 14, and hence had not formed the *mens rea* for the offence. The question for the magistrates was whether this belief was relevant or whether liability was strict as to the child's age. The magistrates decided that liability was strict and therefore D was guilty, despite his belief. The Divisional Court rejected D's appeal but, on further appeal, the House of Lords quashed the conviction. The Lords decided that the offence required *mens rea* as to the age of the child, namely, either an intent to incite a child under 14 or recklessness as to whether the child was under 14 or not.

B v DPP was followed a year later by the House of Lords in *K* (2001). D, aged 26, was charged with carrying out an indecent assault on a girl under 16, contrary to s.14 of the Sexual Offences Act 1956. The question for the trial judge was whether the offence was one of strict liability as to the girl's age. He decided that it was not, relying on *B v DPP*, and therefore D had a good defence if he honestly thought the girl was at least 16 – even if she was, in fact, younger. The prosecution appealed but the House of Lords agreed with the judge. Lord Steyn said that it would have been 'strange' if Parliament in 1956 had wanted to make it a strict liability offence 'where any [sexual] contact takes place between two teenagers of whom one is under 16'. Instead, 'the strong presumption of *mens rea*' enabled the House of Lords to rule that a defendant charged with this offence was guilty only if he knew or realised that the girl was under 16.

Many sex crimes do refer to the age of the victim. Until recently these crimes were contained in a variety of statutes, primarily the Sexual

Offences Act 1956. The law has now been updated and consolidated in the Sexual Offences Act 2003, which contains the following age-based sex crimes:

- rape of a child under 13 (s.5)

- assault of a child under 13 by penetration (s.6)

- sexual assault of a child under 13 (s.7)

- sexual activity with a child under 16 (s.9).

Children under 13

The 2003 Act makes it clear that the s.5 offence (rape) is one of strict liability with regard to the age of the child. Thus, if D has sex with a 12-year-old girl, he is guilty of raping her even if he genuinely – and reasonably – believed that she was, in fact, older. In *G* (2008), the House of Lords confirmed that the s.5 offence was one of strict liability. The elements of the offence are that D (a) intentionally penetrates the vagina, anus or mouth of another person with his penis, and (b) the other person is under 13. Although D must have the intention to 'penetrate', there is no *mens rea* as to V's age, nor is there any *mens rea* as to whether or not V is consenting. In the words of Lord Hoffman, 'The policy of the legislation is to protect children. If you have sex with someone who is on any view a child or young person, you take your chance on exactly how old they are'.

Similarly, the 2003 Act makes it clear that the offences in sections 6 (penetration) and 7 (sexual assault) are also strict liability with regard to V's age. Thus, if D penetrates a 12-year-old girl's vagina with his finger (for example) then he is guilty of the s.6 offence even if he genuinely thought she was older. In *Court* (1989), D, a shop assistant, spanked a 12-year-old girl who had come into the shop, on the bottom outside her shorts about 12 times (he later admitted he had a buttock fetish). This type of case would now be dealt with under s.7, and it would be no defence for D to claim that he thought V was at least 13.

Children under 16

The s.9 offence (sexual activity) is slightly different from the offences in sections 5, 6 and 7. Under s.9, if V is aged under 13 then liability is strict as to V's age but, if V is aged at least 13 but no older than 15, D has a defence if he reasonably believed that V was at least 16. Note the 2003 Act requires D's belief to be reasonable – it is not a defence if D honestly (but unreasonably, perhaps because he was drunk) thought that a 15-year-old girl looked older than she was.

Rebutting the presumption

In *Gammon (HK) Ltd v A-G of Hong Kong* (1985), part of a temporary support on a building site had collapsed. Various parties involved in the building works were charged with deviating in a 'material' way from work shown on an approved plan. The question was whether the parties had to know their deviance was material, or whether liability was strict. The Privy Council held liability was strict. Lord Scarman indicated the matters that a court should consider to determine whether the presumption has been rebutted:

• there is a presumption of law that *mens rea* is required before a person can be held guilty of a criminal offence

• the presumption is particularly strong where the offence is 'truly criminal' in character

• the presumption applies to statutory offences, and can be displaced only if it is clearly or by necessary implication the effect of the statute

• the only situation in which the presumption can be displaced is where the statute is concerned with an issue of social concern

• even where a statute is concerned with such an issue, the presumption of *mens rea* stands unless it can also be shown that creation of strict liability will be effective in promoting the objects of the statute by encouraging greater vigilance to prevent the commission of the prohibited act.

In *Blake* (1997), the Court of Appeal specifically referred to Lord Scarman's five-point test in determining whether the offence in s.1 of the Wireless Telegraphy Act 1949, using a radio station without a licence, was one of strict liability (they decided that it was). In considering whether the presumption has been rebutted, the following factors may be considered.

Statutory language

There are many words in statutes which strongly imply that *mens rea* is required, while many other statutes, or even different sections of the same statute, do not have such words. Where Parliament has failed to include any word that might imply *mens rea*, it can be argued that it deliberately left them out, indicating a desire to create an offence of strict liability. However, even where no such words are used, it is not necessarily decisive (as in *Sweet v Parsley* above).

Verbs

Some verbs imply a mental element. Other verbs are less clear. What about 'permitting'? It is an offence under the Motor Vehicles (Construction and Use) Regulations 1951 if D 'uses or causes or permits to be used' on the road a motor vehicle with defective brakes. In fact, this creates three separate offences. In *James & Son Ltd v Smee* (1955), the Divisional Court held that using a motor vehicle with defective brakes was an offence of strict liability; but the defendant company had been charged with *permitting the use* of the vehicle in question, and this offence was one which 'imports a state of mind'.

Adverbs

The use of adverbs makes it clear that *mens rea* is required. Clearly offences which may be committed only 'maliciously' or 'recklessly' cannot be strict liability. The clearest of all is 'knowingly' – it would surely be impossible for a court to interpret an offence requiring that D act 'knowingly' as one not requiring *mens rea*! The position of 'wilfully' is less clear. The case law is inconsistent, but the leading authority is *Sheppard and Sheppard* (1980), decided in the House of Lords. D was not guilty of 'wilfully neglecting' a child in a manner likely to cause it unnecessary suffering or injury to its health, contrary to s.1 of the Children and Young Persons Act 1933, by simply refraining from getting medical aid and allowing it to die.

Sheppard and Sheppard (1980)

James and Jennifer Sheppard had a young son. They were themselves a young couple in their early twenties. The child died, aged 16 months, of hypothermia associated with malnutrition. The couple, who were of low intelligence and on a meagre income, denied 'wilfully neglecting' the boy in the weeks preceding his death. Although they were convicted, the House of Lords allowed their appeal. The court ruled that a conviction could be imposed only where (a) D knew that there was a risk that the child's health would suffer or (b) where he was unaware of the risk, if he did not care whether the child might be in need of medical care or not.

Lord Diplock accepted their version of events: that they did not realise that the boy was ill enough to need a doctor; they genuinely thought his loss of appetite and failure to keep down his food was due to 'some passing minor upset'.

The statutory context

Assistance may come from *other* sections of the same Act. If *mens rea* words are used in some sections, but not in others, this suggests that

Parliament deliberately created offences of strict liability in the latter sections. In *Cundy v Le Cocq* (1884), D, a publican, was convicted of selling intoxicating liquor to a person who was already drunk, contrary to s.13 of the Licensing Act 1872. Despite the fact that D did not know that the man was drunk, his conviction was upheld, after the Divisional Court examined the other sections of the 1872 Act. Some sections contained the word 'knowingly' while s.13 did not.

Similarly, in *Pharmaceutical Society of Great Britain v Storkwain Ltd* (1986), the defendant company supplied specified drugs on prescriptions, purportedly signed by a Dr Irani. The prescriptions were forged. The company was charged under s.58 of the Medicines Act 1968, which provides that no person shall sell by retail prescription-only medicines except in accordance with a prescription given by an appropriate medical practitioner. There was no suggestion that the company had acted intentionally, recklessly, or even negligently – the forgery was a very good one. But the House of Lords held that the offence was one of strict liability. The presence of words requiring *mens rea* in other parts of the 1968 Act helped the House of Lords to this conclusion.

This test is not, however, decisive. In *Sweet v Parsley*, Lord Reid said that 'the fact that other sections of the Act expressly require *mens rea* . . . is not itself sufficient to justify a decision that a section which is silent as to *mens rea*' creates a strict liability offence. An example of this occurred in *Sherras v De Rutzen* (1895). D, a publican, was convicted under s.16(2) of the Licensing Act 1872, for unlawfully supplying liquor to a policeman on duty. D regularly served officers in uniform if they were off-duty, which was indicated by the officer not wearing an armlet. On the day in question, an officer was in D's bar without an armlet, so D assumed – on this occasion, wrongly – that he was off-duty. The Divisional Court noted that s.16(1) made it an offence for a licensee to 'knowingly' harbour or suffer to remain on his premises any constable on duty. The court therefore imported a similar requirement into s.16(2), despite the absence of any *mens rea* word in that subsection, and quashed D's conviction.

> Is it possible to reconcile the decisions in *Sherras v De Rutzen* and *Storkwain* in terms of fault? The accused in both cases could be regarded as the victims of deception.

The statutory context was taken into consideration by the House of Lords in the recent case of *DPP v Collins* (2006). The House of Lords was asked to decide whether the offence of sending a grossly offensive message by means of a public electronic communications network, contrary to s.127(1)(a) of the Communications Act 2003, was one of strict liability.

Specifically, the question for the Law Lords was whether the prosecution had to prove, on the part of D:

- simply an intent to send a message (which happened to be grossly offensive); or

- an intent to send a grossly offensive message.

Lord Bingham drew comparisons with offences in the surrounding subsections which, he said, explicitly 'require proof of an unlawful purpose and a degree of knowledge'. By contrast, he said, s.127(1)(a) 'provides no explicit guidance on the state of mind which must be proved against a defendant to establish an offence against the subsection'. Lord Bingham therefore concluded that no *mens rea* was required in s.127(1)(a) as to the grossly offensive nature of the message, it was enough to prove that D intended to send messages which 'were grossly offensive and would be found by a reasonable person to be so'. It was irrelevant whether D intended his message to be grossly offensive.

DPP v Collins (2006)
D telephoned his MP and left a number of messages either on his answering machine or with his staff. In those messages D referred to 'wogs', 'Pakis', 'black bastards' and 'niggers'. D was charged with sending grossly offensive messages. At first instance the magistrates decided that, although the messages were offensive, a reasonable person would not have found them *grossly* offensive, and acquitted D. The prosecution appealed, unsuccessfully, to the High Court. A further prosecution appeal to the House of Lords was successful. The Law Lords unanimously decided that the messages were grossly offensive 'applying the standards of an open and just multiracial society'. Moreover, the fact that D himself did not necessarily intend his messages to be grossly insensitive was irrelevant.

'True' crimes and 'quasi' crimes

The courts have drawn a distinction between 'real' or 'true' crimes, on one hand, and 'quasi' crimes, on the other. In *Gammon (HK) Ltd v A-G of Hong Kong* (1985), Lord Scarman, giving the opinion of the Privy Council, said that the presumption of *mens rea* was particularly strong where the offence was 'truly' criminal. In *Wings Ltd v Ellis* (1985), Lord Scarman again said of the Trade Descriptions Act 1968 (which creates various criminal offences that are designed to regulate trading and to protect the consumer) that the entire statute 'belongs to that class of legislation which prohibits acts which are not criminal in any real sense'. These are often referred to as 'quasi-crimes'.

So what distinguishes a 'true' crime (requiring *mens rea*) from a 'quasi' crime (strict liability)? The former category includes offences that could be (very loosely) described as immoral (murder, rape, assault, theft, etc.). The latter are those which involve a technical breach of the law, but it is a breach to which no social stigma, no 'disgrace of criminality', attaches. Most offences of strict liability – relating to driving, food hygiene and public safety – are not inherently immoral. There is nothing inherently immoral in motorway driving at 70.1 mph, as opposed to 69.9 mph, but Parliament has made it an offence, in the interests of public safety. Those who break such laws are punished in order to encourage them, and others, to follow the laws for their own safety. But such people are not really regarded as 'criminals'.

The case of *Harrow London Borough Council v Shah and Shah* (1999) helps to demonstrate this issue. The National Lottery Regulations 1994 provide that 'No National Lottery ticket shall be sold by or to a person who has not attained the age of 16 years'. One day H, who worked at the defendants' newsagent's shop in Harrow, sold a National Lottery ticket to a 13-year-old boy. H thought, reasonably, that the boy was at least 16. The Queen's Bench Divisional Court directed a conviction: the offence was one of strict liability. The court said that the offence was 'plainly' not truly criminal.

Of course, strict liability is not confined to 'quasi' crimes. This test, like all of the tests in this section, provides guidance but is never decisive and must be considered alongside the other tests.

General or specific application?

The judges' perceptions of public policy considerations have greatly influenced the application of strict liability offences in particular situations. If an offence applies only to a specific class of persons, who are engaged in a particular activity, trade or profession, such as food and drugs, liquor, particular industries, etc., the courts are more likely to find that it is strict liability. If it applies to society as a whole, it is more likely to be a 'real' crime (although driving is an exception). This helps to explain cases such as *Storkwain*, above – the prohibition was particular to pharmacists.

Degree of social danger

The greater the social danger, i.e. the more people likely to be affected by commission of the offence, the more likely the presumption of *mens rea* will be rebutted. Hence many strict liability offences relate to industrial activities, pollution, and food hygiene. Crucially, it also explains why driving offences are strict liability even though the vast majority of citizens partake of the activity. In *Alphacell Ltd v Woodward* (1972), which concerned the offence of causing polluting matter to enter a river, contrary to s.2 of the Rivers (Prevention of Pollution) Act 1951, Lord Salmon said, 'It is of the utmost public importance that rivers should not be polluted'.

Alphacell Ltd v Woodward (1972)
Alphacell Ltd had a factory on the banks of a river where they produced manilla fibres, a raw material for paper. Part of the process involved washing the fibres. The dirty water was then piped to two 'settling tanks' on the riverbank, where the water would be cleaned. The tanks were equipped with pumps, designed to prevent overflow into the river. If the pumps failed to work, the tanks would overflow, so every weekend a man was supposed to inspect the pumps. However, over a period of time a quantity of brambles, ferns and leaves were allowed to clog up the pumps until eventually the tanks overflowed and dirty water was released directly into the river. The company was convicted of causing polluting matter to enter a river, contrary to the 1951 Act – despite the presence of the pumps and the man whose job it was to inspect them.

A more recent decision of the House of Lords, *Empress Car Company v National Rivers Authority* (1998), also imposed strict liability on the offence of causing polluting matter to enter controlled waters, contrary to the Water Resources Act 1991. Thus the defendant company was liable for pollution caused by oil escaping into a river – even though an unknown person had opened a tap on a diesel tank. The Lords said that the company was responsible for matters of ordinary occurrence, such as vandalism, but would not be held liable for extraordinary events such as terrorist attack.

In a similar vein, in *Wings Ltd v Ellis* (1985), Lord Scarman decided to construe the offence, in s.14 of the Trade Descriptions Act 1968, for any person in the course of trade or business to 'make a statement which he knows to be false' as one of strict liability. The company had published a holiday brochure in which it was stated, innocently but incorrectly, that a room at the Seashells Hotel in Sri Lanka was air-conditioned. A couple from Plymouth booked a holiday in reliance upon the brochure – and duly suffered the consequences of a holiday in a non-air-conditioned room in sweltering heat and humidity. They complained to trading standards officers on their return, and they brought a prosecution. The House of Lords held that the company was liable. Lord Scarman described the 1968 Act as 'plainly a very important safeguard for those members of the public (and they run into millions) who choose their holidays in this way'.

In *Blake* (1997), the Court of Appeal decided that the offence of operating a radio station without a licence, contrary to s.1 of the Wireless Telegraphy Act 1949, was one of strict liability. Unlicensed radio transmissions were dangerous because they could interfere with radio systems employed by the emergency services and air traffic controllers. And in *Harrow LBC v Shah* (1999), the Divisional Court held that the offence of selling National Lottery tickets to minors was strict liability. The National Lottery Regulations 1994 dealt with an issue of social concern, namely, the problem of young people gambling.

In *Bromley LC v C* (2006), the High Court held that s.444(1) of the Education Act 1996 (the offence of failing to secure school attendance) was one of strict liability. It was therefore no excuse for a mother to take her children out of school during term time without the head teacher's permission even though the mother honestly (and perhaps reasonably) believed that it was beneficial for her children's development. The issue of ensuring school attendance is clearly one of high importance.

Severity of punishment

The courts' approach here reveals no consistency. A low maximum penalty in a statute may indicate that an offence is not 'truly' criminal, and hence liability should be strict. Conversely, a severe penalty, particularly imprisonment, may suggest that the offence deals with a matter of grave social danger, and so liability should be strict. Hence, in *Storkwain*, the maximum penalty of two years' imprisonment did not prevent the House of Lords deciding that liability was strict. Similarly, in *Gammon*, the maximum penalties were a HK$250,000 fine and/or three years' imprisonment. The Privy Council thought this indicated the 'seriousness with which the legislature viewed the offence' – it did not prevent the imposition of strict liability. The most extreme example is *Howells* (1977), where D was charged with possession of a firearm without a certificate contrary to s.1 of the Firearms Act 1968. The Court of Appeal held that the maximum prison term of five years did not preclude strict liability. Other factors, in particular the danger to the community arising from unregistered possession of lethal weapons, justified the decision.

Promotion of standards and law enforcement

The mere fact a statute deals with an issue of social concern will not displace the presumption of *mens rea*. Strict liability must be effective in encouraging vigilance and observance of the law, and promoting standards generally. If it would not have this effect, the offence is probably not strict liability. In *Reynolds v G H Austin and Sons Ltd* (1951), Devlin J said that to punish a private-hire coach company for breaches of the Road Traffic

Act 1934 caused by the acts of the trip organiser, over whom the company had no influence or control, would engage the law 'not in punishing thoughtlessness or inefficiency, and thereby promoting the welfare of the community, but in pouncing on the most convenient victim'.

Similarly, in *Lim Chin Aik* (1963), D had been convicted under s.6(2) of the Immigration Ordinance 1952 of remaining in Singapore after having been denied entry. He had not known about the prohibition, which had not even been published. The Privy Council quashed his conviction.

However, the theory that making offences strict liability encourages better standards has been queried. In *City of Saulte Ste Marie* (1978), the Supreme Court of Canada, observed that:

> If a person is already taking every reasonable precautionary measure, is he likely to take additional measures, knowing that however much care he takes, it will not serve as a defence in the event of breach? If he has exercised care and skill, will conviction have a deterrent effect upon him or others?

A glaring example of the courts imposing strict liability, in a case where it is difficult to see how D could have done much more, is *Smedleys Ltd v Breed* (1974). A Dorset housewife bought a tin of peas from a supermarket. The tin of peas was one of 3.5 million tins that had been processed by Smedley's that year. When the woman opened the tin she found a dead Hawk Moth caterpillar inside. The caterpillar being small, round in shape, green in colour – in fact, looking exactly like a pea – had passed through the tinning process undetected. A prosecution was brought under s.2 of the Food and Drugs Act 1955. The magistrates, although finding that Smedley's had exercised all reasonable care, found the company was nevertheless guilty of the offence, because it was one of strict liability. Appeals to the Divisional Court and House of Lords were unsuccessful.

Impact of the Human Rights Act 1998

In the case of *G* (2008), discussed above, D, a 15-year-boy, had consensual sex with a 12-year-old girl although he honestly believed that she was actually 15. D was charged with the offence under s.5 of the Sexual Offences Act 2003 (rape of a child under 13) and pleaded not guilty. However, after being told that his belief as to V's age was irrelevant, D pleaded guilty. He then appealed on the ground that the s.5 offence was in breach of Article 6(2) of the European Convention of Human Rights, which states that 'Everyone charged with a criminal offence shall be presumed innocent until proved guilty according to law'. The Court of Appeal and House of Lords both dismissed his appeal. Lord Hope explained the position with regard to Article 6(2) as follows:

When Article 6(2) uses the words 'innocent' and 'guilty' it is dealing with the burden of proof regarding the elements of the offence and any defences to it. It is not dealing with what those elements are or what defences to the offence ought to be available.

In other words, the mere fact that a criminal offence – even one as serious as rape of a child – is a strict liability offence does *not* amount to a breach of D's human rights. The Court of Appeal in *Deyemi* (2007) reached the same conclusion in a case involving the offence of possessing a prohibited weapon contrary to s.5 of the Firearms Act 1968.

Deyemi (2007)
The police had found D in possession of an electrical stun-gun (a prohibited weapon). D admitted having it in his possession but said that he thought that it was a torch. The court accepted that this was D's genuine belief. However, D was still found guilty after the trial judge ruled that the s.5 offence was one of strict liability – that is, D's genuine belief that it was not a stun-gun was irrelevant. The Court of Appeal dismissed the appeal and confirmed that the imposition of strict liability was not in breach of D's human rights.

Pros and cons of strict liability

One of the main justifications for imposing liability without fault is the *ease of conviction*. Convictions, especially for regulatory offences, may be difficult to secure if *mens rea* had to be proved. Making an offence strict liability makes for efficient law enforcement and administration of the judicial process. It is only necessary to prove the *actus reus* was carried out; there is no need to prove *mens rea*, which is also more difficult to do and easy to deny.

While this is true, making such offences strict is not necessary for conviction. Legislation *could* be interpreted to involve a reversal of the burden of proof, imposing a presumption of negligence, so that D would be convicted unless they proved that they had not been at fault, i.e. a 'no fault' or 'due diligence' defence could be utilised (see below). If this had been adopted when strict liability was in its infancy it may well have stuck, but whether the position will change now is questionable.

Baroness Wootton, in her book *Crime and the Criminal Law* (1981), argued for the extension of strict liability to all crimes. She wrote, 'If . . . the primary function of the courts is conceived as the prevention of forbidden acts, there is little cause to be disturbed by the multiplication of offences of strict liability'. Of course, what is a 'forbidden act'? If, in murder, it is causing death, a boxer could be liable if his opponent suffers brain damage and dies; a surgeon could be liable if the life-saving heart transplant is successful but complications set in and the patient dies.

This would curtail much human activity – would any surgeons undertake operations carrying any risk of death? Such a law would jeopardise society, not protect it. Leaving it up to the judge to correct this in sentencing does not prevent the fact that the surgeon was convicted of murder. The courts would also be cluttered with blameless people who had caused various 'forbidden acts' but who would end up with an absolute discharge.

One purpose of the criminal law is to deter harmful conduct, but it only makes sense to deter intentional, reckless or negligent behaviour; if the harm occurs even if D takes reasonable care, imposing liability for it will only prevent its occurrence in the future if no-one does the act at all. That would mean no-one driving, operating factories, selling food, etc. – which is ridiculous. The law should encourage care on the part of the people undertaking these activities, but should not discourage them altogether.

In *Storkwain*, Lord Salmon said that strict liability would encourage those who might be potential polluters 'not only to take reasonable steps to prevent pollution but to do everything possible to ensure that they do not cause it'. This is fanciful to say the least.

> Why should a firm take hugely expensive precautions when they are going to be punished if they nevertheless accidentally pollute a river? Would it not make more sense for companies to scrap all precautions and save money to pay any fines imposed?

Sentencing

Another problem with extending strict liability is that it would make sentencing very difficult. The person who *deliberately* pollutes a river is deserving of much harsher punishment than someone who *inadvertently* pollutes a river despite taking the most elaborate and expensive precautions possible. Yet, if the prosecution only have to prove the *actus reus*, mitigating evidence would not come out before the court.

Due diligence defences

A defence of due diligence, or no-negligence, may be available in certain situations. The burden of proof is on D to establish the defence. Due diligence defences appear in many statutes, such as s.24 of the Trade Descriptions Act 1968. In some cases the defence is combined with a third-party defence requiring D to prove both that they, D, exercised due diligence, and the offence was due to the act or default of a third party.

S.24 is an example. It provides that it is a defence for the person charged to prove:

- that the commission of the offence was due to a mistake or to reliance on information supplied to them or to the act or default of another person, an accident or some other cause beyond their control; and

- that they took all reasonable precautions and exercised all due diligence to avoid the commission of such an offence . . .

The defence was relied upon in *Tesco Ltd v Nattrass* (1972). The supermarket chain was accused of the offence under s.11 of the 1968 Act (giving an indication that goods are on sale at a lower price than that at which they are, in fact, on sale). 'Radiant' washing powder had been advertised as on sale at the company's Northwich branch for about 14p whereas the true price was nearer 19p. The company relied upon s.24(1); specifically, they blamed the store manager, a Mr Clement, for not checking the shelves thoroughly. The House of Lords held that the company was entitled to rely upon the defence.

Due diligence defences have been developed by the courts at common law in Australia, Canada and New Zealand. These have general application: that is, they apply to every strict liability offence notwithstanding lack of a statutory defence. According to the Supreme Court of Canada in *City of Sault Ste Marie*, 'The defence will be available if [D] reasonably believed in a mistaken set of facts which, if true, would render the act or omission innocent, or if he took all reasonable steps to avoid the particular event'. Despite the notion of strict liability itself being a common law invention, no court in England has followed these leads. One problem would be in deciding exactly how to structure such a defence.

A due dilligence defence of general application (that is, it would apply to every strict liability offence notwithstanding lack of a statutory defence) could take any one of the several forms. Which of the following (if any) would you adopt?

- D must *prove*, on the balance of probabilities, that he honestly believed in a state of facts which, had they existed, would have made his act innocent

- As above, but D must also *prove* that his belief was *reasonably held*

- D must *produce evidence* that he honestly believed in a state of facts which, had they existed, would have made his act innocent, in which case the Crown must prove beyond reasonable doubt that he had no such belief

- As above, but D must *also* produce evidence that his belief was *reasonably held*, while the Crown may seek to prove beyond reasonable *that his belief was unreasonable.*

Summary

- Crimes of strict liability are those which do not require *mens rea* – intention, recklessness or even negligence – as to one or more elements of the *actus reus.*

- D will have no excuse, no matter how careful he has been (*Callow v Tillstone*; *Smedleys Ltd v Breed*).

- The vast majority of these crimes are statutory, but some are common law, e.g. criminal contempt of court.

- Strict liability was first used in the nineteenth century but even today courts are prepared to hold that recent statutory provisions impose strict liability (*Harrow LBC v Shah and Shah*; *DPP v Collins*).

- There is a presumption of *mens rea* (*Sherras v De Rutzen*; *Sweet v Parsley*; *B v DPP*).

- But the presumption may be rebutted (*Gammon [HK] Ltd v A-G of Hong Kong*).

- The courts will look at a number of factors in deciding whether the presumption has been rebutted – none of which is decisive. These factors include:

  - The statutory language. Certain words are suggestive of *mens rea* (*Sheppard and Sheppard*).

  - The statutory context (*Cundy v Le Cocq*; *Pharmaceutical Society of Great Britain v Storkwain Ltd*; *Sherras v De Rutzen*).

  - Whether the offence was a 'true' or 'quasi' crime; true crimes require *mens rea* (*Wings Ltd v Ellis*; *Harrow LBC v Shah & Shah*).

  - Whether the offence was of general or specific application. Offences of specific application may not need *mens rea.*

– The degree of social danger. The more dangerous the activity, the more likely strict liability will be imposed (*Alphacell Ltd v Woodward*; *Wings Ltd v Ellis*).

– The severity of punishment. Low statutory penalties suggest strict liability, but this is not decisive (*Howells*).

– Whether the imposition of strict liability would promote higher standards and/or law enforcement (*Reynolds v G H Austin and Sons Ltd*; *Lim Chin Aik*).

• The imposition of strict liability does *not* breach D's human rights, in particular, the presumption of innocence (*G*; *Deyemi*).

• Certain statutes contain due diligence defences (*Tesco Ltd v Nattrass*) but there is no common law due diligence defence of general application.

Questions on Part I General principles I

1 'Strict liability offences are necessary in a modern society. They promote high standards of behaviour, protect the public and guard against dangerous activities. In these circumstances it is fair that the prosecution do not have the difficult task of proving *mens rea* (a guilty mind).'

Discuss the validity of this statement using relevant cases to illustrate your answer.

(OCR 2006)

2 'In general, the criminal law prohibits the doing of harm but does not impose criminal liability for an omission. However, there are justifiable exceptions to this general principle.'

Assess the truth of this statement by reference to situations where a failure to act may result in criminal liability.

(OCR 2005)

3 Assume that Parliament has recently passed the Inshore Waters Safety Act. This makes it an offence 'to use or permit to be used a speedboat, launch, jetski or similar motorised craft without a licence from the relevant local authority'.

Jetskis Are Us Ltd, a company which specialises in the hire of jetskis, instructs Sharp, its area manager, to promote the hire of jetskis at all large holiday resorts in the south of England. Sharp telephones the local authority in Crystalwater, a southern coastal town and is told by Crapp, a clerk in the relevant department, that Jetskis Are Us Ltd have been granted a licence but that the official confirmation may be delayed because the computer network at the local authority has crashed. In fact Crapp has made a mistake and Jetskis Are Us Ltd have been refused a licence. Jetskis Are Us Ltd begin hiring out jetskis to the public from the beach at Crystalwater believing that a licence has been granted. Hugh hires a jetski from Jetskis Are Us Ltd on the opening day.

Discuss the criminal liability, including possible strict liability, if any, of Jetskis Are Us Ltd and Sharp for permitting the use of the jetski without a licence, Hugh for using the jetski and of Crapp for aiding and abetting Sharp.

(OCR 2002)

Part 2

Homicide

Figure 1 Unlawful homicide

This is essentially either murder or manslaughter and can be broadly classified as follows:

1. Murder

Unlawful killing of a human being under the Queen's Peace with malice aforethought (*Moloney 1985 HL/Woollin 1998 HL* – note this is *not* a statutory definition).

Malice aforethought – intention to kill or cause the victim serious bodily harm.

2. Manslaughter

There are two categories of manslaughter:

(a) VOLUNTARY and (b) INVOLUNTARY, each of which can be further subdivided:

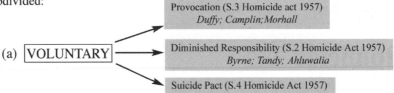

(a) VOLUNTARY

Provocation (S.3 Homicide act 1957)
Duffy; Camplin; Morhall

Diminished Responsibility (S.2 Homicide Act 1957)
Byrne; Tandy; Ahluwalia

Suicide Pact (S.4 Homicide Act 1957)

Although malice aforethought is present the accused successfully pleads a special and partial defence under the Homicide Act 1957.

(b) INVOLUNTARY

The unlawful killing of a human being under the Queen's Peace without malice aforethought

- Killing by an unlawful and dangerous act (constructive manslaughter)
  Church; Newbury and Jones; Goodfellow

- Gross negligence manslaughter (*Stone and Dobinson; Adomako*)

- Subjectively reckless manslaughter (*Lidar*)

Be sure you understand this classification and that murder requires a *specific intent* to kill or do serious harm whereas involuntary manslaughter is a crime of *basic intent*. This will be significant when related to the defence of intoxication.

5 Murder

Introduction

The offence of murder is the most serious of criminal offences and attracts a mandatory life sentence upon conviction. It is associated with some of the most notorious names in the annals of crime: Dr Crippen, Peter Sutcliffe, Dennis Nielsen and Dr Harold Shipman to name but a few. It may, therefore, seem odd that murder is still defined through a whole series of common law decisions that have occurred over the years. There is, for example, no Murder Act in this country. Contrary to popular misconception, s.1 of the Homicide Act 1957 does *not* define murder. The Act mainly deals with a number of special defences that can be pleaded to the charge. To discover the law of murder you have to trace its evolution through a series of important judgments in decided cases since the seventeenth century, culminating in the House of Lords decision in *Woollin* (1998). As with other offences it is essential to appreciate the elements of *actus reus* and *mens rea* that constitute the offence.

Actus reus

The *actus reus* of murder – which is exactly the same for manslaughter – comprises the following four elements:

- Causing the death

- Of another human being

- Under the Queen's Peace

- Within any county of the realm

All of these must be present. If any one of them is missing, there cannot be liability for murder under English law. There used to be a fifth element:

- Within a year and a day

However, this element was deemed surplus to requirements and was abolished in 1996.

Mens rea

The *mens rea* of murder is 'malice aforethought'. This means one of two things:

- An intention to kill (express malice aforethought)

or

- An intention to cause grievous bodily harm (implied malice aforethought).

Either of these states of mind will be sufficient for a conviction. If both are missing, the defendant cannot be convicted of murder – but may well be facing liability for involuntary manslaughter (see Chapter 7).

Causing death

When D is charged with murder (or manslaughter) it is necessary to prove that D, by his acts or omissions, caused V's death. If V dies because of some other cause then the offence has not been committed even though all the other elements of the offence, including the *mens rea*, are present. D may of course be liable for attempt instead (*White* [1910]). The vast majority of reported cases on causation involve homicide (see Chapter 1), but the principles of causation apply equally to any result crime (e.g. criminal damage, various assaults). It does not matter how the death is caused (by shooting, stabbing, drowning, strangling, poisoning, etc.) as long as it is caused by the conduct of the accused.

Another human being

Only human beings can be the victims of murder. This sounds obvious – but there are potential problems with people just beginning, or nearing the end of, their lives. For example, a foetus that is killed in the womb cannot be a victim of murder, though there are other offences: procuring a miscarriage and child destruction.

A person who is already dead obviously cannot be the victim of murder (although the person who shoots a corpse lying under bedclothes, without realising the intended victim is already dead from natural causes, could theoretically be convicted of *attempted* murder – see Chapter 21). However, the correct definition of death has proved elusive. There is conventional death, when the heartbeat and breathing stop. But there is also brain death, when through artificial means the heart continues to beat and air circulates the lungs. Brain death is recognised by the British Medical Association and is the point when life-support machinery will be switched off. In *Malcharek, Steel* (1981), the Court of Appeal referred to this test although they did not have to decide the point. It is likely that if the question arose squarely that the courts would adopt the brain death test (or strictly tests as there are six of them).

The Queen's Peace

This only serves to exclude from homicide cases when enemy soldiers are killed in the course of war.

Within any county of the realm

Murder and manslaughter are exceptional from a jurisdictional point of view in that they are triable in England even if the offence is perpetrated abroad, provided D is a British citizen.

The year-and-a-day rule

There used to be a rule that death had to occur within a year and a day of the original stabbing, strangling, etc. This rule was justified because of the difficulty in establishing causation where there was a long interval between the original wound and V's death. The net result was that if D stabbed or shot someone, but V was kept alive for 367 days before death, D could not be guilty of homicide.

Medical science developed to such an extent that the original justification was no longer valid. The Law Commission recommended the abolition of the rule and in 1996 the Law Reform (Year-and-a-Day Rule) Act 1996 came into force, abolishing the rule (s.1). The reform applies to any 'fatal offence', defined as including murder, manslaughter, infanticide and 'any other offence' of which one of the elements is causing a person's death. The Law Commission recognised the undesirability of an unqualified abolition of the rule in two circumstances (s.2(2)).

- If a very long time had passed since the original incident, it would be undesirable to have the history of the case trawled over again in a homicide trial. It could mean D having to live for years with the threat of a murder charge hanging over him. It makes more sense to prosecute for an assault or wounding charge now, rather than wait for years to see whether V dies or not. Hence, if the injury alleged to cause death was sustained *more than three years* before the death occurred, then homicide proceedings may not be brought except by or with the consent of the Attorney-General.

- If D has already been convicted of a non-fatal offence, or attempt, on the same set of facts, the consent of the Attorney-General is also required.

'Malice aforethought'

The *mens rea* of murder is malice aforethought. This is a technical term which implies neither ill-will nor premeditation. A person who kills out of compassion to alleviate suffering (a so-called 'mercy killing') almost certainly acts with malice aforethought. The term means that D either:

- intended to kill (*express malice*); or

- intended to cause grievous bodily harm (GBH) (*implied malice*).

This was not always entirely clear; but the House of Lords in *Moloney* (1985) confirmed that 'malice aforethought' means an intention to kill or an intention to cause GBH. Thus, it is possible for D to be convicted of murder when he intended some serious injury but did not even contemplate that V's life be endangered.

Intention

In many offences, the *mens rea* required is an 'intention' to cause a particular result. In murder, the *mens rea* is an intention to kill or cause GBH. Other crimes requiring intent include causing grievous bodily harm with intent to do so (see Chapter 8) and theft, where the intent is to permanently deprive the owner of their property (see Chapter 10). However, it is in the context of murder that the vast majority of intent cases have arisen, so it makes more sense to examine the topic here.

There are two forms of intent:

- Direct intent – this is what D desires;

- Indirect or oblique intent – this is not necessarily what D desires but what he foresees will almost certainly happen.

Direct intention

The dictionary definition of intention is to have something as one's aim or purpose. This form of intention is called direct intention. Suppose that D stands to gain under an insurance policy on V's life. He decides to kill V in order to gain the cash. Thus his desire is to kill V; his motive is to get rich. D points a gun at V's head and pulls the trigger. Clearly here D intends V's death. The consequence (death) was actually desired.

This is so even though V is far away, it is dark, D's aim is poor, and D believes that the chances of him hitting V are slim. If – despite the odds! – D succeeds in putting a bullet in V's brain, he will still be guilty as it was his desire and therefore also his intention to kill.

Now suppose that D sees V sitting in his car and shoots at his head. D realises that the bullet will pass through the car windscreen first. It may be said that D also intends to break the window, as it is a *necessary precondition* to killing V. Although V's death remains D's direct intention, he is prepared to accept the criminal damage and therefore also intends to break the windscreen. It is irrelevant that D does not want to break the windscreen.

Oblique intention

Now suppose that D places a bomb under V's airplane seat designed to explode when the plane is 30,000ft up over the mid-Atlantic. The consequence which D desires remains V's death – but what of the other passengers and crew? The other deaths are not a necessary precondition to killing V, but are an *almost inevitable consequence.* If D bothered to think about it, he would conclude that the deaths are practically certain. Thus he may be said to have intended the passengers' and crews' deaths too. This form of intention is described as oblique intention.

However, this scenario invites problems. What degree of probability is required before an undesired consequence, but which D has foreseen, can be said to have been intended? Some would argue none – that once one steps away from foresight of something as 100 per cent *certain to happen* then one is dealing with *risk*, and that means *recklessness*, not intent. Others would argue that very high probability would suffice.

The leading case is now that of the House of Lords in *Woollin* (1998). It is the culmination of several House of Lords and Court of Appeal decisions, dating back to the early 1970s. Various formulae have been proposed, adopted, criticised and dropped again as the courts have struggled to come up with a direction to juries that conveys the correct message. In *Woollin*, Lord Steyn (with whom the other Law Lords agreed) laid down a model direction, for trial judges to use in cases where D's intention is unclear, as follows:

> The jury should be directed that they are not entitled [to find] the necessary intention, unless they feel sure that death or serious bodily harm was a virtual certainty (barring some unforeseen intervention) as a result of [D]'s actions and that [D] appreciated that such was the case.

Woollin (1998)
Stephen Woollin had killed his three-month-old son, Carl Roper, by throwing him against a wall, fracturing his skull. W did not deny doing this, but claimed that he did not have the *mens rea* for murder. W claimed that he had picked the child up after he began to choke

and shaken him, then, in a fit of rage or frustration, had thrown him with some considerable force towards a pram four or five feet away. The trial judge directed the jury that they might infer intention if satisfied that when W threw the child he had appreciated that there was a 'substantial risk' that he would cause serious harm to the child. W was convicted of murder and appealed on the basis that the phrase 'substantial risk' was a test of recklessness, not of intent, and that the judge should have used 'virtual certainty'. The Court of Appeal dismissed the appeal but the House of Lords unanimously reversed that Court's decision, quashed W's murder conviction and substituted one of manslaughter.

The reason that the trial judge directed the jury to 'infer' intention is due to s.8 of the Criminal Justice Act 1967. This states, 'A court or jury in determining whether a person has committed an offence . . . shall decide whether he did intend . . . that result by reference to all the evidence, drawing such inferences from the facts as appear proper in the circumstances'. The statute therefore requires that juries must 'infer' intent. Trial judges across the country used this word faithfully for the next 30 years – but in *Woollin*, the Lords decided that the word 'find' got the point across more clearly.

The model jury direction in *Woollin* was first laid down by Lord Lane CJ in *Nedrick* (1986). That case provides a useful illustration of when D may be said to have an 'oblique' intent. D had a grudge against a woman. In the early hours of the morning, he poured paraffin through the letterbox of her house and set it alight. She survived but her 12-year-old son Lloyd died in the fire. D claimed that he had not intended to harm anyone, merely to wake the woman and frighten her. In the Court of Appeal, D's murder conviction was quashed and one of manslaughter was substituted – like *Woollin*, the jury had not been directed properly. However, it is possible that, had the jury been given the model direction, they may well have decided that D foresaw it as 'virtually certain' that someone – not necessarily Lloyd – would be killed or at least seriously injured, and so convicted D of murder. Many convictions are quashed in the Court of Appeal for technical legal reasons. Students should not be confused that this means that the Court is stating that in their view an accused is completely innocent and sometimes a re-trial is ordered.

An illustration of the sort of case where references to 'oblique' intent should be avoided altogether is *Moloney* (1985). D and his stepfather, V, had been drinking heavily into the early hours of the morning. The two men were heard talking and laughing until 4am when a shot rang out. D phoned the police to say, 'I've just murdered my father'. He said that they had a disagreement over who could load and fire a shotgun the fastest. He had fetched two guns and cartridges. D loaded first, at which point V goaded him to pull the trigger. D did so, apparently without aiming, but shot V in the head. D told the police, 'I just pulled the trigger and he was dead'. The trial judge directed the jury in terms of oblique intent and they convicted of murder. However, on appeal, a manslaughter conviction was substituted. Lord Bridge in the House of Lords stated:

> The golden rule should be that, when directing a jury . . . the judge should avoid any elaboration or paraphrase of what is meant by intent, and leave it to the jury's good sense to decide whether the accused acted with the necessary intent, unless the judge is convinced that, on the facts and having regard to the way that case has been presented . . . some further explanation or elaboration is strictly necessary to avoid misunderstanding . . .

In *Moloney*, the trial judge's direction created unnecessary confusion. The question for the jury was essentially factual. If D knew the gun was pointing at V's head, the jury was surely bound to convict him of murder, on the basis that he must have wanted to shoot V in the head. But, if they thought that D had not realised that the gun was pointing at V's head (given his tired and drunken condition), they should have convicted him of manslaughter (either on the basis that he had committed an unlawful and dangerous act or that he had been grossly negligent – see Chapter 7). Either D had the direct intent to kill, or he had no intent at all other than pulling the trigger. Oblique intent simply did not come into it.

However, *Woollin* does not completely clear up the confusion. Lord Steyn said that, if the jury are satisfied that D foresaw death (or really serious injury) as virtually certain to occur, then they are 'entitled to find' that he intended it. That is, the jury do not *have* to do so – they do not *have* to convict of murder. *Woollin* tells the jury nothing about what factors, if any, to take into account in deciding whether 'to find' intention, once they are sure that D foresaw death or really serious injury.

Intriguingly, in *Woollin*, Lord Steyn also said, at one point, that 'a result foreseen as virtually certain is an intended result'. However, that comment did not form part of the *ratio* of the case. Professor Sir John Smith argued that that 'is what the law should be', but it is not – yet. The law remains that foresight of a virtually certain consequence is not the same thing as intent, and that juries must be left to decide whether D intended a consequence. In *Scalley* (1995), a case which was almost factually identical to *Nedrick*, a jury was directed to convict of murder if they found that D had foreseen death as a virtually certain consequence, which they did. But the Court of Appeal quashed the conviction. The jury should have been told that if they found D had the necessary foresight then they could convict him of murder *but they did not have to.*

However, in *Matthews and Alleyne* (2003), the Court of Appeal upheld two murder convictions despite the fact that the trial judge had equated foresight of a virtually certain consequence with intention. The trial judge had told the jury that, if D and E appreciated that pushing V from a bridge into a river would be virtually certain to result in his death by drowning (because they knew he could not swim), then they 'must have' intended to kill him. The jury convicted and D and E appealed. Given the outcome in *Scalley*, we might have expected the appeal to be successful but the Court of Appeal upheld the convictions. Rix LJ held that, on the particular facts of the case, if the jury were sure that D and E had appreciated the virtual certainty of V's death when they threw him into the river, it was 'impossible' to see how they could not have drawn the inference that D and E intended V's death.

Matthews and Alleyne (2003)

At about 3 o'clock one morning, Jonathan Coles, an 18-year-old A-level student, was pushed from Tyringham Bridge over the River Ouse, where he fell about 25 feet into the river to his death. Coles had been at a Milton Keynes nightclub celebrating a friend's birthday. On leaving the club he was 'picked on' by a group of men, including the two appellants; he was beaten up and his bank-card stolen. What exactly happened next was disputed by the appellants but the jury found that Darren Matthews and Brian Alleyne pushed Coles from the bridge – despite the fact that he had told them he could not swim. Matthews and Alleyne were convicted of murder (as well as robbery and kidnapping) after the trial judge told the jury that if 'drowning was a virtual certainty and [the appellants] appreciated that . . . they must have had the intention of killing him'. Matthews and Alleyne appealed on the basis that this direction went beyond what was permitted by *Nedrick/Woollin* and equated foresight with intention. The Court of Appeal, however, rejected the appeal.

The following propositions can be made about indirect/oblique intention, as follows:

- Intention is a subjective concept. That is, it is entirely dependent on what was going through D's mind at the time he killed V.

- Unless dealing with direct intent, reference *must* be made to what D foresaw would happen as the result of his actions.

- It is only if D foresaw death or really serious injury as 'virtually certain' to happen, that a jury is 'entitled' to find that D intended it to happen.

- Other phrases, such as 'highly probable' or even 'very highly probable', do not satisfy this standard.

- It may be helpful to visualise degrees of foresight in relation to oblique intent where, remember, D does not desire V's death or GBH, but foresees the risk of it occurring, as follows:

Figure 2 Degrees of foresight

Impossible	Unlikely	Possible	Probable	Highly probable	Virtually certain	Certain
↓	↓	↓	↓	↓	↓	↓
		Manslaughter D is subjectively reckless *Lidar* (2000)			Jury can find intent *Woolin*	Murder D has intention

'Grievous bodily harm'

What does 'grievous bodily harm' (GBH) mean? In *DPP v Smith* (1961), Viscount Kilmuir, with whom the rest of the Lords agreed, held that there was no reason to give the words any special meaning: '"Bodily harm" needs no explanation and "grievous" means no more and no less than "really serious".' In *Saunders* (1985), D was charged with inflicting GBH contrary to s.20 of the Offences Against the Person Act 1861 after punching a stranger in the face, breaking his nose. He was convicted after the jury was directed that GBH meant 'serious injury'. The Court of Appeal dismissed the appeal, holding that the omission of 'really' was not significant. This was confirmed in *Janjua and Choudury* (1998). The Court of Appeal held that a trial judge has discretion when directing the jury whether or not to use the word 'really' before the words 'serious bodily harm'.

Manslaughter as an alternative verdict

Whenever murder is charged, there is always the possibility that the prosecution will not be able to prove one of the elements of *actus reus* (in which case an alternative verdict of attempted murder is possible, as in *White* [1910]) or *mens rea* (in which case a verdict of manslaughter is usually available). In *Coutts* (2006), the House of Lords allowed an appeal against a murder conviction on the basis that the jury was not allowed to consider manslaughter as an alternative verdict. D had pleaded not guilty, his defence being that V's death was a tragic accident, but the jury rejected that version of events and therefore convicted him of murder. Lord Rodger explained as follows:

> The jury were told that they had to choose between convicting the appellant of murder and acquitting him on the ground that the victim had died as a result of an accident. On that basis they chose to convict of murder. But the jury should also have been told that, depending on their view of the facts, they could convict him of manslaughter . . . The reality is that, in the course of their deliberations, a jury might well look at the overall picture, even if they eventually had to separate out the issues of murder, manslaughter and accident. So, introducing the possibility of convicting of manslaughter could have changed the way the jury went about considering their verdict.

Coutts (2006)
D was convicted of murder of Jane Longhurst. He admitted having 'consensual asphyxial sex' with Jane, meaning that he had – with her consent – 'tied a pair of tights round her neck'. At some point D had closed his eyes and released the tights, but by that time Jane had died. D said that he did not know how she had died. The prosecution alleged murder, and adduced evidence that D visited pornographic websites 'showing extreme violence towards women' under headings such as 'asphyxiation' and 'strangulation'. The prosecution also contended that he had visited Jane's body in various places where he had stored it for five weeks post-mortem before dumping it in woodland and setting it alight; this was suggestive of D's 'necrophiliac propensities'. At his trial, D claimed that Jane's death was a complete accident but the jury convicted him of murder and he was sentenced to 30 years' imprisonment. The Court of Appeal upheld his conviction but the House of Lords allowed his appeal.

Reform

Reform of murder

In November 2006, the Law Commission (LC) published a Report entitled *Murder, Manslaughter and Infanticide*. In it, among other things, they recommended a new three-tier structure for homicide:

- first-degree murder

- second-degree murder

- manslaughter.

The LC's main point is that the law of murder at present is too wide, by including in the meaning of 'malice aforethought' those who intended to do serious harm but had no idea that V was at risk of death. Hence, according to the LC, first-degree murder should cover all unlawful killings where D was proved to have intent to kill; *or* where D had intent to do serious injury *and* where D was also aware that their conduct posed a serious risk of death. Second-degree murder would include all unlawful killings where:

- D had the intent required for first-degree murder but pleaded one of the partial defences

- D had intent to do serious injury but was *not* aware of a serious risk of death

- D was aware that their conduct posed a serious risk of death and had intent to cause either:
  – some injury, or
  – a fear of injury, or
  – a risk of injury.

The LC did consider the creation of another category of murder, which could be described as 'aggravated murder'. Those could include, for example, serial killers (those who kill on more than one occasion) and/or those who kill using torture. Alternatively, it could include those whose killings cause fear among a group within society; for example, killings with a racist motive. However, the LC decided that, instead of recommending the creation of a new offence, such killings would remain as murder (whether first or second degree) and their aggravating features would be 'best reflected through an uncompromising approach to the length of the minimum custodial sentence imposed'.

In July 2008, the Government responded to the LC's Report. Although the Government intends to implement some of the LC's proposals regarding the partial defences (see Chapter 6), the response to the idea of degrees of homicide was rather unenthusiastic: the Government says that these recommendations 'may be considered at a later stage' – which probably means 'never'.

Reform of intention

In their 2006 Report, the LC also recommend that the *Woollin* direction on oblique intent should be codified (set out in a statute), and that 'intention' should be defined – in full – as follows:

1. A person should be taken to intend a result if he or she acts in order to bring it about.
2. In cases where the judge believes that justice may not be done unless an expanded understanding of intention is given, the jury should be directed as follows: an intention to bring about a result may be found if it is shown that the defendant thought that the result was a virtually certain consequence of his or her action.

However, there is no indication in the Government's July 2008 response to the LC's report that it intends to do anything about this recommendation. It is therefore safe to assume that, for the time being at least, the meaning of intention remains as set out in *Woollin*.

Meanwhile, there have been suggestions that intention should be limited to direct intention, i.e. aim or purpose. This would make the legal definition fit with the word's everyday dictionary meaning. In *Steane* (1947), this approach was adopted by the Court of Criminal Appeal. D was charged with doing acts likely to assist the enemy with intent to assist the enemy, contrary to the Defence (General) Regulations 1939. He was a British film actor resident in Germany prior to World War II who had been arrested when the war broke out and forced, extremely reluctantly, to broadcast propaganda on German radio. Threats had been made to place his wife and children in a concentration camp if he did not comply. The Court quashed his conviction, because of his lack of intent.

Such reform would also provide a clear distinction between intention and recklessness. How is it possible to distinguish a consequence foreseen as 'virtually certain' (which is intended) from one foreseen as 'highly probable' (where D is reckless)? There is no obvious cut-off.

Do you agree that some clear, legal and/or moral distinction should be drawn between the following:

- D1, who causes V's death because that is what he wants to happen, and

- D2 who (in seeking to achieve some other purpose) foresees that V's death is virtually certain to happen, although he desperately hopes that it will not happen.

The approach of the American Law Institute's *Model Penal Code* (similar to the Law Commission's Criminal Code Bill – the difference is that several American states have adopted at least part of the Code into legislation) is to distinguish between 'intention' and 'knowledge'. Thus, the *Code* states that 'a person acts intentionally . . . when . . . it is his conscious object to . . . cause such a result' and that 'a person acts knowingly . . . when . . . he is aware that it is practically certain that his conduct will cause such a result.'

One state that has adopted the *Code* is Alaska, where it is first-degree murder to kill 'with intent to cause the death of another person', but second-degree murder for a person to kill 'knowing that his conduct is substantially certain to cause death'. The state of New Hampshire, however, distinguishes between 'purposely' killing and 'knowingly' killing.

Summary

- To be liable for murder, D must cause the death of another human being, under the Queen's Peace, within any county of the realm, with malice aforethought.

- The requirement that death occur within 'a year and a day' was abolished in 1996.

- Malice aforethought means an intention to kill or cause grievous bodily harm (*Moloney*).

- 'Grievous' bodily harm means 'really serious' bodily harm (*DPP v Smith*).

- If there is proof that D wanted or desired death or really serious injury then he intended it. This is 'direct' intent.

- If there is proof that D foresaw death or really serious injury as virtually certain to happen without necessarily wanting or desiring it, then the jury is 'entitled to find' that D intended it (*Woollin*). This is 'indirect' or 'oblique' intent. Foresight of a virtually certain consequence is not the same thing as intent (*Scalley*) – the jury must be left to 'find' intent.

6 Voluntary manslaughter

General introduction

The verdict of voluntary manslaughter is unique. Firstly it is not a specific charge in itself but rather arises from a charge of murder to which a special and partial defence has been pleaded. These special and partial defences will be considered below but are called *special* since they may only be pleaded in defence to murder and *partial* because a successful plea results, not in acquittal but in a conviction for manslaughter. This allows the judge to exercise discretion in choosing the appropriate sentence depending upon all the circumstances of the individual case.

The defences are contained in the Homicide Act 1957, which was passed at a time when capital punishment was the mandatory sentence for murder. It was acknowledged that many murders were spontaneous rather than planned and that most occurred within close relationships. Consequently the defences of provocation, suicide pact and infanticide were justifiable insofar as they mitigated the otherwise harsh consequences of a murder conviction. The defence of diminished responsibility was introduced partially as an admission that the law relating to mental abnormality was inadequate and outdated. Those who were accused of murder and suffered from certain mental conditions, for example psychopaths, did not fall within the rules relating to insanity and were liable to conviction and would be hanged; this despite the fact that they had been diagnosed as unable to control their actions due to their mental condition.

Neither provocation nor diminished responsibility (DR) involve a denial of *mens rea* for murder (i.e. the intent to kill or cause GBH). Indeed, the whole point of these defences is that D did have the intent required for murder. If the prosecution were unable to prove this, then D could, at most, be convicted of some form of involuntary manslaughter (see Chapter 7). Thus, it is clearly wrong for a trial judge to direct the jury that provocation or DR are not available when D admitted having the intent to kill or cause GBH. This happened in *Smith* (2002), where D admitted intentionally shooting V but claimed provocation. The Privy Council quashed D's murder conviction and substituted one of manslaughter, because the trial judge should have allowed the jury to consider evidence of provocation.

A   Provocation

Important note about law reform

By the time you read this, provocation will probably have been abolished by Parliament. At the time of writing this book, the Coroners & Justice Bill was making its way through Parliament and had already cleared the House of Commons. If passed, this Bill will abolish provocation but replace it with a new defence of 'loss of control'. The reasons for this reform and the details of the proposed new defence are set out at the end of this section.

Introduction

Provocation is a defence only to murder. Even when D successfully pleads provocation as a defence to murder, it reduces liability only to manslaughter. Provocation existed – indeed still exists – at common law. The common law rule has been *modified* but *not replaced* by s.3 of the Homicide Act 1957.

Homicide Act 1957
3. Where on a charge of murder there is evidence on which the jury can find that the person charged was provoked (whether by things done or by things said or by both together) to lose his self-control, the question whether the provocation was enough to make a reasonable man do as he did shall be left to the jury; and in determining that question the jury shall take into account everything both done and said according to the effect it would have on a reasonable man.

Provocation therefore consists of two questions:

- Did D lose his self-control? (a subjective question)

- Would the reasonable man have lost his self-control? (an objective question)

Before tackling those questions, which are both for a jury alone, there is a preliminary question, which is for the judge alone – was there enough evidence of provocation for the defence to be left to the jury to consider?

What can amount to provocation?

Under the 1957 Act, provocation need not be something illegal, or wrongful. It simply has to be something 'done' or 'said'. In *Doughty* (1986),

D's murder conviction was quashed on the ground that provocation should have been left to the jury. He had killed his 19-day-old son after the child would not stop crying. The Court of Appeal held that it should have been left to the jury to decide whether the baby's crying was provocation by 'things done'.

Provocation may *come from or be directed at* third parties. In the following cases the Court of Appeal held that the trial judge had wrongly denied D the defence even though:

- D was provoked by his wife's lover into shooting her – *Davies* (1975);

- D was provoked by his father's abusive treatment of D's brother into killing the father with a sledgehammer – *Pearson* (1992).

The subjective question

The first question for the jury is: was D provoked to lose his self-control? If D kept his cool, then it is unnecessary to consider the objective question. If D is unusually phlegmatic or emotionless and retains his cool (even when the reasonable man would have lost his), then the defence is not available.

A 'sudden and temporary loss of self-control'

In *Ibrams and Gregory* (1981) and *Thornton (No. 1)* (1992), the Court of Appeal approved the classic test of Devlin J in *Duffy* (1949) that there must be 'a sudden and temporary loss of self-control, rendering the accused so subject to passion as to make him or her for the moment not the master of his mind'. In *Ibrams and Gregory*, Lawton LJ said:

> Indeed, circumstances which induce a desire for revenge are inconsistent with provocation, since the conscious formulation of a desire for revenge means that a person has had time to think, to reflect, and that would negative a sudden temporary loss of self-control, which is the essence of provocation.

Ibrams and Gregory (1981)

Ibrams was sharing a flat with his fiancée, Laura. An ex-boyfriend of hers, John Monk, regularly visited the flat and terrorised them. The police were contacted on 7 October, but did nothing. Thus, on 10 October, Ibrams, Laura and a friend called Gregory met and agreed a plan for dealing with Monk. The plan was to get him drunk and encourage him to go to bed with Laura. The two men would then burst in and attack Monk while he was in bed. The plan was carried out on 12 October and Monk was killed. The Court of

Appeal upheld their murder convictions. There was no evidence that Monk had done anything after 7 October to provoke them. The interval of time between the last act of provocation, combined with the pre-formulated plan, negatived their claims of loss of self-control.

In *Baille* (1995), the Court of Appeal stressed that the question whether D had lost his self-control at the time of the killing was one for the *jury*. The judge's task was simply whether there was *evidence* that D had lost his self-control. D had learnt from his son that a drug dealer, M, had threatened his son with violence. D armed himself with a shotgun and drove around to M's house. There was an altercation, which resulted in D shooting and killing M. D pleaded provocation, partly based on being told of the threats by his son. The judge directed the jury to ignore the possible provoking effect of the threats, because any loss of self-control induced earlier *must have ceased* by the time of the shooting. The Court of Appeal allowed D's appeal: there was evidence of provocation, it was then for the jury to determine whether D had lost self-control at the time of the shooting.

Cumulative provocation

Evidence of provocation is not confined to the last act or word before the killing. There may have been previous acts or words which, when added together, cause D to lose self-control, even though the last act on its own may have been 'relatively unprovocative if taken in isolation', according to Lord Goff in *Luc Thiet Thuan* (1997). All the evidence of provocation must be left to the jury to consider (*Humphreys* [1995]).

'Slow burn'

The defence of provocation developed from traditional, male ideas of reacting instantly to violence with further violence. Consequently, the defence struggles to cope when it is a woman who kills. It has been argued that, in domestic violence cases, the 'sudden and temporary loss of self-control' test is inappropriate. Where a woman who has suffered years of violence and abuse finally seizes her opportunity when the husband is asleep or drunk or both, and kills him, she may not be reacting to any particular act or incident, but rather the accumulation of years of abuse. Although the situation does call for mitigation, the courts in such cases have consistently upheld the *Duffy* test. Consequently, battered women who kill face life sentences for murder. The leading cases are *Thornton (No. 1)* (1992) and *Ahluwalia* (1992).

Thornton (No. 1)
Sara and Malcolm Thornton's marriage quickly degenerated, Sara suffering physical abuse from Malcolm, who was jealous and possessive and a heavy drinker. One night, Sara returned home to find her husband lying on the sofa. He called her a 'whore'. She went into the kitchen, found a bread-knife, sharpened it, and returned to the living room. Malcolm said that he would kill Sara when she was asleep. She replied she would kill him first, and stabbed him in the stomach. Sara was convicted of murder and her appeal was dismissed. Her years of provocation were ignored; at the crucial time she was not suffering a 'sudden temporary loss of self-control'. The fact she had gone to the kitchen to fetch, and sharpen, the knife, were crucial factors.

In *Ahluwalia*, D was also the long-term victim of an abusive and violent marriage. One night, her husband threatened her with violence the next day unless she paid a bill; he then went to bed and fell asleep. Later, D doused him in petrol and set him alight. He died six days later. D was convicted of murder but, on appeal, argued that the *Duffy* test was inappropriate in battered woman cases. However, the Court of Appeal rejected her appeal on this ground. The court did stress that the requirement was that D's reaction had to be 'sudden' as opposed to 'immediate', but pointed out that 'the longer the delay and the stronger the evidence of deliberation on the part of the accused, the more likely it will be that the prosecution will negative provocation'.

The objective question

The jury must be satisfied that the reasonable man would (1) have lost self-control, and (2) done as D did.

Who is the 'reasonable man'?

Before the Homicide Act 1957, judges consistently held that the reasonable man was an adult with normal physical and mental attributes. This led to some very harsh decisions. In *Bedder v DPP* (1954), where a prostitute taunted D about his impotence – something that he was, unsurprisingly, very sensitive about – with the result that he lost his self-control and stabbed her to death, the House of Lords upheld his murder conviction. The Lords approved a direction that the jury had to consider what effect the provocation would have had on the ordinary person with no sexual hang-ups (presumably, very little).

This decision was not reversed until *DPP v Camplin* (1978). The House of Lords held that *Bedder* had, in fact, been overruled by s.3 of the 1957

Act. Lord Diplock, giving a model direction with which the rest of the House agreed, concluded that:

> A proper direction to a jury ... should state ... that the reasonable man ... is a person having the power of self-control to be expected of an ordinary person of the sex and age of the accused, but in other respects sharing such of the accused's characteristics as they think would affect the gravity of the provocation to him; and that the question is not merely whether such a person would in like circumstances be provoked to lose his self-control but also whether he would react to the provocation as the accused did.

DPP v Camplin (1978)
Mohammed Khan, a middle-aged man, had sexually abused Paul Camplin, a 15-year-old boy, at his flat in Halifax – and then laughed at him. At this, Camplin lost his self-control and hit Khan over the head with a chapati-pan, twice, splitting his skull wide open. Camplin was charged with murder. The trial judge directed the jury to consider the effect that Khan's provocation may have had on the *reasonable man*, as opposed to a *reasonable 15-year-old boy*. The jury convicted but the Court of Appeal quashed the conviction and the House of Lords rejected the prosecution's appeal, overruling *Bedder* in the process. The jury should have been told to assess the impact of the provocation on a *reasonable 15-year-old boy*.

The *Camplin* distinction (1978–2000)

Thus, *Camplin* allowed juries to take account of D's characteristics when deciding whether the reasonable man may have lost self-control. Lord Diplock's direction divides the objective question into two separate and distinct issues:

- the gravity of the provocation: theoretically, any of D's characteristics may be relevant

- the power of self-control: this remained a 'purely' objective standard (only D's sex and age were relevant).

This distinction was confirmed by the House of Lords in *Morhall* (1996) and by a majority of the Privy Council in *Luc Thiet Thuan* (1997). In *Smith* (2000), however, a majority of the House of Lords (Lords Clyde, Hoffman and Slynn), decided that the objective test should not be divided up in the way suggested by Lord Diplock.

The majority's view

A majority of the Law Lords in *Smith* decided that to draw a distinction between the two parts of the objective test would be very difficult for juries and thus probably unworkable. Lord Hoffman described the effect of the distinction as requiring the jury to perform 'mental gymnastics'.

The minority's view

Lord Millett and Lord Hobhouse dissented, and their decisions were described by Professor Sir John Smith as 'completely convincing'. He argued that allowing juries to consider evidence of a depressive illness when deciding on the standard of self-control possessed by the reasonable man effectively eliminated the objective element altogether.

Reinstatement of the *Camplin* distinction (2005)

In the years immediately after *Smith*, the Court of Appeal was obliged to follow the majority's decision in *Smith*. However, in June 2005, an unusually large nine-member Privy Council gave judgment in an appeal from the Court of Appeal of Jersey in *Attorney-General of Jersey v Holley*. The statutory defence of provocation there (Art. 4, Homicide (Jersey) Law 1986) is identical to that in the Homicide Act 1957. A majority of the Privy Council (Lords Bingham, Hoffman and Carswell dissenting) disagreed with the majority view in *Smith* (2000) and instead confirmed that the decision in *Luc Thiet Thuan* (1997) was correct. Referring to the majority's view in *Smith*, Lord Nicholls said:

> This majority view ... is one model which could be adopted in framing a law relating to provocation. But their Lordships consider there is one compelling, overriding reason why this view cannot be regarded as an accurate statement of English law ... However much the contrary is asserted, the majority view does represent a departure from the law as declared in s.3 of the Homicide Act 1957. It involves a significant relaxation of the uniform, objective standard adopted by Parliament. Under the statute the sufficiency of the provocation is to be judged by one standard, not a standard which varies from defendant to defendant. Whether the provocative act or words and the defendant's response met the 'ordinary person' standard prescribed by the statute is the question the jury must consider, not the altogether looser question of whether, having regard to all the circumstances, the jury consider the loss of self-control was sufficiently excusable. The statute does not leave each jury free to set whatever standard they consider appropriate in the circumstances by which to judge whether the defendant's conduct is 'excusable'. On this short ground their Lordships, respectfully but firmly, consider the majority view expressed in the *Morgan Smith* case is erroneous.

Holley (2005)

Dennis Holley, a chronic alcoholic, lived with his long-standing girlfriend, Cherylinn Mullane, also an alcoholic, in a flat in St Helier, Jersey. Their relationship was described in court as 'stormy' and frequently violent. On the fateful day the pair of them had been drinking heavily both at home and in a nearby pub. In the late afternoon, D made to leave the flat with an axe, apparently to chop some wood. At this point, V said to him, 'You haven't got the guts'. At this, D killed her with the axe. The sole issue at the trial was provocation, which was rejected by the jury, and D was convicted of murder. On appeal, however, the Court of Appeal of Jersey allowed his appeal, on the basis that since the trial the House of Lords in *Smith* had changed the law of provocation, and substituted a manslaughter conviction. Following an appeal against that decision by the Attorney-General of Jersey, the Privy Council held that the decision in *Smith* was wrong. Lord Nicholls said that 'evidence that [D] was suffering from chronic alcoholism was not a matter to be taken into account by the jury when considering whether in their opinion, having regard to the actual provocation and their view of its gravity, a person having ordinary powers of self-control would have done what [D] did'.

The *Holley* decision created a conflict in the authorities as, strictly speaking, the Privy Council cannot overrule decisions of the House of Lords. However, in *James, Karimi* (2006), a five-member Court of Appeal confirmed that the decision in *Holley* had overruled *Smith*. Giving judgment, Phillips LJ said there were circumstances in which a decision of the Privy Council could take precedence over a decision of the House of Lords, and in the case itself he said that 'this court must be bound in those circumstances to prefer the decision of the Privy Council to the prior decision of the House of Lords'. The Court of Appeal did certify two questions for decision by the House of Lords, namely:

1. Can an opinion of the judicial board of the Privy Council take precedence over an existing opinion of the judicial committee of the House of Lords, and if so, in what circumstances?
2. Is the majority of the opinion in *Holley* to be preferred to the majority decision in *Morgan Smith*?

Subsequently, the House of Lords' appeal committee refused leave to appeal. That would seem to confirm once and for all that the decision in *Smith* has been overruled.

We can therefore say that the law now is, once more, the same as it was in *Camplin* and *Morhall*: only D's age and sex are relevant when assessing the **level of self-control** to be expected of the reasonable man. However, it is very important to appreciate, even after *Holley*, that characteristics of the accused – both mental and physical – are potentially relevant when assessing the **gravity of the provocation**. There are two circumstances in which such characteristics may be relevant.

- First, when the characteristics are the target of the provocation. In *Holley* itself, Lord Nicholls stated that 'mental infirmity of the defendant, if itself the subject of taunts by the deceased, may be taken into account as going to the gravity of the provocation'.

- Second, where the characteristics are not the target of the provocation but their mere existence increases its gravity. In *Holley*, Lord Nicholls decided that the decisions in cases such as *Ahluwalia* (1992), discussed below, were correct in allowing psychological characteristics (such as battered woman syndrome) to be attributed to the reasonable man (or woman) for the purposes of assessing gravity, even where those characteristics were not the subject of taunts.

This latter point of law was central to the decision of the Court of Appeal in *Gregson* (2006). D had stabbed his stepfather, V, to death with a kitchen knife. Charged with murder, D pleaded provocation on the basis that he had 'received sustained verbal abuse, insults and put-downs from [V] over a number of years' culminating one night in the fatal attack. D put forward two potential characteristics: epilepsy and depression. The trial judge, however, ruled that these were irrelevant in assessing the gravity of the provocation to the reasonable man. This was because V's abuse was targeted at D's unemployment status (V would often refer to D as a 'waste of space' and a 'loser') rather than D's epilepsy and depression. D was convicted of murder but appealed, successfully. The Court of Appeal ruled that D's characteristics were potentially relevant, even though D had not been taunted about them. The key point was that the reasonable man *with* depression and epilepsy might have perceived V's abusive behaviour as more provocative than the reasonable man *without* depression or epilepsy. Giving judgment for the Court, Smith LJ said, 'We think that his illnesses were potentially relevant because [D] could well have had a heightened sense of grievance about the insults because he felt that, due to his depression and epilepsy, it was not his fault he was out of work.'

The Camplin distinction also represents the law in both Canada and Australia. In *Hill* (1986), the Supreme Court of Canada decided that, while certain characteristics of the accused could be attributed to the reasonable man for the purposes of determining the gravity of the provocation, the standard of self-control should be determined simply according to the reasonable man of D's age and sex. This distinction existed 'in order to ensure that in the evaluation of the provocation defence there is no fluctuating standard of self-control against which accused are measured'. This was confirmed by the Canadian Supreme Court in *Thibert* (1996). To similar effect, see the High Court of Australia in *Stingel* (1990) and *Masciantonio* (1995).

Attributing characteristics to the 'reasonable man'

In *DPP v Camplin*, Lord Diplock said that the reasonable man shared 'such of the accused's characteristics as [the jury] think would affect the gravity of the provocation'. Ever since, there has been a steady flow of cases through the Court of Appeal and House of Lords examining this question. The key cases are as follows.

- *Ahluwalia* (1992) (which was considered above in the context of the subjective question). The Court of Appeal decided that Battered Woman Syndrome, a psychological condition caused by enduring years of domestic violence, could be a relevant characteristic because a battered woman might well perceive threats of violence more seriously than a woman who had never suffered physical violence before.

- *Dryden* (1995). The Court of Appeal decided that D's eccentricity and obsessiveness were relevant characteristics which could well have exacerbated the provocation that he had suffered (local government planning officers had attempted to demolish D's self-built bungalow).

- *Humphreys* (1995). The Court of Appeal thought that D's immaturity and attention-seeking traits were relevant characteristics which may have worsened the gravity of the provocation that she had experienced (taunting from V, D's partner and pimp, concerning D's unsuccessful suicide attempt).

- *Morhall* (1995). The House of Lords decided that characteristics may not be withdrawn from the jury's consideration simply because they were self-induced (such as, in this case, addiction to glue-sniffing). Lord Goff, with whom the rest of the House agreed, said that the reasonable man shared whichever of D's characteristics were capable of affecting the gravity of the provocation (in this case, nagging from D's friend, V, about his addiction).

Psychological characteristics

You will note that in the first three cases in the above list, the characteristics were of a psychological (as opposed to physical) quality.

This creates an overlap with, and potential confusion between, the defences of provocation (where the burden of proof is on the prosecution to disprove the defence beyond reasonable doubt) and diminished responsibility (where the burden of proof is on the defence to prove the case on the balance of probabilities; see below). However, when Lord Taylor CJ addressed this point in *Thornton (No. 2)* (1996), he stressed that psychological characteristics were relevant in the provocation defence:

> What characteristics of a defendant should be attributed by the jury to the notional reasonable person and how far the judge should go in assisting the jury to identify those characteristics are issues which have been clarified in a number of decisions . . . *Ahluwalia*, *Humphreys* and *Morhall* make clear that mental as well as physical characteristics should be taken into account.

In *Luc Thiet Thuan* (1997), a majority of the Privy Council disagreed with this line of cases and held that psychological characteristics were not relevant in the context of provocation – and should be left exclusively to diminished responsibility (DR). Their reasoning was that, allowing D to rely on psychological characteristics in the context of provocation undermined DR and subverted Parliament's intention (in the Homicide Act 1957). Lord Goff said that it was 'extraordinary' that D could raise some psychological condition (such as a depressive illness) in support of a plea of DR and then, if that defence failed, rely on the same condition to support a plea of provocation.

This criticism has not been followed by either the Court of Appeal or the House of Lords. Indeed, in *Holley* (2005), the Privy Council itself accepted that D's characteristic – chronic alcoholism – was relevant to the defence of provocation, albeit only in the context of assessing the gravity of the provocation to the reasonable man and not when assessing the level of self-control to be expected.

Are any characteristics irrelevant?

Prior to *Smith*, certain characteristics were deemed to be irrelevant because they were incompatible with the concept of the 'reasonable man'. In *DPP v Camplin*, Lord Simon stated that a trial judge may tell a jury that D is not entitled to rely on 'his exceptional excitability or pugnacity or ill-temper or on his drunkenness'. Similarly in *Smith* (2000), Lord Clyde stated that 'such characteristics as an exceptional pugnacity or excitability will not suffice. Such tendencies require to be controlled'. Lord Hoffman also said that 'male possessiveness and jealousy should not today be an acceptable reason for loss of self-control leading to homicide'.

Would the reasonable man have lost self-control and done as D did?

At common law there was a requirement that D's reaction to provocation had to bear a reasonable relationship to the provocation. However, in *DPP v Camplin* (1978), the House of Lords declared that this rule could not survive s.3 of the 1957 Act, because otherwise the provision that provocation could arise from words alone would be meaningless. The question for the jury to consider is whether the reasonable man, having lost his self-control, would have done as the defendant did. All of D's behaviour is to be considered; not just the immediate act of killing. This is made clear from the facts of *Clarke* (1991). D, having been provoked, head-butted and strangled V. She may have still been alive at this point but D, panicking, electrocuted her as well. The Court of Appeal held the judge had rightly allowed the jury to ignore the electrocution. The jury should consider everything which is not 'too remote', which some factors, such as disposal of the body, might be.

A more recent example of this point occurred in *Van Dongen* (2005). D had been convicted of murder after the trial judge refused to leave his defence of provocation to the jury. The Court of Appeal upheld the conviction, even though there was evidence of both provocative conduct from V and a loss of self-control by D, because the Court was satisfied that the reasonable man would not have reacted to the provocation in the same way. D had admitted killing V by kicking him in the head as he lay on the ground 'scrunched up in a foetal position' – this was not something the reasonable man would have done.

The 'reasonable man' test in provocation: summary

The objective test in the provocation defence has been in existence since the nineteenth century. However, it has undergone a remarkable transformation in that time. The table overleaf summarises the developments since before the Homicide Act 1957 to the present day.

Procedure

If D wishes to rely on the defence, they must provide evidence of provocation. The onus is then on the prosecution to prove that D was *not* provoked. If there is evidence of provocation, the judge must direct the jury to consider it. Often, the defence will raise self-defence only, a tactical move, hoping for an acquittal. (While provocation only reduces murder to manslaughter; self-defence leads to a complete acquittal – see Chapter 19.) Where this happens, the judge remains obliged to direct the jury on provocation regardless of what the defence wants.

In *Rossiter* (1994), D stabbed her husband to death. She had been exposed to a great degree of verbal abuse and physical violence from him on the day in question but she refused to admit that she had deliberately stabbed him, maintaining that it was self-defence. The Court of Appeal quashed her murder conviction and substituted manslaughter. There was evidence, particularly the number of stab wounds (over 20), from which the jury could have concluded that she had lost her self-control. The judge should have left the defence to them.

Nevertheless there *must* be *some* evidence of provocation to bring the judge's duty into play. If there is no evidence of provocation, it is not up to the judge to direct the jury on what would be a hypothetical, speculative possibility. In *Acott* (1997), D was charged with the murder of his elderly mother. He claimed that she had fallen and her injuries were the result of this plus his desperate efforts to resuscitate her. However, he was convicted of murder. On appeal, he argued that the judge should have directed the jury on provocation. However, both the Court of Appeal and the House of Lords rejected his appeal. There was simply *no evidence* of provocation.

Acott was applied by the Court of Appeal in *Miao* (2003). D admitted killing his partner, V, but denied doing so intentionally. He also claimed that V had accused him of having an affair and had slapped and kicked him (in other words, he claimed that there was evidence of provocation). However, the judge declined to leave provocation to the jury as the evidence was 'minimal'. D was convicted of murder and the Court of Appeal, following *Acott*, upheld his murder conviction.

Criticism of the provocation defence

In October 2003, the Law Commission (LC) published a Consultation Paper, '*Partial Defences to Murder*' (Law Com No. 173), which identified several criticisms that may be made of the provocation defence. The LC observed that the issue of the 'reasonable man' had been before the House of Lords/Privy Council four times since 1978 (and of course it has since been back to the Privy Council again, with *Holley* [2005]). The LC claimed that this 'demonstrates fundamental problems with the concept of the reasonable man'. However, that was not the only problem. Other, specific criticisms made include:

- Provocative conduct now has a very wide meaning. The LC cited *Doughty* (1986) as an authority for the proposition that entirely innocent behaviour can support the defence. This, the LC said, was 'contrary to one of the fundamental rationales of the defence, which is that [V] contributed to [D]'s lethal loss of temper'.

- Anger is elevated to a status higher than other emotions such as fear, despair, compassion or empathy. According to the LC, it is morally questionable that killings following loss of temper should be dealt with as manslaughter and not killings caused by fear, despair and so on.

Case	Year	Decision	Comment
DPP v Bedder	1954	The reasonable man is an adult, sharing none of D's characteristics.	A 'purely' objective test, this is seen as very harsh now and was overruled by *Camplin*.
DPP v Camplin	1978	The reasonable man 'shares' those characteristics with D which affect the gravity of the provocation. Splits the test into two sub-questions: gravity of the provocation and level of self-control.	First move towards softening the objectivity of the test. The *Camplin* distinction that the gravity of the provocation and level of self-control are separate issues means that the latter remains 'purely' objective (only sex and age relevant).
Dryden/ Humphreys	1995	Characteristics may be psychological as well as physical.	Further softening of the objectivity of the test. Risks confusion with DR.
Morhall	1996	Characteristics may be self-induced, e.g. addiction to glue-sniffing.	Further softening of the objectivity of the test. Maintains the *Camplin* distinction.
*Luc Thiet Thuan**	1997	Psychological characteristics (e.g. brain disorders, depression) belong to DR not provocation.	This would help to maintain the objectivity of the test. Also provides a clearer separation between provocation and DR.
Smith	2000	*Camplin* distinction between gravity of provocation and level of self-control abolished. No longer any requirement to refer to the 'reasonable man'.	Significantly softened the objective test. Virtually any characteristic of D could be regarded as relevant. Strong dissenting minority, with academic support, complained that abolishing the *Camplin* distinction was a mistake.
Holley	2005	*Smith* not followed, albeit by the Privy Council. *Camplin* distinction restored along with requirement to refer to the 'reasonable man'.	Creates conflict of authorities as, strictly speaking, the Privy Council cannot overrule the House of Lords.
James, Karimi	2006	Court of Appeal follows *Holley* in preference to *Smith*. House of Lords refuses leave to appeal.	Conflict in authorities resolved. *Smith* overruled. All of D's characteristics are potentially relevant, but only when assessing the gravity of the provocation.

*Privy Council decision, so persuasive only. Not followed in subsequent cases.

- The 'sudden and temporary loss of control' criterion is flawed. It makes the defence biased in favour of male defendants, who react to provocation 'in violent anger', as opposed to female defendants, who are more likely to 'kill with premeditation from fear rather than rage'.

- The defence has been stretched by the courts over the last ten years to accommodate 'slow burn' killings in domestic abuse cases, such that it is now difficult to exclude revenge killings from the scope of the defence.

Reform of the provocation defence

In their 2003 paper, the LC suggested two broad options for reform: abolition (to be combined with the abolition of the mandatory life sentence for murder) and modification. The vast majority of the responses to consultation indicated widespread support for the retention of provocation, albeit not necessarily in its present state. In 2004, therefore, the LC proposed a radical new definition of provocation in its Report, *Partial Defences to Murder*. The LC essentially repeated this definition in its 2005 Consultation Paper, *A New Homicide Act for England & Wales?* and again in its 2006 Report, *Murder, Manslaughter and Infanticide.*

In July 2008, the Government announced its response to the LC's proposals. These are set out in a Ministry of Justice consultation paper, entitled *Murder, Manslaughter & Infanticide: proposals for reform of the law*. In summary, the Government stated that it wished to:

- Abolish provocation as a defence

- Introduce a new partial defence where D lost control and killed in response to:
  1. a 'fear of serious violence'; and/or
  2. things done or said (or both) which caused D to have a 'justifiable sense of being seriously wronged' (to apply only in exceptional circumstances).

The Coroners and Justice Bill

In December 2008, these proposals were put to Parliament, as part of the Coroners and Justice Bill. The Bill was amended by the House of Commons and, at the time of writing, the relevant clauses, 44–46, state as follows:

---

44. *Partial defence to murder: loss of control*
(1) Where a person ('D') kills or is a party to the killing of another ('V'), D is not to be convicted of murder if:

(a) D's acts and omissions in doing or being a party to the killing resulted from D's loss of self-control,

(b) the loss of self-control had a qualifying trigger, and

(c) a person of D's sex and age, with a normal degree of tolerance and self-restraint and in the circumstances of D, might have reacted in the same or in a similar way to D.

(2) For the purposes of subsection (1)(a), it does not matter whether or not the loss of control was sudden.

(3) In subsection (1)(c) the reference to 'the circumstances of D' is a reference to all of D's circumstances other than those whose only relevance to D's conduct is that they bear on D's general capacity for tolerance or self-restraint.

(4) Subsection (1) does not apply if, in doing or being a party to the killing, D acted in a considered desire for revenge.

(5) On a charge of murder, if sufficient evidence is adduced to raise an issue with respect to the defence under subsection (1), the jury must assume that the defence is satisfied unless the prosecution proves beyond reasonable doubt that it is not.

(6) For the purposes of subsection (5), sufficient evidence is adduced to raise an issue with respect to the defence if evidence is adduced on which, in the opinion of the trial judge, a jury, properly directed, could reasonably conclude that the defence might apply.

(7) A person who, but for this section, would be liable to be convicted of murder is liable instead to be convicted of manslaughter.

(8) The fact that one party to a killing is by virtue of this section not liable to be convicted of murder does not affect the question whether the killing amounted to murder in the case of any other party to it.

45. Meaning of 'qualifying trigger'
(1) This section applies for the purposes of s.44.

(2) A loss of self-control had a qualifying trigger if subsection (3), (4) or (5) applies.

(3) This subsection applies if D's loss of self-control was attributable to D's fear of serious violence from V against D or another identified person.

(4) This subsection applies if D's loss of self-control was attributable to a thing or things done or said (or both) which:
(a) constituted circumstances of an extremely grave character, and
(b) caused D to have a justifiable sense of being seriously wronged.

(5) This subsection applies if D's loss of self-control was attributable to a combination of the matters mentioned in subsections (3) and (4).

(6) In determining whether a loss of self-control had a qualifying trigger:
(a) D's fear of serious violence is to be disregarded to the extent that it was caused by a thing which D incited to be done or said for the purpose of providing an excuse to use violence;
(b) a sense of being seriously wronged by a thing done or said is not justifiable if D incited the thing to be done or said for the purpose of providing an excuse to use violence;
(c) the fact that a thing done or said constituted sexual infidelity is to be disregarded.

(7) In this section references to 'D' and 'V' are to be construed in accordance with s.44.

46. Abolition of common law defence of provocation
(1) The common law defence of provocation is abolished and replaced by sections 44 and 45.

(2) Accordingly, the following provisions cease to have effect:
(a) section 3 of the Homicide Act 1957.

Points to note (assuming the Bill is passed in its present form)

- The new defence will require a 'loss of self-control': s.44(1)(a). However, the *Duffy* test of a 'sudden and temporary' loss of self-control will be abolished (s.44(2)).

- A simple 'loss of self-control' test allows for D to undergo a 'slow burn' reaction, as seen in cases like *Ahluwalia*. However, the defendant in *Ahluwalia*, like those in *Ibrams & Gregory* and *Thornton* would not succeed with the new 'loss of control' defence as, in all of those cases, there was no loss of self-control (sudden or otherwise).

- The loss of self-control must have a 'qualifying trigger': s.44(1)(b) and s.45. (See below for more detailed discussion.)

- The 'reasonable man' is renamed as the 'normal person': s.44(1)(c). The new test is whether a person of D's sex and age, with a 'normal' degree of tolerance and self-restraint might have reacted in the same or in a similar way.

- The 'normal' person is to be placed 'in the circumstances of D'. However, circumstances 'whose only relevance to D's conduct is that they bear on D's general capacity for tolerance or self-restraint' are explicitly excluded: s.44(3). This confirms *Camplin/Holley*. In its 2006 Report, the LC gave alcoholism as an example of an excluded circumstance. The LC also stated that characteristics such as intoxication, irritability and 'excessive jealousy' would be excluded. The Ministry of Justice referred to these points in its 2008 report without comment and may be taken to agree with the LC.

- Other 'circumstances' are allowed. Presumably this will include D's characteristics, where relevant.

- The new defence will not be available if D 'acted in a considered desire for revenge': s.44(4).

- The burden of proof will be on the prosecution (as with the present provocation defence), but D must raise 'sufficient' evidence: s.44(5). This confirms the decisions in cases such as *Acott* and *Miao*. Whether evidence is 'sufficient' is a question for the trial judge: s.44(6). This also confirms current practice.

- The defence will be partial, reducing murder to manslaughter: s.44(7).

The 'qualifying triggers'

- There are two 'qualifying triggers'

- The 'fear of serious violence' trigger will be available only where V is the source of the violence and the threat is targeted at D or 'another identified person': s.45(3). This appears to be consistent with cases such as *Pearson* (where D was provoked by violence from V aimed at D's younger brother).

- The 'things done or said' trigger will be available only where the thing(s) said or done 'constituted circumstances of an extremely grave character': s.45(4). In its 2008 Paper, the Ministry of Justice gave an example of such an 'extremely grave' circumstance: where D is raped by V and then mocked afterwards by V. This example is clearly based on the facts of

Camplin. The 'extremely grave' test would clearly exclude cases like *Doughty* (where D claimed that he was provoked by his crying baby son). But would it also exclude cases such as *Baillie* (where D claimed that he was provoked by his son telling him about his drug dealer) and *Morhall* (where D was nagged about his glue-sniffing addiction)? These are not exactly routine events, but are they 'extremely grave'? An act of 'sexual infidelity' is to be disregarded: s.45(6)(c). This would exclude cases such as *Davies* (where D claimed that he was provoked into killing his wife by seeing his wife's lover).

- A loss of control triggered by a combination of both 'fear of serious violence' and 'things done or said' will also suffice (s.45(5)). The case of *Humphreys* provides an example where both 'qualifying triggers' may have been present. D believed that V (her violent boyfriend/pimp) and his friends were going to gang-rape her and hence she had a 'fear of serious violence'; she also claimed that V had mocked her suicide attempt – this is a 'thing said' which could constitute 'circumstances of an extremely grave character'.

- Neither trigger will be available if D incited the thing done or said 'for the purpose of providing an excuse to use violence': s.45(6).

- The Ministry of Justice's Consultation Paper had suggested that the new defence should not be available if D's 'loss of self-control' was 'predominantly attributable to conduct engaged in by D which constitutes one or more criminal offences'. This was designed to prevent, for example, gang-related killings from falling within the scope of either of the triggers. However, the present version of the Bill does not include this provision.

Summary

- Provocation is a common law defence but is regulated by s.3 of the Homicide Act 1957.

- It is a defence only to murder and reduces D's liability to manslaughter.

- There must be some evidence of provocation (which is a question for the judge) before the defence can be left to the jury (*Acott*; *Miao*). It is then up to the prosecution to disprove the defence.

- Provocation may be by things done, or things said, or both. There are no limitations on these concepts. The provocation does not necessarily have to come from V (*Davies*), nor does it need to have been directed at D (*Pearson*).

- There is a subjective element and an objective element.
  The subjective element – was D provoked to lose his self-control? – requires that D must have undergone a 'sudden and temporary loss of self-control' (*Duffy*; *Ibrams and Gregory*; *Ahluwalia*; *Thornton (No. 1)*).

- But 'sudden' does not mean 'instant' and in cases, particularly those involving domestic violence characterised by 'slow burn' reactions, the defence may be available despite a lengthy time delay (*Ahluwalia*).

- The courts recognise cumulative provocation (*Humphreys*).

- The objective element means that the jury must be satisfied that the reasonable man might also have lost self-control.

- The reasonable man shares whichever of D's characteristics as would affect the gravity of the provocation to D, but in assessing the power of self-control to be expected of the reasonable man, only D's age and sex are relevant (*Camplin*; *Morhall*; *Holley*).

- Characteristics may be psychological as well as physical (*Ahluwalia*; *Dryden*; *Humphreys*). Characteristics may even be self-induced (*Morhall*).

B   Diminished responsibility

Introduction

The defence of diminished responsibility (DR) evolved in the courts of Scotland as a common law defence. However, it was introduced into English law only by s.2 of the Homicide Act 1957.

Homicide Act 1957
2 (1) Where a person kills or is party to a killing of another, he shall not be convicted of murder if he was suffering from such abnormality of mind (whether arising from a condition of arrested or retarded development of mind or any inherent causes or induced by disease or injury) as substantially impaired his mental responsibility for his acts and omissions in doing or being party to the killing.

(2) On a charge of murder, it shall be for the defence to prove that the person charged is by virtue of this section not liable to be convicted of murder.

DR operates as a limited defence, in two ways. First, it may only be pleaded to a charge of murder. Second, it only reduces liability from murder to manslaughter. However, this allows the judge full discretion on sentencing. Some defendants may receive an absolute discharge, others probationary or suspended sentences, while in appropriate circumstances some will receive hospital or guardianship orders under the Mental Health Act 1983. Others may still face imprisonment, with some receiving life sentences for manslaughter (about 15 per cent of cases).

S.2(1) breaks down into three components:

- An abnormality of mind

- Arising from certain specified causes

- Which substantially impairs mental responsibility.

The defence must establish all three elements before D can avoid a murder conviction. But there are no further requirements. For instance, the fact that a killing was premeditated does not destroy a plea of DR (*Byrne* [1960]).

'Abnormality of mind'

Although medical evidence is important, the decision whether D was suffering such an abnormality is one for the jury. In *Byrne* (1960), D was a sexual psychopath who suffered violent, perverted sexual desires, which he found difficult, if not impossible, to control. He strangled a girl in a YWCA hostel in Birmingham and then mutilated the body. He was convicted of murder, but the Court of Criminal Appeal reduced his conviction to manslaughter. Lord Parker CJ said that 'Abnormality of mind ... means a state of mind so different from that of ordinary human beings that the reasonable man would term it abnormal'.

The definition is much wider than that of insanity under the M'Naghten Rules (see Chapter 15). Crucially, for psychopathic defendants like Byrne, DR recognises the so-called 'irresistible impulse' defence, a plea that D should be excused liability because of an inability, or even difficulty, to control impulses. This has never been allowed as part of the insanity defence but, since *Byrne*, is at least a defence to murder. In fact, the impulse need not be *irresistible*; it is sufficient that D's difficulty in controlling his impulses is *substantially greater than normal.*

The Court of Criminal Appeal approved the medical witnesses' description of Byrne's condition as amounting to 'partial insanity'. Earlier cases had used expressions such as 'not quite mad but a borderline case'. Unsurprisingly, such directions created a risk of confusion with the insanity defence. The position was only resolved in *Seers* (1984), where the judge had directed the jury that DR was available only to those who were 'partially insane' or 'on the borderline of insanity'. D, who suffered a depressive illness, was convicted of murder, but the Court of Appeal substituted manslaughter. While a depressive illness could amount to an abnormality of mind, few people would consider it to be on the 'borderline of insanity'. In future, judges should keep to Lord Parker CJ's direction in *Byrne* and avoided references to 'insanity' altogether.

The specified causes

Although there is nothing in s.2 to rule out any other causes, D's abnormality of mind should be attributable to one of the causes listed in s.2:

- a condition of arrested or retarded development of mind; or

- any inherent cause; or

- induced by disease; or

- induced by injury.

The judge should attempt to tailor the direction to fit the facts of the case. In most cases it would not be particularly helpful for the judge to direct the jury by simply reading out s.2 in full; only those causes that could be relevant should be mentioned.

The courts have generally been prepared to allow a wide range of mental conditions to provide a basis for DR pleas. The abnormality of mind does not have to have any degree of permanence, provided that it existed at the time of the killing and that it substantially diminished D's responsibility. Factors such as jealousy and rage have been used to support the defence. Mercy killers not infrequently receive verdicts of not guilty to murder on grounds of DR.

'A condition of arrested or retarded development of mind'

Mental deficiency was accepted as an 'abnormality of mind' in *Speake* (1957).

'Any inherent cause'

The words 'any inherent cause' clearly have a wide scope. The word 'inherent' in s.2 does *not* require that the condition be an inherited one. Nor need it have been present from birth (*Gomez* [1964]). The following have all been accepted as inherent causes:

- psychopathy

- paranoia

- epilepsy

- depression

- pre-menstrual tension.

In *Jama* (2004), the Court of Appeal held that Asperger Syndrome (AS), an autistic spectrum disorder in which sufferers have 'grave difficulty in developing relationships' and are 'self-centred and [do] not empathise with other people', constituted an 'abnormality of mind' for the purposes of DR.

'Induced by disease'

'Disease' is wide enough to cover mental, as well as physical, diseases. In *Sanderson* (1993), S was convicted of murder after the judge's direction to the jury to the effect that the defence had to show injury to the brain. On appeal, the Court of Appeal accepted that the defence did *not* have to show some physical injury. The physical condition of the brain, though not irrelevant, was a question for evidence only. In any event, 'any inherent cause' would cover functional mental illness.

The courts in England were slow to accept Battered Woman Syndrome, despite its recognition as a psychological condition, especially in the United States, as providing a basis for a successful defence of DR. However, in *Ahluwalia* (1993) – considered above under provocation – the Court of Appeal actually allowed her appeal against a murder conviction on the basis of such a condition.

'Induced by injury'

This would include physical blows to the head, for example, that left D suffering brain damage.

> Is physical violence essential before someone can be said to have suffered an 'injury'? What else could cause an 'injury'?

Other factors

The basic position here is that if D pleads DR he may not support this plea with any evidence of abnormality derived from factors not listed in s.2. Where the evidence suggests that D suffered from one of the causes within s.2, *plus* another factor which falls outside of s.2, then the judge should direct the jury to ignore the effects of the inadmissible cause. This unfortunately means that the jury must answer a hypothetical question. This problem raises itself most often when D claims that he was intoxicated *and* had an abnormality of mind due to a specified cause (see below).

'Substantially impaired . . . mental responsibility'

The expression 'diminished responsibility' does not actually appear in s.2 itself; rather it is used in a marginal note in the Homicide Act. Instead, s.2 uses the phrase 'substantially impaired . . . mental responsibility'. In *Byrne*, the Court of Criminal Appeal said that the question of whether D's impairment could be described as 'substantial' was a question of degree and, hence, although medical evidence was not irrelevant, one for the jury. In *Lloyd* (1967), the trial judge, Ashworth J, directed the jury as follows:

> Substantial does not mean total, that is to say, the mental responsibility need not be totally impaired, so to speak, destroyed altogether. At the other end of the scale substantial does not mean trivial or minimal. It is something in between and Parliament has left it to you and other juries to say on the evidence, was the mental responsibility impaired and if so, was it substantially impaired?

The effect of intoxication

This is a tricky area of law. There is often conflicting medical evidence, which can create confusion in the mind of the jury – and sometimes the judge! The case of *Sanderson* (1993) illustrates some of the difficulties in this area. D was a regular user of cocaine and heroin. He admitted killing his girlfriend with a hockey stick. The only issue was whether he was guilty of murder or manslaughter. The prosecution and defence psychiatrists disagreed:

- *Defence*: D was suffering *paranoid psychosis* – a mental illness – which was already present, irrespective of his drug abuse. It was an 'inherent cause' and, although exacerbated by cocaine abuse, was an abnormality of mind in its own right.

- *Prosecution*: D was suffering from paranoia caused purely by his *cocaine abuse*. There was no 'disease'. Furthermore, cocaine or heroin abuse could not damage the physical structure of the brain in the way that alcohol could; hence, there was no 'injury'.

D was convicted of murder and appealed. The Court of Appeal quashed the conviction because of contradictions in the judge's summing-up which might have confused the jury. However, it is not difficult to see how the jury would have struggled to reach a verdict in this case, with so much conflicting evidence presented to them.

There are two distinct situations to consider:

- D killed whilst intoxicated *and* whilst suffering some unrelated 'abnormality of mind'.

- D killed whilst some suffering an 'abnormality of mind' *caused* by intoxication.

The defendant was intoxicated and was also suffering some unrelated 'abnormality of mind'

A plea of DR may not be supported with evidence of intoxication. In *Fenton* (1975), Lord Widgery CJ said, 'We do not see how self-induced intoxication can of itself produce an abnormality of mind due to inherent causes'. In *Gittens* (1985), D suffered from depression for which he sought and received medical treatment. One night he consumed a large amount of drink and anti-depressant pills. In this state he clubbed his wife to death and then strangled his stepdaughter. The Court of Appeal quashed his murder conviction and substituted one of manslaughter because of a misdirection to the jury about the role of intoxicants. Lord Lane CJ said the jury should be directed to disregard the effect of the alcohol or drugs. Then the jury should consider whether D, had he been sober, would have been suffering from such abnormality of mind as substantially impaired his mental responsibility.

In *Egan* (1992), there was evidence that D was mentally abnormal. One day he drank fifteen pints of beer plus some gin and tonics, then bludgeoned an elderly woman to death. The Court of Appeal, agreeing with the trial judge's direction, said that 'the vital question' for the jury was whether D's abnormality of mind was such 'that he would have been under diminished responsibility, drink or no drink'.

In *Dietschmann* (2003) – the first DR case to be heard by the House of Lords – the decisions in *Fenton*, *Gittens* and *Egan* were confirmed. Lord Hutton suggested the following model direction for future juries in murder trials where the evidence suggests that D was suffering an admissible 'abnormality' and was intoxicated as well (emphasis added):

You may take the view that both [D]'s mental abnormality and drink played a part in impairing his mental responsibility for the killing and that he might not have killed if he had not taken drink. [If so] the question for you to decide is this: has [D] satisfied you that, *despite the drink*, his mental abnormality substantially impaired his mental responsibility for his fatal acts, or has he failed to satisfy you of that? If he has satisfied you of that, you will find him not guilty of murder but you may find him guilty of manslaughter. If he has not satisfied you of that, the defence of [DR] is not available to him.

Dietschmann (2003)

Anthony Dietschmann admitted killing Nicholas Davies by punching, kicking and stamping on his head in what was described as a 'savage attack'. At the time of the killing, D was heavily intoxicated in addition to suffering from an 'adjustment disorder', a 'depressed grief reaction' to the recent death of his aunt Sarah, with whom he also had a 'close emotional and physical relationship'. On the night in question the two men had been dancing at a party when D claimed that V's flailing arm had broken his watch, a gift from Sarah before she died. D also appeared convinced that V had gone to the cemetery and urinated on Sarah's grave. At his trial for murder, D relied on DR based on the adjustment disorder. The prosecution case, however, was that the alcohol had been a significant factor as a disinhibitor and that, if D had been sober, he would probably have exercised self-control. The trial judge directed the jury to allow the defence only if they were satisfied that D would still have killed V had he been sober. The jury convicted of murder. D appealed and, although the Court of Appeal dismissed the appeal, he was successful in the House of Lords. The question for the jury was not whether D, had he been sober, *would have killed*, but whether he, had he been sober, *would still have been suffering from an abnormality of mind*. Those were very different questions.

Dietschmann was followed by the Court of Appeal in *Hendy* (2006). D admitted killing V whilst intoxicated on alcohol. At his trial for murder, evidence was adduced that D had brain damage, possibly caused by a head injury as a child, and a psychopathic disorder. D was convicted of murder but the Court of Appeal allowed the appeal on the basis that the jury had not been directed in accordance with Lord Hutton's model direction (above) on the interplay between underlying mental abnormality and intoxication.

The defendant was suffering an 'abnormality of mind' caused by intoxication

This may happen in two situations:

'Injury'

First, where D's long-term alcohol and/or drug abuse has actually led to brain damage or psychosis, this would almost certainly be held to amount to an 'injury' within s.2. The leading case is *Tandy* (1989). Watkins LJ said 'If . . . alcoholism had reached the level at which her brain had been injured by the repeated insult from intoxicants so that there was gross impairment of . . . judgment and emotional responses, then the defence was available.'

For obvious reasons, the *immediate* effects of taking alcohol or drugs cannot be classed as an 'injury'. In *Di Duca* (1959), it was unsuccessfully argued that the toxic effect of alcohol on the brain was an 'injury' for the purposes of s.2. This decision was confirmed in *O'Connell* (1997) concerning the effect on D's brain of sleeping pills.

'Disease'

Alcoholism and/or drug addiction may amount to a 'disease'. However, the courts have been reluctant to accept that simply being an alcoholic suffices and have imposed further conditions. In *Tandy* (1989), Watkins LJ said that if D were able to establish that the alcoholism had reached the level where her drinking had become involuntary, so that she was no longer able to resist the impulse to drink, then DR would be available. Thus, as well as simply being an alcoholic, D must also have a craving for drink or drugs to the extent that drinking becomes 'involuntary'.

Tandy (1989)
Linda Tandy was an alcoholic and had been for a number of years. She usually drank only barley wine or *Cinzano*. However, over the course of one day she drank 90 per cent of a bottle of vodka, a beverage that she had not drunk before but which is significantly stronger than either barley wine or *Cinzano*. That evening she strangled her 11-year-old daughter, after she told her mother that Tandy's second husband had sexually interfered with her. The judge directed the jury to decide whether Tandy was suffering from an abnormality of mind, as a direct result of her alcoholism, or whether she was simply drunk. She was convicted of murder. The Court of Appeal dismissed the appeal. Tandy had not shown that her brain had actually been injured, nor had she proven that her drinking was 'involuntary'.

Despite criticism of this decision, the Court of Appeal followed *Tandy* in *Inseal* (1992) where D was again convicted of murder despite medical evidence that he was suffering from 'alcohol dependence syndrome'. However, in a more recent decision, the Court of Appeal has shown more sympathy for alcoholic defendants who kill. In *Wood* (2008), the Court held that the 'rigid' principles established in *Tandy* had to be 're-assessed' in light of the House of Lords' decision in *Dietschmann*. The Court stated:

> The sharp effect of the distinction drawn in *Tandy* between cases where brain damage has occurred as a result of alcohol dependency syndrome and those where it has not is no longer appropriate.

The Court went on to lay down the following principles:

- Alcohol dependence syndrome is a disease or illness which may amount to an 'abnormality of mind'. Whether it does or not is a matter for the jury to decide.

- It is not essential that brain damage has occurred – although if it has, it will be easier for D to prove that he or she has an 'abnormality of mind'.

- If D's syndrome does amount to an 'abnormality of mind', then the jury must consider whether D's mental responsibility was substantially impaired.

- In deciding that question, the jury should focus 'exclusively' on the effect of alcohol consumed by D as a 'direct result of his illness or disease' but the jury should 'ignore the effect of any alcohol consumed voluntarily'.

Commenting on *Wood* in the *Criminal Law Review*, Professor Andrew Ashworth states:

> If there is no proof of brain damage it is still open to the jury to decide that the alcohol dependency syndrome amounted to an 'abnormality of mind' within s.2. If they do so, then the next question is whether that abnormality 'substantially impaired' D's responsibility, discounting any effects of alcohol consumed voluntarily. So the jury are left to determine how much of D's drinking derived from his alcohol dependency and how much was 'voluntary'. This is a fearsomely difficult question to ask.

Wood (2008)
After a day's heavy drinking, Clive Wood killed V in a frenzied attack with a meat cleaver. At Wood's murder trial, four psychiatrists agreed that Wood suffered from alcohol dependency syndrome, but the trial judge told the jury that a verdict of manslaughter based on DR was open to them only if D's consumption of alcohol was truly involuntary, and that simply giving in to a craving for alcohol was not involuntary drinking. D was convicted of murder but the Court of Appeal quashed his conviction and substituted a verdict of manslaughter.

Procedure

Initially, it was thought that the judge's task was simply to read s.2 and leave it up to the jury. However, it has since been made clear that trial judges must direct the jury as to the meaning of s.2. As with insanity, D bears the burden of proving the defence, on the balance of probabilities. If the defence rely on another defence that puts D's abnormality of mind in issue, like automatism, then it would seem the prosecution can seek to show this is DR. But the prosecution may not seek to raise DR or insanity unless the defence has first put D's state of mind in issue.

Originally the courts took the view that DR had to be proved to the jury, and could not be accepted by a trial judge. Again the position has since changed. Now D may plead guilty to manslaughter on the ground of DR. The judge has to decide whether to accept the plea. The judge should do so only where medical evidence is clear. A plea of guilty to manslaughter was correctly refused in *Ahmed Din* (1962). Din had stabbed his lodger seven times with a hacksaw and then cut off the man's penis. D pleaded guilty to manslaughter, based on paranoia, but the judge thought that there was insufficient evidence of an abnormality of mind and left the defence to the jury, who returned a verdict of guilty of murder. The Court of Criminal Appeal dismissed the appeal.

According to research by Dell, *Diminished Responsibility Reconsidered* (1982), in practice 80 per cent of pleas of guilty to manslaughter are accepted. Of all pleas refused, most are because the prosecution's medical experts disputed the application of the defence. Where the case does go to trial, there is about a 60 per cent chance of conviction for murder. Thus the overall failure rate of the defence is quite small, around 10 per cent.

Where D pleads DR but it is rejected by the jury, the Court of Appeal may, if it believes the murder conviction to be unsupported by the evidence, quash it and substitute one of manslaughter. In *Matheson* (1958), the medical experts agreed that D was suffering an abnormality of mind but the jury rejected the defence. The Court of Criminal Appeal quashed the murder conviction. Where there was 'unchallenged' evidence of abnormality of mind and substantial impairment of mental responsibility, and 'no facts or circumstances appear that can displace or throw doubt on that evidence' then the court was 'bound' to say that the conviction was unsafe.

Importance of medical evidence

Medical evidence is crucial to the success of the defence. In *Byrne* (1960), it was said that while there is no statutory requirement that a plea be supported by medical evidence, the question of what actually caused the abnormality of mind did, however, 'seem to be a matter to be determined on expert evidence'. This view has been supported ever since.

Where D was suffering a condition that was not, at the time of the trial, regarded by psychiatrists as a mental condition the defence will be unavailable but, if the condition subsequently becomes so regarded, a conviction may be quashed. In *Hobson* (1998), D was tried for the murder of her abusive partner in 1992. The trial judge refused to leave DR to the jury and they convicted. However, in 1997 she appealed, claiming that the evidence at trial supported a DR defence, namely Battered Women's Syndrome (BWS). The Court of Appeal, allowing the appeal and ordering a retrial, noted that BWS was not recognised as a mental disease until 1994, two years after her trial.

Reform

Reform of diminished responsibility

In its 2005 Consultation Paper, *A New Homicide Act for England & Wales?*, the Law Commission (LC) recommended a re-definition of DR, a point it repeated in its 2006 Report *Murder, Manslaughter and Infanticide.* In July 2008, the Ministry of Justice published its own report on the subject, *Murder, Manslaughter & Infanticide: proposals for reform of the law*, in which it agreed to implement the LC's proposals. In November 2008, these proposals were presented to Parliament in the Coroners & Justice Bill (the same Bill as discussed above in the context of provocation). At the time of writing, the Bill contains the following definition of DR which, if enacted, will replace the present s.2(1) of the Homicide Act 1957.

---

(1) A person ('D') who kills or is a party to the killing of another is not to be convicted of murder if D was suffering from an abnormality of mental functioning which:
(a) arose from a recognised medical condition,
(b) substantially impaired D's ability to do one or more of the things mentioned in subsection (1A), and

(c) provides an explanation for D's acts and omissions in doing or being a party to the killing.
(1A) Those things are:
  (a) to understand the nature of D's conduct;
  (b) to form a rational judgment;
  (c) to exercise self-control.
(1B) For the purposes of subsection (1)(c), an abnormality of mental functioning provides an explanation for D's conduct if it causes, or is a significant contributory factor in causing, D to carry out that conduct.

Points to note:

- Only s.2(1) of the Homicide Act 1957 is to be replaced.

- The phrase 'abnormality of mind' is to be deleted, replaced with a more specific requirement of 'abnormality of mental functioning'.

- The 'abnormality' must be based on 'a recognised medical condition' – thereby removing the present list of 'arrested or retarded development of mind', 'inherent cause', 'disease' and 'injury'. This is unlikely to make a great deal of difference in practice, however, as most DR cases under the present s.2(1) are based on 'a recognised medical condition' – alcoholism, depression, epilepsy, psychosis, schizophrenia, etc.

- The Ministry of Justice rejected the LC's suggestion in its 2006 Report that 'developmental immaturity in a D under the age of 18' should be an alternative source of 'abnormality of mental functioning'. The Government thought that there was 'a risk that such a provision would open up the defence too widely'. In any event, the Government believes that the phrase 'recognised medical condition' is wide enough to 'cover conditions such as learning disabilities and autistic spectrum disorders which can be particularly relevant in the context of juveniles', as in the case of *Jama* (2004).

- The test (under the present s.2(1)) that D's 'mental responsibility' be 'substantially impaired' will be abolished. The Ministry of Justice accepted the LC's criticism that the phrase 'mental responsibility' is too vague. Under the new s.2(1), D will have to show more specifically that what has been 'substantially impaired' was their ability to (a) understand the nature of their conduct and/or (b) form a rational judgment and/or (c) exercise self-control.

- The requirement that D's 'abnormality of mental functioning' 'provides an explanation' for the killing means that there must be a causal connection between the 'abnormality' and the killing. However, although the 'abnormality' must be *a* reason for D killing, it need not necessarily be the *only* reason for doing so. It will be enough if D's 'abnormality' was 'a significant contributory factor'.

- Section 2(2) of the Homicide Act 1957 will be retained, so the burden of proof will remain on the defence.

- Section 2(3) is also retained, so the defence will remain partial, reducing D's liability to voluntary manslaughter.

Summary

- Diminished responsibility is a limited defence. It is available only to murder and reduces liability only to manslaughter. The burden of proving the defence rests with the defence, on the balance of probabilities.

- It is a statutory defence, introduced by s.2 of the Homicide Act 1957.

- The defence must prove that D was suffering an abnormality of mind, arising from certain specified causes, which substantially impaired D's mental responsibility.

- A plea of guilty to manslaughter based on the defence may be accepted but only where the evidence is plain.

- Where the defence goes to the jury, medical evidence is crucial (*Byrne*). If there is strong medical support for the defence but the jury ignores it, the Court of Appeal may quash a murder conviction and substitute one of manslaughter (*Matheson*).

- 'Abnormality of mind' means a 'state of mind so different from that of ordinary human beings that the reasonable man would term it abnormal' (*Byrne*).

- The abnormality of mind should be the result of a condition of arrested or retarded development of mind or any inherent cause, or be induced by disease or injury.

- Substantial does not mean total, nor does it mean trivial or minimal (*Lloyd*).

- Intoxication is irrelevant to the defence. Juries should be directed to ignore the effect of alcohol or drugs when considering whether D has an 'abnormality of mind' (*Fenton*; *Gittens*; *Egan*; *Dietschmann*; *Hendy*).

- Alcoholism or 'alcohol dependence syndrome' may amount to a disease or illness. If so, DR is available, provided there is evidence of brain damage and/or where some or all of D's intoxication resulting from the syndrome is regarded by the jury as involuntary (*Wood*).

C   Suicide pact

S.4(1) of the Homicide Act 1957 provides a defence to the survivor of a suicide pact. Again it is a partial defence, available in murder cases only and reducing the liability to one of manslaughter. 'Suicide pact' is defined in s.4(3) of the Act as 'a common agreement between two or more persons having for its object the death of all of them'. As with diminished responsibility, the burden of proof is on the defence and the standard of proof is on the balance of probabilities.

7   Involuntary manslaughter

General introduction

The term 'involuntary manslaughter' encompasses a variety of situations where death has occurred as a result of the conduct of the accused and in circumstances where it has been deemed appropriate to find the accused criminally responsible for that death. However, it should never be confused with the verdict of voluntary manslaughter since the accused will not have intended to kill or cause grievous bodily harm.

The student must appreciate that the offence of involuntary manslaughter covers a diversity of circumstances. At one end of the spectrum is very blameworthy behaviour involving a high risk of death or serious injury, but falling short of murder because the element of intention is lacking. At the other extreme the death may verge upon careless conduct which is nevertheless so blameworthy as to be considered criminal.

The maximum sentence for the offence is life imprisonment and the judge has discretion in handing out the appropriate type and length of sentence up to that maximum. It is not unknown for a non-custodial sentence to be given for an involuntary manslaughter conviction.

There have been many proposals for the reform of involuntary manslaughter through legislation but most forms of involuntary manslaughter remain subject to common law principle. The one exception is corporate manslaughter, where Parliament has recently passed the Corporate Manslaughter and Corporate Homicide Act 2007, discussed below.

A   Constructive manslaughter

Introduction

D will be guilty of constructive manslaughter if he kills by doing an act that is both 'unlawful' and 'dangerous'. It is called constructive manslaughter because the liability for death is built or 'constructed' from the unlawful and dangerous act from which the death has flowed, even though the risk of death may never have been contemplated by the accused. For this reason the offence has often been criticised for being potentially harsh. On the other hand the death of an innocent victim has been caused by the unlawful and dangerous actions of the accused. The degree of blameworthiness will be reflected in the sentence.

The *actus reus* of constructive manslaughter

The *actus reus* of constructive manslaughter requires D to commit an unlawful act which causes death.

D must commit an unlawful 'act'

There is one crucial difference between the *actus reus* of murder and that of constructive manslaughter. Given that constructive manslaughter requires an unlawful and dangerous *act*, it follows that, if D *omits* to act, he cannot be guilty of this form of manslaughter. In *Lowe* (1973), D was convicted of both neglecting his child and manslaughter. The trial judge had directed the jury that if they found Lowe guilty of the neglect offence they had to find him also guilty of manslaughter. The Court of Appeal quashed his manslaughter conviction.

D must commit an 'unlawful' act

D must commit an 'unlawful' act to be found guilty of the offence of constructive manslaughter. Indeed, this is where the expression 'constructive' manslaughter comes from – D's liability is 'constructed' by adding together various elements, as follows:

Unlawful act + dangerousness + death = constructive manslaughter

The unlawful act must be a crime (as opposed to a civil wrong or tort). In *Lamb* (1967), D's manslaughter conviction was based on the unlawful act of assault. This offence will be considered in Chapter 8 but, briefly, it requires that D do or say something to cause V to apprehend immediate unlawful violence. The Court of Appeal quashed D's conviction because there was no evidence that V had been put in fear. Sachs LJ said that D's act was not 'unlawful in the criminal sense of the word'.

> *Lamb* (1967)
> Terry Lamb had shot his best friend with a revolver. The shooting was completely accidental. Although Lamb knew that the gun was loaded, and had pulled the trigger whilst pointing it at his friend, both men thought – wrongly – that it would not fire. There were two bullets in the five-chamber cylinder, but no bullets in the chamber opposite the barrel. Both men failed to appreciate that the cylinder revolved *before* the hammer struck the back of the mechanism.

The unlawful/criminal act will, typically, be a battery – defined as the intentional or reckless application of unlawful force to another person (see Chapter 8). In *Larkin* (1943), a constructive manslaughter conviction based upon the crime of assault was upheld. At a party, D had threatened another man with a razor. D's somewhat dubious account of what happened next was that a drunken woman swayed against him and cut her throat by accident! He was charged with the manslaughter of the woman. The trial judge directed the jury that threatening a man with a naked razor in order to scare him was an unlawful act and the jury convicted.

Possibly the classic case of constructive manslaughter occurs during a fight when D punches V, who falls backwards and bangs his head on the pavement, with fatal results. Inevitably, the case law has thrown up less obvious examples. These include:

- administering a noxious substance (drugs or other substances), contrary to s.23 of the Offences Against the Person Act (OAPA) 1861 – *Cato* (1976)

- affray – *Carey and Others* (2006)

- arson – *Goodfellow* (1986); *Willoughby* (2004)

- burglary – *Watson* (1989)

- criminal damage – *DPP v Newbury and Jones* (1977)

- robbery – *Dawson and Others* (1985).

You will note that it is possible for offences against property to suffice for the 'unlawful' act. In *DPP v Newbury and Jones*, two 15-year-old boys pushed a paving stone from a bridge onto the cab of a train. The stone smashed through the cab window, hit a guard and killed him. The House of Lords upheld their manslaughter convictions, without specifying upon which offence, exactly, this was based. The most obvious is criminal damage.

In *Goodfellow*, D wanted to be moved from his council house in Sunderland. There was little chance of the council moving him as he was some £300 in rent arrears. He therefore planned to set the house on fire in such a way that it would look like a petrol bomb attack. He poured petrol over the sideboard, chair and walls of the living room, then set it alight. The fire got out of control and his wife, son and another woman all died. The Court of Appeal upheld his manslaughter conviction, based on the unlawful act of arson (criminal damage by fire).

D's unlawful act must cause V's death

The normal rules of causation apply (see Chapter 1). In *Mitchell* (1983), which was considered in Chapter 1, Staughton LJ said 'although there was no direct contact between [D] and [V], she was injured as a direct and immediate result of his act ... The only question was one of causation: whether her death was caused by [D]'s acts. It was open to the jury to conclude that it was so caused.'

However, there have been problems in a number of constructive manslaughter cases involving deaths resulting from drugs overdoses, where the prosecution has alleged that the victim's drug dealer should face liability for manslaughter. In the earliest case, *Cato* (1976), D injected V with a mixture of heroin and water. V overdosed and died, and D was convicted of manslaughter. The Court of Appeal upheld the conviction on the basis that D's unlawful act of administering a noxious substance (heroin) contrary to s.23 OAPA 1861 actually caused V's death.

However, should the same result follow if D gives the drug to V, who then takes it himself (and overdoses and dies)? Put simply, on these facts, has D caused V's death? In *Dalby* (1982), the Court of Appeal answered this question 'No'. D had given drugs to V, who proceeded to take them in a highly dangerous form and quantity, overdosed and died. D was convicted of manslaughter but the Court of Appeal allowed the appeal. V's self-administration of the tablets broke the chain of causation.

This line of thinking was confirmed in *Dias* (2002), involving similar facts to *Dalby*. The leading case is now *Kennedy* (2007), a decision of the House of Lords, the facts of which appear in Chapter 1. The House of Lords quashed D's conviction of constructive manslaughter on the basis that V's self-injection of the heroin which D had given to him broke the chain of causation.

Thus, the situation involving drug dealers is that:

- where D actually injects V with a drug, and V dies, then D may face liability for constructive manslaughter (*Cato*); but

- where D hands over the heroin-filled syringe and V self-injects (and dies), then D is not liable for constructive manslaughter (*Dalby*; *Dias*; *Kennedy*).

1. Do you agree that the facts in *Cato* (1976) are sufficiently different from those in *Dalby* (1982), *Dias* (2002) and *Kennedy* (2007) to justify imposing a constructive manslaughter conviction on Ronald Cato but not on Derek Dalby, Fernando Dias and Simon Kennedy?

2. What alternative form of involuntary manslaughter could be used to impose liability on a drug dealer in the *Dalby/Dias/Kennedy* situation? (Refer back to Chapter 2 and the discussion of *Evans* [2009].)

The *mens rea* of constructive manslaughter

The *mens rea* of constructive manslaughter has two elements, both of which must be present:

- the fault required to render D's act unlawful

- dangerousness.

Unlawfulness

In order to be guilty of constructive manslaughter, D must commit an unlawful act, which must be a crime – so D must have the required *mens rea* for that crime. If the offence is assault or battery, D must have acted intentionally or recklessly. This was another reason for quashing D's conviction in *Lamb* (1969). As D did not think that the gun would fire when he pulled the trigger, he had not been reckless as to whether his friend would be harmed, still less had he intended it; therefore there was no *mens rea* for assault.

Of course, if the underlying unlawful act is one of strict liability, no *mens rea* is required at all. This point was decided in *Andrews* (2003), involving the offence in s.58 of the Medicines Act 1968, the unauthorised administration of specified medicinal products, which is a strict liability offence. This case is factually similar to *Cato* (1976), in that D injected V with insulin (which is used in the treatment of diabetes). The insulin had been prescribed for someone else but V agreed to the injection as it can produce a 'rush'. Tragically, V died soon afterwards. D was convicted of constructive manslaughter and his appeal was dismissed. Note that, as D actually injected V, the decision in *Andrews* (2003) survives that in *Kennedy* (2007). As V did not self-inject the insulin, there was no break in the chain of causation.

It is important to note that there is no further mental element for constructive manslaughter. In *DPP v Newbury and Jones* (1977), the House of Lords explicitly held that there was no requirement that D foresee that his acts may cause death or even injury.

'Dangerousness'

In *Church* (1965) – the facts of which appear in Chapter 1 – the Court of Criminal Appeal laid down an objective test for dangerousness:

An unlawful act causing the death of another cannot, simply because it is an unlawful act, render a manslaughter verdict inevitable. For such a verdict inexorably to follow, the unlawful act must be such as all sober and reasonable people would inevitably recognise must subject the other person to, at least, the risk of some harm resulting therefrom, albeit not serious harm.

In *DPP v Newbury and Jones* (1977), the House of Lords was specifically asked whether D needed to have foreseen harm in order to be guilty of constructive manslaughter. The court answered 'No', emphasising that 'dangerousness' is a purely objective test.

All the circumstances are relevant to the *Church* test. This includes those known to D, as well as those that would have been known by the hypothetical 'sober and reasonable' person, had they been present. In *Watson* (1989), D burgled the house of a frail, 87-year-old man, Harold Moyler. When Harold came to investigate he was abused verbally. However, Harold was so distressed by what had happened that he died of a heart attack 90 minutes later. D was convicted of manslaughter. Although the Court of Appeal quashed his conviction (on the basis that the heart attack may have been caused by all the subsequent commotion), they upheld the jury's finding that the burglary was 'dangerous' – or at least it became dangerous as soon as Harold's age and condition would have become apparent to the reasonable person.

However, in *Dawson and Others* (1985), manslaughter convictions were quashed because the Court of Appeal decided that an attempted armed robbery was not 'dangerous'. When the three defendants arrived at a petrol station, masked and armed with a pickaxe handle and replica gun, the attendant – who had a heart condition – managed to sound the alarm but later died from a heart attack. The Court of Appeal held that this was not manslaughter – the reasonable person could not have been aware of the attendant's 'bad heart'.

In *Carey and Others* (2006), the Court of Appeal reached a similar decision to that in *Dawson and Others*. This time the court decided that a single punch thrown at an apparently healthy 15-year-old girl was not sufficiently dangerous to support a manslaughter conviction.

Carey & Others (2006)
Aimee Wellock, a 15-year-old girl, had been out with friends when her group was approached by another group of teenage girls including the three defendants. The defendants attacked Aimee's group, and Aimee was punched once. She then ran away after being threatened with further violence, but collapsed after running about

100m and died of an undiagnosed heart complaint aggravated by the running. The defendants were convicted of affray and constructive manslaughter but their manslaughter convictions were quashed on appeal. The Court of Appeal held that the count of manslaughter should have been withdrawn from the jury as the only physical harm to V (a single punch) did not cause her death. Although there were other threats of violence in the course of the affray they were not dangerous, inasmuch as a reasonable person would not have foreseen their causing any physical harm to V.

More recently, in *Lynch* (2007), the Court of Appeal upheld D's conviction of manslaughter despite V's death being at least partly attributable to an unknown heart defect. D had punched V four times in the head and V died later in hospital. Thus, D had committed an unlawful act (battery) and it was also 'dangerous' in the sense that punching someone four times in the head was objectively likely to subject V to at least the risk of some harm, regardless of whether or not V had a defective heart condition. D could not, therefore, use V's condition to escape liability. (This case should instead be seen as another example of D having to take V as she found him, the principle established in *Blaue* [1975] which was examined in Chapter 1.)

According to the *Church test*, V must be subjected to 'the risk of some harm'. What does this mean? Will a shock or a fright suffice? In *Dawson and Others*, the Court of Appeal thought that 'harm' included 'injury to the person through the operation of shock emanating from fright'. What does this mean exactly?

Summary

- D will be guilty of constructive manslaughter if he kills by doing an act that is both 'unlawful' and 'dangerous'.

- Constructive manslaughter requires an unlawful and dangerous 'act' – thus, if D omits to act, they cannot be convicted of this offence (*Lowe*).

- The unlawful act must be a criminal offence, typically battery, but it could be arson, burglary, robbery or criminal damage.

- D's unlawful act must be a cause of V's death. The normal rules on causation apply (*Mitchell*).

- D must have both the *actus reus* and *mens rea* of that criminal offence. If they do not, there can be no conviction of constructive manslaughter (*Lamb*).

- The act must be 'dangerous', which means doing an act that the reasonable person would inevitably recognise must subject V to the risk of some harm (*Church*). It is an objective test (*DPP v Newbury and Jones*).

- 'Harm' includes 'injury to the person through the operation of shock emanating from fright' (*Dawson and Others*) as long as the risk of some harm was apparent to the accused or the reasonable person (*Watson*; *Carey and Others*).

B   Gross negligence manslaughter

Introduction

According to the leading case, *Adomako* (1995), the elements of this form of involuntary manslaughter, are:

- the existence of a duty of care

- breach of that duty causing death

- gross negligence which the jury consider justifies criminal conviction.

Adomako (1995)
V was a patient undergoing an operation for a detached retina. He was totally paralysed, and the only part of his body visible was his eyes. Oxygen was supplied through a tube. An array of machines monitor the patient's condition.

It was the job of D, an anaesthetist, to watch the machines while the surgeons operated. After the tube accidentally became disconnected, D failed to notice anything wrong for several minutes, until V went into cardiac arrest and the ECG display (which monitors the patient's heartbeat) showed a flat line. He died six months later from hypoxia (lack of oxygen to the brain). D was charged with manslaughter. The prosecution called two witnesses who described D's failure to react as 'abysmal' and said that a competent anaesthetist would have recognised the problem 'within 15 seconds'. D was convicted of gross negligence manslaughter and the Court of Appeal and House of Lords upheld his conviction.

Duty of care

The criminal law recognises certain duty situations – see Chapter 2. *Adomako* itself involved a breach of duty owed by a hospital anaesthetist towards a patient – imposed under a *contract of employment*. Other cases involving doctors facing gross negligence manslaughter charges include *Bateman* (1925) and *Misra and Srivastava* (2004). In *Adomako*, the House of Lords approved *Stone and Dobinson* (1977) – where the defendants had undertaken a duty of care. The *Miller* principle was used as the basis of the duty in the recent gross negligence manslaughter case of *Evans* (2009), which was examined in Chapter 2. *Evans* decides that a duty may be imposed on those who *create or contribute to a life-threatening situation*.

So is the ambit of the offence limited to those who, for whatever reason, have either undertaken or had a duty imposed upon them – or should it be wider? In *Adomako*, Lord Mackay LC actually said that the 'ordinary principles of law of negligence apply to ascertain whether or not D has been in breach of a duty of care towards the victim'. That being so, it logically follows that those same principles should apply in determining those persons to whom a duty is owed. These principles are to be found in the leading negligence case of *Donoghue v Stevenson* (1932), where Lord Atkin in the House of Lords said:

> You must take reasonable care to avoid acts or omissions which you can reasonably foresee would be likely to injure your neighbour. Who then is my neighbour? The answer seems to be – persons who are so closely and directly affected by my act that I ought reasonably to have them in contemplation as being so affected when I am directing my mind to the acts or omissions which are called into question.

This clearly goes much further than the traditional duty situations identified in Chapter 2. If this analysis is correct, then this form of manslaughter has a very wide scope indeed.

In *Wacker* (2003), the Court of Appeal, following *Adomako*, confirmed that the question whether or not a duty of care was owed for the purposes of gross negligence manslaughter was determined by 'the same legal criteria as governed whether there was a duty of care in the law of negligence'. However, this did *not* include the tortious principle of *ex turpi causa* (according to which the participants in a criminal enterprise did not owe a duty of care to each other).

> *Wacker* (2003)
>
> Perry Wacker was a lorry driver. He had agreed to smuggle 60 illegal immigrants from the Netherlands into the UK, the last leg of their journey from China. The plan involved the 60 immigrants entering a container which would be loaded into Wacker's lorry and sealed. Before the lorry reached the Belgian port of Zeebrugge where it was to board the North Sea ferry, Wacker closed a vent, the only means of ventilation into the container. The purpose of doing so was to make it more difficult for anyone to discover the smuggling operation. There was no possibility of those inside opening either the container door or the vent and the lack of fresh air had tragic consequences. Five hours later, when the lorry was offloaded at Dover, customs officials ordered the container to be opened and found 58 dead bodies and only two survivors. Wacker was convicted of 58 counts of manslaughter. The Court of Appeal rejected his plea that he did not owe the Chinese immigrants a duty of care.

In *Willoughby* (2004), the Court of Appeal followed and confirmed *Wacker*. The Court decided that D, a participant in a joint enterprise (here, the intentional arson attack on a pub) owed the other participant a duty of care.

Breach of duty

The next issue is at what point D breaks that duty. In civil law, D is judged against the standard of the reasonable person performing the activity involved. If D is driving a car, for example, they must reach the standard of the reasonable driver. If D is a doctor, they are judged against the standard of the reasonably competent doctor – no more, no less.

Gross negligence

Simply proving that D has been in breach of a duty owed to another person and caused that person's death will not lead inevitably to liability for gross negligence manslaughter. Something more is required. In *Adomako*, the House of Lords confirmed that the correct test for this extra element was 'gross negligence'. This confirmed a line of case law dating back to *Bateman* (1925), which also involved negligent treatment by a doctor which caused the patient to die. In *Bateman*, Lord Hewart LCJ explained that, in order to establish criminal liability for gross negligence, 'the negligence of the accused went beyond a mere matter of compensation between subjects and showed such disregard for the life and safety of others as to amount to a crime against the state and conduct deserving punishment'.

This passage may be criticised for being somewhat vague: it tells the jury to convict if they think that D's negligence was bad enough to amount to the crime. However, the *Bateman* test received approval from the House of Lords in *Andrews v DPP* (1937), which involved death caused by extremely negligent driving. In *Adomako* (1995), Lord Mackay LC approved the *Bateman* test, stating that it was for the jury 'to consider whether the extent to which [D's] conduct departed from the proper standard of care incumbent on him . . . was such that it should be judged criminal'. Lord Mackay acknowledged that the test 'involves an element of circularity', but was adamant that the matter had to be left to the jury: 'an attempt to specify that degree [of badness] more closely is I think likely to achieve only a spurious precision'.

In *Andrews*, Lord Atkin at least offered some guidance on exactly how 'bad' D's negligence has to be. He said that 'a very high degree of negligence is required to be proved'. He added that 'mere inadvertence' by D would never suffice for criminal liability; D must have had 'criminal disregard' for others' safety, or 'the grossest ignorance or the most criminal inattention'.

In *Misra and Srivastava* (2004), the Court of Appeal held that the ingredients of gross negligence manslaughter involved no uncertainty which offended against Article 7 of the European Convention on Human Rights. It had been argued that the implementation of the ECHR into British law via the Human Rights Act 1998 meant that the principles set out in *Adomako* were no longer good law. Judge LJ disagreed with that argument. He said (emphasis added):

> The question for the jury was not whether the D's negligence was gross and whether, *additionally*, it was a crime, but whether his behaviour was grossly negligent and *consequently* criminal. This was not a question of law, but one of fact, for decision in the individual case . . . [Gross negligence manslaughter] involves an element of uncertainty about the outcome of the decision-making process, but not unacceptable uncertainty about the offence itself. In our judgment the law is clear. The ingredients of the offence have been clearly defined, and the principles decided in the House of Lords in *Adomako*. They involve no uncertainty.

Misra and Srivastava (2004)
Amit Misra and Rajeev Srivastava were senior house officers at Southampton General Hospital responsible for the post-operative care of a young man called Sean Phillips who had undergone surgery to repair his patella tendon on 23 June 2000. He became infected

with staphylococcus aureus but the condition was untreated and he died on 27 June. It was alleged that V died as a result of D and E's gross negligence in failing to identify and treat the severe infection from which he died. The Court of Appeal dismissed their appeals.

What state(s) of mind will amount to 'gross negligence'?

This is obviously a question of crucial importance, and it has caused the courts considerable difficulty over the years. When *Adomako* was heard in the Court of Appeal in 1993, Lord Taylor CJ attempted to provide a list of what states of mind could be considered to be 'grossly negligent'. However, when the case reached the Lords, Lord Mackay rejected Lord Taylor's proposals to list the different states of mind. The Lord Chancellor said that 'the circumstances to which a charge of [gross negligence] manslaughter may apply are so various that it is unwise to attempt to categorise or detail specimen directions'. Lord Mackay LC did say that, depending on the circumstances of the case, it might be 'perfectly appropriate' to use the word 'reckless' when directing a jury – but in the 'ordinary connotation of that word'. This harks back to what Lord Atkin said in *Andrews v DPP* (1937) – 20 years before *Cunningham* and 44 years before *Caldwell* – when he offered this explanation of 'gross negligence':

> Probably of all the epithets that can be applied 'reckless' most nearly covers the case . . . but it is not all-embracing, for 'reckless' suggests an indifference to risk, whereas the accused may have appreciated the risk, and intended to avoid it, and yet shown in the means adopted to avoid the risk such a high degree of negligence as would justify a conviction.

However, this begs the question, risk of what, exactly? For some time there was doubt as to what exactly the risk had to involve before D could be said to have been grossly negligent. Was it death, or serious injury, or something else? The authorities were not entirely consistent. It is now clear: the risk must be of **death**. This was established in *Misra and Srivastava* (2004), considered above, where the Court of Appeal stated that:

> Where the issue of risk is engaged . . . it is now clearly established that it relates to the risk of death, and is not satisfied by the risk of bodily injury or injury to health. In short, the offence requires gross negligence in circumstances where what is at risk is the life of an individual . . . As such it serves to protect his or her right to life.

Summary

- There are four elements to this form of involuntary manslaughter: the existence of a duty of care; breach of that duty; gross negligence which the jury consider justifies criminal conviction; and death caused by the breach.

- A duty of care will certainly be held to exist in doctor/patient situations (*Bateman*; *Adomako*) and in situations where D had or assumed responsibility for the welfare of another person (*Stone and Dobinson*, *Evans*).

- Duties may, however, be owed in other situations, e.g. motorists owe a duty to other road users (*Andrews*).

- A person who creates or contributes to a life-threatening situation may be held to owe a duty to anyone in that situation (*Evans*).

- Breach of duty is the same as in civil law, that is, falling below the standard to be expected of the reasonable person (*Adomako*).

- Liability will be imposed only where D was 'grossly negligent' – this is a question for the jury to decide (*Andrews*; *Adomako*).

- Gross negligence includes, but is not limited to, deliberate risk-taking. Where there is an issue of risk, the risk must be of death (*Misra*).

C   Subjective reckless manslaughter

In *Lidar* (2000), the Court of Appeal held that there is a third limb of involuntary manslaughter – reckless manslaughter. The Court said that there was nothing in *Adomako* (1995) to suggest that subjective reckless manslaughter had been abolished. The *actus reus* elements of this crime are simply that D causes V's death (there is no requirement that D owed V a duty of care). The *mens rea* elements are that:

- D must have foreseen a risk of serious injury or death occurring. The type of recklessness is therefore the subjective, *Cunningham* form.

- D must have assessed that risk as at least highly probable to occur.

Lidar (2000)

D had driven his car over 200 metres with V hanging half-out of a car window. Eventually V's feet were caught in a wheel and he was pulled out of the car and was run over and killed. At D's trial for manslaughter, the trial judge directed the jury using subjective recklessness as the standard (i.e. that the jury should convict D if satisfied that he had foreseen a highly probable risk that V would suffer at least serious injury). D was convicted and appealed, arguing that the judge should have referred exclusively to gross negligence. The Court of Appeal upheld D's conviction.

D   Corporate manslaughter

There has been much discussion in recent years about the difficulty of imposing manslaughter liability in cases where a corporation has allegedly caused death. There have been several high-profile examples in recent years, such as the Zeebrugge ferry disaster in March 1987. The North Sea car ferry, the *Herald of Free Enterprise*, had left the port of Zeebrugge in Belgium heading for Dover with its bow doors still open. Within minutes, as the ferry picked up speed and water poured through the open doors, the ferry capsized and 187 people were drowned. The Crown Prosecution Service brought manslaughter charges against P&O Ferries Ltd (the company that owned and operated the ferry), but the trial collapsed. The problem was that, under the law as it then was, it was necessary to 'identify' a person within the organisation with a 'controlling mind' – usually, someone in a senior management position – on whom blame could be placed. Although there had clearly been serious mistakes made by the company, it was not possible to identify anyone in particular within P&O's management structure who could be blamed.

Other examples include the King's Cross underground station fire in London in November 1987, which caused 31 deaths; the Piper Alpha oil platform disaster in July 1988 (167 fatalities); the Clapham rail crash in December 1988 in which 35 people died; the Southall rail crash in September 1997 (seven deaths); and the Ladbroke Grove rail crash in October 1999 (31 deaths). None of these cases resulted in any convictions for manslaughter, although in the Ladbroke Grove case, Network Rail and Thames Trains were collectively fined £6m for breach of health and safety regulations.

One case in which there was a successful prosecution was *R v Kite & OLL Ltd* (1994). Peter Kite was the managing director of an outdoor pursuits centre, OLL Ltd. His staff (some of whom were unqualified) had told him that they were concerned about safety measures in relation to canoeing expeditions that were often undertaken in Lyme Bay on the south-west coast of England, but he had done nothing about it. Four sixth-formers from a school in Plymouth were drowned when their canoes capsized in heavy seas. Both Peter Kite and OLL Ltd were convicted of gross negligence manslaughter. In this case it was easy to identify Peter Kite as the 'controlling mind' of OLL Ltd since the organisation was so small.

However, with larger organisations it was much more difficult for courts to apply the 'identification' principle. Indeed, the larger the organisation, the more likely it was to have sophisticated management structures behind which it was possible for senior management to hide.

Eventually the Law Commission produced a Report in 1996, *Legislating the Criminal Code: Involuntary Manslaughter* (Law Com 237), which recommended the introduction of a specific crime of corporate killing. The Home Office produced its own report four years later, *Reforming the Law on Involuntary Manslaughter: the Government's Proposals* (2000), which was then followed by the introduction into Parliament of a Bill. Finally, in July 2007, the Corporate Manslaughter and Corporate Homicide Act 2007 was passed.

Section 1(1) of the 2007 Act creates a specific offence of 'corporate manslaughter' under which an 'organisation' is guilty 'if the way in which its activities are managed or organised (a) causes a person's death, and (b) amounts to a gross breach of a relevant duty of care owed by the organisation to the deceased'. Section 1(2) identifies various 'organisations' including corporations, partnerships, police forces and many government departments. Section 1(3) states that liability under s.1(1) will follow only if the way in which the organisation's activities are managed or organised by its 'senior management' is a 'substantial element in the breach'.

A 'relevant duty of care'

This is explained in great detail in s.2 of the 2007 Act. It is closely linked to the meaning of 'duty' in the civil law of negligence. The Act identifies several duty situations: a duty owed to employees (s.2(1)(a)); a duty owed as occupier of premises (s.2(1)(b)); a duty owed in connection with the supply by the organisation of goods or services (s.2(1)(c)(i)). These duties would clearly apply to the organisations in the various disasters listed above, where the victims were either employed by or receiving a service from the organisations concerned. A number of situations, including emergencies and certain military, policing, law-enforcement and child protection activities are excluded from the scope of s.2 by sections 3–7.

A 'gross breach'

A breach of duty is a 'gross' breach if the organisation's conduct 'falls far below what can reasonably be expected of the organisation in the circumstances' (s.1(4)(b)). When a jury is required to decide this point, s.8 applies. Section 8(2) states that the jury **must** consider whether the organisation failed to comply with any relevant health and safety legislation and, if so, (a) how serious that failure was and (b) how much of a 'risk of death' it posed. Section 8(3) adds that the jury **may** also (a) consider the extent to which there were 'attitudes, policies, systems or accepted practices' within the organisation that were 'likely to have encouraged' or 'produced tolerance' of such a failure and (b) have regard to any health and safety guidance that relates to the alleged breach.

'Senior management'

This refers to the persons in an organisation who play 'significant roles' in 'the making of decisions about how the whole or a substantial part of its activities are to be managed or organised, or the actual managing or organising of the whole or a substantial part of those activities' (s.1(4)(c)).

Causation

The organisation must be proved to have caused the victim's death. No definition is provided in the Act, so presumably the normal rules of causation (see Chapter 1) apply to the new offence.

Implications of conviction

Under the 2007 Act, the Crown Court has the power to impose an unlimited fine on an organisation found guilty of corporate manslaughter (s.1(6)). In addition, the court has the power to make a 'remedial order' requiring the organisation to correct the breach that caused the death (s.9(1)) and to make a 'publicity order' compelling the defendant to publicise details of their offence, including the size of any fine imposed and whether a 'remedial order' was made (s.10(1)).

Evaluation

At the time of writing, it remains to be seen whether the 2007 Act will make it easier to bring successful prosecutions for corporate manslaughter, now that it is no longer necessary to 'identify' a specific individual director or senior manager. However, perhaps giving the jury power to consider an organisation's 'attitudes' towards health and safety enforcement (under s.8) might make successful prosecutions more likely.

Reform of involuntary manslaughter

In its 2005 Consultation Paper, *A New Homicide Act?*, the Law Commission (LC) proposed that reckless manslaughter (defined as occurring where

D acted with 'reckless indifference' to causing death) should be upgraded to second-degree murder (refer back to the Reform section at the end of Chapter 5).

The LC also proposed that the remaining two forms of involuntary manslaughter should be retained, albeit with some changes from the present law. The LC proposed that D should be guilty of manslaughter when:

- D committed a criminal act, intending to cause physical harm or with foresight that there was a risk of causing physical harm. This essentially replaces constructive manslaughter. The main difference is that the LC proposal requires foresight by D of at least a risk of causing harm (the present *Church* test of dangerousness is based on whether 'all sober and reasonable people' would recognise the risk)

- Death occurred as a result of D's conduct falling far below what could reasonably be expected in the circumstances, where there was a risk that D's conduct would cause death, and this risk would have been obvious to a reasonable person in D's position. D must have had the capacity to appreciate the risk. (This essentially describes what is presently gross negligence manslaughter.)

The LC repeated these proposals in their 2006 report, *Murder, Manslaughter and Infanticide.*

Questions on Part 2 Homicide

I Sarev owes Dipak £40,000 as the result of a gambling debt. When Sarev refuses to pay, Dipak is very angry and decides to frighten Sarev. One night, he cuts the brake fluid pipe beneath Sarev's car hoping that Sarev will be involved in a crash that will scare him into repaying the debt. Outside Sarev's house there is a steep hill with a sharp bend at the bottom. Next morning Sarev drives down the hill but is unable to slow down as he approaches the sharp bend. The car collides at speed with a stone wall and Sarev is critically injured and knocked unconscious.

An ambulance arrives within ten minutes to take Sarev to hospital. Unfortunately, the paramedics, John and Carol, who are the crew on the ambulance, fail to close the rear door of the ambulance correctly and, as it accelerates away, the stretcher on which Sarev is lying is thrown out onto the road. Sarev is run over and killed by a van driven by Ron that is travelling closely behind the ambulance.

Discuss Dipak's liability for the murder of Sarev.

(OCR 2006)

2 Andy has been diagnosed as an alcoholic and is receiving treatment for his condition. He lives with his girlfriend, Barbara. They frequently drink together and then have arguments over trivial matters during which Barbara often tells Andy he is useless and pathetic.

One day, Barbara returns home late and finds Andy in the garage repairing his car. Andy is drunk. When he asks her where she has been she tells him she has been in bed all day with another man. Andy becomes enraged and shouts, 'I'll kill you' at Barbara. She replies, 'Don't be stupid, you haven't got the guts'. Andy immediately hits her over the head with a heavy spanner he is holding, killing her instantly.

Discuss Andy's potential liability including any defences that he may have available to him under the Homicide Act 1957.

(OCR 2007)

3 'The law relating to involuntary manslaughter continues to be muddled and unjust. Reform of this type of homicide is overdue.'

Assess the accuracy of this statement.

(OCR 2007)

4 Clive belongs to a terrorist organisation. They have informed the police that they are determined to use tactics that will disrupt the public, if necessary, in order to further their aims. They give a secret password to the police which will verify that any future telephone calls they make are genuine and not a hoax.

Clive telephones the police in London to say that he has placed a bomb in Paddington police station and confirms that the call is genuine by giving the password. He adds that the bomb is timed to explode in 15 minutes. The operator mistakenly thinks that Clive has said '50 minutes'. The telephone operator immediately communicates this information to his superior and the station is completely cleared without panic within ten minutes.

David, a bomb disposal expert, approaches the locker after 15 minutes in the mistaken belief that the bomb will not explode for at least 30 minutes but is seriously injured when the bomb explodes. David is rushed to hospital in an ambulance where he is given emergency treatment. After a few days David is still in a critical condition and then develops a secondary infection for which he is given an antibiotic drug. Unfortunately David is highly allergic to the drug and dies the following day.

Advise Clive who has been charged with the murder of David.

(OCR 2002)

Part 3

Offences against the person

8 Non-fatal offences against the person

Introduction

There are a number of offences against the person, with distinctions made according to the seriousness of the injuries caused and D's mental state at the time of causing them (intent or recklessness). The offences are, in ascending order of seriousness:

- Assault – contrary to s.39 of the Criminal Justice Act 1988 (CJA)

- Battery – also contrary to s.39 CJA

- Assault occasioning actual bodily harm – contrary to s.47 of the Offences Against the Person Act 1861 (OAPA)

- Inflicting grievous bodily harm – contrary to s.20 OAPA

- Wounding – also contrary to s.20 OAPA

- Causing grievous bodily harm with intent to do so or with intent to resist arrest – contrary to s.18 OAPA

- Wounding with intent to do grievous bodily harm or with intent to resist arrest – also contrary to s.18 OAPA

Note that there is no offence of 'wounding with intent to wound'. It may also strike you as odd that the relevant sections in the statute are 18, 20 and 47. This is because the OAPA was a 'consolidating' statute, one that drew together a wide range of non-fatal offences contained in older legislation into one new statute (sections 23 and 24 deal with poisoning, for example).

Assault and battery are summary offences and can be tried only in the magistrates' court with a maximum sentence of six months' imprisonment. The offences under s.47 and s.20 are 'either way' and so can be tried either in the magistrates' court or the Crown Court; if tried 'on indictment' in the Crown Court, the maximum penalty is five years' imprisonment. The offences under s.18 are the most serious and must be tried in the Crown Court; the maximum sentence is life imprisonment.

For convenience, the following abbreviations will be used throughout this chapter:

* ABH = actual bodily harm

* GBH = grievous bodily harm

* OAPA = Offences Against the Person Act 1861

* CJA = Criminal Justice Act 1988

Assault and battery

Assault and battery are separate crimes, under s.39 of the Criminal Justice Act 1988. This was confirmed in *DPP v Little* (1992), where a single charge alleging that D 'did unlawfully assault and batter' V was held to charge two offences and was therefore bad for 'duplicity' (different offences have to be charged separately).

The terminology can be confusing. To 'assault' someone is usually taken, in ordinary language, to mean 'commit a battery against'. However, in legal terms, an 'assault' means to cause V to apprehend force (for example, shaking a fist at someone's face is an assault), while a 'battery' means to actually apply force to V (for example, punching someone in the face is a battery). Often the two crimes will be committed very close together – drawing your fist back (assault), throwing a punch and connecting with V (battery). Hence the common references to someone committing 'assault and battery'.

Assault

An assault is any act whereby D causes V to (*Fagan v Metropolitan Police Commissioner* [1968]):

* Apprehend

* Immediate

* Force

Apprehend

It is necessary that V 'apprehends' force. The word is used in preference to 'fears', because it would severely restrict the law of assault if it had to be proven that V was scared. Aiming a punch at the World Heavyweight Boxing Champion may well make him 'apprehend' force but he would certainly not 'fear' it.

To 'apprehend' something means to be aware of it, so to apprehend force simply means that V has to be aware that something violent is about to happen. If D's acts are unobserved by V, because it is dark or D approaches from behind, or V is blind or asleep, then there will be no assault. But if V apprehends force then it does not matter if – in fact – V was not in danger. In *Logdon v DPP* (1976), D showed V a gun in his office desk drawer and said that it was loaded. Although it was, in fact, a fake, this was not obvious from its appearance and V was frightened. D was convicted of assault and the Divisional Court upheld the conviction. But if V had known the gun to be a fake, or that it was real but unloaded, then there would be no assault (see *Lamb* [1967] – Chapter 7). Similarly, there would not be an assault if it was obvious that D had no means of carrying out their threat; for example, by gesticulating at the passengers of a moving train from beside the track.

Immediate

This requirement means that a threat to use force in the future cannot be an assault. However, the courts have tended to take a generous view of immediacy. In *Smith v Superintendent of Woking Police Station* (1983), the Divisional Court decided that D had committed an assault by standing in V's garden, looking at her in her nightclothes through her bedroom window at about 11pm. Kerr LJ said that it was sufficient that D had instilled in V an apprehension of what he might do next. Obviously, as she was inside the house and he was in the garden, he was not in a position to attack her that very second. But nevertheless V had thought that 'whatever he might be going to do next, and sufficiently immediately for the purposes of the offence, was something of a violent nature'.

In *Ireland* (1997), D had made a number of silent phone calls to three women. The House of Lords upheld his convictions of assault occasioning actual bodily harm. There was sufficient evidence that the victims had apprehended immediate force, because they did not know from where D was making the phone calls; they did not know what D was going to do next, which was sufficient for assault in *Smith*, above.

In *Constanza* (1997), on similar facts to *Ireland*, the Court of Appeal expanded the immediacy test ever-so-slightly. Schiemann LJ held that it was sufficient for the Crown to have proved an apprehension of force 'at some time not excluding the immediate future'. The Court of Appeal, however, did point out that V knew D lived nearby and that 'she thought that something could happen at any time'.

Force

Force does not mean violence. A touch would suffice. See *Collins v Wilcock* (1984), below.

Assault by words alone

It used to be the law that something more than words was required. But in *Ireland* (1997), Lord Steyn said:

> The proposition that a gesture may amount to an assault, but that words can never suffice, is unrealistic and indefensible. A thing said is also a thing done. There is no reason why something said should be incapable of causing an apprehension of immediate personal violence, e.g. a man accosting a woman in a dark alley saying, 'Come with me or I will stab you'.

The words need not necessarily be oral, as in Lord Steyn's example. In *Constanza*, the Court of Appeal held that words in a written form (such as letters, emails or texts) could amount to an assault. Schiemann LJ pointed out that what was important was that V apprehended force. How that apprehension got there was 'wholly irrelevant'.

Words may negative an assault

Words may negative behaviour that would otherwise be an assault. In *Tuberville v Savage* (1669), a civil case, D placed one hand on his sword, saying, 'If it were not assize time, I would not take such language from you'. This was held not to be an assault. V knew he was not in danger because the assize judges were in town.

However, in *Light* (1857), where D raised a sword over his wife's head and said, 'Were it not for the bloody policeman outside, I would split your head open', this *was* held to be an assault. Someone in her situation would surely have been put in fear – she had only D's word that he was not going to 'split her head open'. If, even fleetingly, it crossed her mind that she was in danger, this was an assault, no matter how convincing D was in stating that she was not in danger. The justification offered for upholding the convictions in *Smith*, *Ireland* and *Constanza* was that the victims did not know what D was going to do next. Presumably Light's wife did not know what D was going to do next either.

Battery

This is the application of force to the person. Battery does not presuppose an assault. A blow to the back of the head, taking V completely by surprise, is a battery. The merest touching without consent is a battery. In

Collins v Wilcock (1984), Robert Goff LJ said, 'It has long been established that any touching of another person, however slight, may amount to a battery'.

Of course, every day thousands, if not millions, of people squash onto crowded commuter trains and buses, or squeeze into almost-full lifts. Some physical contact with other people is inevitable. According to Robert Goff LJ, they all commit battery! Except that they do not: the answer is that most touchings are not 'batteries' because implied consent is given to all the touching which is inevitable in the ordinary course of everyday life (see further Chapter 9).

Is there a requirement of hostility?

In *Faulkner v Talbot* (1981), Lord Lane CJ said that a battery 'need not necessarily be hostile, rude or aggressive, as some of the cases seem to indicate'. However, Croom-Johnson LJ in *Wilson v Pringle* (1986), a civil case, stated that a touching had to be 'hostile' in order to be a battery. In *Brown and Others* (1993), the House of Lords approved *Wilson v Pringle*. Lord Jauncey described hostility as 'a necessary ingredient'. Lord Mustill, dissenting, said that 'hostility cannot . . . be a crucial factor which in itself determines guilt or innocence, although its presence or absence may be relevant when the court has to decide *as a matter of policy* how to react to a new situation' (emphasis added). It is suggested that this latter view is the correct one.

Is there a requirement of directness?

Most batteries are directly applied to V's person, usually by striking that person with a fist or some object, throwing a missile at them, or shooting them. But it is not essential. In *Martin* (1881), D placed an iron bar across the doorway of a theatre, put out the lights and then created general panic and confusion. Various theatregoers were injured. D was convicted of inflicting GBH – but the court accepted that in doing so he had also committed battery. A more recent example of this principle is *Haystead* (2000). D punched a woman who was holding a small child in her arms. As a result of the blows, she dropped the boy on the ground. D was charged with assaulting the boy, and the Divisional Court upheld his conviction of battery, even though no direct physical contact had occurred between D and the boy.

'Reasonable punishment' of children – a defence only to battery

There is one defence in English law which is unique to battery: reasonable punishment of children. Section 58 of the Children Act 2004 states that force used on a child cannot be justified on the ground that it constituted 'reasonable punishment' in relation to any offence under:

- s.18 or s.20 OAPA (wounding and causing GBH)

- s.47 OAPA (ABH) or

- s.1 of the Children and Young Persons Act 1933 (cruelty to persons under 16).

As no reference is made to battery, it is clear that a defence of 'reasonable punishment' does apply as long as no more than physical contact is used.

Actual bodily harm

S.47 of the Offences Against the Person Act 1861 provides that 'Whosoever shall be convicted on indictment of any assault occasioning actual bodily harm shall be liable to imprisonment for not more than five years'.

'Actual bodily harm'

In *Donovan* (1934), the Court of Criminal Appeal said that 'actual bodily harm' in s.47 bore its ordinary meaning. It included 'any hurt or injury' that interfered with the 'health or comfort' of V. This hurt or injury did not need to be permanent though it had to be 'more than merely transient or trifling'. The definition is deliberately broad. Very slight physical injuries have been held to fall within it, including minor bruises and abrasions. In *Chan-Fook*, the Court of Appeal stated that the injury 'should not be so trivial as to be wholly insignificant'.

In *DPP v Smith* (2006), the High Court held that the cutting of hair without an individual's consent constituted ABH. Sir Igor Judge declared:

> In my judgment, whether it is alive beneath the surface of the skin or dead tissue above the surface of the skin, the hair is an attribute and part of the human body. It is intrinsic to each individual and to the identity of each individual ... Even if, medically and scientifically speaking, the hair above the surface of the scalp is no more than dead tissue, it remains part of the body and is attached to it. While it is so attached, in my judgment it falls within the meaning of 'bodily' in the phrase 'actual bodily harm'. It is concerned with the body of the individual victim.

'Occasioning'

This is purely a question of causation (see Chapter 1). In *Roberts* (1972), D had tried to remove the coat of his female car passenger and she had jumped out of the motor vehicle to escape. She suffered grazing and concussion for which she was detained in hospital for three days. The jury was directed to convict provided that V's injury was the natural consequence of D's conduct, in the sense that it could have reasonably been foreseen. D's conviction was upheld. In *Notman* (1994), where D ran into V and slightly injured his ankle, D was convicted after the trial judge directed the jury that it was sufficient if his conduct was a 'substantial cause' of V's injury. The Court of Appeal upheld his conviction.

Wounding and grievous bodily harm

Offences Against the Person Act 1861
18. Whosoever shall unlawfully and maliciously by any means whatsoever wound or cause any grievous bodily harm to any person with intent to do some grievous bodily harm to any person or with intent to resist or prevent the lawful apprehension or detainer of any person, shall be guilty of [an offence], and being convicted thereof shall be liable to imprisonment for life.

20. Whosoever shall unlawfully and maliciously wound or inflict any grievous bodily harm upon any other person, either with or without any weapon or instrument, shall be guilty of [an offence triable either way], and being convicted thereof shall be liable to imprisonment for five years.

Caution is advised here. There are many similarities, but some differences, between the two offences. In terms of the *actus reus*, both offences share the common expressions 'wound' and 'grievous bodily harm' but while s.20 uses the verb to 'inflict', s.18 uses the verb to 'cause'. The *mens rea* is very different (see below).

Wound

To constitute a 'wound', the continuity of the skin must be broken. There are two layers of the skin, an outer layer known as the epidermis or cuticle, and an inner layer called the dermis. It is not enough that the cuticle is broken if the inner layer remains intact. Purely internal bleeding will not suffice for a 'wound'. In *JCC (a minor) v Eisenhower* (1984), the Divisional Court ruled that internal rupturing of blood vessels in the eye caused by an air-pistol pellet was not a 'wound' because the injury was purely internal.

Grievous bodily harm

The meaning of this expression was considered in Chapter 5, on murder, because it has a common meaning in homicide and non-fatal offences. Essentially, according to Viscount Kilmuir in *DPP v Smith* (1961), 'bodily harm needs no explanation and "grievous" means no more and no less than "really serious"'. In *Saunders* (1985), where D was convicted of inflicting GBH despite the trial judge omitting the word 'really', the Court of Appeal still upheld the conviction.

In *Bollom* (2003), the Court of Appeal held that, in deciding whether injuries were 'grievous', it was necessary to take into account the effect of those injuries on V, which meant taking into account V's age.

Bollom (2003)

Stephen Bollom had been convicted of causing GBH with intent to Alex, the 17-month-old daughter of his partner, Carrie-Ann Jones. The injuries included abrasions on her legs and numerous bruises to her arms, legs and stomach. He appealed, arguing that the trial judge had wrongly allowed the jury to take into account Alex's age in determining whether the injuries were 'grievous'. The Court of Appeal decided that it would be wrong to ignore V's age, health or 'any other particular factors' in deciding whether injuries amounted to really serious harm. However, the court found the trial judge had made another, different error when directing the jury and quashed Bollom's conviction under s.18 (substituting a conviction under s.47 instead).

Inflict and cause

Until 1997 there was much judicial and academic discussion about what differences, if any, there were between the word 'inflict', which appears in s.20, and 'cause', which appears in s.18. The general consensus was that 'cause' was a wider concept. As recently as *Mandair* (1995), the House of Lords had maintained that the words 'inflict' and 'cause' had different meanings. However, in *Burstow* (1997), the Lords unanimously ruled that the two words should be treated as synonymous. Lord Hope said that 'for all practical purposes there is, in my opinion, no difference between these words . . . the words "cause" and "inflict" may be taken to be interchangeable'.

Mens rea of s.18

Intention

Under s.18, intention is critical to a conviction. Intention has the same meaning as in the law of murder. Where D intends to cause GBH to P, but misses and accidentally causes harm to Q, then he may be convicted under s.18 (this is one application of the 'transferred malice' doctrine, see Chapter 1).

Maliciously

Because s.18 requires 'intent', is the word 'malicious', which appears in s.18, redundant? Remember, according to the leading recklessness case, *Cunningham* (1957), 'maliciousness' means 'intentionally or recklessly'. The answer is: it depends. S.18 really divides up into four crimes, as follows:

• Causing GBH with intent to do GBH

• Wounding with intent to do GBH

• Causing GBH with intent to resist arrest

• Wounding with intent to resist arrest

Where the charge is causing GBH with intent to do GBH, then Diplock LJ in *Mowatt* (1968) was absolutely right when he said, 'In s.18 the word "maliciously" adds nothing'. However, where any of the other crimes are charged, then the word is very important. D would not be liable under s.18 if, with intent to resist arrest, they *accidentally* injured a policeman – with no foresight of the injuries. To be guilty, D must intend to resist arrest and intend, or be reckless whether, a wound or GBH is caused.

You should note that there is no offence under s.18 of 'wounding with intent to wound'. This point was confirmed very recently in *Taylor* (2009), where D's conviction under s.18 was quashed because the trial judge had directed the jury to convict if they were satisfied that D had wounded with intent to do GBH or with intent to wound. The Court of Appeal allowed the appeal (although substituting a conviction under s.20) because, although there was evidence that D had intended to wound V, there was no evidence to suggest that D had intended to do GBH. Thomas LJ said that an 'intent to wound is insufficient. There must be an intent to cause really serious bodily injury. It is not necessary for us to set out why that was so because the statutory language is clear'.

Included offences

S.6(3) of the Criminal Law Act 1967 allows for the conviction of an alternative offence to the one charged 'where the allegations in the indictment expressly or by necessary implication include' that offence. In *Savage* (1992), the Lords ruled that s.47 was included in s.20; and in *Mandair* (1995) the Lords ruled that s.20 was included in s.18. This is very likely to happen where the jury is satisfied that wounding or GBH has been caused but are not convinced beyond reasonable doubt that D intended GBH. This was the situation in *Taylor* (2009), above.

Psychiatric injury

Psychiatric injury as ABH

In *Chan-Fook* (1994), the Court of Appeal held that 'bodily harm' was capable of including psychiatric injury, although it did not include mere emotions such as fear, distress, panic or a hysterical or nervous condition. Hobhouse LJ said,

> The body of the victim includes all parts of his body, including his organs, his nervous system and his brain. Bodily injury therefore may include injury to any parts of his body responsible for his mental and other faculties.

> *Chan-Fook* (1994)
> Chan-Fook suspected that V had stolen his fiancée's engagement ring. C-F dragged him upstairs and locked him in a second floor room. V tried to escape but was injured when he fell to the ground. C-F was charged under s.47. It was alleged that even if V had not been physically injured, the trauma he had suffered prior to the escape bid would amount to ABH. However, there was no medical evidence to support this, only V's claim that he felt abused, frightened and humiliated. The trial judge directed the jury that a hysterical or nervous condition was capable of being ABH. C-F was convicted. On appeal, the Court of Appeal quashed the conviction. Although the court held first that ABH was capable of including psychiatric injury, what V had suffered did not qualify.

In *Ireland* (1997), Lord Steyn in the House of Lords approved the decision in *Chan-Fook* (1994), saying that 'the ruling ... was based on principled and cogent reasoning and it marked a sound and essential clarification of the law'. He said that 'one can nowadays quite naturally speak of inflicting psychiatric injury'. D's convictions in that case were upheld, as there was much stronger evidence of psychiatric injury: his victims had suffered palpitations, breathing difficulties, cold sweats, anxiety, inability to sleep, dizziness and stress. In *Constanza* (1997), the Court of Appeal unanimously rejected D's appeal against a s.47 conviction for causing ABH in the form of clinical depression and anxiety.

Psychiatric injury as GBH

Once it had been accepted in *Chan-Fook* that psychiatric injury could amount to 'actual' bodily harm, it logically followed that serious psychiatric injury could amount to 'grievous' bodily harm. In *Burstow* (1997), D had mounted a sustained campaign of harrassment against Tracey Sant, with whom he had had a very brief relationship three years earlier. This mainly consisted of silent telephone calls and hate mail, but there was other, more eccentric behaviour. Eventually, she was diagnosed as suffering severe depression. D was convicted of inflicting GBH and the Court of Appeal and the House of Lords dismissed his appeal.

In *Dhaliwal* (2006), the Court of Appeal decided that for non-physical harm to amount to 'bodily' harm for the purposes of s.20 OAPA 1861 there had to be evidence of a recognisable psychiatric illness. Purely psychological harm would not be sufficient.

Need for psychiatric evidence

Expert evidence is required before someone can be convicted of causing ABH or GBH where the harm alleged is psychiatric in nature. In *Morris* (1998), where the facts were similar to *Burstow*, the trial judge allowed the case to go to the jury – without any psychiatric evidence. The judge was happy to leave it to the jury to say whether or not V's symptoms – sleeping difficulties, nightmares, cold sweats, nausea, stomach ache and joint pains – amounted to ABH. The Court of Appeal quashed D's conviction – although it did order a retrial.

Transmission of disease

Until recently, English criminal law did not regard the transmission of disease through sexual intercourse as an offence. This situation was because of the nineteenth-century case of *Clarence* (1888). Charles Clarence had sex with his wife, Selina (with her consent), even though he knew that he had gonorrhoea (a venereal disease) and yet without telling her. He was convicted by a jury of inflicting GBH and assault occasioning ABH but his appeal was allowed.

This was because, at the time of *Clarence*, the word 'inflicting' had a narrower meaning than it does now. The court ruled that to 'inflict' harm upon another person implied that an assault had taken place. However, because the court also decided that Selina had consented to sex with Charles, he had not assaulted her. Therefore there was no possibility of a conviction under either s.47 or s.20 OAPA. (The consent aspect of the case will be examined further in Chapter 9.) This narrow interpretation of the word 'inflict' was changed only more than a century later by the House of Lords in *Ireland* and *Burstow* (1997), discussed earlier, when it was held that to 'inflict' simply means to 'cause'. Although *Ireland* and *Burstow* involved stalking, the new, wider, interpretation of 'inflict' paved the way for *Clarence* to be overruled in 2004.

In the meantime, however, an important decision was made by the Supreme Court of Canada in *Cuerrier* (1998). The case involved the prosecution of D for two counts of 'aggravated assault' (equivalent to ABH in English law). He had unprotected sex with two women, even though he knew that he had the human immunodeficiency virus (HIV), and passed the disease on to them. He was convicted and the Supreme Court upheld his conviction, distinguishing *Clarence* (which, despite being an English case, forms a precedent in Canadian law) and holding that D had committed assault.

Back in England, in *Dica* (2004), the Court of Appeal took the opportunity to decide that *Clarence* was wrongly decided. In *Dica*, the facts of which are virtually identical to *Cuerrier*, D was convicted by a jury of two counts of inflicting 'biological' GBH contrary to s.20 OAPA and, although his convictions were quashed by the Court of Appeal because of a judicial misdirection, the Court took the opportunity to overrule *Clarence*. Judge LJ held as follows:

> The effect of this judgment . . . is to remove some of the outdated restrictions against the successful prosecution of those who, knowing that they are suffering HIV or some other serious sexual disease, recklessly transmit it through consensual sexual intercourse, and inflict GBH on a person from whom the risk is concealed and who is not consenting to it. In this context, *Clarence* has no continuing relevance.

The Court of Appeal did, however, order a retrial at which D was again convicted of inflicting 'biological' GBH by a different jury. The case of *Dica* (and a very similar case, *Konzani* [2005], where *Dica* was followed) will be examined in more detail in Chapter 9, when the consent issue will be explored.

In 1993, the Law Commission proposed that the intentional or reckless transmission of disease should be a criminal offence as part of a Report on reform of this area. However, in 1998, the government also published a Report on reform of non-fatal assaults and a draft Bill containing four new offences to replace those in the Offences Against the Person Act 1861 and the Criminal Justice Act 1988. One of the proposed new offences is 'intentional serious injury', and the Report indicates that intentional transmission of a serious disease comes within that new offence. However, disease transmission is specifically excluded from the other offences. There were two reasons for this:

- 'it would be wrong to criminalise the reckless transmission of normally minor illnesses such as measles or mumps'; and

- 'the law should not seem to discriminate against those who are HIV positive, have AIDS or viral hepatitis or who carry any kind of disease.

Nor do we want to discourage people from coming forward for diagnostic tests and treatment ... because of an unfounded fear of criminal prosecution.'

The report concluded that the offence would be used only 'in those rare and grave cases where prosecution would be justified'. Presumably, cases like *Cuerrier*, *Dica* and *Konzani*, where life-threatening illnesses are transmitted during sex, would satisfy the criteria of 'rare and grave cases'. The government's report and draft Bill will be considered fully at the end of this chapter.

Stalking

Several of the cases considered above – *Burstow*, *Constanza*, *Ireland*, *Morris* – involved what is commonly known as 'stalking', loosely defined as a sustained campaign of harrassment. At the time when these cases were brought, England had no laws designed to deal effectively with the problem. Section 1 of the Malicious Communications Act 1988 contains an offence of making threats or sending indecent or grossly offensive messages by letter or 'electronic communication', but it is a summary offence with a maximum sentence of six months' imprisonment. This compares with five years' imprisonment for inflicting GBH or ABH, the charges in *Burstow* and *Ireland* respectively. It is little wonder, therefore, that the House of Lords was prepared to modify established law on assault (the immediacy requirement; the question whether words alone constituted an assault) in order to uphold the convictions.

In 1996, the Home Office published a consultation paper in which it recognised the scale of the problem – at least 7,000 victims had contacted the National Anti-Stalking and Harassment (NASH) helpline in less than two years. A year later, specific anti-stalking legislation was brought into force, in the form of the Protection from Harassment Act 1997. There are two offences: harassment (s.1), and causing fear (s.4).

- *Harassment*: it is an offence for a person to 'pursue a course of conduct which amounts to the harassment of another'. The definition section (s.7) provides that 'references to harassing a person include alarming the person or causing the person distress'.

- *Causing fear*: A person whose course of conduct causes another to fear, on at least two occasions, that violence will be used against him is guilty of an offence.

S.7 also provides that 'course of conduct' must 'involve conduct on at least two occasions' and that 'conduct' includes speech.

Mens rea of non-fatal offences

Intention or recklessness

It is now firmly established that *all* of the non-fatal offences – other than s.18, where proof of intent is essential – may be committed recklessly, as well as intentionally. The word 'maliciously', which appears in s.20 and s.18, means 'intentionally or recklessly' (*Cunningham* [1957]).

In *Venna* (1976), it was argued on appeal that assaults and batteries, including s.47 ABH, could be distinguished from statutory offences requiring 'malice'. It was argued that as s.47 makes no reference to 'malice' or, indeed, any form of *mens rea*, that recklessness was insufficient and only intention would suffice. Four police officers were struggling to arrest D when he lashed out with his legs, kicked one of the officers in the hand and broke a bone. He was convicted after the trial judge directed the jury to convict if they believed he had kicked out 'reckless as to who was there, not caring one iota as to whether he kicked anybody'. Unsurprisingly, the Court of Appeal rejected his appeal. James LJ said, 'In our view the element of *mens rea* in the offence of battery is satisfied by proof that the defendant intentionally or recklessly applied force to the person of another.'

What type of recklessness is required?

The form of recklessness established in *Cunningham* and approved by the Court of Appeal in *Venna* is the subjective form. Following a period of doubt triggered by the decision of the Divisional Court in *DPP v K (a minor)* (1990), the House of Lords clarified the position in respect of s.20 in *DPP v Parmenter* (1992). Lord Ackner, giving the unanimous decision of the House, said, '*Cunningham* correctly states the law in relation to the word "maliciously" . . . in order to establish an offence under s.20 the prosecution must prove either that [D] intended or that he actually foresaw that his act would cause harm.'

What degree of harm must be foreseen?

The next question is, what *degree* of harm need D to have foreseen? This is particularly important where D is accused of either s.47 or s.20. Where those offences are concerned, there is no requirement that D foresee the harm that they in fact cause, whether a broken nose or a bleeding lip. With s.47, it is enough that D foresees that their acts might result in the application of force to V, or that V is made apprehensive of force being applied. This was decided by the Court of Appeal in *Roberts* (1972) and approved by the Lords in *Savage* (1992). With s.20, it is enough that D foresees that their acts might cause 'some physical harm to some other person', according to the Court of Appeal in *Mowatt* (1968), also confirmed in *Savage* (1992).

D slaps V across the face. He anticipates that V's cheek may be stung. But, D forgot that he was wearing a ring, and V's face is cut deeply. According to the above cases, D faces liability for ABH and/or wounding, each carrying a maximum five years' imprisonment. Is this fair? Should there be a requirement that D foresee the actual injuries caused? Do the above decisions really reflect the courts' insistence that liability for assaults must be decided 'subjectively', using *Cunningham* recklessness, as opposed to 'objectively'?

Reform

In 1993 the Law Commission published a Report, *Offences Against the Person and General Principles*, which contained a draft Criminal Law Bill. In their report, the Commission made three specific criticisms:

- complicated, obscure and old-fashioned language

- complicated and technical structure

- complete unintelligibility to the layman.

Hence the proposed new legislation did away with nineteenth-century terminology including words like 'maliciously' and 'grievous'. However, the Bill was never enacted – but, in 1998, the Labour Government produced its own report, *Violence: Reforming the Offences Against the Person Act 1861*, and a draft Offences Against the Person Bill. The draft Bill proposed that all the existing offences be scrapped and that four new offences take their place. These are the same as the Law Commission proposed in 1993. The offences are (starting with the least serious):

- Assault

- Intentional or Reckless Injury

- Reckless Serious Injury

- Intentional Serious Injury

'Assault'

Clause 4(1) states that it will be an offence if D:

(a) intentionally or recklessly applies force to or causes an impact on the body of another, or

(b) he intentionally or recklessly causes the other to believe that any such force or impact is imminent.

Clause 4(2) provided that no offence is committed 'if the force or impact, not being intended or likely to cause injury, is in the circumstances such as is generally acceptable in the ordinary conduct of daily life and [D] does not know or believe that it is in fact unacceptable to the other person'.

This seems to restate the law on assault and battery as it currently stands with no significant changes at all. Clause 4(1)(a) is what we now call 'battery', clause 4(1)(b) is what we now call 'assault'. Clause 4(2) states the general rule of implied consent laid down by Robert Goff LJ in *Collins v Wilcock* (1984) – see Chapter 9.

'Injury'

The word 'harm' in the OAPA offences would be replaced by 'injury'. Clause 15(1) defined 'injury' as meaning (a) physical or (b) mental injury. Clause 15(2) and (3) defined both terms further:

- Physical injury includes pain, unconsciousness and any other impairment of a person's physical condition.

- Mental injury includes any impairment of a person's mental health.

'Serious'

Neither the draft Criminal Law Bill nor the draft Offences Against the Person Bill defined 'serious'. The Home Office Report stated that the Government would be 'content for the courts to decide what is appropriate in individual cases'. The reform would affect the offences of wounding under s.18 and s.20 in particular. The *actus reus* of those crimes is satisfied on proof of a break in the continuity of the skin – that is, even minor cuts will suffice. But the new offences of intentional and reckless serious injury require 'serious injury' as their *actus reus* – so only those wounds that can be described as 'serious' will lead to liability. Minor cuts would be downgraded to the category of intentional or reckless injury.

'Recklessness'

The proposed new offence of reckless serious injury and reckless injury would require proof that D foresaw 'serious injury' and 'injury', respectively. This would abolish the rule established in *Mowatt* (1968) for s.20 and in *Roberts* (1972) for s.47 that D need not foresee the consequences required for the *actus reus*.

Figure 3 Reform of non-fatal offences: summary

Present offences	Proposed new offences	Changes (if any)	Maximum penalty
Wounding, causing GBH with intent, s.18 OAPA	Intentional serious injury	Only wounds that are 'serious' will satisfy the *actus reus*	Life (no change)
Wounding, inflicting GBH, s.20 OAPA	Reckless serious injury	As above. Plus, foresight of risk of 'serious injury' required for *mens rea*	7 years (+2 years)
ABH, s.47 OAPA	Intentional or reckless injury	Foresight of 'injury' required for *mens rea*	5 years (no change)
Assault and Battery, s.39 CJA	Assault	None	6 months (no change)

Summary

- There is a range of offences against the person.

- Assault is an offence under s.39 of the Criminal Justice Act 1988 (CJA). It is defined as intentionally or recklessly causing another person to apprehend immediate force (*Fagan*).

- Battery is also an offence under s.39 CJA. It is defined as the intentional or reckless application of force to another person (*Fagan*).

- Assault occasioning actual bodily harm (ABH) is an offence contrary to s.47 of the Offences Against the Person Act 1861 (OAPA).

- Wounding or inflicting grievous bodily harm (GBH) are offences contrary to s.20 OAPA.

- Wounding or causing GBH with intent to do GBH or with intent to resist arrest are offences contrary to s.18 OAPA. There is no offence of wounding with intent to wound (*Taylor*).

- For an assault, although V must apprehend 'immediate' force, it is sufficient if V does not know what D is going to do next (*Smith v Superintendent of Woking Police Station; Ireland; Constanza*).

- Assault may be committed by words alone, whether spoken (*Ireland*) or written (*Constanza*). But words may also negative assault (*Tuberville v Savage*).

- ABH has a wide meaning (*Donovan*; *Chan-Fook*). It includes psychiatric injury (*Chan-Fook*; *Ireland*).

- Wounding means that the continuity of the skin must be broken (*Moriarty v Brookes*). Purely internal bleeding is not a 'wound' (*JCC [a minor] v Eisenhower*).

- GBH means really serious harm (*DPP v Smith* [1961]) or just serious harm (*Saunders*). It includes psychiatric injury (*Burstow*) but psychological harm does not suffice (*Dhaliwal*). The transmission of a serious disease through sexual intercourse can lead to liability for inflicting 'biological' GBH (*Dica*; *Konzani*).

- There is no practical distinction between 'inflicting' GBH and 'causing' GBH (*Burstow*).

- The word 'maliciously' in s.20 and s.18 means intentionally or recklessly.

- The subjective *Cunningham* test for recklessness applies to all non-fatal offences (*Savage*; *DPP v Parmenter*), including those that do not expressly require 'malice' (*Venna*).

- In s.47 it is sufficient *mens rea* that D foresees that their acts might result in force being applied to V, or that V is made apprehensive of force being applied to them. D does not have to have foreseen the degree of harm required for the *actus reus*, i.e. ABH (*Roberts*; *Savage*).

- In s.20 it is sufficient *mens rea* that D foresees that their acts might cause 'some harm to some other person'. D does not need to have foreseen the degree of harm required for the *actus reus*, i.e. wounding or GBH (*Mowatt*; *Savage*).

- The draft Offences Against the Person Bill (1998) would abolish all of the above offences and replace them with four new offences: assault, intentional or reckless injury, reckless serious injury and intentional serious injury. 'Injury' would include physical or mental injury.

9   Consent

Introduction

One thing that should become apparent upon reading this chapter is that the availability of the defence of consent has attracted a good deal of public debate in recent years. This is because consent often involves balancing the freedom of the individual against considerations of public policy as interpreted by the courts.

It is a cornerstone of English law that those charged with a criminal offence have a right to defend themselves. We have already seen that a person charged with murder may seek to raise a special and partial defence to that particular charge; for example, provocation or diminished responsibility. There are other so-called general defences such as insanity, automatism, intoxication and mistake which may be pleaded as a defence to most crimes. These are considered in Part 5. The defence of consent will be dealt with here since it is inseparably linked with offences against the person. It is the very essence of all assaults that they are done against V's will. Once the accused raises the defence, the onus of proving lack of consent rests on the Crown (*Donovan* [1934]). Submission (through force, threats or fraud) is *not* the same thing as consent.

It is assumed that you will already have read the preceding chapter, on assaults and aggravated assaults. The same abbreviations will be used, i.e.:

- ABH = actual bodily harm

- GBH = grievous bodily harm

- OAPA = The Offences Against the Person Act 1861. References to s.18, s.20 and s.47 are all to this Act.

General principles

Consent is (depending on the circumstances) a defence to:

- all non-fatal offences against the person, from assault and battery to causing GBH with intent; and

- all sexual offences including indecent assault and rape. Although rape is not examined in this book, some important consent cases involve the offence.

It may be a defence to constructive manslaughter (*Slingsby* [1995]) but is never a defence to murder. No one can consent to being killed. The tragic case of *Pretty v DPP* (2002) confirmed that euthanasia is a criminal offence in England. The case was argued using the European Convention of Human Rights, specifically articles 2, 3, 8 and 9. Both the House of Lords and the European Court of Human Rights agreed that the offence of assisting suicide (under s.2 of the Suicide Act 1961) was *not* contrary to the Convention. The decision of the courts can be summarised as follows:

- Article 2 (right to life) – Pretty argued that a 'right' to life meant that a person could choose when and how to end that life. The courts disagreed: article 2 provided a guarantee that no individual should be deprived of life by intentional human intervention.

- Article 3 (prohibition of torture) – Pretty argued that denying her the right to die constituted 'torture or inhuman or degrading treatment or punishment'. The courts disagreed: while article 3 should not be given a narrow interpretation, it could not be taken to convey the idea that the State had to guarantee to individuals a right to die.

- Article 8 (respect for private and family life) – Pretty argued that the principle of personal autonomy meant that all individuals had a right (enforceable against the State) to choose to die. The courts disagreed: the article protected individuals from unnecessary interference by the State in how they led their lives, not the manner in which they wished to die.

- Article 9 (freedom of thought and conscience) – Pretty argued that she was entitled to manifest her belief in assisted suicide by having her husband commit it. The courts disagreed: the article was not designed to give individuals the right to perform any acts in pursuance of whatever beliefs they might hold.

Pretty (2002)
Diane Pretty, a mother-of-two from Luton, suffered from motor neurone disease, which eventually left her paralysed from the neck down, unable to speak and able to communicate only using a computer. She decided that her life was no longer worth living;

unfortunately, by this stage, her condition had advanced so far that she was physically incapable of taking her own life. Instead, she asked the Director of Public Prosecutions to guarantee her husband, Brian Pretty, immunity from prosecution if he was to assist her in committing suicide. This would allow her to die at home and with as much dignity as possible. The DPP refused and Mrs Pretty challenged him. She was unsuccessful.

Postscript. Diane Pretty died in a Luton hospice in May 2002, a matter of days after the Strasbourg Court rejected her last appeal. She had been experiencing breathing difficulties for several days and, as a result of being heavily sedated, had slipped into a coma-like state.

Why is euthanasia illegal?

The House of Lords heard a similar case in June 2009. In *Purdy* (2009), Debbie Purdy, 45, suffered from progressive multiple sclerosis. She knew that it was inevitable that her condition would deteriorate until life became unbearable, in which case she wanted to be helped to travel to another country where assisted suicide was legal (probably Switzerland). She brought a judicial review seeking to clarify the law on whether her husband would be prosecuted under s.2 of the Suicide Act 1961 if he was to assist her to travel. Like Diane Pretty before her, Debbie Purdy relied on her right to privacy in Article 8. However, this time, the Lords accepted Mrs Purdy's arguments and ordered the DPP to clarify the circumstances in which a prosecution would be brought under s.2 of the 1961 Act.

Consent must be real

The fact that V apparently consents to D's act does not mean that the law will treat that consent as valid. If V is a child, or mentally disabled, this apparent consent may not suffice. The issue is whether V was unable to comprehend the nature of the act. The leading case involving children is *Burrell v Harmer* (1967). D was convicted of ABH after tattooing two boys aged 12 and 13 with the result that their arms became inflamed and painful. The Divisional Court held that there was no consent as the boys did not understand the nature of the act. Presumably they understood what a tattoo was, but they would not have understood the level of pain involved.

The Mental Capacity Act 2007 provides useful guidance on the ability of people generally to give consent. Section 2(1) of the Act states that 'a person lacks capacity in relation to a matter if at the material time he is unable to make a decision for himself in relation to the matter because of an impairment of, or a disturbance in the functioning of, the mind or brain'. Section 3(1) states that a person is 'unable to make a decision' when he is unable to (a) understand the information relevant to the decision; (b) retain that information; (c) use or weigh that information as part of the process of making the decision; or (d) communicate his decision (whether by talking, using sign language or any other means).

Consent and mistake

An honestly-held (and not necessarily reasonable) belief that V was consenting will be a good defence, as this would deny proof that D carried out an unlawful assault. This is subject to the rules on intoxicated mistakes (see Chapter 17).

Consent obtained by fraud

Fraud does not necessarily negative consent. It does so in only two situations, if it deceives V as to:

• the identity of the person; or

• the 'nature' or 'quality' of D's act.

Richardson (1998) involved the first situation. D was a dentist who had been suspended by the General Dental Council. However, she continued to treat patients until she was eventually detected and prosecuted. She was convicted of six counts of ABH, on the basis that her fraud as to her continued entitlement to practise negatived her patients' consent. The Court of Appeal, though describing her behaviour as 'reprehensible', allowed the appeal. The patients were consenting to treatment by her. It was irrelevant that they would not have consented had they known the truth.

Tabassum (2000) is an example of the second situation. D had examined the breasts of a number of women after telling them that he was medically qualified, when in fact he was not. The Court of Appeal upheld convictions of 'indecent assault' (contrary to s.14 of the Sexual Offences Act 1956; subsequently replaced by the offence of 'sexual assault' in s.3 of the Sexual Offences Act 2003). The Court decided that the women had consented to D touching their breasts (and therefore understood the 'nature' of D's act). However, because they had done so only because they thought it was for a medical purpose, as opposed to a sexual purpose, they had been deceived as to the 'quality' of D's act. Hence, there was no consent and D was guilty of assault.

Prior to *Tabassum*, the courts had taken a narrower approach to this question. Before fraud vitiating consent could be established, the prosecution had to prove that D had deceived V as to both the 'nature' *and* 'quality' of his act. This helps to explain the decision in *Clarence* (1888), examined in Chapter 8. When Charles had sex with his wife Selina and infected her with gonorrhoea, the court decided that she had given her consent to having sex (the nature of the act) and so her consent was genuine. The fact that she had been deceived as to the 'quality' of the act (arguably sex with a diseased man is of a different 'quality' from sex with someone who has no such disease) was not enough to vitiate her consent. Therefore there was no assault.

The approach established in *Clarence* survived for over a century. The developments that led to its abolition began in Canada, in *Cuerrier* (1998), also examined in Chapter 8. In that case, the Supreme Court of Canada introduced the idea of 'informed consent' into Canadian criminal law where sexually transmitted diseases were involved. Justifying the decision, L'Heureux-Dubé J said that 'those who know they are HIV-positive have a fundamental responsibility to advise their partners of their condition and to ensure that their sex is as safe as possible'.

Then, after *Tabassum* (2000) held that fraud could vitiate consent if V was deceived as to either the 'nature' or 'quality' of D's act, *Clarence* was finally overruled by the Court of Appeal in *Dica* (2004). The court decided that, when D, knowing he had HIV, had unprotected sex with V, and failed to reveal this fact to her, the latter was giving consent to the 'nature' of the act but not necessarily to its 'quality'. Judge LJ said that 'to the extent that *Clarence* suggested that consensual sexual intercourse of itself was to be regarded as consent to the risk of consequent disease, again, it is no longer authoritative'. The Court of Appeal rejected the argument that, just because V had consented to unprotected sex, she had also automatically consented to the risk of contracting a potentially fatal disease. The Court decided that, in theory at least, V could consent to such a risk, but D would have to inform her of the fact of his disease first so that she could make an informed decision.

The doctrine of informed consent has therefore now been introduced into English criminal law; at least in the context of sexual intercourse where D knows that he has a potentially fatal disease and fails to reveal this fact to V.

Dica (2004)
Mohammed Dica had been diagnosed with HIV in 1995. Despite this knowledge, he had unprotected sex on a number of occasions with two women, V and W, who had been willing to be sexual partners with D but were unaware of his condition at the time. V claimed that D insisted that they have unprotected sex because he

had had a vasectomy. According to V, each time they had sex, D said, 'Forgive me in the name of God'. After some time V noticed that her glands were swollen; she went to hospital and was diagnosed with HIV. W's story was similar. D was charged with two offences of inflicting GBH, contrary to s.20 OAPA. He denied the offences contending that any sexual intercourse which had taken place had been consensual. The trial judge made two legal rulings:

- that it was open to the jury to convict D of the charges, notwithstanding the decision in *Clarence*;

- that any consent by V and W was irrelevant and provided no defence as a matter of law, because of the serious nature of the disease. He therefore withdrew the issue of consent from the jury.

D was convicted in October 2003. The Court of Appeal allowed D's appeal, but only on the basis that the trial judge had erred in withdrawing the issue of consent from the jury. If V and/or W had, in fact, consented to the risk of contracting HIV, that would provide a defence under s.20. Although the court thought it unlikely that V and W would consent to having unprotected sex with D if they knew that D was HIV positive, this was nevertheless a question of fact for the jury to decide (not a question of law for the judge). However, the Court ordered a retrial.

Postscript: At D's retrial in March 2005 – when the issue of consent was left to the jury to decide – he was again convicted of inflicting 'biological' GBH and sentenced to 4½ years in prison. He then appealed against that conviction and sentence, unsuccessfully, to the Court of Appeal.

The *Dica* ruling was relied on shortly afterwards in the similar case of *Konzani* (2005). D had been convicted of inflicting 'biological' GBH on three women over a three-year period. At his trial, the jury rejected his plea that the victims all consented to the risk of catching HIV because they agreed to have unprotected sex with him. The Court of Appeal dismissed his appeal. The Court said that D had 'deceived' the three women and there was 'not the slightest evidence, direct or indirect, from which a jury could begin to infer that [D] honestly believed that [the victims] consented to that specific risk [of contracting HIV].'

Consent obtained by duress

A threat to imprison or otherwise harm V if he did not 'consent' would invalidate that consent.

Limitations on consent

There are limits to anyone's right to consent to the infliction of harm upon themselves. In *Attorney-General's Reference (No. 6 of 1980)* (1981), two youths, aged 17 and 18, decided to settle an argument with a bare-knuckle fist fight. One had sustained a bloody nose and a bruised face. Following acquittals, the Court of Appeal held that the defence of consent was not available in this situation. Lord Lane CJ said, 'It is not in the public interest that people should try to cause or should cause each other actual bodily harm for no good reason.'

In *Brown and Others* (1994), the majority's view was that consent was always a good defence to charges of assault and battery, but not to any offence involving ABH, GBH or wounding unless a recognised exception applied. If, therefore, the allegation is that D committed no more than a simple battery, then consent is always a defence. This is an unavoidable conclusion, as Robert Goff LJ made clear in *Collins v Wilcock* (1984):

> Generally speaking, consent is a defence to battery; and most of the physical contacts of ordinary life are not actionable because they are impliedly consented to by all who move in society and so expose themselves to the risk of bodily contact. So nobody can complain of the jostling which is inevitable in, for example, a supermarket, an underground station or a busy street; nor can a person who attends a party complain if his hand is seized in friendship, or even if his back is (within reason) slapped. Although such cases are regarded as examples of implied consent, it is more common nowadays to treat them as falling within a general exception embracing all physical contact which is generally acceptable in the ordinary conduct of daily life.

However, if D is alleged to have gone beyond a battery and committed ABH (or worse), then the situation changes dramatically. No one impliedly consents to a risk of actual bodily harm just because they are out shopping or at a party. Consent to ABH (or worse) can be given, but only in certain situations. Various courts have suggested lists of activities which carry the risk of serious injury, but where consent would nevertheless provide a good defence to charges of ABH, GBH and wounding. A non-exhaustive list reads as follows:

● contact sports including boxing

● surgery

- 'horseplay'

- tattooing and branding

- 'vigorous' sexual activity (but not sado-masochism)

- haircuts

These situations will now be examined in greater detail.

Contact sports
Boxing
No prosecutions have ever been brought in respect of public boxing matches conducted within the *Queensberry Rules*. The high entertainment value and popularity of the sport is taken to justify V's consent to D trying to punch him or her very hard about the face and upper body. However, fights conducted in other circumstances have regularly been held to amount to batteries (*Attorney-General's Reference [No. 6 of 1980]*). This is especially true of bare-knuckle fights staged for 'entertainment' purposes. Any entertainment value they may have is far outweighed by the risk of injury to the fighters. In *Coney* (1882), prosecutions were brought against various spectators at a bare-knuckle prize-fight, for aiding and abetting (see Chapter 20) the unlawful activities. One question for the Court for Crown Cases Reserved was whether the consent of the participants negated the unlawful element of assault. Cave J said that 'a blow struck in sport [wrestling or boxing with gloves] is not an assault' but that 'a blow struck in a prize-fight is clearly an assault'.

Other contact sports
With other contact sports such as football, rugby and ice-hockey, a clear distinction must be drawn between two situations. An off-the-ball incident is, in principle, no different from any other assault. There is no suggestion that players consent, impliedly or otherwise, to the use of force in such situations. In *Billinghurst* (1978), D punched an opposing player, V, in the face in an off-the-ball incident during a rugby union match in South Wales. V's jaw was fractured in two places and D was convicted of inflicting GBH under s.20.

Problems arise where the alleged assault occurs on-the-ball, during play. The players in contact sports impliedly consent to D doing what the rules of the particular game permit. Perhaps a breach of the rules ought to establish at least a *prima facie* case; but in any given contact sport game there may be dozens of fouls. Even if only the most serious were prosecuted, the sports would be seriously affected.

The rules themselves provide only a guide as to what has been consented to. In *Moore* (1898) it was said that, 'no rules or practice of any game whatever can make lawful that which is unlawful by the law of the land'. Therefore, where an alleged assault has occurred during play, this should be assessed independently of the rules.

In *Barnes* (2004), the Court of Appeal held that prosecutions should be brought against a player who injured another player in the course of a sporting event only if his conduct was 'sufficiently grave to be properly categorised as criminal', where what had occurred had gone beyond what the injured player could reasonably be regarded as having accepted by taking part in the sport.

Lord Woolf CJ said that in all contact sports, the participants impliedly consent to the risk of certain levels of harm. However, what was implicitly accepted in one sport would not necessarily be covered by the defence in another sport. In highly competitive sports, such as rugby, football and ice-hockey, conduct outside the rules could be expected to occur in the 'heat of the moment' and, even if the conduct justified a warning or a sending off, it still might not reach the threshold level required for it to be criminal. That level was an objective one and did not depend upon the views of individual players. The following factors were all likely to be relevant in determining whether D's actions went beyond the threshold:

- the type of sport

- the level at which it was played, whether amateur or professional

- the nature of the act

- the degree of force used

- the extent of the risk of injury

- D's state of mind.

Whether conduct reached the required threshold to be criminal would therefore depend on all the circumstances. There would be cases that fell within a 'grey area' and then the jury would have to make their own determination as to which side of the line the case fell. In such a situation the jury would need to ask themselves, among other questions, whether the contact was so 'obviously late and/or violent' that it could not be regarded as 'an instinctive reaction, error or misjudgment in the heat of the game'.

Barnes (2004)

Mark Barnes was convicted of inflicting GBH under s.20 OAPA following a tackle in the course of an amateur football match. The prosecution alleged that it was the result of a 'late, unnecessary, reckless and high crashing tackle'. D claimed that the tackle was a fair, if hard, challenge in the course of play and that any injury caused was accidental. The Court of Appeal allowed the appeal.

In *Ciccarelli* (1989) the Ontario Court of Appeal in Canada considered the significance of the whistle having been blown to stop play during an ice-hockey match before the alleged assault occurred. The whistle had just blown for offside against D when another player, V, who had been skating across to block him, was unable to stop and they collided. D retaliated, using his stick to hit V over the head three times. The officials intervened to separate the pair but D punched out at them too. He was convicted of assault and his appeal was dismissed.

Should the criminal law concern itself with incidents on the field of play? One view is that it should: 'the law does not stop at the touchline'. Another view is that sporting violence should be left exclusively to the various sporting bodies to deal with. What do you think?

Surgery

With 'reasonable surgical interference' there is really no issue of consent as a defence to bodily harm, given that *no harm* is caused or inflicted. But in surgery there is certainly a 'wounding', and the patient must consent to that. Consent to any recognised surgical procedure is effective; this includes sex-change operations and probably cosmetic surgery.

'Horseplay'

The courts have accepted that 'horseplay' is another area in which consensual assaults, even where quite serious injury is caused, may be legally tolerated. Society accepts that community life, such as in the playground, involves risks of deliberate physical contact, but that the criminal law should not get involved. The defence was successfully used in:

- *Jones and Others* (1986) – boys injured having been tossed into the air by schoolmates; and (more controversially),

- *Aitken and Others* (1992) – where serious burns, amounting to grievous bodily harm, were caused to a new RAF officer as part of a bizarre 'initiation ceremony'.

Tattooing and branding

Getting a tattoo can be a very painful experience but the tattooist does not commit ABH because consent is a valid defence. In *Wilson* (1997), the Court of Appeal extended this to branding, holding that it was no more hazardous than a tattoo.

Wilson (1997)
Alan Wilson had branded his initials onto his wife's buttocks using a hot blade. She regarded the branding as 'a desirable personal adornment', and had apparently originally requested that the branding be on her breasts. It was her husband who persuaded her to have the branding on her buttocks instead. The matter came to light only when her doctor reported the incident to the police. Wilson was convicted of ABH but the Court of Appeal allowed the appeal.

'Vigorous' sexual activity

During sexual intercourse and related activities there is obviously bodily contact during which injuries may inadvertently occur. However, these injuries would not amount to battery or ABH (or worse) as long as the bodily contact was consented to. This is the case even where the sexual activity is what may politely be termed 'vigorous'. In *Slingsby* (1995), D had penetrated the vagina and rectum of a girl he had met at a nightclub with his hand *with her consent*. However, she suffered internal cuts caused by a ring on D's hand. These injuries were neither intended nor foreseen by D. V was unaware how serious these cuts were and she later died of septicaemia (blood poisoning). Was D therefore liable for constructive manslaughter, based on the unlawful act of battery? The answer was 'No'. The judge held that it was clear that all of D's acts on the night in question were consented to by V and, consequently, there was no battery.

In *Meachen* (2006), V had suffered serious internal injuries caused by D, who was charged with a number of offences, including inflicting GBH under s.20. D admitted penetrating V's anus with his fingers but claimed that V had consented and that the injuries were accidental. However, D was convicted after the trial judge (following the decision in *Emmett* [1999], discussed below) ruled that V's consent in the circumstances was legally irrelevant. However, the Court of Appeal applied *Slingsby* (1995) instead and quashed the conviction under s.20. Thomas LJ said that D's case was that V had consented to 'vigorous sexual activity which involved her desire to have him insert fingers into her anus and that the very serious injury caused was as a result of her activity'. The Court ruled that 'it could not in the circumstances be correct to hold as a matter of law that consent was no defence to the charge under s.20'.

Sado-masochism

Thus, the **inadvertent** infliction of injury during 'vigorous' sexual activity is not an offence (*Slingsby*; *Meachen*). However, the law does not readily tolerate the idea of consent being a defence to the **deliberate** infliction of injury for the sexual gratification of either party. In *Donovan* (1934), D, for his sexual gratification, had beaten a 17-year-old prostitute, with a cane, 'in circumstances of indecency'. When examined by a doctor two days later, she was found to have seven or eight red marks on her buttocks. The doctor concluded she had had a 'fairly severe beating'. D was convicted of common and indecent assault. The Court of Criminal Appeal quashed his conviction, but only because it had not been left to the jury to decide whether D had intended to cause bodily harm – the suggestion being that the girl's consent would not have been legally effective because of the sado-masochistic nature of the beating.

In the Court of Appeal in *Brown and Others* (1992), Lord Lane CJ said that 'the satisfying of sado-masochistic libido does not come within the category of good reason nor can the injuries be described as merely transient or trifling'. In the House of Lords, Lord Templeman said, 'The violence of sado-masochistic encounters involves the indulgence of cruelty by sadists and the degradation of victims. Such violence is injurious to the participants and unpredictably dangerous.'

Brown and Others (1994)
Anthony Brown and the other appellants belonged to a group of sado-masochistics who, over a 10-year period, willingly and enthusiastically participated in acts of violence against each other for sexual pleasure. Many of these acts took place in rooms designed as torture-chambers. The activities included branding with wire or metal heated by a blow-lamp, use of a cat o'nine tails and genital torture. All the activities were carried out in private with the consent of the passive partner or 'victim'. There were no complaints to the police, no medical attention was ever sought and no permanent injury suffered. The police discovered the activities by accident. All members were charged with various offences, including ABH under s.47 and wounding under s.20. They were convicted and their appeals dismissed by the Court of Appeal and House of Lords (albeit by 3:2).

In *Brown and Others* (1994), the question of consent was approached differently by the Law Lords. The majority clearly viewed what occurred as acts of violence with a sexual motive, as opposed to sexual acts that inadvertently involved violence. This led them to conclude that what had happened was *prima facie* unlawful. The majority then considered whether the defence applied; they concluded that it did not. Lord Lowry commented that homosexual sado-masochism could not be regarded as a 'manly diversion', nor was it 'conducive to the enhancement or enjoyment of family life or conducive to the welfare of society'. For Lord Jauncey the corruption of young men was a real danger to be considered. Yet no one was induced or coerced into the activities.

The minority, meanwhile, decided that the activities in question were *prima facie* lawful. Both Law Lords decided that a victim could give valid consent to ABH but not GBH. Lord Mustill identified and analysed the specific policy considerations that might point towards criminal liability, including the risk of infection, in particular AIDS, and decided that this did *not* justify criminalising all sado-masochistic activity. He observed that, as medical evidence suggested that consensual sex was the main cause of transmission of the HIV virus, what grounds were there for criminalising what had happened in the *Brown* case? (*Note*: Lord Mustill's comments now have to be read in the light of the Court of Appeal's decisions in *Dica* [2004] and *Konzani* [2005], discussed above.) Lord Slynn thought that the whole area was for Parliament to decide.

The impact of the Human Rights Act 1998

The enactment of the Human Rights Act 1998 has not affected this area too greatly. In *Laskey, Jaggard and Brown v UK* (1997), the European Court of Human Rights (ECHR) in Strasbourg upheld the judgment in *Brown and Others*. It had been argued that the criminalisation of private sado-masochistic activities constituted a breach of Article 8(1) of the European Convention on Human Rights, which provides that 'everyone has the right to respect for his private and family life'. However, like many of the rights protected by the Convention, it is not absolute. Article 8(2) adds that public authorities may interfere with the exercise of this right provided it is necessary in the interests of national security or public safety or the economic well-being of the country, for the prevention of disorder or crime, for the protection of health or morals, or for the protection of the rights and freedoms of others.

In *Laskey*, the ECHR ruled that, once conduct had gone beyond a potential risk with a sufficient degree of seriousness, the involvement of the authorities could not possibly amount to a breach of Article 8(1). In the most recent case in this area, *Emmett* (1999), the Court of Appeal applied the decisions in *Brown and Others* and *Laskey*. D was convicted of two counts of ABH on his girlfriend. The couple enjoyed sado-masochistic sex. One day, during sex, D had placed a plastic bag over her head and tied it tightly around her neck. As a result of lack of oxygen, she nearly lost consciousness, suffered bruising to the neck and ruptured blood vessels in her eyes. A month later, D poured lighter fluid over her left breast and ignited it. As a result of that injury, D persuaded her to go to the doctor, who reported D to the police. The Court of Appeal dismissed D's appeals against conviction.

Haircuts

In *DPP v Smith* (2006), discussed in Chapter 8, the High Court decided that cutting hair amounted to assault occasioning ABH. It follows that all haircuts are *prima facie* illegal unless V has given their consent!

Reform

The Law Commission's draft Criminal Law Bill (1993) and their Consultation Paper, *Consent in the Criminal Law* (1995), did not propose any radical changes in the law of consent. The Bill's definition of assault includes a proviso in clause 6 (2) that:

No such offence is committed if the force or impact, not being intended or likely to cause injury, is in circumstances such as is generally acceptable in the ordinary conduct of daily life and the defendant does not know or believe that it is in fact unacceptable to the other person.

This is very similar to the legal situation now. The Consultation Paper states that 'we recommend that the intentional [and reckless] causing of seriously disabling injury to another person should continue to be criminal, even if the injured person consents to such injury or to the risk of such injury'. This also maintains the present legal requirement.

However, the Commission did recommend that the intentional or reckless causing of injury to another person, falling short of the 'seriously disabling' variety, would not be criminal, if the other person had consented to it. This shifts the law slightly, as in *Brown and Others* (1994) the House of Lords had ruled that injury amounting to ABH, or worse, could be consented to only if there was a good reason for it. As the proposed offence of causing injury is designed to replace that of ABH, then the law will be relaxed if the Commission's proposals are ever adopted.

Summary

- Consent is a potentially valid defence to all assaults, including sexual assaults and rape, and even manslaughter (*Slingsby*) but not murder. Euthanasia is still a crime in English law (*Pretty*; *Purdy*).

- The alleged victim must be capable of giving a valid consent (*Burrell v Harmer*).

- Where consent is obtained by D's fraud, this will usually not vitiate the consent unless V is deceived as to D's identity (*Richardson*) or where V is deceived either as to the 'nature' or 'quality' of D's act (*Tabassum*).

- A doctrine of 'informed consent' applies in cases where D knows that he has a fatal disease (such as HIV) which can be transmitted sexually but fails to inform his sexual partner(s). Although V may have consented to unprotected sexual intercourse, V has not necessarily consented to the risk of contracting a fatal disease (*Cuerrier*; *Dica*; *Konzani*).

- Persons can consent to assault and battery, in any circumstances.

- Where the charge is ABH, GBH or wounding (the aggravated assaults), then V's consent is valid only if there was a legally recognised 'good reason' (*Attorney-General's Reference [No. 6 of 1980], Brown and Others*).

- 'Good reasons' include: contact sports (*Barnes*), surgery, 'horseplay' (*Jones and Others*; *Aitken and Others*), tattooing and branding (*Wilson*) and 'vigorous' sexual activity (*Slingsby*; *Meachen*).

- Sado-masochistic activity is not considered to be a good reason (*Donovan*; *Brown and Others*; *Emmett*).

- In sporting contests, consent is no defence if the assault occurred 'off-the-ball' (*Billinghurst*). In 'on-the-ball' incidents during contact sports, V is taken to impliedly consent to the risk of injury. D's act must cross a 'threshold' of seriousness which is assessed objectively, and depends on several factors including the type of sport, the level at which the game is played, the degree of force used, etc. (*Barnes*).

Questions on Part 3 Offences against the person

NB Many questions on offences against the person are invariably combined with potential defences which may be available to the accused. In some cases they occur alongside other offences. These should be answered only after the chapters on defences (Chapters 14–19) have been studied and where examples of further questions appear.

1 'The law on consent as a defence has been decided according to considerations of public policy rather than being developed in a reasoned and logical way.'

Critically evaluate the truth of this statement.

(OCR 2006)

2   Two strangers, Mike and John, have been drinking next to each other for two hours in a pub when Mike accidentally spills John's drink. John is annoyed and responds by picking up Mike's pint glass and pouring the remainder of the contents over Mike's head, soaking Mike's shirt in the process. Mike loses his temper and raises his arm to strike John but is immediately restrained by the pub landlord, Barry, who grabs Mike's arm. They are now both very angry with each other and agree to step outside to settle their differences. Once on the pavement they continue arguing and John punches Mike in the face, knocking him to the ground and causing a small cut to his eye. Enraged, Mike picks up a stone from the gutter and throws it at John, who ducks. The stone misses John and smashes the pub window.

Consider what offences, if any, have been committed by both Mike and John.

(OCR 2002)

3   Kate and Mark are partners. Kate reluctantly allows him to 'brand' the letter 'M' on her thigh with a piece of hot wire as a token of their love. The pain is so great that Kate lashes out uncontrollably and strikes Mark in the face, breaking his glasses and cutting his eyebrow. Mark is now so annoyed that he retaliates by hitting out at Kate, catching her in the face and causing her nose to bleed. Kate storms out saying she will never forgive him for hitting her. For the next three months Mark telephones Kate at her parents' house as many as ten times a day. Each time he threatens her that she will 'regret it' if she ever decides to go out with another man. Kate becomes so frightened and depressed by Mark's behaviour that she cannot leave the house and gives up her job. One day, she desperately confronts him in the pub and, after a brief argument during which he again raises his fist to her, she grabs his mobile phone from the table in front of them and throws it onto the floor, causing the case to crack.

Consider what offences, if any, have been committed by Kate and Mark and discuss whether either of them may put forward a defence.

(OCR 2004)

Part 4

Offences against property

10 Theft and making off

Introduction

Theft and other related offences were codified in the Theft Act 1968. Some aspects of the legislation, particularly those dealing with deception offences, proved to be unsatisfactory and in 1978 a further Theft Act was passed in order to remedy these difficulties. Even since then, the courts have been frequently asked to interpret the various statutory provisions and their application. Consequently the law in this area is once again, for the student, a challenging mixture of legislation and case law.

S.1(1) of the Theft Act 1968 provides that 'A person is guilty of theft if he dishonestly appropriates property belonging to another with the intention of permanently depriving the other of it'. Sections 2–6 of the Theft Act 1968 go on to explain what the various component parts of this definition mean – but that is all they do. A common misunderstanding with theft is that there are separate offences contained in these sections – do not make this mistake! There is no offence of 'appropriation', no crime of 'dishonesty' – they are simply elements that go together to make up the crime of theft.

The *actus reus* comprises three elements:

- Appropriation (s.3)

- Property (s.4)

- Belonging to another (s.5)

The *mens rea* comprises two elements:

- Dishonesty (s.2)

- An intention to permanently deprive the owner (s.6)

Another of the more common misconceptions in this area of law is that the second element of the *mens rea* belongs in the *actus reus* list, i.e. that for a theft conviction the owner must, in fact, be permanently deprived of their property. This is not the case. There is no requirement that the defendant 'get away' with property before it becomes stolen. The accused simply has to 'appropriate' it with the intention of permanently depriving the owner of it.

This could, for example, lead to a theft conviction if D picks up a chocolate bar in a supermarket and slips it into their pocket – even if they are stopped from leaving the store – because the intention was present at the moment of the 'appropriation'. Of course, as with many elements of the *mens rea*, proving that D had the intent is another matter – this is why many store detectives allow suspected thieves to leave the shop before stopping them. Nevertheless, as a *matter of law*, theft is committed as soon as all the above elements are present.

'Appropriation'

Section 3(1) of the Theft Act 1968 states that 'Any assumption by a person of the rights of an owner amounts to an appropriation'. The 1968 Act does not provide any definition of the 'rights of an owner'. However, one fundamental question is whether s.3(1) relates to *all* the rights, or merely any of the rights. In *Morris* (1984), counsel argued for the former, but Lord Roskill was unimpressed: 'It is enough for the prosecution if they have proved ... the assumption by the defendant of any rights of the owner of the goods in question'. That is not to say that simply touching an item of property amounts to *theft*, of course – it may not be dishonest – but it could be an 'appropriation'.

Relevance of consent or authority

The question of whether D appropriates property when he does so with the authorisation or consent of the owner has troubled the courts for years. In *Lawrence* (1972), the House of Lords decided it was still an 'appropriation'.

Lawrence (1972)

On arrival at Victoria Station in London, an Italian student, Occhi, who spoke little English, showed Alan Lawrence, a taxi-driver waiting outside, a piece of paper on which was written an address in Ladbroke Grove. The address was not far and should have cost 50p. Lawrence, however, said that it was a long journey and would be expensive, at which point Occhi proferred a £1 note. Lawrence said this would not be enough, so Occhi opened his wallet and Lawrence removed a further £1 and a £5 note. Lawrence was convicted of theft, and on appeal the argument that he had not appropriated the money because he took it with Occhi's consent was rejected by both the Court of Appeal and a unanimous House of Lords.

After a period of doubt triggered by certain *dicta* of Lord Roskill in *Morris*, the House of Lords resolved the issue in *Gomez* (1993) by giving their approval to *Lawrence*. Lord Keith said that 'an act may be an appropriation notwithstanding that it is done with the consent of the owner'. Where an honest shopper places goods in a shopping basket, this is not theft, said Lord Keith, but it is an appropriation. Lord Browne-Wilkinson added that he regarded 'the word "appropriation" in isolation as being an objective description of the act done irrespective of the mental state of either the owner or the accused'.

The *Lawrence/Gomez* definition of 'appropriation' is very wide indeed. So wide, in fact, that for a while the Court of Appeal struggled to accept what the House of Lords very clearly said. In *Gallasso* (1993), for example, Lloyd LJ said that 'Lord Keith did not mean to say that every handling is an appropriation. Suppose, for example, the shopper carelessly knocks an article off the shelf; if he bends down and replaces it on the shelf nobody would regard it as an act of appropriation'. However, it seems clear that that is exactly what Lord Keith said and also exactly what he meant to say.

Later, in *Mazo* (1997), the Court of Appeal stressed that in *Gomez*, V's apparent consent had actually been obtained by deception. The Court in *Mazo* seemed to be suggesting that the *ratio* in *Gomez* be limited to such cases, that is, where an apparent consent was obtained by deception. However, despite these suggestions, in *Hinks* (2001), the House of Lords confirmed and even extended even further the wide definition of 'appropriation'. The Lords decided (by a 3:2 majority) that the receipt of a gift is capable of amounting to an 'appropriation' of property for the purposes of theft. Karen Hinks had befriended John Dolphin, a 53-year-old man of below average IQ who was described as naïve and trusting. He was also wealthy, having inherited money from his father, but had no idea of the value of his assets. Every day over a period of six months, Dolphin withdrew £300 from his building society account and paid it into Hinks' account. Eventually, after about £60,000 had been transferred in this way, Hinks was convicted of theft. The Court of Appeal and House of Lords upheld Hinks' conviction. Lord Steyn said that he 'would not be willing to depart from the clear decisions of the House in *Lawrence* and *Gomez*'.

Appropriation by keeping or dealing

S.3(1) of the Theft Act 1968 states that 'appropriation' extends to the situation where D has come by property, innocently or not, though without stealing it, but later assumes a right to it by 'keeping' or 'dealing with it as owner'.

'Keeping'

It will be an 'appropriation' by D if they borrow property from V – some item of DIY equipment, for example – and then refuse to return it, or simply hang on to it in the hope that V will forget about it. D is therefore guilty of theft if they do this with the *mens rea* required.

'Dealing with property as owner'

This would deal with a variation on the situation above where D sells V's DIY equipment. Having borrowed the equipment in the first place meant that D was in lawful possession of it, but they would dishonestly appropriate it by selling it, i.e. by 'dealing with' the property as if they owned it.

The exception in favour of bona fide purchasers

Every year hundreds of proprietors of second-hand shops will innocently buy stolen property. Does s.3(1) of the Theft Act 1968 make them thieves if they subsequently discover that the property was stolen, but decide to keep the property or otherwise deal with it, by selling it on to a customer? The answer is 'No'. S.3(2) of the 1968 Act imposes a limitation in favour of persons who purchase property 'in good faith'.

Appropriation as a continuing act

Is 'appropriation' an instantaneous act, or does it continue over time? If the latter is correct, for how long does it continue? At one extreme, 'appropriation' might be said to continue as long as the stolen property remains in D's possession. This would, however, create difficulties for the offence of handling stolen goods. The courts have therefore taken the view that an 'appropriation' continues for as long as the thief can sensibly be regarded as being in the act of stealing.

The leading case is *Atakpu and Abrahams* (1993). D and E had a plan to travel to Frankfurt, Germany, hire a number of expensive cars using false papers, drive them to England and sell them there. The plan worked perfectly and they duly arrived in Dover with two Mercedes and a BMW. However, customs officers were suspicious and they were arrested and charged with conspiracy to steal. On appeal against conviction they argued that no appropriation had taken place in England. The Court of Appeal allowed the appeals. The cars had clearly been stolen in Germany. Once property had been stolen, any further dealing with it did not amount to an 'appropriation' within s.3(1) of the Theft Act. This was so even if the property was stolen abroad. Although, generally speaking, it was for the common sense of the jury to decide how long 'appropriation' continued so that the thief could be sensibly regarded as in the act of stealing, this was not possible in the present case. Ward J said that no jury 'could reasonably arrive at a conclusion that the theft of these motor cars was still continuing days after the appellants had first taken them'.

'Property'

What can be stolen?

S.4(1) of the Theft Act 1968 provides that 'property includes money and all other property, real or personal, including things in action and other intangible property'.

'Real property'

'Real property' means land. However, s.4(2) goes on to say that 'a person cannot steal land, or things forming part of land and severed from it' except in a limited number of situations. One of these is where D 'appropriates anything forming part of the land by severing it or causing it to be severed'. This could include removing topsoil, or trees and plants, or any structure on the land. Thus, in a case in 1972, a man was prosecuted for stealing Cleckheaton Railway Station near Leeds by dismantling and removing it.

S.4(3) provides that wild mushrooms or flowers, fruit or foliage picked from a plant (which in turn includes shrubs or trees) growing wild on any land cannot be stolen – unless D picks them 'for reward or for sale or other commercial purpose'.

Personal property

The vast majority of theft cases involve personal property. In *Kelly and Lindsay* (1998), D, a sculptor, was accused of stealing various body parts from the Royal College of Surgeons where he worked as a laboratory assistant. When arrested he told police that he wanted to 'understand death' and that he had treated all the body parts with respect. He was convicted and on appeal it was argued that parts of bodies were not, in law, capable of being property and therefore could not be stolen. The Court of Appeal dismissed the appeals.

'Things in action'

A 'thing in action' is property that does not exist in a physical state – it cannot be seen or touched – but can be claimed by legal action. Examples include:

● bank accounts;

● shares;

● intellectual property rights (copyrights, patents, trade marks, design rights, etc.).

What cannot be stolen?

Electricity

Electricity cannot be stolen (*Low v Blease* [1975]). Instead, s.13 of the Theft Act 1968 provides a separate offence of making dishonest use, wasting or diverting electricity.

Confidential information

Although confidential information has value, and can be sold, it is not 'property'. In *Oxford v Moss* (1979), D, a civil engineering student at Liverpool University, acquired a draft of his examination paper. He read the contents and then returned it. It was agreed that he had never intended to permanently deprive the University of the paper itself. Instead, he was charged with theft of the information on the paper (the examination questions). The magistrates dismissed the charge and the prosecution's appeal was dismissed.

Wild creatures

Genuinely wild animals are 'property', but cannot be stolen, according to s.4(4) of the Theft Act 1968. The only occasions when a wild animal can be stolen is if it:

• has been tamed; or

• is 'ordinarily kept in captivity'; or

• has been reduced into possession and possession of it has not since been lost or abandoned.

Hence, all pets and zoo creatures, as well as something like a tame fox, can be stolen. Pets and zoo animals may be stolen even after they have escaped because they are 'ordinarily kept in captivity'. See *Cresswell and Currie v DPP* (2006), discussed in Chapter 11, for explanation of 'reduced into possession'.

Value of the property irrelevant

It is no defence for D to argue that there was no property stolen because the property is practically worthless in commercial terms.

'Belonging to another'

S.5(1) of the Theft Act 1968 provides that 'property shall be regarded as belonging to any person having possession or control of it, or having any proprietary right or interest'. In the vast majority of cases D, having no interest in the property, steals from someone who both owns and possesses the property in question. But s.5(1) is wide enough to allow D to steal property which at the relevant time is owned, possessed, or controlled, by different people. So if P lends a book to Q, who shows it to R, and D then grabs it, D has stolen the book from R (who was in possession) and Q (who was in control) and P (who had ownership).

Ownership and 'possession or control'

It is impossible for D to steal property that is wholly owned, possessed and controlled by D themselves. This seemingly self-evident proposition has nevertheless been tested in court. In *Powell v McRae* (1977), D, a turnstile operator at Wembley Stadium, dishonestly accepted £2 from a member of the public and admitted him even though he (D) was fully aware that entrance was by ticket only. He was convicted of theft of the £2 from his employers, but his conviction was quashed by the Divisional Court. By no stretch of language could it be said that the money 'belonged to' his employers. D was simply the recipient of a bribe; he was not a thief.

However, given the possible separation of ownership, possession and control, s.5(1) means that D may, in certain circumstances, steal his own property. In *Turner (No. 2)* (1971), D took his car to a garage for repair. He was to pay for the repairs on his return a few days later. When the repairs were practically completed the car was left on the road outside the garage. During the night D surreptitiously took the car using a duplicate key. He was charged with theft of the car. He claimed that, as the car did not 'belong' to anyone other than himself, he could not steal it, but he was held liable. The Court of Appeal upheld the conviction.

'Control'

D may be guilty of theft if he appropriates property that was under V's 'control'. This is illustrated by *Woodman* (1974). D and two accomplices drove a van to a disused factory near Bristol owned by a company called English China Clays, and removed a large amount of scrap metal. D was convicted of theft and the Court of Appeal upheld the conviction. Even though the factory had been closed for some two and a half years, the premises were surrounded by a barbed-wire fence and several notices stating 'Private Property', 'Keep Out' and 'Trespassers will be prosecuted'. The Court decided that this showed that English China Clays was still in control of the site – and therefore also in 'control' of the scrap metal.

Rostron and Collinson (2003) is similar. D and E were discovered by police officers in the middle of the night in the car park of a golf course in Leicestershire wearing diving suits and in possession of a sack of wet golf balls, which had been retrieved from a lake on the course. They were convicted of theft of the golf balls and appealed, contending that the balls had been abandoned by their original owners (the golfers) and thus the removal of them did not amount to the appropriation of property belonging to another. However, the Court of Appeal upheld the convictions, because the golf balls now belonged to the golf club, which had 'control' of them.

'Any proprietary right or interest'

Property may also be stolen from anyone having 'any proprietary right or interest' in it. Once it is established that someone has a proprietary interest, it does not matter that this is precarious or short-lived. It does not matter that someone exists who has a better right to the property than V – one thief may, indeed, steal from another thief.

Joint ownership

Even when D owns property jointly with V, he is still capable of stealing it from him. Thus a partner (in a firm of solicitors, for example) could steal partnership property, even though it is jointly owned by himself.

Property received for a particular purpose

It is clear that in many situations D may be convicted of theft even where he has acquired legal ownership of property, if he was under 'an obligation' to deal with 'that property' in a particular way. In this situation, s.5(3) provides that 'the property or proceeds shall be regarded (as against him) as belonging to the other'.

Suppose D operates a Christmas fund, into which members of a club pay sums during the year, on the understanding that D returns it in a lump sum at Christmas. D, however, misappropriates the money. It is clear that D now owns the money – there is no suggestion that D should return the exact same notes and coins to the members – but s.5(3) would allow D to be treated as a thief. The members of the club retain a proprietary interest in that money.

The obligation must be legal

The obligation referred to must be a legal, as opposed to a moral, obligation.

The obligation is to deal with 'that property'

In some cases D's conduct will not amount to theft because of the requirement that D deals with 'that property' in a particular way. In *Hall* (1972), D was a partner in a firm of travel agents. He had received money from various customers as deposits for air trips to America. The flights were never arranged and the money, which had been paid into the agency's general trading account, was never returned. D was charged with stealing the customers' money. The Court of Appeal, albeit reluctantly, quashed his convictions. There was no evidence that the customers imposed an obligation on D to deal with the cash in any particular way. The agency simply had an obligation to the customers to provide a holiday in due course. For liability in such a case, it would have to be shown that D was obliged to maintain a fund representing V's deposit and not simply pay the money into a general account.

'Proceeds'

While D may not be under an obligation to deal with particular property, he may be under an obligation to deal with the 'proceeds' of the property instead. In *Wain* (1995), D had raised over £2,800 for a charity, which he initially paid into a separate bank account. When the charity asked for the money he was unable to produce it; by this time he had withdrawn the money for his own purposes. His conviction for theft was upheld. McCowan LJ said that D was 'plainly under an obligation to retain, if not the actual notes and coins, at least their proceeds, that is to say the money credited in the bank account which he opened for the trust with the actual property'.

Property acquired by mistake

S.5(4) of the 1968 Act provides that:

Where a person gets property by another's mistake, and is under an obligation to make restoration (in whole or in part) of the property or its proceeds or of the value thereof, then to the extent of that obligation the property or proceeds shall be regarded (as against him) as belonging to the person entitled in restoration, and an intention not to make restoration shall be regarded accordingly as an intention to deprive that person of the property or proceeds.

There has been confusion about the application of s.5(4). It led to an incorrect acquittal in *Attorney-General's Reference (No. 1 of 1983)* (1985). D was an officer with the Metropolitan Police. Her salary was paid into her bank account by direct debit. On one occasion the Met mistakenly overpaid her. She was charged with theft but the judge directed an acquittal. The Court of Appeal, however, held that this case was covered by s.5(4). Although, as a matter of civil law, she became owner of the money as soon as it was paid into her account, she remained under an 'obligation' to restore it to the Met.

The Court of Appeal has held that, as with s.5(3), the obligation must be a legal one. In *Gilks* (1972), Cairns LJ said, 'In a criminal statute, where a person's criminal liability is made dependent on his having an obligation, it would be quite wrong to construe that word so as to cover a moral or social obligation as distinct from a legal one.'

Gilks (1972)

Gilks called into a Ladbrokes' betting shop and placed a number of bets. One of these was on a horse called Fighting Scot, which did not get anywhere. Instead the race was won by a horse called Fighting Taffy. However, the relief manager, mistakenly believing that Gilks had backed Fighting Taffy, paid him £106. Gilks kept the cash and was charged with theft. On appeal, he argued that s.5(4) did not apply. Because gambling contracts are not, as a matter of contract law, legally enforceable, D was under no legal obligation to repay the money. The Court of Appeal agreed: the obligation had to be a legal one.

Ownerless property

A person cannot steal property that is not owned by anyone at the time of the appropriation. This includes property which, although capable of ownership, has never actually been owned by anyone, as well as property that was owned once but has become ownerless.

Lost property and abandoned property

It is insufficient that property is simply lost; it must have been abandoned before it can be said to be ownerless. Abandonment is not lightly inferred: property is abandoned only when the owner is indifferent as to any future appropriation of the property by others. The Court of Appeal accepted in *Rostron and Collinson* (2003), discussed above, that the golf balls in the lake had been abandoned by the golfers who had hit them into the lake (but the balls then became the property of the golf course instead).

It is not enough that D has no further use for property. Thus a householder who leaves rubbish outside their house awaiting collection by the local authority has not abandoned it. Property is not abandoned just because the owner has lost it and given up looking for it. The more valuable the property, the less likely it is that the owner has abandoned the hope of ever seeing it again.

'Dishonesty'

The next element that must be proved is that D was dishonest.

Situations covered by s.2(1)

The 1968 Theft Act does not provide a definition of dishonesty. Instead, it provides that in three situations D is not to be regarded as being dishonest if they appropriate the property in the belief that:

- they have in law the right to deprive the other of it, on behalf of themselves or of a third person (s.2(1)(a)); or

- they would have the other's consent if the other knew of the appropriation and the circumstances of it (s.2(1)(b)); or

- the person to whom the property belongs cannot be discovered by taking reasonable steps (s.2(1)(c)).

Belief in a 'right to deprive'

If D believes he has a legal right to appropriate V's property, he is not dishonest, no matter how unreasonable that belief. An example is provided by *Holden* (1991). D was charged with theft of scrap tyres from Kwik-Fit, where he had previously been employed. He claimed that other people had taken tyres with the permission of the supervisor. The depot manager, however, gave evidence that taking tyres was a sackable offence. The jury was directed that D was guilty unless he had a reasonable belief that he had a right to take the tyres. The Court of Appeal quashed the conviction: a person was not dishonest if he believed – reasonably or not – that he had a legal right to do what he had done. The question was whether he had – or might have had – an honest belief that he was entitled to take the tyres. The reasonableness (or otherwise) of the belief was no more than evidence as to whether D actually held that belief.

Belief in the 'other's consent'

Suppose D and V share a flat and, one night, D realises that he has no money to spend in the pub. V is away but D finds V's wallet containing money. If D removes £20 from the wallet genuinely thinking that V would not object were he around and knew of the circumstances, then D is not dishonest under s.2(1)(b). The belief may be unreasonable: again, the crux is whether D genuinely believed that V would have consented.

Belief that the owner 'cannot be discovered'

Although s.2(1)(c) does not refer to this situation explicitly, it seems to relate most clearly to the situation where D finds property. If D does find property, and comes to the honest conclusion that the owner cannot be discovered by taking reasonable (as it appears *to him*) steps, then D's appropriation of the property will not be dishonest. The reasonableness (or otherwise) of D's belief is, yet again, no more than evidence as to whether he actually held that belief.

In *Small* (1988), D was convicted of the theft of a car. He claimed that he believed it had been abandoned, because it had been parked in the same place, at an angle on a corner, every day for two weeks, during which time it had not moved at all. On inspection he discovered that the doors were unlocked and the keys were in the ignition. The car appeared to be in a 'forlorn' state: the petrol tank was empty, the battery was flat, as was one tyre; the windscreen wipers did not work. Having filled the tank with petrol he managed to get it started and drove off in it. He did not consider at any time that it was stolen until he observed the police flashing their lights at him, at which point he 'panicked' and ran off. The Court of Appeal quashed the conviction. There was evidence that D might have believed that the car had been abandoned. The question was whether he had – or might have had – an honest belief that the owner could not be traced.

Situations not covered by s.2(1)

Where D's situation does not fall within s.2(1) does not mean they are dishonest. Rather, they will be subject to the general test of dishonesty. The initial question that arises concerns who should determine honesty. There are three possibilities:

- the defendant (a purely subjective test) – Option 1

- the magistrates or jury (a purely objective test) – Option 2

- some combination of the two – Option 3.

During the 1970s the Court of Appeal toyed with Options 1 and 2, before plumping for Option 3 in *Ghosh* (1982). Lord Lane CJ said:

> In determining whether the prosecution has proved that the defendant was acting dishonestly, a jury must first of all decide whether according to the ordinary standards of reasonable and honest people what was done was dishonest. If it was not dishonest by those standards, that is the end of the matter and the prosecution fails. If it was dishonest by those standards, then the jury must consider whether D himself must have realised that what he was doing was by those standards dishonest.

The problem with having 'dishonesty' decided by magistrates or by a jury on a case-by-case basis is that it is unpredictable. This was clearly demonstrated in the recent case of *DPP v Gohill and Walsh* (2007). A magistrates' court acquitted the two defendants of theft on the basis that, according to the magistrates' idea of the standards of reasonable and honest people, G and W had not acted dishonestly. The prosecution appealed and the High Court reversed the acquittal. The High Court described the magistrates' decision as 'perverse'.

If a bench of magistrates and the judges of the High Court cannot agree – *in the same case* – on what are the ordinary standards of reasonable and honest people, what hope is there for two different juries from reaching agreement?

DPP v Gohill and Walsh (2007)

G and W worked for HSS Hire, a company that hired out tools and equipment to the public. On a number of occasions when customers had returned the equipment after use, G and/or W had waived the hire charge, altering the computer records to show that the equipment had been faulty so that no hire charge was applicable. On those occasions, the customers normally 'tipped' G and/or W £5 or £10, which the pair then split between themselves. Eventually G and W were caught and charged with theft from HSS. The magistrates decided that they were not dishonest and therefore not guilty; but this decision was reversed on appeal to the High Court.

No precedent is ever created by the deliberations of a jury, so each jury or bench of magistrates must approach the question anew, with no earlier cases to look to for guidance. Questions of fact, determined by a jury, may not be appealed, unlike questions of law. They are therefore not open to consideration and correction by the appeal courts.

In your view, was Robin Hood (who stole from the rich and gave to the poor) dishonest 'according to the ordinary standards of reasonable and honest people'? (see above)

D's willingness to pay not conclusive of honesty

S.2(2) of the Theft Act 1968 provides that 'a person's appropriation of property belonging to another may be dishonest notwithstanding that he is willing to pay for the property'. The effect of s.2(2) is that D may be guilty of theft where he appropriates property and pays for it. Very often the fact that D has paid, or was willing to pay, for property will be strong evidence that he was not dishonest, often on the basis that he genuinely believed V would consent to the appropriation, but it is not conclusive.

'Intention to permanently deprive'

Stealing requires an intention to permanently deprive. It is unnecessary for there to be permanent deprivation *in fact*; theft is committed even if there is no danger of V ever losing his property, provided D had the intent that he would. Conversely, the fact that there is permanent deprivation does not make something theft if D did not have the intent. The intent *must* be present at the time of the appropriation.

Circumstantial evidence will be necessary in many cases to determine whether D had the intent or not. In such cases where intent is not obvious it will be for the jury to infer intent from the evidence. For example, if D borrows V's lawnmower and it is found in D's garden, in full view of V or anyone else, the inference that D intended to permanently deprive V of it will not be easy. On the other hand, if D is discovered respraying V's car that he took without permission, the inference will be much easier.

Money

Where D takes money, say from his employer's cash-till, intending to replace an equivalent amount in due course, could it be argued that, as he had intended to repay the money, albeit not the exact notes and/or coins taken, then there was no intention to deprive the owner of the money? In *Velumyl* (1989), the Court of Appeal held that D *does* have such an intent. D, a company manager, took £1,050 from an office safe without authority. He said that a friend owed him money; when this money was repaid he would replace the money in the safe. The Court of Appeal upheld his theft conviction. He had the intention of permanently depriving the company of the money because he had no intention of returning the objects that he had taken. His intention was to return objects of equivalent value, which was not a defence to theft. D had taken something that he was not entitled to take without the consent of the owner and could not force upon the owner a substitution to which the latter had not consented.

Intending to treat property as your own to dispose of regardless of the other's rights

Section 6(1) of the Theft Act 1968 provides that 'a person appropriating property belonging to another without meaning the other permanently to lose the thing itself is nevertheless to be regarded as having the intention of permanently depriving the other of it if his intention is to treat the thing as his own to dispose of regardless of the other's rights'.

Section 6(1) need be invoked only where D ultimately expects the property to find its way back into the hands of the owner. There are two main situations:

- D takes V's property with the intention of *selling it* back to him. In *Lloyd and Others* (1985), Lord Lane CJ cited an old case – in which D took fat from a candlemaker and then offered it for sale to the same man – as an example of a situation where s.6(1) would apply today.

- D takes V's property with the intention of *ransoming it*. This is illustrated by the recent case of *Raphael and Johnson* (2008). D and E had taken a Ford Focus car belonging to V, then telephoned V a few days later offering to return the car if he would pay them £500. The jury found that D and E had an intention to permanently deprive V of his property and the Court of Appeal agreed.

Unfortunately confusion has been caused by judges referring to s.6(1) in straightforward theft cases that simply did not require it. The prime example is *Cahill* (1993). D picked up a package of newspapers from outside a newsagent's shop, only to drop it soon after (when he noticed that police officers were watching). He was charged with theft. His story was that he was going to dump the papers on a friend's doorstep for a joke. The trial judge directed the jury in terms of s.6 – but got the wording wrong and forced the Court of Appeal to allow D's appeal. However, it was not necessary for the judge to refer to s.6(1) at all. The question for the jury should simply have been, did D intend that the package be lost to the newsagent for ever? If D knew that this would be the effect of depositing the package on the friend's doorstep, that would have been sufficient intent even though D's only purpose was the bizarre practical joke.

In *Cahill*, the judge's reference to s.6(1) allowed D to escape liability on appeal. The opposite happened in *DPP v Lavender* (1994). D had taken doors from council property undergoing repair and used them to replace damaged doors on his girlfriend's council flat. He was charged with theft but argued he had no intention to permanently deprive. Magistrates dismissed the charge but the Divisional Court disagreed. The question was whether D intended to treat the doors as his own, regardless of the owner's rights; the answer to this was 'Yes'.

> Was D a thief? Was he treating the doors as his own? Or was he in fact treating the doors as the Council's? At most, D was 'guilty' of rearranging the Council's property; is this theft?

'Regardless of the other's rights'
What if D takes V's property and is completely indifferent as to whether V ever sees it again? It could be argued that D did not *intend* V to be permanently deprived of their property, hence s.6(1) provides that it is sufficient if D intends to 'treat the thing as his own to dispose of regardless of the other's rights'.

In *Marshall, Coombes and Eren* (1998), D, E and F were caught obtaining London Underground (LU) day tickets from people who had passed through the exit barriers, then selling them on to other people. They were all convicted of theft of the tickets and appealed, on the basis that there was no intention to permanently deprive. The Court of Appeal upheld the convictions. By acquiring and re-selling the tickets the men had demonstrated an intention to treat the tickets as their own to dispose of regardless of LU's rights.

> What 'rights' did the London Underground have over the tickets?

Borrowing or lending

S.6(1) of the Theft Act 1968 goes on to provide that 'a borrowing or lending of (the thing) may amount to (treating the thing as his own to dispose of regardless of the other's rights) if, but only if, the borrowing or lending is for a period and in circumstances making it equivalent to an outright taking or disposal'.

It is therefore clearly not theft if D merely borrows property from V. This is illustrated by the recent case of *Mitchell* (2008). D, who was escaping from the police, used threats to hijack V's car which he later abandoned. D was convicted of robbery (theft with the use of force or the threat of force – see Chapter 11) and appealed. The Court of Appeal quashed his conviction, because there was no evidence of an intention on D's part to *permanently* deprive V of his property. This is correct: after all, if D in a case such as *Mitchell* was guilty of the theft of V's car then all 'joyriding' cases, which are dealt with under s.12 of the Theft Act 1968 (taking a conveyance without the owner's consent) would also amount to theft, rendering s.12 redundant.

However, there may be situations where D merely borrows property from V, fully intending to return the property to V, but where D could nevertheless be liable for theft. This is where the borrowing is 'for a period or in circumstances making it equivalent to an outright taking or disposal'. An example would be the taking of a battery with the intention of returning it only when its power is exhausted. In *Lloyd and Others* (1985) Lord Lane CJ said:

> The second half of s.6(1) is intended to make clear that a mere borrowing is never enough to constitute the necessary guilty mind unless the intention is to return the 'thing' in such a changed state that it can truly be said that all its *goodness* or *virtue* has gone.

Lloyd and Others (1985)
D worked as a projectionist at an Odeon cinema. E and F ran a pirate video operation. Over a period of months D surreptitiously removed a number of films from the cinema and lent them to E and F who quickly copied them onto a master tape from which they

produced large numbers of pirate videos. The films were taken out of the cinema for only a few hours at a time. Eventually the three men were caught red-handed in the process of copying *The Missionary*. They were convicted of conspiracy to steal but the Court of Appeal quashed the convictions. Applying the above test to the facts, Lord Lane CJ held that the films had not been stolen. The particular films had 'not themselves been diminished in value at all', there was still virtue in them.

A problem arises if D takes property, and returns it in a changed state where *some* of its goodness or virtue has gone. It is clear that if D takes V's football ticket, intending to return it after the match, then D is guilty of theft although V may well recover the ticket because by then it is simply a piece of paper with no intrinsic value. However, what happens if D takes V's season ticket and returns it after half the season, or even just one game? Does this amount to theft? There do not appear to have been any cases on this issue, but s.6(1) as explained in *Lloyd* would suggest that it is not theft, as the circumstances must make the borrowing 'equivalent to an outright taking or disposal' and it can hardly be said to be outright if a substantial proportion of the value still remains.

Making off without payment

Section 3 of the Theft Act 1978 was introduced in order to cover a loophole situation in the 1968 Act. Where D obtains ownership and possession of property from V, then decides not to pay for it, he is not guilty of theft because by the time he formed the dishonest intention, the property belonged to D. This conduct, commonly referred to as 'bilking', is now provided for as follows. S.3(1) states that 'a person who, knowing that payment on the spot for any goods supplied or services done is required or expected from him, dishonestly makes off without having paid as required or expected and with intent to avoid payment of the amount shall be guilty' of making off without payment.

Actus reus
The *actus reus* elements of the offence are that D:

● Makes off

● Without having paid as required or expected

● For any goods supplied or services done

'Makes off'

'Makes off' is not limited to D leaving by stealth but includes situations where D openly runs off, typically by jumping out of a taxi and running away. To 'make off' means that D must actually leave premises or the point at which payment was expected. For example, if D is caught climbing through a hotel window, he will not have made off (though he may well be guilty of an attempt). In *McDavitt* (1981), D refused to pay his bill for a meal at a restaurant after an argument with the manager. He got up and walked towards a door where he was advised not to leave as the police had been called. At this point he went to the toilet and remained there until the police arrived. He was charged with making off without paying from the restaurant but, at the end of the prosecution case, the judge told the jury to acquit as D had not 'made off'.

Without having paid as required or expected

D's departure must be made without paying. If D hands over forged bank notes he does not 'pay'. On the other hand, where D pays with a cheque supported by a guarantee card then there is no offence even if he has no funds in his account, because the bank will be obliged to honour the cheque. Similarly, where D pays by credit card, even if he does so without authority because it has been withdrawn or the card is stolen, there is no offence as the card company will honour the debt.

If D leaves a hotel or restaurant (for example) without paying, having obtained the consent of the owner to defer payment to some future date, then they have not 'made off without having paid as required or expected'. That is, there is no *actus reus*. Therefore, even if D acted dishonestly, and never intended to pay, no offence under s.3 has been committed. This happened in *Vincent* (2001). During the summer of 1998, D stayed at two hotels in Windsor, for a total of five weeks. He left both hotels without fully paying his bills, which totalled £1,300, after persuading both hotel owners to postpone payment. D told them that he was temporarily short of cash but was owed money. When payment was not forthcoming D was charged with two counts of making off. The judge directed the jury that if D obtained the agreements to postpone payment dishonestly, then the *actus reus* of the offence had been committed. D was convicted but the Court of Appeal quashed his convictions. The hotel owners had agreed to postpone payment, which meant that the *actus reus* had not been committed. The fact that D may have acted dishonestly was a question of *mens rea* only.

Goods supplied or services done

Goods must be 'supplied' to D, although it is not necessary that the goods be delivered to them. It is sufficient that D is permitted to take the goods;

for example, by filling their petrol tank at a self-service filling station, or taking items from a supermarket shelf. Where services are involved, the service must be 'done'. This typically involves letting hotel rooms, supplying meals in restaurants, or valeting D's car. Allowing D to use a facility, such as parking their car in a car park, would be regarded as a service 'done', so that D would commit the offence if they drove away without paying.

> An interesting problem arises if D were charged under s.3 after having sneaked into a cinema to watch a film and then leaving without paying. Could this be regarded as a service 'done'?

Excluded goods and services
S.3(3) provides that there is no offence committed 'where the supply of the goods or the doing of the service is contrary to law, or where the service done is such that payment is not legally enforceable'. Examples involving the supply of goods being contrary to law include prohibited drugs, alcohol and cigarettes (where D is under 18). Examples of the supply of services being contrary to law would include the situation where D leaves a brothel or an unlicensed casino without paying his debts.

Mens rea
The *mens rea* elements of the offence are:

• Dishonesty

• Knowledge that payment on the spot was required or expected

• Intent to avoid payment of the amount.

Dishonesty
The *Ghosh* (1982) test applies.

Knowledge that payment on the spot was required or expected
D must make off knowing that payment was 'required' or 'expected'. If, for example, D honestly believed that goods were supplied or the service done on credit, and that they would be invoiced later they would not be guilty. Similarly, a foreigner who travels on a bus without paying, because in their country all public transport is free, would not commit the offence because they would not believe that payment was required or expected of them. Two cases involving passengers running away without paying for taxi journeys illustrate what is meant by this element of the offence.

- In *Troughton v Metropolitan Police* (1987), D got into a taxi and asked to be taken to 'Highbury, North London'. He did not give an address. Unable to get an address from D, the exasperated driver drove to the nearest police station, where D got out and ran off. He was convicted but the Divisional Court quashed his conviction.

- In *Aziz* (1993), the taxi had reached the requested destination but D refused to pay a £15 taxi fare. At this the driver set off to drive him back to the point where he had been picked up but, *en route*, decided to drive to a police station. D forced the car to stop and ran off. On appeal, he claimed that the driver's announcement that he was returning meant that his requirement to pay had ceased but the Court of Appeal rejected the argument and upheld the conviction.

The crucial differences in these cases was that in *Troughton v Metropolitan Police* the journey had never been completed, whereas in *Aziz* it had been completed. The former driver's failure to take D to his destination amounted to a breach of contract, and he was therefore unable to 'require' or 'expect' payment, whereas the fact that the latter driver had then driven off somewhere else was irrelevant, D knew that payment was still required.

Intent to avoid payment of the amount

It was originally believed that the offence was committed where D's intention in making off was merely to avoid payment *at that time*, even though he intended to pay later. However, in *Allen* (1985), the House of Lords held that an intention to avoid payment permanently is required.

Allen (1985)
Chris Allen booked a hotel room for ten nights from 15 January 1983. He stayed on thereafter and finally left on 11 February, without paying his bill of £1,286.94, and leaving behind his belongings. He telephoned two days later to say that he was in financial difficulties and arranged to return to the hotel on 18 February to collect his belongings and to leave his passport as security. He was, however, arrested on his return. At his trial Allen denied that he acted dishonestly and said that he genuinely expected to pay his bill from various business ventures. The Court of Appeal quashed the conviction and the Lords upheld that decision.

Summary

- A person is guilty of theft if they dishonestly appropriate property belonging to another with the intention of permanently depriving the other of it.

- Any assumption of any of the rights of an owner amounts to an appropriation (*Morris*).

- An act may be an appropriation notwithstanding that it is done with the consent of the owner (*Lawrence*; *Gomez*). A gift may therefore constitute an appropriation (*Hinks*).

- Appropriation includes keeping property and dealing with it as if you were the owner.

- Appropriation is not necessarily instantaneous but may be treated as continuing for as long as the thief can sensibly be regarded as being in the act of stealing (*Atakpu and Abrahams*).

- Property is defined widely (*Kelly and Lindsay*), including personal and intangible property, although real property can be stolen only in certain circumstances.

- Property belongs to any person having possession or control of it, or having any proprietary right or interest in it.

- D cannot steal their own property if they own, possess and control it (*Powell v McRae*) but they can steal property that they own if it is temporarily in the possession or control of another (*Turner (No. 2)*).

- If D received property and was under a legal obligation to deal with it in a particular way, then either the property itself or the proceeds of it shall be regarded as belonging to another. Because the obligation is to deal with 'that property', D will not be guilty if they were not obliged to deal with it in a particular way (*Hall*) but they may be under an obligation to deal with the proceeds instead (*Wain*).

- Property received by mistake may be treated as belonging to another if D was under a legal obligation to make restoration of it (*Gilks*, *Attorney-General's Reference (No. 1 of 1983)*).

- D must be proved to have been dishonest. The Theft Act 1968 gives three illustrations of when D is not dishonest, all of which depend on D's genuine belief. The Act does *not* define when D is dishonest. This is left to the courts – the test is that laid down in *Ghosh*.

- D must intend to permanently deprive the owner of their property. Taking money from a till is theft even if D intends to replace the cash eventually because the actual notes and coins will be different (*Velumyl*).

- Even if D intended V to get their property back, D still has the required intention to permanently deprive if their plan was to sell, or ransom, the property back to V (*Raphael and Johnson*).

- Borrowing V's property is not theft (*Mitchell*). But D may nevertheless have the required intention if their intention was to return the property in such a changed state that it can truly be said that *all its goodness* or *virtue* has gone (*Lloyd*).

- 'Making off without payment' is designed to plug a loophole in the definition of theft. D is guilty if he dishonestly makes off, knowing that payment on the spot for any goods supplied or services done is required or expected from them but without having paid as required or expected, and with intent to permanently avoid payment of the amount (*Allen*).

- To 'make off' is to leave the place where payment was required or expected (*McDavitt*)

- 'On the spot' means 'at that time' not 'at that particular place' (*Troughton v Metropolitan Police*; *Aziz*).

11 Robbery

Introduction

S.8 of the Theft Act 1968 provides that 'a person is guilty of robbery if he steals, and immediately before or at the time of doing so, and in order to do so, he uses force on any person or puts or seeks to put any person in fear of being then and there subjected to force'.

The *actus reus* of robbery

'Steals'

Robbery is an aggravated form of theft; it is therefore necessary to prove theft. If D has not committed theft he cannot be convicted of robbery even though he uses force to deprive V of the property. This may occur if D honestly believes that he has a right to the property and is, therefore, not dishonest (*Robinson* [1977]). In such cases D could, of course, be charged with the appropriate offence against the person. In *Robinson*, D had approached a man who owed his wife money, brandishing a knife. After a struggle, D grabbed a £5 note. When he was charged with robbery, the judge directed the jury that it was necessary for D to have honestly believed that he was entitled to get his money in that particular way. The jury convicted but the Court of Appeal quashed the conviction.

Robbery is complete when D has appropriated the property. There is no requirement that D succeed in 'getting away' with the property (*Corcoran v Anderton* [1980]).

> *Corcoran v Anderton* (1980)
> Chris Corcoran and a friend, P, agreed to steal a handbag from a woman, Mrs Hall, whom they had seen walking along the street in Manchester. P hit her in the back and tugged at her bag to release it, while Corcoran participated. Mrs Hall released the bag and it fell to the ground but in doing she also fell to the ground. She screamed and at this, the pair ran off empty handed. Mrs Hall recovered her bag. Corcoran was subsequently convicted of robbery. He appealed but the Queen's Bench Division upheld the conviction. An appropriation did not require either defendant to have sole control of the handbag.

'Force'

In *Dawson and James* (1976), D nudged a man so that he lost his balance, at which point E, who was in position just behind V, was able to take his wallet. The Court of Appeal held that 'force' was an ordinary word and was therefore to be determined by the jury. This approach was confirmed in *Clouden* (1987), below.

'On any person'

Prior to the 1968 Act, robbery required that force be used to overpower V or to make them give up their property. This is no longer the case and robbery may be committed, for example, by wrenching a shopping bag from V's grasp, as in *Clouden*. The Court of Appeal held that, in applying force to the bag, D was taken to apply force to the woman as well. In most cases, the person on whom the force is used or against whom it is threatened will be the same person against whom theft is committed. However, the Act does not limit robbery to this situation. Thus, if D threatens P and takes jewellery belonging to Q, P's wife, then this will also be robbery.

Threat of force

S.8 of the Theft Act 1968 defines robbery as including the situation where D 'puts . . . any person in fear of being then and there subjected to force'. Thus, a threat of future force will not suffice for robbery (although it may constitute blackmail, contrary to s.21 of the 1968 Act).

In *Bentham* (2005), D broke into the house of his former employer, V. He put his fingers into his jacket pocket to give the appearance that he had a gun in there, approached V and demanded money and jewellery from him, threatening to shoot him if he did not comply. V did hand over some money. Shortly afterwards, D was charged with robbery and pleaded guilty. It was clear that D was guilty of robbery as he had sought to put V 'in fear of being then and there subjected to force'. The fact that it was only his fingers did not matter for the offence of robbery.

However, it is not necessary that V be aware of the threat; or, if they are aware, that they are in fact fearful. The Act simply requires that D '*seeks* to put' them in fear of force. Thus, if V is blind and does not see D waving a knife at them while D takes their wallet, this is nevertheless robbery. The point that V need not actually fear force was crucial to the recent case of *B and R v DPP* (2007). Here the High Court upheld robbery convictions on the basis that the defendants had sought to put V in fear of force, even though V did not actually fear it. This has to be correct, otherwise V's bravery (or lack of it) would determine D's guilt.

B and R v DPP (2007)

B and R were part of a group of 11 or 12 boys who had approached V and surrounded him. Various items including money and a watch were taken. B and R were convicted of robbery despite V stating at the trial that he did not feel threatened or scared. B and R appealed without success to the High Court. The Court held that a threat of force could be express or implied, by either words or conduct. Here there had been an implied threat of force. The fact that V did not actually feel threatened, or in fear, did not mean that the defendants had not sought to put him in fear.

'Immediately before or at the time of' stealing

Given that theft is complete as soon as property is appropriated, a problem may arise where D uses force to effect their escape with stolen property. That is, the use of force is arguably not 'immediately before or at the time of' the theft and, therefore, there is no robbery. To tackle this problem, the courts are prepared to treat appropriation as a continuing act. In *Hale* (1978), D and E forced their way into a house owned by Mrs Carrett after she answered the door to them. D put his hand over her mouth to stop her from screaming, while E went upstairs where he found a jewellery box. Before leaving the house, they tied her up. D was charged with, and convicted of, robbery. On appeal, he argued that, as theft was complete as soon as E laid hands on the box, any force used when tying Mrs Carrett up was irrelevant, but this had not been made clear to the jury. That is, he had not used force 'at the time of' the stealing, but afterwards. The Court of Appeal dismissed the appeal. Eveleigh LJ said:

> To say that the conduct is over and done with as soon as he laid hands on the property ... is contrary to common-sense and to the natural meaning of words ... the act of appropriation does not suddenly cease. It is a continuous act and it is a matter for the jury to decide whether or not the act of appropriation has finished ... As a matter of common sense [D] was in the course of committing theft; he was stealing.

In *Lockley* (1995), D, caught shoplifting, had used force on a store security man who was trying to stop him to make good his escape. It was argued on appeal against his robbery conviction that the decision of the House of Lords in *Gomez* (1993), considered in Chapter 10 above, had impliedly overruled *Hale*. However, the Court of Appeal confirmed the continuing application of the *Hale* principle: it is for the jury to decide whether the appropriation was still continuing while D was endeavouring to escape and, hence, whether the use of force was 'at the time of' the theft. Of course a line must be drawn somewhere, but the matter is one for the jury to decide.

'In order to' steal

The force, or the threat of force, must be used 'in order to' steal. Thus, if D punches V in a fight, knocking him unconscious, and then removes his watch, this would not be robbery, as the force was not used 'in order to' steal.

The *mens rea* of robbery

Obviously D must steal, so this requires the *mens rea* of theft. See Chapter 10.

Summary

- To be guilty of robbery a person must 'steal', thus they must commit theft. If there is no theft, for whatever reason, there is no robbery (*Robinson*).

- As in theft, there is no requirement that D escape with the property (*Corcoran v Anderton*). It is sufficient if D appropriates property, belonging to another, dishonestly with the intention of permanently depriving the other of it.

- The use of force is not actually essential for robbery. Robbery may also be committed if D puts or seeks to put any person in fear of being then and there subjected to force (*Bentham*; *B & R v DPP*).

- However, if the allegation is that 'force' was used, this is an ordinary word that can simply be left to the jury (*Dawson and James*).

- Force must be used 'immediately before or at the time of' stealing – but the appropriation element of theft is a continuing act and it should be left to the jury to decide when it has stopped (*Hale*; *Lockley*).

- Force must be used 'on any person' – but force can be used on property, e.g. a bag snatch is robbery (*Clouden*).

- D must use force, or put or seek to put any person in fear of being then and there subjected to force, 'in order to' steal. Simply using force, and then later stealing something from the same person, does not amount to robbery.

12 Burglary

Introduction

Burglary replaced the old offence of breaking and entering. Section 9 of the Theft Act 1968 creates two separate offences of burglary. In many, if not most, cases D will commit both offences – but they are separate.

Theft Act 1968
9 (1) A person is guilty of burglary if –

(a) he enters any building or part of a building as a trespasser and with intent to commit any such offence as is mentioned in subsection (2) below; or
(b) having entered any building or part of a building as a trespasser he steals or attempts to steal anything in the building or that part of it or inflicts or attempts to inflict on any person therein any grievous bodily harm.

(2) The offences referred to in subsection (1) (a) above are offences of stealing anything in the building or part of a building in question, of inflicting on any person therein any grievous bodily harm and of doing unlawful damage to the building or anything therein.

(4) References in subsections (1) and (2) above to a building ... shall also apply to an inhabited vehicle or vessel, and shall apply to any such vehicle or vessel at times when the person having a habitation in it is not there as well as at times when he is.

Actus reus of burglary

The *actus reus* elements – which are common to both burglary offences – are that D must have:

- Entered

- A building or part of a building

- As a trespasser.

Furthermore, depending on exactly what it is that D is alleged to have done, the word 'therein' requires some explanation.

'Entry'

The 1968 Act does not explain what is meant by 'entry'. In *Collins* (1973), the Court of Appeal offered some guidance. The facts of the case are unusual to say the least. D did not deny climbing a ladder, wearing only his socks, and entering the bedroom of an 18-year-old girl in the middle of the night and having sex with her. However, he claimed that, whilst balanced on the windowsill, the girl had sat up and then knelt on the bed before putting her arms around his neck and pulling him into the bed. Apparently, the girl – who had been drinking – had assumed that D was her boyfriend paying her an 'ardent nocturnal visit'! It was only after they had started to have sex that she discovered that D was not her boyfriend, slapped his face and demanded that he leave. When he was charged with burglary (entry with intent to rape), contrary to s.9(1)(a), he denied having entered the building as a trespasser, on the basis that he was still outside the building when the girl pulled him into the bedroom.

Although he was convicted, the Court of Appeal quashed the conviction. Edmund-Davies LJ said that the jury had to be 'entirely satisfied' that D had to make an 'effective and substantial' entry into the building before a conviction was possible. The Court made it very clear that D did not have to have his entire body inside the building before he had entered it.

The 'substantial and effective entry' test was modified in *Brown* (1985). D was observed with the top half of his body inside a shop window rummaging around, and was convicted of burglary (entry with intent to steal), contrary to s.9(1)(a). The Court of Appeal held that all that was required was that D had made an 'effective' entry, and that this was a question of fact for the jury.

This approach suggests that what is an effective entry in some circumstances may not be in others. While D's entry is effective for stealing goods if he can reach into a shop window, it will rarely, if ever, be effective for inflicting grievous bodily harm.

More recent developments suggest that the requirement that entry be 'effective' has also been removed. In *Ryan* (1996), D was discovered stuck in the downstairs window of an elderly man's house in the middle of the night. His head and right arm were inside the house but the rest of his body was in the garden. He was completely trapped and the fire brigade had to be called to release him. The Court of Appeal upheld his conviction of burglary (entry with intent to steal), contrary to s.9(1)(a). The Court dismissed his argument that his actions were incapable of amounting to entry because he could not have stolen anything. The question had correctly been left to the jury.

Do you agree that Ryan had made an 'entry' into the old man's house?

'Any building or part of a building'
The maximum sentence that may be imposed depends on the type of building entered. The maximum penalty for conviction on indictment is 14 years if the building in question is a 'dwelling'. For other buildings, the maximum is ten years.

'Building'
The word is not defined in the 1968 Act but it must be a fairly permanent structure. A temporary, prefabricated structure would probably be a 'building'; a tent is not. It is not clear when a structure under construction becomes a 'building'. If D wanders onto a building site and enters a partly finished house with no roof or fittings and causes criminal damage, have they entered a 'building'? Similarly, does there come a point when a dilapidated and/or partly demolished house ceases to be a 'building'? At present there is no answer to these questions.

'Inhabited' vehicles, such as caravans, or vessels, like houseboats, are buildings. There is no requirement that the occupier has to be in at the time when D enters. But would a caravan be 'inhabited', and therefore a building, if it was left empty for months, as many holiday caravans are during the winter? The answer may be that a caravan or houseboat is a building only if it is *actively* occupied. Meanwhile, vehicles such as mobile libraries, blood transfusion centres and army recruitment offices are not buildings as they are not 'inhabited'.

The cases of *B and S v Leathley* (1979) and *Norfolk Constabulary v Seekings and Gould* (1986) involved similar facts but different outcomes. In each case the defendants had been accused of burgling a large container that was being used to provide storage space. Were they 'buildings'? In *B and S* it was held that the container was a 'building' because it had been in the same place (a farmyard) resting on railway sleepers for two or three years; it had locked doors and an external electricity supply. The court rejected the defence that the container was not a building because it did not have foundations. The defendants were therefore guilty of burglary. In *Seekings and Gould*, two lorry trailers had been driven into a Budgens supermarket site to provide temporary storage space during refurbishment. They had locked shutters and an external electricity supply and had been in the same place for about a year. However, it was held that these containers were merely 'vehicles' because they were still on wheels. To be guilty of burglary, vehicles have to be 'inhabited' and, as no-one was actually living in these containers, the defendants were acquitted of burglary.

'Part of a building'

It is sufficient that D enters 'part of a building' as a trespasser. D may have permission to enter parts of a building but not others; they may commit burglary if they enter those other parts. A guest in a hotel has permission to enter their own room and communal rooms (the foyer, bar, restaurant, for example), but not other guests' rooms or parts of the hotel used exclusively by staff. If D were to enter another guest's room or the manager's office intending to steal, this could be burglary.

'Part of a building' does not necessarily mean a separate room; any separate section of a room will suffice. In *Walkington* (1979), D entered Debenhams department store in Oxford Street, London one evening. It was 20 minutes before closing time and the store was quiet. On the first floor was a three-sided counter, with a till, the drawer of which was partially open. D entered the counter area, opened the drawer and, after looking inside and finding it empty, slammed it shut and left the store whereupon he was arrested. He was convicted of burglary (entry with intent to steal) contrary to s.9(1)(a) and the Court of Appeal upheld the conviction. Whether the counter area was a 'part' of a building was a question of fact for the jury.

'As a trespasser'

Whether D is charged under s.9(1)(a) or (b), it is essential that D entered a building, or part of a building, as a trespasser. If D, having lawfully entered a shop, remains behind after closing by hiding somewhere, then moves throughout the display area he will not be a trespasser unless he leaves that 'part' of the shop and enters another 'part'.

Trespass is a civil concept, a tort. It basically means being on someone else's property without their permission or without some legal right to be there. While the tort of trespass may be committed negligently, the crime of burglary requires *mens rea*, and this means that D must enter the building, or part of the building, either:

• intending to trespass; or

• being reckless whether or not he is trespassing.

In *Collins* (1973), Edmund-Davies LJ said (emphasis added):

> There cannot be a conviction for entering premises 'as a trespasser' ... unless the person entering does so *knowing* that he is a trespasser and nevertheless deliberately enters, or, at the very least, *is reckless* as to whether or not he is entering the premises of another without the other party's consent.

The form of recklessness in burglary is subjective. In *Collins*, D's conviction was quashed after the trial judge directed the jury that civil trespass was sufficient; the question of D's *mens rea* had not therefore been left to the jury. Further, D's entry must be voluntary. Thus there would be no trespass if D stumbled into a building, or was dragged into a building against his will.

Permission to enter

The person who is in possession of a building, or part of it, is the person who may give permission to others to enter. The person in possession may authorise others to give permission to enter. A husband who owns the family home expressly, or more usually impliedly, authorises his wife and children to invite people into the house. Those people do not enter as trespassers, even if the husband does not know about the entry.

The person in possession may, equally, forbid the entry of certain persons, for example his daughter's boyfriend. If the boyfriend nevertheless enters, and either knows or thinks that the father has refused him permission to be there, he enters as a trespasser. If he were then to steal some item of property he would commit burglary.

Exceeding consent

A question arises about the limit of consent to enter a building. A father might well consent to his 15-year-old daughter's boyfriend coming round to see her – but almost certainly does not consent to them having sex in her bedroom. Would this make the boyfriend a trespasser? Suppose D, who is grown up and left home, still has consent to enter his father's house. One night he enters the house and steals a television set. Is consent impliedly limited in some way, so that D is a trespasser and hence a burglar?

In *Jones and Smith* (1976), where this exact situation occurred (although Chris Smith, along with his friend John Jones, actually stole two televisions from Alfred Smith's house), the Court of Appeal answered this question, 'Yes'. James LJ said that in such cases the prosecution had to prove that D 'entered with the knowledge that entry was being effected against the consent or in excess of the consent that had been given'.

This suggests that, where D is given permission to enter for one purpose (say to look after a flat while the owner is away on holiday), but enters for another (say to have wild parties), then D will enter as a trespasser. There is no requirement that the latter entry be for an unlawful purpose. Of course, if D merely enters a flat in order to have wild parties this will not necessarily make him a burglar! Similarly, if D has permission to enter one part of a building, but then enters another, he will be trespassing. A TV repairman may be invited into the living room but, if he then enters the kitchen to search for money, he would enter that room as a trespasser.

The courts have never had to tackle the issue of where the limit of permission to enter shops is drawn. However, it would seem that D, a shoplifter, may commit burglary if he enters a shop intending to steal from the very outset. The shopkeeper's permission to enter is impliedly limited to the purpose of inspecting and/or purchasing goods. A conviction under s.9(1)(a) would be unlikely, given the problem of proof, unless D were to confess or was found to have gone equipped for shoplifting. A conviction under s.9(1)(b) would seem more feasible once D has actually appropriated goods.

'Therein'

Both offences of burglary under s.9(1)(a) and (b) refer to entering a building, etc., and either intending to commit various offences or actually committing them 'therein'. This word is ambiguous. Does it mean that the property to be stolen, destroyed or damaged, or the person to be harmed, has to be inside the building already? Or is it sufficient that they arrive there at the same time as D, or even later? If the latter interpretation is correct it would mean that if D and E both entered a building together as trespassers intending to steal, and D then stole E's jacket, D would be guilty of burglary (under s.9(1)(a) and (b)). However, as the purpose of the offence is the protection of persons or property in buildings, the former, more restrictive interpretation, appears more correct.

The *mens rea* of burglary

The *mens rea* required depends on whether D is charged with the s.9(1)(a) or (b) offence.

Section 9(1)(a): intent to commit another offence

Under s.9(1)(a) it must be proved that D, when entering a building or part of a building, had the intention to commit one of the offences referred to in s.9(2):

- theft

- criminal damage (strictly the 1968 Act refers to 'unlawful damage' but this presumably means the offence of criminal damage, which was only introduced by the Criminal Damage Act 1971)

- GBH.

It is crucial for liability under s.9(1)(a) that D is proven to have formed the intent (to steal, do unlawful damage or inflict GBH) before entering. This point was emphasised in the recent case of *Bennett* (2007). D was convicted under s.9(1)(a) after the trial judge told the jury that they could convict if they were sure that D 'entered as a trespasser into that house and that when he was in there he intended to steal property'. The Court of Appeal accepted that this was a misdirection, as it suggested that D was still guilty even if he formed the intent after entering the house, which is not the law. However, the Court upheld D's conviction on the basis that the only plausible reason for D to have entered the house at all was because he intended to steal.

A conditional intent will suffice. In *Attorney-General's References (Nos. 1 and 2 of 1979)* (1979), there were two cases. D1 was caught inside a house. D2 was caught fiddling with a set of French windows. Both claimed that they planned to steal whatever they could find 'lying around' (D's actual words in the second case). D1 was charged with burglary and D2 with attempted burglary; in each case the trial judge directed an acquittal. However, the Court of Appeal held that the trial judges had got the law wrong. It was no defence to burglary for D to claim that he had not intended to steal any specific objects. An intention to steal whatever there was worth stealing is, nevertheless, an intention to steal.

Presumably, applying this argument, D also commits burglary if he enters a building with intent to inflict GBH on anyone he *finds* sitting around inside. As far as guilt is concerned it would not matter that no one was, in fact, inside; it is D's intent that defines the offence.

If D enters a building as a trespasser with intent to kill, is he a burglar? If D enters a building as a trespasser with intent to commit robbery, is he a burglar?

Section 9(1)(b)

Under s.9(1)(b), the actual offences of theft, the infliction of GBH, or an attempt to commit either, must be proven. D must have the requisite *mens rea* states for these. Suppose D enters a house, as a trespasser, intending to commit criminal damage. Once inside he gets distracted by a magazine and starts reading it. Subsequently, he absent-mindedly places the magazine into his bag and leaves. Whilst he is certainly guilty under s.9(1)(a), has he committed burglary contrary to s.9(1)(b)?

Trespass with intent to commit a sexual offence

Section 63(1) of the Sexual Offences Act 2003 abolished the type of burglary under s.9(1)(a) of the Theft Act 1968 where D enters a building (or part of a building) with intent to rape anyone therein (the crime with which D in *Collins* [1973] was charged). It is replaced with a new offence – 'trespass with intent to commit a sexual offence'. Under the new offence,

D is guilty if he trespasses on any premises with intent to commit a relevant sexual offence on the premises. D must know or be reckless as to the trespass. Note the following similarities and differences between the two offences:

- D must still be a trespasser (this is part of the *actus reus*), and must know, or be reckless whether, he is trespassing (this is part of the *mens rea*).

- There is no requirement that D 'enter' a 'building' or 'part of a building'. It is enough if he is trespassing 'on any premises'. The word 'premises' is not fully defined in the 2003 Act. Section 63(2) states that 'premise includes a structure or part of a structure', while 'structure' is defined as including a 'tent, vehicle or vessel or other temporary or movable structure'. This is clearly a wider concept than 'building'.

- There is no requirement that D intend to commit 'rape'. An intention to commit a 'relevant sexual offence' is sufficient. This refers to all the other offences in Part 1 of the 2003 Act, including rape (s.1), assault by penetration (s.2), sexual assault (s.3), sexual activity with a child (s.9), incest (ss.25, 64 and 65), exposure (s.66), voyeurism (s.67), sex with an animal (s.69) and sex with a corpse (s.70).

An example of the new trespass offence is *Fulton* (2006). V, a 60-year-old lady, answered a knock at her front door. She found D at the door; he forced his way into her hallway and said to her, 'Have you ever seen a man wank?' He then said, 'Please look', took his penis out and began masturbating. V was frightened but eventually managed to push D out of the door. D was convicted of trespass with intent to commit a sexual offence.

Summary

- There are two offences of burglary under s.9 of the Theft Act 1968.

- In either case, D must have entered a building or part of a building as a trespasser.

- Under s.9(1)(a), D must have entered with the intent to commit theft, criminal damage or grievous bodily harm. D must have formed the intent prior to entering (*Bennett*). A conditional intent will suffice (*Attorney-General's References [Nos. 1 and 2 of 1979]*).

- Under s.9(1)(b), D must have entered and then gone on to steal, inflict grievous bodily harm, attempted to steal or attempted to inflict grievous bodily harm.

- 'Entry' does not require that D get the whole of his body inside (*Collins*; *Brown*).

- 'Entry' is an issue simply left to the jury to decide (*Ryan*). It does not appear that the entry has to be either 'substantial' or effective' (*Ryan*).

- A 'part' of a building does not have to be a separate room. Whether D has entered a 'part' of a building is a jury question (*Walkington*).

- 'Trespass' means to enter a building or part of a building without the consent of the person in possession.

- D must trespass either knowingly or recklessly (*Collins*).

- D may have consent to enter but still be a trespasser if he exceeds that consent (*Jones and Smith*).

- Section 63(1) of the Sexual Offences Act 2003 replaces the type of burglary where D enters a building with intent to rape with a new offence of 'trespass with intent to commit a sexual offence'.

13   Criminal damage

Introduction

The 'offence' of criminal damage was introduced in 1971 to replace the old offence of malicious damage. There are really four main criminal damage offences: criminal damage, aggravated criminal damage, arson and aggravated arson.

- *Simple criminal damage* occurs if D intentionally or recklessly destroys or damages property belonging to another.

- *Aggravated criminal damage* occurs if D intentionally or recklessly destroys or damages their own or someone else's property, intending or being reckless whether life would thereby be endangered.

- *Arson* occurs if D intentionally or recklessly destroys or damages property, by fire.

- *Aggravated arson* occurs if D intentionally or recklessly destroys or damages property, by fire, intending or being reckless whether life would thereby be endangered.

Criminal damage

Criminal Damage Act 1971
1 (1) A person who without lawful excuse destroys or damages any property belonging to another intending to destroy or damage any such property or being reckless as to whether any such property would be destroyed or damaged shall be guilty of an offence.

'Destroys or damages'

This is a question of fact and degree. It includes physical harm, whether permanent or temporary, and the permanent or temporary impairment or usefulness of property. It may occur in many ways. One test would seem to be whether the owner of property is put to expense in cleaning or repairing the property (*Roe v Kingerlee* [1986], in which the Divisional Court held that mud smeared on the wall of a police station cell could, in law, amount to 'damage' to the wall). Thus, in *Hardman v Chief Constable of Avon and Somerset* (1986), drawing or painting on the pavement even with water-soluble chalks or paints was 'damage' because the local authority was put to expense in cleaning the pavement. But spitting on a policeman's coat does not constitute damage where the spittle can be removed with a damp cloth (*A (a juvenile) v R.* [1978]). However, if the policeman's coat had required dry-cleaning then spitting would have been damage.

The nature of the property may also be relevant. In *Morphitis v Salmon* (1990) the Divisional Court held that a scratch to a scaffolding bar could not constitute damage as it involved no impairment of its value or usefulness. But a scratch to the bonnet of a car would be damage as the owner would expect to have this repaired.

In *Fiak* (2005), D was convicted of criminal damage after stuffing a blanket down a toilet whilst being held in a prison cell (on suspicion of assaulting a police officer) and flushing it repeatedly. He appealed on the basis that, as the water was clean, both the blanket and the cell floor would dry and would therefore be undamaged. However, the Court of Appeal upheld his conviction, applying *Morphitis v Salmon*. The court held that the 'simple reality' was that the blanket could not be used until it had been dried and the flooded cell was out of action until the water had been cleared. Both had sustained damage for the purposes of the Criminal Damage Act 1971.

Alteration, tampering, etc.

Property can be damaged where it is simply tampered with, or parts are removed from it, especially if the property is machinery so that it no longer works. Where D has removed parts from a machine he should be charged with damaging the machine, not the parts, unless they have also been damaged.

Damage to computer programs

The Computer Misuse Act 1990, s.3(6), provides that 'For the purposes of the Criminal Damage Act 1971 a modification of the contents of a computer shall not be regarded as damaging any computer or computer storage medium unless its effect on that computer or computer storage medium impairs its physical condition'. Instead, a new offence of 'unauthorised modification of computer material' has been created by s.3(1) of the 1990 Act.

'Property'

Criminal Damage Act 1971
10 (1) In this Act 'property' means property of a tangible nature, whether real or personal, including money and –

> *(a) including wild creatures which have been tamed or are ordinarily kept in captivity, and any other wild creatures or their carcasses if, but only if, they have been reduced into possession which has not been lost or abandoned or are in the course of being reduced into possession; but*
> *(b) not including mushrooms growing wild on any land or flowers, fruit or foliage of a plant growing wild on any land.*

This is similar to the definition of property in s.4 of the Theft Act 1968, with some differences. First, land cannot be stolen, though it can, and often is (especially arson to buildings) damaged. Second, wild plants and flowers cannot be damaged but they can, in certain circumstances, be stolen. Third, property in the 1971 Act is confined to tangible property.

In *Cresswell and Currie v DPP* (2006), the High Court explained the meaning of 'reduced into possession' in s.10(1)(a). The Court stated that:

> Merely to entice a wild animal, whether it be a badger or a game bird or a deer, to a particular spot from time to time by providing food there, even with the objective ultimately of killing it in due course, does not form part of a course normally of reducing it into possession.

Cresswell and Currie v DPP (2006)
One night, Fiona Cresswell and Donald Currie destroyed four badger traps set by the government Department for Environment, Food and Rural Affairs (DEFRA) on a farm in Cornwall. The defendants were charged with criminal damage to the traps but claimed that they were acting in order to protect other property – the wild badgers – from being caught and later killed (DEFRA was researching suspected links between wild badgers and bovine tuberculosis, a disease affecting cattle). If this argument was accepted it would provide the defendants with a lawful excuse, under s.5(2)(b) of the 1971 Act (see below). This depended on the court accepting that the wild badgers were also 'property', which in turn required the court to accept that they were being 'reduced into possession' by DEFRA by trying to trap them. This argument was rejected. The Court held that the badgers were not being 'reduced into possession' until they actually entered a set trap.

'Belonging to another'
S.10(2) of the 1971 Act provides that property belongs to another if that person has:

• custody or control of it; or

- has any proprietary right or interest in it; or

- has a charge on it.

It is possible for D to commit criminal damage of property which he actually owns if V has a proprietary interest in it. Suppose D hires his car to V but tampers with the engine; this may be criminal damage as V has a proprietary interest in the car.

'Intention'

Under s.1(1) it must be proved that D intended to damage property belonging to another. If D honestly intended to damage their own property, but mistakenly damaged V's, then that is insufficient for liability. In *Smith* (1974), D, the tenant in a flat, damaged certain fixtures that he had installed when removing wiring for his stereo equipment. He believed that the fixtures belonged to him, when in law they had become the property of the landlord. His conviction was quashed because he did not intend to 'damage property belonging to another'.

'Recklessness'

See Chapter 3.

Aggravated criminal damage

Criminal Damage Act 1971
1 (2) A person who without lawful excuse destroys or damages any property, whether belonging to himself or another –

(a) intending to destroy or damage any property or being reckless as to whether any property would be destroyed or damaged; and
(b) intending by the destruction or damage to endanger the life of another or being reckless as to whether the life of another would be thereby endangered;

shall be guilty of an offence.

Professor Sir John Smith criticised the inclusion of the aggravated offence because it introduced *an offence against the person* into the Criminal Damage Act 1971, a statute designed to deal with offences against property. The decision in *Merrick* (1995) illustrates this point. In that case, D was convicted of aggravated criminal damage when, in removing old electrical equipment, he left live wires exposed for about six minutes. The Court of Appeal held that this created a risk of endangering life, and D had been reckless with respect to that risk. If D had left live wires exposed when installing new equipment, there would be no offence, because there would have been no damage! Yet the dangerous situation is exactly the same. Surely, both situations should be illegal (i.e. an offence of creation of danger to life, for example), or neither.

Actus reus

This is largely the same as for criminal damage, although the property may belong to D himself. If D, frustrated that his car will not start, starts shooting at it with a rifle, being reckless as to whether anyone might get hit by flying glass or metal, he might be liable under s.1(2).

No requirement that life be endangered in fact

The fact that lives were not, in fact, endangered is irrelevant if it was D's intention to endanger life or, more likely, that he was reckless whether life would be endangered. In *Sangha* (1988), D, who had been drinking all day, set fire to a mattress and two chairs in his neighbour's flat in Southall. The flat, which was gutted, was unoccupied at the time. Moreover, the block itself was of a particular design, such that the occupants of neighbouring flats were not, in fact, endangered. When charged under s.1(2), D argued that this meant he was not reckless as to whether life would be endangered. However, the Court of Appeal upheld his conviction. Tucker J said that the fact that there were 'special features' which prevented a risk of death from materialising was 'irrelevant'.

Mens rea

he Crown must prove that D's state of mind was one of the following:

- *intent* to damage property, and *intent* by that damage to endanger the life of another; or

- *intent* to damage property, and *recklessness* as to whether life would thereby be endangered; or

- *recklessness* as to whether property would be damaged, and *recklessness* as to whether life would thereby be endangered.

D must intend that, or be reckless whether, life would be endangered by the damage that they cause, not by the means employed to cause the damage. This point was established in *Steer* (1988). D had fired a rifle through V's bungalow window. His conviction of aggravated criminal damage was quashed – it had not been proven that he had been reckless whether lives would be endangered by the damage, i.e. by shards of broken glass flying around, as opposed to being endangered by the act which caused the damage, namely the bullets.

Steer was distinguished in two Court of Appeal cases heard in 1995, *Webster, Asquith and Seamans* and *Warwick*. In the former case, the three defendants pushed a heavy stone from the parapet of a railway bridge onto the roof of a passenger train, showering the passengers with debris; in the latter case D had thrown bricks at a police car from a stolen car, smashing the rear window and showering the officers with broken glass. In both cases the court decided that the defendants had been reckless whether lives would be endangered by the damage they had caused and upheld their convictions.

> D drops a brick from a motorway flyover onto the windscreen of a car travelling at 70mph in the middle lane. The brick hits the passenger side of the windscreen and shatters it; the brick lands on the passenger seat. The driver, who was alone in the car, swerves in shock but manages to avoid hitting other cars and eventually regains control, moves over onto the hard shoulder and stops. If D is charged with aggravated criminal damage, would you convict him?

'Without lawful excuse'

There are two 'lawful excuses' contained in s.5(2) of the 1971 Act.

• Belief in consent (s.5(2)(a))

• Belief that other property was in immediate need of protection (s.5(2)(b))

S.5(3) states that 'it is immaterial whether a belief is justified or not, provided it is honestly held'. It need not be a reasonable belief – though the more unreasonable the belief, the more likely that D will simply not be believed. However, if D's belief was the result of extreme intoxication, it will nevertheless provide them with a good excuse under s.5(2). Indeed, in *Jaggard v Dickinson* (1980), the court accepted a defence under s.5(2)(a) based on a drunken belief that would in all probability never have been accepted had D been sober at the time. Once D has adduced evidence of lawful excuse, the onus is on the prosecution to disprove it.

Belief in consent: s.5(2)(a)

Under s.5(2)(a), D has a lawful excuse if, at the time of the alleged criminal damage they believed that the person(s) 'whom he believed to be entitled to consent to the destruction of or damage' – not necessarily the owner – either:

- had so consented; or

- would have done so if they had known of the destruction or damage and its circumstances.

If D honestly believes that the owner of property (or some other person entitled to give consent) has consented to their damaging property, then no offence of criminal damage is committed. In *Denton* (1982), D, a cotton mill worker, thought that his employer had asked him to set fire to the mill and the machinery in order to make a fraudulent insurance claim. One evening D entered the mill and set fire to the machinery, and caused £40,000 damage. The Court of Appeal quashed his conviction, applying s.5(2)(a).

The 'person entitled to consent' must be a human being or corporate body. In *Blake v DPP* (1993), D, a vicar, had been convicted of criminal damage. Using a marker-pen he wrote a Biblical quotation on a concrete pillar at the Houses of Parliament, as part of a protest against the use of military force in Kuwait and Iraq. In his defence he claimed to be carrying out the instructions of God, and so had a lawful excuse under s.5(2)(a). This meant that God was the person entitled to consent to the damage of property. This defence was rejected and D's conviction was confirmed.

Belief that other property was in immediate need of protection: s.5(2)(b)

D is not guilty of criminal damage if they destroyed or damaged property 'in order to protect property belonging to himself or another', provided they believed that:

- the other property was 'in immediate need of protection'; and

- the means of protection adopted were 'reasonable having regard to all the circumstances'.

In order to protect property

It is for the court to determine whether, as a matter of law, D's purpose was to protect property. If D has some ulterior motive other than protecting their or another's property then this defence will not be available. In *Hunt* (1978), D, who assisted his wife in her post as deputy warden of a block of old people's flats, set light to some bedding in order, he claimed, to draw attention to the state of a defective fire alarm. The judge withdrew the defence; this was upheld in the Court of Appeal. The act was not done to protect property.

The case of *Hill* (1988) provides a good illustration of the application of s.5(2)(b). The Court of Appeal held that the correct approach was to decide whether it could be said, as a matter of law, on the facts believed by D, that the damage or destruction had been done in order to protect property or a right or interest in property.

> *Hill* (1988)
> Valerie Hill was a member of CND (the Campaign for Nuclear Disarmament). She claimed that, by cutting the fence surrounding the US naval base at Brawdy, a strategic military target, she was protecting her nearby home from blast-damage or radiation fall-out in the event of a Russian nuclear missile strike on the base. If enough people cut the fence and irritated the Americans enough they might move the base somewhere else. However, she was convicted and the Court of Appeal dismissed her appeal, holding that her purpose was not to protect her property but to get the US navy out.

In *Blake v DPP* (1993), above, D also claimed he was damaging government property in order to protect the property of others (i.e. civilians in Kuwait and Iraq). This was also rejected. D's damage was not capable of protecting property in those countries.

In April 2000, a criminal damage case was brought against Lord Melchett, a director of Greenpeace, and several members of that organisation, accusing them of damaging genetically modified (GM) crops in a Norfolk field. They did not deny the damage but relied upon s.5(2)(b), claiming that the damage was done in order to protect non-GM crops in neighbouring fields from contamination with airborne GM pollen. The judge at Norwich Crown Court allowed the defence to go to the jury, but the jury was unable to agree on a verdict and a retrial was ordered. At the retrial, the new jury acquitted.

Hill was followed in *Kelleher* (2003). The Court of Appeal in this case again decided that the property allegedly in need of protection was far too remote from the property which D damaged for him to be able to rely upon the defence.

> *Kelleher* (2003)
> D went to the Guildhall Gallery, in London, armed with a cricket bat which he used to try to knock the head off a statue of Lady Thatcher, the former Prime Minister. This was unsuccessful but he tried again using a metal stanchion used to support the rope around the statue. This time he was successful. The statue was damaged beyond repair and D was charged with £150,000 worth of criminal

damage. He did not deny the damage but claimed he had a lawful excuse – he claimed to have 'strong and sincerely felt concerns' about certain policies of the USA, the UK and other western countries which, he claimed, were 'leading the world towards its eventual destruction'. In particular, he was concerned about the threat of globalisation, and 'prevailing materialistic values and the influence which major corporations seem to be able to exercise over supposedly democratic governments'. By destroying Thatcher's statue he hoped to raise public awareness of his views, which might make the world a safer place. The trial judge ruled that this belief – however genuine – did not raise the defence as there was no specific property that D could believe was in need of immediate protection. The jury convicted and the Court of Appeal upheld his conviction.

The adoption of an objective test for this question is odd: how can a purpose be anything other than subjective? The position should be that if D honestly believed they were protecting their or another's property, s.5(2)(b) should apply (subject to the two questions below). The fact that, objectively, their chosen methods are incapable of achieving their purpose is, really, irrelevant.

D must believe that they are acting in order to protect 'property'. If D is acting in order to protect human life, for example, they are not covered by the Act. In *Baker and Wilkins* (1997), B and W were charged with causing criminal damage to the door of a house, in which they believed B's daughter was being held, in order to rescue her. On appeal against conviction they argued s.5(2)(b), unsuccessfully.

Belief that property was in immediate need of protection
It is up to D to provide evidence that they held this belief, and for the prosecution to disprove that they held it. While D's beliefs may be (objectively) wholly unreasonable, this is not fatal to the defence; but the more unreasonable D's beliefs appear, the less likely it is that the court will believe them.

D must adduce evidence that they believed the other property was in *immediate* need of protection. In *Hill* (1988), above, D was forced to admit that she did not expect a nuclear bomb 'to fall today, or tomorrow', which clearly counted against her.

Belief that the means adopted were reasonable having regard to all the circumstances
In *Hill* (1988), the Court of Appeal held that the test is whether, on the facts as D believed them to be, the measures taken could be said,

objectively, to amount to something reasonably done to protect D's property or some right or interest of his in property. That is, it is not for D to say that he thought the means adopted were reasonable but whether the court thinks that they were.

No application to the aggravated offence

The provisions of s.5(2) do not apply to aggravated criminal damage. Thus, the fact that D believes that he has consent, or believes other property is in immediate need of protection, is irrelevant if D damages or destroys property intending to be or being reckless whether life be endangered.

Arson and aggravated arson

Criminal Damage Act 1971
1 (3) An offence committed under this section by destroying or damaging property by fire shall be charged as arson.

Actus reus

For arson there must be some damage or destruction 'by fire'. The damage need not be severe. It would be sufficient that wood was charred, or that some material was singed. However, it would seem that blackening property by smoke would be insufficient, as there is no damage or destruction 'by fire'.

Mens rea

To be liable for arson, D must intend to destroy or damage property, or be reckless whether property is destroyed or damaged, by fire. Similarly, to be liable for aggravated arson, D must intend to endanger life, or be reckless whether life be endangered, by fire.

Summary

- There are four main criminal damage offences: criminal damage, aggravated criminal damage, arson and aggravated arson. There are also related offences of threatening criminal damage and possessing anything with intent to commit criminal damage.

- Damage is defined very widely – property is damaged if the owner of property is put to expense in cleaning or repairing it (*Roe v Kingerlee*).

- With the aggravated offence, D must intend to be or be reckless whether life be endangered by the damage itself, not by the means of causing the damage (*Steer*; *Webster*; *Asquith and Seamans*; *Warwick*).

- There is no requirement that anyone's life be endangered in fact (*Sangha*).

- Two defences of lawful excuse are available – but only if D is charged with criminal damage, not aggravated criminal damage.

- D may have a defence to criminal damage if he honestly believed that he had consent to damage or destroy property (*Denton*).

- D may have a defence to criminal damage if he did it in order to protect other property provided he honestly believed that the other property was in immediate need of protection, and that the means adopted to do so were reasonable.

- Whether D acted in order to protect other property is a question of law (*Hunt*; *Hill*).

Questions on Part 4 Offences against property

1 Fred is often forgetful. He draws his weekly pension from the post office and is overpaid £10 by the cashier. Fred thinks his pension must have been increased but meets his friend Jim who tells him there has, in fact, been no increase. Fred goes to his local supermarket and spends the extra £10 buying lottery tickets. While shopping he absent-mindedly places a small bottle of whisky in his coat pocket. At the checkout he only pays for the items in his shopping trolley.

   On his way home Fred sees some apples growing in a residential garden. He leans into the garden, picks three apples and puts them in his basket. Feeling tired, he sits down on a bench in the park where he falls asleep. John, a passer-by, sees the apples in Fred's basket, takes one and eats it.

   When he gets home Fred discovers the whisky in his pocket but decides to keep it.

   Discuss the liability of Fred and John for theft.

   (OCR 2007)

2 Hugh and Keith, who are both aged 18, are cocaine addicts sharing a squat. They frequently steal goods which they sell to finance their habit. Hugh knows that his father, Colin, has put a mountain bike in the shed at the top of his garden saying that he doesn't use it any more. One night, Hugh sneaks round to his father's house and takes the bike with a view to selling it. Keith drinks half a bottle of whisky and, while Hugh is out, searches through Hugh's jacket intending to take any money he might find. He doesn't find any so he drinks the rest of the bottle of whisky and walks down to the local supermarket. There he places several items inside his coat unaware that Aziza, a store

detective, is watching him. As soon as he passes the cash till without paying for any of the items Aziza stops him. Keith pushes Aziza aside causing her to fall and bruise her arm. Keith then runs out of the store.

Advise Hugh and Keith of their criminal liability.

(OCR 2000)

3   Graham goes to his favourite corner store. In the shop he places some items of food in the wire shopping basket that is provided for shoppers. He also hides a small bottle of whisky in his coat pocket. Next, he takes a label from the case of a high-priced CD that is in the charts and switches it with the label from a specially reduced CD on the shelf below and places it in the basket. He then goes to the checkout and only pays for the items in the basket.

Outside the shop Graham sees a mountain bike that was there when he went in and which he also remembers seeing there at the same time the previous week. He rides home on it alongside a canal. On the way he notices a personal CD player on a table on board a canal longboat that is moored to the towpath. He climbs aboard and takes the CD player. He leaves the bike leaning against a fence at the end of his road and goes home.

Discuss Graham's criminal liability.

(OCR 2004)

Part 5

Defences

General introduction

This Part of the book deals in detail with those defences that are often termed 'general defences'. We have already seen that there are special and partial defences that may be raised on a murder charge and that the defence of consent has specific relevance to offences against the person. In addition, s.2 of the Theft Act provides the so-called 'partial dishonesty defences' which may allow a jury to conclude that a defendant on a charge of theft has not acted in a dishonest manner when appropriating property belonging to another.

Lest this should appear confusing, the following chart may assist in clarifying when particular defences may be raised in the context of various offences.

Figure 4 Table showing the relationship between offences/defences

Offence	Duress	Diminished responsibility	Provocation	Automatism	Insanity	Intox	Self defence
				Defence			
Murder	no defence	guilty of voluntary manslaughter	guilty of voluntary manslaughter	acquittal	special verdict hospital	guilty of involuntary manslaughter	acquittal
Involuntary manslaughter	acquittal	no	no	acquittal	special verdict discretion	no defence	acquittal
s.18	acquittal	no	no	acquittal	special verdict discretion	guilty of s.20	acquittal
s.20, s.47 and battery	acquittal	no	no	acquittal	special verdict discretion	no defence	acquittal

14 Intoxication

Introduction

Beginning on a Sunday morning and continuing until Monday night, Robert Majewski went on a 36-hour drugs and drink marathon. Over that time he consumed a combination of barbiturates, amphetamines (speed), and alcohol. On the Monday evening he got involved in a pub brawl and assaulted a customer, the manager and several police officers sent to deal with him. He was eventually arrested and charged with three offences of assault occasioning actual bodily harm and three offences of assaulting a police officer in the execution of his duty. His defence was that he was suffering from the effects of the alcohol and drugs at the time. He claimed that he was intoxicated, that this prevented him from foreseeing the consequences of his actions, that he was not, therefore, reckless in the *Cunningham* sense, and hence not guilty.

Would you allow him a defence?

Although Robert Majewski's intake of intoxicants was fairly extreme, hundreds if not thousands of people get involved in drink- and/or drug-related violence every week. Everyone knows that alcohol and other intoxicants affect our ability to think clearly and coolly, to react appropriately in certain situations. Alcohol is described as a 'depressant'. This does not mean that it makes you depressed! But it does 'depress' your inhibitions and other, more sophisticated, brain functions. If alcohol and/or drugs were to be allowed as a defence to crimes such as assault, rape and criminal damage (on the basis that it prevented D from foreseeing the consequences of his or her actions), then a very dangerous message would be sent out: basically, the more intoxicated you get, the stronger your potential defence! Unsurprisingly, therefore, the law does not allow intoxication as a general defence.

In *DPP v Majewski* (1977), D was convicted of all charges after the trial judge directed the jury that they should ignore the effect of drink and drugs. Effectively they were told to look at what he did and convict him if satisfied that he would have had the necessary *mens rea* had he been completely sober. The Court of Appeal and House of Lords upheld his convictions.

Legal principle *vs* public policy

Intoxication is not a true defence, like duress: it is no excuse for D to say that they would not have acted as they did but for their intoxication. Instead, it is a means of putting doubt into the minds of the jury as to whether D formed the necessary *mens rea*. Alcohol and many other drugs – barbiturates, amphetamines (speed and 'E'), hallucinogens (LSD), tranquillisers – all have an influence on a person's perception, judgment and self-control, and their ability to foresee the consequences of their actions. In extreme cases, D may be so drunk that they are rendered an automaton.

Generally, if enough members of the jury form a reasonable doubt as to D's *mens rea* then they are required to acquit. This creates a dilemma for the law. Application of legal principle would mean that the more intoxicated D became, the better their chances of acquittal. Policy demands the opposite. The law has tried to achieve a compromise, but perhaps inevitably it is policy that has prevailed.

D's intoxication must be extreme in order to prevent them from foreseeing *any* of the consequences of their actions. Lord Simon in *DPP v Majewski*, however, was not convinced that matters should be left entirely to the jury. He thought that, without special rules for intoxicated defendants, the public would be 'legally unprotected from unprovoked violence where such violence was the consequence of drink or drugs having obliterated the capacity of the perpetrator to know what he was doing or what were its consequences'.

Of course the criminal law should seek to protect the public from violence. But surely the number of cases where D might escape conviction – if the matter were simply left to the jury – would be very few. The approach of the leading courts in New Zealand (*Kamipeli* [1975]) and Australia (*O'Connor* [1980]) has been to leave the question of D's intoxication to the jury in all cases. The result has not been a proliferation of acquittals.

As well as protecting the public, the law must protect the rights of the individual, including D. However, this issue did not unduly trouble Lord Elwyn-Jones LC in *DPP v Majewski*. His attitude was that those who caused harm while intoxicated should not be allowed to go unpunished. He said, 'If a man of his own volition takes a substance which causes him to cast off the restraints of reason and conscience, no harm is done by holding him answerable criminally for any harm he may do while in that condition.'

The evidential burden

D is required to adduce evidence of intoxication before the matter becomes a live issue. The question of whether D's intoxication is sufficient is a question of law for the judge. In *Groark* (1999), D had, apparently, consumed 10 pints of beer before striking V in the face with a 'knuckleduster'. He was charged with wounding with intent to do GBH under s.18 OAPA. At trial he gave evidence that he had known what he was doing but that he had acted in self-defence. The judge, therefore, did not direct the jury as to intoxication and D was convicted of the s.18 offence. The Court of Appeal dismissed his appeal: because D had not raised the defence, then there was no obligation on the judge to do so.

> Compare the approach of the Court of Appeal in *Groark* (1999) with that of the same court in *Rossiter* (1994), which was considered in Chapter 6. Both cases involved defendants pleading self-defence (as a tactical move, hoping for an acquittal) but having that defence rejected and appealing against their convictions. Rossiter's appeal was successful because the judge should have directed the jury on provocation; Groark's appeal was dismissed. But why? If there is an obligation on the judge to direct the jury on provocation, why not on intoxication?

Voluntary intoxication

The present law is comparatively lenient. Until the mid-nineteenth century, voluntary intoxication was not regarded as any form of defence at all. But as time passed the courts began to relax the strict approach. In *DPP v Beard* (1920), Lord Birkenhead considered the situation where D pleaded intoxication to deny malice aforethought, the *mens rea* for murder. He concluded that, if D was rendered incapable of forming the intent to kill or cause GBH, then he would not be guilty of murder, but would be guilty of manslaughter. He emphasised that intoxication was merely a means of demonstrating that D lacked, on a particular charge, the mental element necessary:

> Where a specific intent is an essential element in the offence, evidence of a state of drunkenness rendering the accused incapable of forming such an intent should be taken into consideration in order to determine whether he had in fact formed the intent necessary to constitute the particular crime.

This principle has remained largely unchanged since, though it is now firmly accepted that D need not be incapable of forming intent; it is sufficient if they do not in fact do so. Conversely, D may be very drunk indeed and yet still form the *mens rea* required. According to *Sheehan* (1975), where D raises intoxication in an attempt to show lack of *mens rea*, the jury should be directed as follows:

The mere fact that the defendant's mind was affected by drink so that he acted in a way in which he would not have done had he been sober does not assist him at all, provided that the necessary intention was there. A drunken intent is nevertheless an intent.

This was essentially the outcome in *Groark*, above. Indeed, the cases where any defendant has successfully avoided conviction on account of intoxication are very rare.

A more recent example of 'drunken intent' is *Heard* (2007). D had been charged with sexual assault, under s.3 of the Sexual Offences Act 2003. This requires, among other things, that D touch V 'intentionally'. D did not deny touching V but argued that it was unintentional; he asked that evidence of intoxication be taken into account to support his argument. However, the trial judge ruled that D's behaviour demonstrated that the touching was intentional (despite evidence of D being intoxicated) and therefore D had no defence. The Court of Appeal agreed.

Heard (2007)

The police had been called to Lee Heard's house where he was found in an 'emotional state'. He was obviously drunk and had cut himself, and so the police took him to hospital. There, he became abusive and began singing and was taken outside to avoid disturbing others. Shortly afterwards, he 'began to dance suggestively' in front of one of the policemen. He then 'undid his trousers, took his penis in his hand and rubbed it up and down' the policeman's thigh. At that point he was arrested. The next day, after he had sobered up, he claimed to be unable to remember what had happened but did accept that when he was ill or drunk he sometimes might 'go silly and start stripping'. D was charged with and convicted of intentional sexual touching, and the Court of Appeal upheld his conviction. Hughes LJ said, 'On the evidence the appellant plainly did intend to touch the policeman with his penis.'

Basic and specific intent

In *Beard* Lord Birkenhead used the expression 'specific intent'. By this he meant that where a particular crime required a particular intent to be proven, then the case was not made out until that proof was achieved. At no point did Lord Birkenhead refer to anything called 'basic intent'. Nevertheless, his analysis was developed into a legal doctrine, according to which crimes divide into two categories. In *Bratty* (1963), Lord Denning said,

If the drunken man is so drunk that he does not know what he is doing, he has a defence to any charge, such as murder or wounding with intent, in which a specific intent is essential, but he is still liable to be convicted of manslaughter or unlawful wounding for which no specific intent is necessary, see *Beard*'s case.

In *DPP v Majewski* (1977), Lord Elwyn-Jones LC said that 'self-induced intoxication, however gross and even if it has produced a condition akin to ... automatism, cannot excuse crimes of basic intent such as ... assault'. One objection to the denial of the intoxication defence in basic intent crimes is based on s.8 of the Criminal Justice Act 1967. This statutory provision requires juries, when deciding whether D was reckless, to consider 'all the evidence' before deciding whether D foresaw the results of their actions. However, in *DPP v Majewski*, Lord Elwyn-Jones LC dismissed this argument. He said that when s.8 refers to 'all the evidence' it means only 'all the relevant evidence'. Because intoxication was irrelevant as far as basic intent crimes are concerned, then evidence of intoxication was also irrelevant.

Do you agree with Lord Elwyn-Jones on this point?

Distinguishing basic and specific intent offences

DPP v Majewski, then, confirms the distinction between crimes of specific and basic intent. However, it does not tell us which offences belong in which category. One explanation that was rejected in *Majewski* is the 'fallback' argument. This would limit specific intent crimes to those where D, were he to be acquitted because of intoxication, would convict himself only of some lesser offence of basic intent. Many specific intent offences do have this fallback; to use the examples given by Lord Denning in *Bratty*, murder has the fallback of manslaughter, wounding with intent has the fallback of unlawful wounding. However, some specific intent crimes, like theft, do not have a fallback crime. Instead, the approach that has prevailed is that:

• specific intent crimes can only be committed intentionally

• basic intent crimes may be committed recklessly.

In *Caldwell* (1982), Lord Diplock stated that 'self-induced intoxication is no defence to a crime in which recklessness is enough to constitute the necessary *mens rea*'. The courts have now assigned most crimes to one category or another, as follows.

Crimes of specific intent

- Murder

- Wounding or causing GBH with intent (s.18 OAPA)

- Theft

- Robbery

- Burglary

- Attempts

Crimes of basic intent

- Manslaughter (involuntary)

- Wounding or inflicting GBH (s.20 OAPA)

- ABH (s.47 OAPA)

- Assault and battery

- Sexual assault (s.3 Sexual Offences Act 2003)

- Criminal damage

Heard (2007), the facts of which were given above, demonstrates a different approach to the task of deciding whether an offence is one of 'specific' or 'basic' intent. The Court of Appeal concluded that the offence of sexual assault in s.3 of the Sexual Offences Act 2003 is one of basic intent, despite the fact that s.3 requires proof that D touched V 'intentionally'. This appears to contradict the explanation (in *Caldwell*, above) of specific and basic intent offences, so it is necessary to explore this important judgment carefully. It seems clear that the Court of Appeal wanted, for policy reasons, to classify the offence of sexual assault as one of *basic* intent, to ensure that drunken defendants could not use intoxication as an excuse. The problem is the requirement in s.3 of the word 'intentionally', which normally indicates a crime of *specific* intent. According to Hughes LJ in the Court of Appeal, 'The first thing to say is that it should not be supposed that every offence can be categorised *simply* as either one of specific intent or of basic intent ... The offence of sexual assault, with which this case is concerned, is an example.' He went on:

It is necessary to go back to *Majewski* in order to see the basis for the distinction there upheld between crimes of basic and of specific intent. It is to be found most clearly in the speech of Lord Simon. [His] analysis was that crimes of specific intent are those where the offence requires proof of purpose or consequence, which are not confined to, but amongst which are included, those where the purpose goes beyond the *actus reus*. We regard this as the best explanation of the sometimes elusive distinction between specific and basic intent . . . By that test, element (a) (the touching) in sexual assault is an element requiring no more than basic intent. It follows that voluntary intoxication cannot be relied upon to negate that intent.

Therefore, *Heard* provides an alternative definition of 'specific' intent: where the prosecution must prove some 'purpose' on the part of D which 'goes beyond the *actus reus*'. Using this test, sexual assault is basic intent because D's purpose (touching V) does not 'go beyond' the *actus reus* (which is also touching V). Some examples of a specific intent crime using this test are:

- theft, where D's 'purpose' must be to permanently deprive V of their property (whereas permanent deprivation in fact is not part of the *actus reus* of theft);

- burglary, under s.9(1)(a) of the Theft Act 1968, where D's 'purpose' is to steal, commit unlawful damage or grievous bodily harm, but the *actus reus* is simply entering a building as a trespasser.

On the other hand, under the 'purpose' test, murder is not specific intent because D's purpose (V's death) does not go beyond the *actus reus* (which is, of course, V's death). Nor would causing GBH with intent under s.18 OAPA 1861, because again D's purpose (causing GBH) and the *actus reus* (causing GBH) are exactly the same. That would be an extraordinary result of the *Heard* judgment (it would also contradict the decisions in *Beard* and *Lipman*, where murder was held to be a crime of specific intent). It is therefore submitted that the *Heard* 'purpose' test is designed to supplement, but not replace, the traditional test set out in *Caldwell*, above.

To recap: the question that arose in *Heard* was whether the offence of sexual assault in s.3 of the Sexual Offences Act 2003 is one of specific intent because the offence requires proof of 'intent' as opposed to 'recklessness'. The Court of Appeal answered that question 'No'. This decision has implications for other offences in the Sexual Offences Act 2003, in particular rape (s.1) and assault by penetration (s.2), both of which require D to 'intentionally' penetrate V. Although the offence in s.2 is new, rape is not, and there is caselaw pre-dating the 2003 Act which establishes that rape is a crime of basic intent (*Fotheringham* [1988], discussed in Chapter 17, below). However, the definition of rape prior to the 2003 Act included the word 'reckless' as part of the *mens rea* whereas the new definition of rape in the 2003 Act does not. So has the re-definition of rape in the 2003 Act converted the offence from basic to specific intent? As yet, there have been no cases dealing with this point but, it is submitted, the answer must be 'No', based both on public policy arguments (protecting the public from drunken rapists) and the decision in *Heard*.

The fact that the law surrounding the distinction between basic and specific intent remains unclear means that cases are still reaching the appeal courts involving arguments about whether a particular offence is 'specific' or not. For example, in *Carroll v DPP* (2009), D tried to persuade the High Court that the offence of being drunk and disorderly in a public place, contrary to s.91 of the Criminal Justice Act 1967, was an offence of 'specific intent' and therefore intoxication would provide a good defence. This was on the basis that he was so drunk that he had not intended to be 'disorderly'. Unsurprisingly, the court rejected his argument, holding that there was no requirement of *mens rea* at all relating to disorderly behaviour (in other words, liability was strict).

Intoxication and basic intent offences

Although it is clear that intoxication is not a defence to a 'basic intent' crime, it is not so clear what exactly happens if D does plead intoxication as a defence to such a crime. There are some passages in *DPP v Majewski* that suggest that D will be automatically guilty, merely because he committed the *actus reus* of a basic intent offence whilst drunk. That is, his intoxication substitutes for the *mens rea* of the offence; his intoxication is conclusive proof that he was reckless. For example, Lord Elwyn-Jones LC said that when D reduced himself to an intoxicated condition this

> supplies the evidence of *mens rea*, of guilty mind certainly sufficient for crimes of basic intent. It is a reckless course of conduct and recklessness is enough to constitute the necessary *mens rea* in assault cases . . . The drunkenness is itself an intrinsic, an integral part of the crime.

The other Law Lords either agreed or made speeches to the same effect. However, in other cases, the courts have adopted a softer approach. According to the Court of Appeal in *Richardson and Irwin* (1999), merely committing the *actus reus* of a basic intent offence whilst intoxicated should not simply invite an automatic conviction.

Richardson & Irwin (1999)

D, E and V were all students at Surrey University. One night, after drinking about five pints of lager each, they returned to D's accommodation and began indulging in 'horseplay' – something the group did regularly – during the course of which V was lifted over the edge of a balcony and dropped about 10 feet, suffering injury. D and E were charged with inflicting GBH. The prosecution case was that they had foreseen a risk that dropping V from the balcony might cause him harm but, nevertheless, took that risk. Their defence was that V had consented to the horseplay and/or that his fall was an accident. The jury was directed to consider each man's foresight of the consequences on the basis of what a reasonable, sober man would have foreseen. D and E were convicted but the Court of Appeal quashed the convictions. The question was *not* what the reasonable, sober man would have foreseen, but what these particular men *would have foreseen had they not been drinking.* Clarke LJ, showing commendable insight into modern student psychology, said that 'the defendants were not hypothetical reasonable men, but University students'.

Thus, the rule in 'basic intent' crimes appears to be that the jury should be directed to assume that D was sober, and assess what D would have foreseen in that condition. They should not consider what the reasonable man would have foreseen. Of course this is still a hypothetical question, but it is better (from the defence point of view) than the suggestions in *DPP v Majewski* that simply being drunk is automatically reckless.

Involuntary intoxication

The *Majewski* rules apply only where D was *voluntarily* intoxicated. The rules are relaxed when D becomes intoxicated without his knowledge or against his wishes. D is not entitled to be automatically acquitted but is entitled to have the evidence of intoxication considered, even where the offence is one of basic intent. If the intoxication negatives *mens rea* he is entitled to an acquittal but, if not, he remains liable, even though he would not have acted as he did had he remained sober.

In *Kingston* (1995), the House of Lords confirmed this proposition after the Court of Appeal had cast doubt upon it. The Court of Appeal had allowed D's appeal against a conviction of indecent assault contrary to s.14 of the Sexual Offences Act 1956 (a basic intent offence) on the basis that it was not his fault that he had become drunk. Academic reaction to this approach was mixed (to put it mildly). In the end the House of Lords reversed the decision of the Court of Appeal and restored the conviction.

Kingston (1995)

Barry Kingston, 48, was known to have paedophiliac and homosexual tendencies. Kevin Penn, who had been hired by former business associates of Kingston, blackmailed him. P had lured a 15-year-old boy to his flat and drugged him. While the boy was asleep, P invited K to abuse him. This he did, and P photographed and tape-recorded him doing it. K claimed that he could remember nothing about the night's events, and it appeared that P may have drugged his coffee. K was convicted of indecent assault, following a direction that the jury could convict if sure that, despite the effect of any drugs, he had still formed the *mens rea* of indecent assault. The Court of Appeal quashed the conviction but, following the Crown's appeal, the House of Lords restored the conviction.

Note that the offence of indecent assault has now been abolished and replaced with sexual assault under s.3 of the Sexual Offences Act 2003 (the offence with which D in *Heard* [2007] was convicted).

There are four main situations where D's intoxication will be treated as involuntary, namely where the intoxicating substance was:

● taken under medical prescription; or

● commonly known to have a 'soporific or sedative' effect; or

● taken by D without his knowledge; or

● taken under duress.

Where any one of these is the case, then D will be entitled to have his evidence of intoxication considered, even where the crime is one of 'basic intent'.

Drugs taken under medical prescription

In *Bailey* (1983), the Court of Appeal held that there was a distinction between intoxication arising from consumption of alcohol and 'certain sorts of drugs to excess', on one hand, and intoxication arising from the unexpected side-effects of therapeutic substances, on the other. Griffiths LJ said, 'The question in each case will be whether the prosecution have proved the necessary element of recklessness.' If D knew that taking some medicine was 'likely to make him aggressive, unpredictable or uncontrolled' then it would be open to a jury to find him reckless and hence guilty.

Bailey (1983)

John Bailey, a diabetic, had struck his ex-girlfriend's new boyfriend over the head with an iron bar causing a 10-inch cut. He was charged with wounding (a basic intent offence). He said that he had taken insulin but failed to take food afterwards, which triggered a loss of consciousness and that he therefore had no *mens rea*. The trial judge directed the jury that, as his condition was self-inflicted, it was no defence, and they convicted. On appeal, the Court of Appeal held that the judge's direction was wrong. Provided it was not due to alcohol or drugs, intoxication *could* provide a defence to a crime of basic intent. The question was whether Bailey's conduct, in the light of his knowledge of the likely results of taking insulin but not eating afterwards, had been sufficiently reckless to establish the *mens rea* necessary for the offence.

'Soporific or sedative' drugs

The next situation involves drugs that do not have an inhibition-lowering (e.g. alcohol) or mind-expanding (e.g. LSD) effect, but instead have a 'soporific or sedative' effect. An example would be intoxication caused by tranquillisers. In such cases, the jury should again be directed to consider whether the taking of the drug was reckless. In *Hardie* (1985), D was depressed because his girlfriend had told him to move out of their flat. Before leaving, he took some of her Valium tablets. He returned to the flat that night and set fire to a wardrobe in the bedroom. He was charged with arson, but said that he did not know what he was doing because of the Valium. The jury was directed to ignore the effects of the tablets and they convicted. However, the Court of Appeal quashed the conviction. Parker LJ said:

> Valium is ... wholly different in kind from drugs which are liable to cause unpredictability or aggressiveness ... if the effect of a drug is merely soporific or sedative the taking of it, even in some excessive quantity, cannot in the ordinary way raise a conclusive presumption against the admission of proof of intoxication ... such as would be the case with alcoholic intoxication or incapacity or automatism resulting from the self-administration of dangerous drugs.

This implies that there *may* be situations where D realises that there is a risk that morphine or Valium, instead of soothing him or calming him down, might induce 'aggressive, unpredictable conduct'. If the jury thinks that such is the case, and that D went on to take that risk, he could be said to be reckless.

Lack of knowledge

Intoxication is involuntary when, for example, D's soft drink has been drugged or 'laced' without his knowledge, as in *Kingston* itself. It is imperative that D did not know that he was taking an intoxicating substance. It is no defence for D to claim that he did not know exactly what effect an intoxicating substance would have on him. Otherwise, people experimenting with drugs would be able to claim a defence. In *Allen* (1988), D was given some home-made wine, which he did not realise had a particularly high alcohol content. As a result he became extremely drunk and in that state carried out a serious sexual assault. He was convicted of buggery and indecent assault and the Court of Appeal upheld the convictions. There was no evidence that Allen's drinking was anything other than voluntary.

However, D may be able to rely upon a defence of involuntary intoxication when his drink is spiked with an entirely different type of intoxicant. In *Eatch* (1980), D had smoked a small amount of cannabis and then drunk a can of beer to which another, stronger drug had been added without his knowledge. The judge directed the jury that it was up to them to decide whether D's condition was 'due solely to voluntary intoxication'.

Intoxication under duress

Although the question has not been judicially considered in England, there is American authority for the proposition that 'intoxication under duress' should be regarded as involuntary.

'Dutch courage'

In *Attorney-General for Northern Ireland v Gallagher* (1963), D decided to kill his wife, bought a knife and a bottle of whisky, drank much of the whisky in order to provide himself with 'Dutch courage', then killed her with the knife. He was convicted of murder, the jury deciding that he had formed the specific intent for murder at the time of the stabbing, despite being drunk, and this was upheld by the House of Lords. Lord Denning, however, went on to consider, obviously *obiter*, what the outcome would have been if the jury had decided that D was too drunk to form the specific intent when he stabbed his wife. He concluded that D would not be entitled to a defence:

> If a man, whilst sane and sober, forms an intention to kill and makes preparation for it knowing it is a wrong thing to do, and then gets himself drunk so as to give himself Dutch courage to do the killing, and whilst drunk carries out his intention, he cannot rely on this self-induced drunkenness as a defence to murder, not even as reducing it to manslaughter.

Intoxication and other defences

Insanity

Where intoxication produces insanity as defined in the M'Naghten Rules (see Chapter 15) then those latter rules apply. In *Davis* (1881), where D claimed that a history of alcohol abuse had caused the disease called *delirium tremens*, and based his defence on insanity, Stephen J directed the jury that, 'Drunkenness is one thing and disease to which drunkenness leads are different things'. This was approved by the House of Lords in both *DPP v Beard* and *Gallagher*. Some American states allow an insanity defence where intoxication has produced temporary insanity.

Automatism

An act done in a state of (non-insane) automatism (see Chapter 16) will negative criminal liability *except* where the state is self-induced; this is most obviously the case where it is due to intoxication. In such cases the normal *DPP v Majewski* approach applies. *Lipman* (1970) is the clearest example of this. Robert Lipman and his girlfriend, Claudie Delbarre, had taken the hallucinogenic drug LSD before falling asleep in her flat. During the night Lipman went on a 'trip', where he thought he was at the centre of the Earth under attack from snakes. When he awoke, Claudie was dead. She had been strangled and had 8 inches of sheet stuffed into her mouth. Lipman was convicted of manslaughter, even though at the time of the killing he was an automaton, and the Court of Appeal confirmed the conviction. In *Sullivan* (1984), Lord Diplock stated that the defence of automatism did not apply when 'self-induced by consuming drink or drugs'.

Developments in Canada: the rule in Daviault

There has been a very interesting development in Canada in this area. The law relating to intoxication as a defence in Canada is essentially the same as in England, with crimes divided into specific intent and basic intent categories. However, in *Daviault* (1995) the Supreme Court of Canada held that a defence of intoxication could be available for a person charged with a basic intent offence, if the intoxication was so extreme as to have produced a state of automatism. The burden of proof would be on D to prove this automatism, on the balance of probabilities. The sort of extreme drunkenness required, for the new rule to apply, would obviously be very rare. Expert evidence would be required to confirm that D was probably in an automatic state. Having established this new rule, the Court quashed D's conviction of sexual assault and ordered a retrial. The trial judge had naturally ruled out evidence that D was intoxicated, although this was fairly extreme: he had consumed a bottle of brandy and several bottles of beer.

> Do you prefer the approach of the English Court of Appeal in *Lipman*, or that of the Canadian Supreme Court in *Daviault*, to self-induced automatism?

Diminished responsibility

The impact of intoxicants on the defence of diminished responsibility was considered in Chapter 6.

Mistake

The issue of intoxicated mistakes will be dealt with in Chapter 17.

Reform

In January 2009, the Law Commission (LC) published a Report entitled *Intoxication and Criminal Liability* (Law Com No. 314) including a draft Bill. In the Report, the LC makes a number of recommendations for reform of the intoxication defence. The key recommendations can be summarised as follows:

General points

- References to 'specific intent' and 'basic intent' should be abolished.

- The distinction between voluntary and involuntary intoxication should be retained.

- Where D relies on the intoxication defence (whether voluntary or involuntary), there should be a presumption that D was **not** intoxicated. Hence, D would have to produce evidence that he or she was intoxicated. This essentially confirms the present law, as set out in *Groark* (1999).

- However, if D is taken to have been intoxicated, there should then be a second presumption that D was voluntarily intoxicated. Therefore, if D contends that he or she was involuntarily intoxicated, D would have to prove this (albeit on the balance of probabilities). This is a completely new set of legal principles.

Voluntary intoxication

- There should be a 'general rule' that would apply when D is charged with an offence the *mens rea* of which is 'not an integral fault element'

– for example, if the *mens rea* 'merely requires proof of recklessness' – and D was voluntarily intoxicated at the time of allegedly committing it.

- The 'general rule' is that D should be treated as having been aware of anything which D would have been aware of but for the intoxication. This is an attempt to place on a statutory basis the principle set out in *Richardson and Irwin* (1999).

- Certain *mens rea* states – which the LC refers to as 'integral fault elements' – should be excluded from the 'general rule'. These are: intention, knowledge, belief (where that is equivalent to knowledge), fraud, and dishonesty.

- Thus, the 'general rule' would not apply to murder, wounding or causing GBH with intent (s.18 OAPA), theft, robbery and burglary (all of which require intent). In such cases, 'the prosecution should have to prove that D acted with that relevant state of mind'. This essentially confirms the present law, as set out in cases like *Beard* (1920) and *Lipman* (1970).

- D should **not** be able to rely on a genuine mistake of fact arising from voluntary intoxication in support of a defence, unless D would have held the same belief had he not been intoxicated. This is consistent with the Court of Appeal's stance on intoxicated mistakes in the context of self-defence in *O'Grady* (1987), *O'Connor* (1991) and *Hatton* (2005), all discussed in Chapter 19. But it would entail overruling the High Court's decision in *Jaggard v Dickinson* (1980), discussed in Chapter 13, involving intoxicated mistakes about whether the owner of property would consent to it being damaged.

Involuntary intoxication

- There should be 'a non-exhaustive list of situations which would count as involuntary intoxication'. The LC gives four examples, so that D would be involuntary intoxicated if they could prove (on the balance of probabilities) that they took an intoxicant:
  1. without consent (such as the spiking of soft drinks with alcohol);
  2. under duress;
  3. which they 'reasonably believed was not an intoxicant';
  4. for a 'proper medical purpose'.

- Where D was involuntarily intoxicated, then D's intoxication should be taken into account in deciding whether D acted with the requisite *mens rea*. This essentially confirms the present law, as set out in *Kingston* (1995).

237

- D should also be able to rely on a genuine mistake of fact arising from involuntary intoxication in support of a defence.

- The distinction drawn between 'dangerous' and 'soporific' drugs should be abolished – thus, if D became intoxicated having taken 'soporific' drugs such as Valium (unless 'for a proper medical purpose') then this would be classed as voluntary intoxication. This would entail overruling the Court of Appeal decision in *Hardie* (1985).

Summary

- With the defence of intoxication, two crucial distinctions must be made: between voluntary and involuntary intoxication, and between crimes of specific intent and basic intent.

- Involuntary intoxication is a defence to crimes of specific intent and basic intent (*Kingston*).

- Voluntary intoxication is a defence to a crime of specific intent (*Beard*; *Lipman*) but is never a defence to a crime of basic intent (*DPP v Majewski*).

- Voluntary intoxication means the consumption of alcohol and other drugs generally known to make people aggressive, unpredictable or uncontrolled ('dangerous' drugs).

- Involuntary intoxication occurs if D consumes an intoxicating substance under medical advice (*Bailey*), consumes an intoxicant commonly known to be 'soporific or sedative' (*Hardie*), does not know they are consuming an intoxicant, perhaps because their soft drink has been spiked (*Kingston*), or if they are forced into consuming it.

- When D pleads intoxication, whether voluntary or involuntary, they may still be convicted if, despite their intoxicated state, they formed the *mens rea* required (*Sheehan* – voluntary; *Kingston* – involuntary).

- Specific intent crimes are those that can only be committed intentionally – e.g. murder, wounding or causing GBH with intent, theft, robbery, burglary.

- Basic intent crimes are those that may be committed recklessly – e.g. manslaughter, malicious wounding, inflicting GBH, ABH, assault and battery, criminal damage.

- Sexual assault (*Heard*) and, probably, rape are also basic intent crimes despite the fact that neither can be committed recklessly.

- If D plans a specific intent crime but then becomes intoxicated so as to give themselves the 'Dutch courage' to commit it, they are still guilty of that specific intent crime (*Attorney-General for Northern Ireland v Gallagher*).

- Intoxication producing insanity is insanity (*Davis*) but intoxication producing automatism is still intoxication (*Lipman*).

Figure 5 Intoxication flowchart

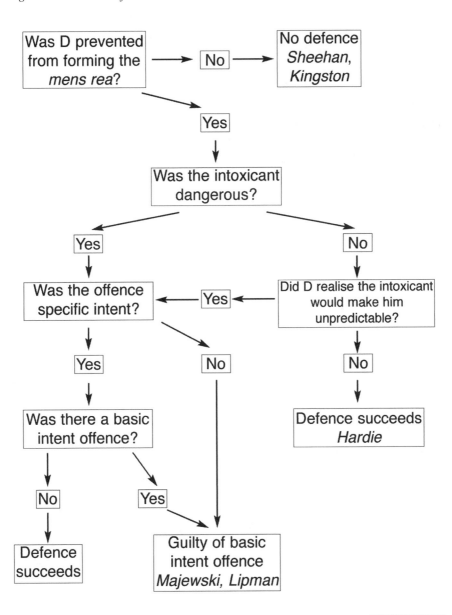

15   Insanity

Introduction

Despite everything that is written about the insanity defence, it is rarely used. Its importance had been much reduced, particularly in murder cases, by the abolition of the death penalty, and the introduction of the diminished responsibility defence.

The M'Naghten rules

The law of insanity in England is contained in the M'Naghten Rules, the result of the deliberations of the judges of the House of Lords in 1843. Media and public outcry at the acquittal of one Daniel M'Naghten led to the creation of the Rules as an attempt to clarify the defence. The joint opinion of 14 Law Lords is not binding as a matter of strict precedent. Nevertheless, the Rules have been treated as authoritative of the law ever since. The 'general part' of the Rules is as follows:

> *The jurors ought to be told in all cases that every man is presumed to be sane, and to possess a sufficient degree of reason to be responsible for his crimes, until the contrary be proved to their satisfaction; and that to establish a defence on the ground of insanity it must be clearly proved that, at the time of the committing of the act, the party accused was labouring under such a defect of reason, from disease of the mind, as not to know the nature and quality of the act he was doing, or, if he did know it, that he did not know he was doing what was wrong.*

M'Naghten (1843)
Daniel M'Naghten was charged with the murder of Sir Robert Peel's secretary, Edward Drummond. M'Naghten was described as 'an extreme paranoiac entangled in an elaborate system of delusions', which led him to believe he was being persecuted by the 'Tories', who were to blame for various personal and financial misfortunes. He had intended to murder Sir Robert himself. Medical witnesses testified that he was insane. The jury accepted his plea and found him not guilty on the grounds of insanity, though he was committed to Broadmoor (where he remained until his death 20 years later).

The Divisional Court has held that the defence is available only where *mens rea* is an element of the offence. In *DPP v H* (1997), D was charged with driving with excess alcohol – a strict liability offence. There was evidence that he was suffering 'manic depressive psychosis'. The magistrates acquitted him on insanity grounds. The prosecution appealed to the Divisional Court – where it was held that the magistrates should have convicted.

'Defect of reason'

The phrase 'defect of reason' implies that D's powers of reasoning must be impaired, as opposed to a failure by D to use those powers. In *Clarke* (1972), Ackner J said that the Rules apply only to 'persons who by reason of a "disease of the mind" are deprived of the power of reasoning. They do not apply and never have applied to those who retain the power of reasoning but who in moments of confusion or absent-mindedness fail to use their powers to the full'.

Clarke (1972)
May Clarke went into a supermarket. She selected three items, including a jar of mincemeat, and put them into her own bag. She left the store without paying for them and was charged with theft. She claimed to have lacked the *mens rea* of theft (the intention to permanently deprive) on the basis of absent-mindedness caused by diabetes and depression. She had no recollection of putting the items into her bag. She did not even want the mincemeat as neither she nor her husband ate it. The trial judge ruled that this amounted to a plea of insanity, at which point she pleaded guilty. On appeal, her conviction was quashed: she had not been deprived of her powers of reasoning but had simply failed to use them.

'Disease of the mind'

'Disease of the mind' is a legal, not a medical, term. In *Kemp* (1957), D made an entirely motiveless and irrational attack on his wife with a hammer. He was charged with inflicting grievous bodily harm. He was suffering from arteriosclerosis, or hardening of the arteries, causing a congestion of blood on the brain. This produced a temporary loss of consciousness, during which time D attacked. He admitted that he was suffering a 'defect of reason', but argued that this did not arise from a 'disease of the mind'. He argued that arteriosclerosis was a physical, as opposed to mental, disease. A physical disease which caused the brain cells to deteriorate would be a disease of the mind but, until that happened, his condition was a temporary interference with the working of the brain, comparable with concussion. Therefore, the true defence was automatism entitling him to an acquittal. Devlin J, rejecting this argument, held that:

> The law is not concerned with the brain but with the mind, in the sense that 'mind' is ordinarily used, the mental faculties of reason, memory and understanding. If one read for 'disease of the mind' 'disease of the brain', it would follow that in many cases pleas of insanity would not be established because it could not be proved that the brain had been affected in any way, either by degeneration of the cells or in any other way. In my judgment the condition of the brain is irrelevant and so is the question whether the condition is curable or incurable, transitory or permanent.

Sane and insane automatism

The law draws a distinction between two causes of automatism:

- Automatism caused by a 'disease of the mind' (insane automatism). Here the M'Naghten Rules apply, and the verdict should be one of not guilty by reason of insanity.

- Automatism *not* caused by a 'disease of the mind' (sane automatism). Here the verdict is an acquittal – unless D's condition was self-inflicted, e.g. by drink or drugs, as in *Lipman* (1970).

The question of whether D's condition is sane or insane automatism is one of law for the judge (*Bratty* [1963]). Judges base their decision on medical evidence. However, because disease of the mind is a legal concept, judges will also take account of policy. There have been two distinct approaches:

- The continuing danger theory, which says that any condition likely to present a recurring danger to the public should be treated as insanity;

- The external cause theory, which says that conditions stemming from the psychological or emotional makeup of the accused, rather than from some external factor, should lead to a finding of insanity.

The two theories are clearly closely linked and overlap to a considerable degree: an internal cause is more likely to recur than an external one. The continuing danger theory was the test used by English courts until 1973. Although the external cause theory was introduced into English law from New Zealand as a qualification to that test, it has since developed into a test in its own right. This has had unhappy consequences, particularly for sleepwalkers.

The continuing danger theory

The leading authority is the House of Lords case of *Bratty* (1963). D had killed an 18-year-old girl by removing one of her stockings and strangling her with it. When arrested he did not deny doing it but said that 'something terrible came over me . . . I had some terrible feeling and then a sort of blackness'. He claimed that it happened during an epileptic seizure. The trial judge ruled that this amounted to an insanity plea; the House of Lords upheld this. Lord Denning said:

> It seems to me that any mental disorder which has manifested itself in violence and is prone to recur is a 'disease of the mind'.

Lord Denning approved *Kemp* (1957) but disapproved of the earlier case of *Charlson* (1955). There, D had hit his 10-year-old son on the head with a hammer and thrown him into a river. D was charged with various offences including inflicting grievous bodily harm. Medical evidence suggested that he was suffering from a cerebral tumour that left him liable to motiveless outbursts of impulsive violence over which he would have no control. The jury acquitted after the judge directed them to consider only automatism. Under Lord Denning's direction, above, D would have been found not guilty by reason of insanity.

The converse of Lord Denning's test should not be taken to represent the law. Thus, even where there is no danger of recurrence, a condition may still amount to a disease of the mind. In *Burgess* (1991), Lord Lane CJ said that 'a danger of recurrence may be an added reason for categorising the condition as a disease of the mind' but it was not a prerequisite. Thus, the greater the likelihood of recurrence, the more likely a condition will be treated as a disease of the mind; but presence or otherwise of recurrence is not conclusive.

The first automatism case to reach the House of Lords after *Bratty* was *Sullivan* (1984). Lord Diplock, like Lord Denning before him, suggested a test based upon the likelihood of recurrence. He said that it was irrelevant whether the source of D's defect of reason was 'organic, as in epilepsy, or functional, or whether the impairment itself is permanent or is transient and intermittent, provided that it subsisted at the time of the commission of the act'.

Sullivan (1984)
Patrick Sullivan had suffered from epilepsy since childhood. He had been known to have fits and to show aggressiveness to anyone coming to his aid. One day he was sitting in a neighbour's flat with a friend of his, Mr Payne, aged 80. The next thing he remembered

243

was standing by a window; Mr Payne was on the floor, injured. Sullivan was charged with assault. The judge ruled that his plea of automatism, based upon an epileptic seizure, amounted to a 'disease of the mind'. To avoid hospitalisation, Sullivan pleaded guilty. This was accepted and the Court of Appeal and House of Lords rejected his appeals against conviction.

The external factor theory

In 1973, the Court of Appeal adopted the external factor theory, first used by the New Zealand Court of Appeal in *Cottle* (1958). This theory was not designed to replace the recurring danger theory but to complement it. Simply put, if a disorder is internal to D, then there is a greater chance of recurrence. In *Quick* (1973), Lawton L said:

> A malfunctioning of the mind of transitory effect caused by the application to the body of some external factor such as violence, drugs, including anaesthetics, alcohol and hypnotic influences cannot fairly be said to be due to disease.

In *Sullivan*, Lord Diplock also gave his support to the external factor theory. He agreed that sane automatism might be available 'in cases where temporary impairment results from some external physical factor such as a blow on the head causing concussion or the administration of an anaesthetic for therapeutic purposes'. In *Hennessy* (1989), Lord Lane CJ confirmed both the external factor and recurrent danger theories. D claimed to be having marital problems that left him suffering stress, anxiety and depression. These, he argued, were external causes. Lord Lane CJ rejected the argument. He said that 'stress, anxiety and depression . . . constitute a state of mind which is prone to recur. They lack the feature of novelty or accident, which is the basis of the distinction drawn by Lord Diplock in *Sullivan*'. The external factor theory has also been approved by the Supreme Court of Canada (*Rabey* [1980]).

Applying the law

In *Quick*, Lawton LJ said that 'it seems to us that the law should not give the words "defect of reason from disease of the mind" a meaning which would be regarded with incredulity outside a court'. How has this *dictum* been applied in practice?

Epilepsy

Epilepsy is a functional disease of the brain, characterised by seizures. It affects several hundred thousand people in the UK. Yet, in both *Bratty* and *Sullivan*, the House of Lords held that epileptics were legally insane.

Diabetes

Diabetes is a disorder of the pancreas, which results in erratic quantities of the insulin hormone being produced. Injections of insulin are needed to control the body's blood-sugar level. If the blood-sugar level gets too high or too low, a seizure may result. There are two types of diabetic seizure, which may eventually lead to a loss of consciousness. Prior to the onset of coma, however, the sufferer may become uncontrollably aggressive and violent. The two seizure types are:

- *Hypoglycaemia* (low blood-sugar), caused by taking too much insulin or by taking insulin and failing to eat afterwards;

- *Hyperglycaemia* (high blood-sugar), caused by failing to take any or enough insulin.

In the cases of *Quick* (1973) and *Hennessy* (1989), each defendant was a diabetic.

Quick (1973)
William Quick, a nurse at a mental hospital, had taken his insulin one morning but had eaten little afterwards. That afternoon he attacked a patient, causing him two black eyes, a fractured nose, a split lip and bruising. Another nurse found Quick sitting astride the patient, glassy-eyed and apparently unable to talk. He pleaded not guilty to assault; he had suffered a hypoglycaemic episode and could not remember what he had done. The judge ruled that this was a plea of insanity. Quick pleaded guilty and appealed. The Court of Appeal quashed his conviction. The cause of his automatic state was not his diabetes, but his insulin; as this was an external factor, automatism should have been left to the jury.

Hennessy (1989)
Andrew Hennessy was seen getting into a car, which had earlier been reported stolen, and driving away. He was charged with taking a motor vehicle without consent and driving while disqualified. In court, he said that he had not taken his insulin for three days, had suffered a hyperglycaemic episode, and did not remember taking the car. The judge ruled that his plea amounted to insanity. Hennessy pleaded guilty and appealed. The Court of Appeal, however, upheld his conviction. Since it was the diabetes that had caused his automatic state, the judge had been correct to rule that his defence had been insanity.

This creates a highly anomalous situation. One diabetic, who falls into a hypoglycaemic state is setting up automatism and should be acquitted (*Quick*); another diabetic, who falls into a hyperglycaemic state, must be treated as pleading insanity (*Hennessy*). If only to achieve consistency, any form of diabetic seizure should be regarded as a disease of the mind. It is a mental disorder that is prone to recur. The strange distinction has occurred because of the emphasis placed upon the external factor theory in *Quick*. It is not the theory itself which is wrong, but the application of it. What really caused Quick's automatic state? The insulin was a cause – but the *underlying* cause was his diabetes. In 1973, when *Quick* was decided, those found insane faced indefinite hospitalisation. Perhaps Lawton LJ was reluctant to say that an epileptic was insane and send him to Broadmoor. But in 1991, compulsory hospitalisation was abolished (for all cases except murder). It is time to recognise that *Quick* was wrongly decided.

Somnambulism

Somnambulism or sleepwalking is a sleep disorder, very common in children but also found in about 2 per cent of adults. For a long time acts committed whilst asleep were treated as raising sane automatism. However, the position has changed, as a result of the courts' emphasis, since *Quick* and *Sullivan*, on the external factor theory. In *Burgess* (1991), Lord Lane CJ said that sleepwalking was 'an abnormality or disorder, albeit transitory, due to an internal factor'.

Burgess (1991)
One evening, Barry Burgess and Katrina Curtis were in Burgess' flat watching videos. They both dozed off, and during the night he attacked her while she slept, hitting her with a wine bottle and the video recorder – which he had unplugged – and then grasping her by the throat. She suffered cuts to her head. To a charge of unlawful wounding, Burgess pleaded automatism on the basis that he had been sleepwalking. The trial judge ruled he was pleading insanity and the jury returned the special verdict. The Court of Appeal dismissed his appeal.

The Supreme Court of Canada, in *Parks* (1992), took a very different view. D had got up in the middle of the night, dressed, got into his car and then drove 15 miles to the home of his in-laws where he stabbed and killed his mother-in-law and severely injured his father-in-law. Throughout this whole sequence of events he was, apparently, sleepwalking. He was charged with murder and attempted murder. At his trial, the judge left automatism to the jury, who acquitted on all charges. The Supreme Court upheld these acquittals. The leading judge held that 'accepting the medical evidence, the respondent's mind and its functioning must have been impaired at the relevant time but sleepwalking did not impair it. The cause was the natural condition, sleep.'

Another judge pointed out that the external cause theory was 'meant to be used only as an analytical tool, and not as an all-encompassing methodology'. Sleepwalking was not suited to analysis under the external cause theory. 'The particular amalgam of stress, excessive exercise, sleep deprivation and sudden noises in the night that causes an incident of somnambulism is, for the sleeping person, analogous to the effect of concussion upon a waking person, which is generally accepted as an external cause of non-insane automatism.'

Hence, leading courts in England and Canada have found totally different solutions to the same problem! That is not to say that one case must be right and the other wrong: there are distinguishing features. In *Parks*, there was evidence that D was under considerable pressure and stress at work, which may have triggered his sleepwalking. The implication is that, when those stresses were removed, he would not repeat his actions, i.e. there was less evidence that he might repeat his behaviour.

Dissociation

Dissociative states are medically classified as 'hysterical neuroses'. The most prominent feature is a 'narrowing' of the field of consciousness, commonly accompanied or followed by amnesia. There may be dramatic, but temporary, personality changes. A 'fugue' – wandering state – is also possible. The body remains capable of carrying out complex, purposive actions. The condition is brought on by psychological reasons, such as overwhelming emotion. The leading cases on this problem come from overseas: Canada and Australia.

In *Rabey* (1977), D had developed an attraction towards a girl. When he discovered that she regarded him as 'nothing', he hit her over the head with a rock and began to choke her. He was charged with causing bodily harm, and pleaded automatism, based on dissociation. He argued that the dissociative state was a psychological blow, akin to being physically struck on the head, and hence not a disease of the mind. The trial judge ordered an acquittal but the Ontario Court of Appeal allowed the prosecution appeal. The judge said that the 'ordinary stresses and disappointments of life which are the common lot of mankind do not constitute an external cause ... the dissociative state must be considered as having its source primarily in [D's] psychological or emotional make-up'.

Note here that Lord Denning's test in *Bratty* is satisfied: where D has such a fragile personality that everyday situations are liable to make them violent, then the likelihood of recurrence is high. In *Burgess* (1991), considered above, the Crown psychologist suggested that D had not been sleepwalking at all, but had fallen into a dissociative state caused by emotional trauma (he was in love with the unfortunate Miss Curtis). The Court of Appeal, like the Canadian court in *Rabey*, thought that even if this was so, the defence was still insanity: the disappointment or frustration caused by unrequited love was not to be equated with something like concussion.

In *Rabey*, the judge referred to the 'ordinary stresses ... of life'. The position, presumably, is different when there is an *extraordinary* stress. The shock of seeing a loved one murdered, for example, could cause a dissociative state in anyone. Consequently, where an event is deemed, objectively, to be extraordinary, then this qualifies it as an external cause entitling D to an acquittal. This seems to be the explanation of the decisions in *T* (1990) and *Falconer* (1990), considered in Chapter 16. In *Falconer*, the High Court of Australia distinguished mental states which 'may be experienced by normal persons', from those which are 'never experienced by or encountered in normal persons'. The former implies sane automatism, the latter insanity. Rather than concentrating exclusively on whether the cause was internal or external, the Court suggested a radical, new distinction, between the reaction of:

- a sound mind to external stimuli including stress (sane automatism); and

- an unsound mind to its own delusions or to external stimuli (insane automatism).

Rabey was followed by the Supreme Court of Canada in *Stone* (1999), where D pleaded automatism to the murder of his wife. D's evidence was that he had experienced a 'whoosh sensation' washing over him after his wife had insulted him, during which he stabbed her 47 times. The trial judge held that, if anything, this was a defence of insanity. D was convicted of manslaughter and appealed. The Supreme Court held that the trial judge was correct. Bastarache J said that 'evidence of an *extremely shocking trigger* will be required to establish that a normal person might have reacted to the trigger by entering an automatistic state, as the accused claims to have done'.

'Disease of the mind': a summary

On the whole, the courts in England have restricted the automatism defence. The defendant who pleads automatism based on epilepsy, diabetes or even sleepwalking faces being labelled as insane. This is perhaps justifiable where D has committed acts of violence. Yet not all the cases have involved violence, for example *Hennessy* (though it must be conceded that *Hennessy* was a danger to the public, driving in his condition).

Arguably, the label of insanity should not extend beyond those who, although they do not realise what they are doing, carry out acts of a violent or dangerous nature. This would cover offenders like Bratty and Burgess, who were acting in a purposive manner. On the other hand, *Sullivan*, who happened to strike someone while thrashing around during an epileptic fit, was not so acting. *Sullivan* seems to enjoy the 'feature of novelty or accident' which characterises automatism. The courts have not made such a distinction, but it would provide justice without jeopardising the policy of social protection.

Until recently, the insanity verdict meant indefinite hospitalisation, and left defendants like Quick, Sullivan and Hennessy pleading guilty to offences when all the evidence pointed to a total lack of *mens rea*. With the Criminal Procedure (Insanity and Unfitness to Plead) Act 1991 relaxing the restrictions available to the judge as to disposal following the special verdict, the insanity defence becomes a more realistic prospect. Nevertheless there remains the stigma of being labelled insane. A new verdict is long overdue. Clause 35 of the Law Commission's Criminal Code Bill (1989) contains such a verdict – 'mental disorder'.

'Nature and quality of the act'

For this limb of the defence to work, D must not know the 'nature and quality' of their act as a result of their 'defect of reason'. Two examples often used are:

- D cuts a woman's throat under the delusion that they are cutting a loaf of bread;

- D chops off a sleeping man's head because they have the deluded idea that it would be great fun to see the man looking for it when he wakes up.

In both examples, D has killed someone but is not guilty of murder by reason of insanity. Although D lacks *mens rea* (they did not intend to kill or cause GBH), because this lack of *mens rea* is due to a 'disease of the mind', they are not entitled to an acquittal but the special verdict instead. If, on the other hand, D kills a man whom D believes, because of some paranoid delusion, to be stalking them, then D is still responsible for their act because their delusion has not prevented them from understanding that they are committing murder.

'Wrong'

If D claims he did not realise that what he was doing was 'wrong', what exactly does that mean? 'Wrong' is an ambiguous concept. It could mean:

- Legally wrong (Option 1); or

- Morally wrong (Option 2); or

- Both legally and morally wrong (Option 3); or

- Either legally or morally wrong (Option 4)

In M'Naghten, the Lords seemed to support Option 1, when they said that D was sane 'if he knew . . . that he was acting contrary to law; by which expression we . . . mean the law of the land'. However, they foresaw a problem with that: if a jury was to be directed 'solely and exclusively' with reference to 'the law of the land', this might confuse a jury into thinking that ignorance of the law was a defence, when it is not. So, the Lords concluded that 'if the accused was conscious that the act was one which he ought not to do, and if that act was at the same time contrary to the law of the land, he is punishable'. This seemed to indicate Option 3. Then, in *Codere* (1916), the Court of Criminal Appeal stated that D would be denied the defence if he knew his act was wrong 'according to the ordinary standard adopted by reasonable men'. This indicated that Option 2 was correct. This confusing and contradictory mess was finally resolved by the Court of Criminal Appeal in *Windle* (1952), when they supported Option 1. Lord Goddard CJ said that 'there is no doubt that . . . "wrong" means contrary to the law'.

> *Windle (1952)*
> Windle was unhappily married to a woman, some 18 years his senior, who was always speaking of committing suicide and who, according to medical evidence at the trial, was certifiably insane. Eventually he killed his wife by giving her 100 aspirins. On giving himself up to the police, Windle said, 'I suppose they will hang me for this?' Despite medical evidence that he was suffering from a form of communicated insanity known as *folie à deux*, both sides agreed that this statement showed he was aware of acting unlawfully. The defence was withdrawn from the jury, Windle was convicted of murder. The Court of Criminal Appeal upheld the conviction.

If the facts of *Windle* occurred now, what defence (other than insanity) would you advise him to plead?

In *Johnson* (2007), the Court of Appeal was invited to reconsider the decision in *Windle*. However, although the court agreed that the decision in *Windle* was 'strict', they felt unable to depart from it, believing that if the law was to be changed it should be done so by Parliament. Latham LJ stated:

> The strict position at the moment remains as stated in *Windle* ... This area, however, is a notorious area for debate and quite rightly so. There is room for reconsideration of rules and, in particular, rules which have their genesis in the early years of the 19th century. But it does not seem to us that that debate is a debate which can properly take place before us at this level in this case.

Johnson (2007)

D suffered from delusions and auditory hallucinations. One day, armed with a large kitchen knife, he forced his way into V's flat and stabbed him four times (fortunately, V recovered). Following his arrest, D was assessed by two psychiatrists who diagnosed him as suffering from paranoid schizophrenia. They agreed that D knew that his actions were against the law; however, one psychiatrist asserted that D did not consider what he had done to be 'wrong in the moral sense'. The trial judge declined to leave the insanity defence to the jury, and D was convicted of wounding with intent. He appealed, but the Court of Appeal upheld his conviction.

The position therefore is: Option 1. If D did not realise his act was illegal then he is entitled to the special verdict. If D knew his act was illegal, then he is guilty. This is the case even if D is suffering from delusions which cause him to believe that his act was morally right.

Suppose D believes his mother is possessed and being tortured by demons. He has enough of a grasp on reality to realise that killing her is the crime of murder, but is nevertheless convinced that to do so would be 'right', in the moral sense of the word. He tries to kill her but fails to do so. If charged with attempted murder (where there is no diminished responsibility defence) should he be guilty or have the defence of insanity?

In Australia and Canada, meanwhile, the highest courts have refused to follow *Windle* and decided that morality, and not legality, is the concept behind the use of 'wrong'; that is, Option 2 (*Stapleton* [1952] – High Court of Australia; *Chaulk* [1990] – Supreme Court of Canada). Finally, in Northern Ireland, the defence of insanity is available if the defendant is prevented from appreciating that what they are doing is either morally wrong or illegal: that is, Option 4.

> What should 'wrong' mean – legally, morally, either or both?

The presumption of sanity

If D wishes to raise the insanity defence he must do more than simply introduce evidence to that effect and invite the prosecution to rebut it. Instead the defence are required to prove that D was insane, albeit on a balance of probabilities. This proposition stems from M'Naghten itself. It was confirmed in the celebrated case of *Woolmington v DPP* (1935), where Viscount Sankey said:

> Throughout the web of the English Criminal Law one golden thread is always to be seen, that it is the duty of the prosecution to prove the prisoner's guilt subject to . . . the defence of insanity.

However, just because the courts have adopted a presumption of sanity does not explain *why* the legal burden of proving D's insanity lies on D. A presumption of sanity need mean no more than that D bears a burden of introducing evidence of insanity, sufficient to raise a reasonable doubt. This is the position with other defences, such as provocation and duress. But remember that in diminished responsibility the burden of proof is also on D.

'Irresistible impulses'

Until the early twentieth century, a plea of 'irresistible impulse', that D was physically unable to control his actions, was a good defence. However, in *Kopsch* (1925), the law was changed. Lord Hewart CJ described the irresistible impulse argument as a 'fantastic theory' which, if it were to become part of the law, 'would be merely subversive'. The reluctance of the courts to recognise a defence of irresistible impulse is based on two grounds:

• the difficulty of distinguishing between an impulse caused by a disease of the mind, and one motivated by greed, jealousy or revenge

• the view that the harder an impulse is to resist, the greater is the need for a deterrent.

In 1953, the Royal Commission on Capital Punishment suggested adding a third limb to the M'Naghten Rules, that D should be considered insane if at the time of his act he 'was incapable of preventing himself from committing it'. Although this was not taken up, the Commission report led to the introduction of the diminished responsibility defence; this, in turn, has allowed the irresistible impulse defence into murder (*Byrne* [1960]).

In the United States, irresistible impulse defences are accepted. The American Law Institute's Model Penal Code (not unlike the Law Commission's Criminal Code Bill [1989], except that this has been converted into legislation in many states) includes a defence of insanity. This is available if, as a result of mental disease or defect, D lacks 'substantial capacity' either to appreciate the criminality/wrongfulness of his conduct or to 'conform his conduct to the requirements of law'. This version of the defence was widely adopted at one time but, in the immediate aftermath of the attempted assassination of President Reagan by John Hinckley in 1982, the American Congress passed the Insanity Defense Reform Act 1984. This removed the irresistible impulse defence in cases where D was charged with federal crimes.

The special verdict

If D is found to have been insane then the jury should return a verdict of 'not guilty by reason of insanity' (s.1, Criminal Procedure (Insanity) Act 1964), otherwise referred to as the *special verdict*. Until quite recently this verdict obliged the judge to order D to be detained indefinitely in a mental hospital. In many cases the dual prospect of being labelled 'insane' and indefinite detention in a special hospital such as Broadmoor discouraged defendants from putting their mental health in issue. In some cases it led to guilty pleas to offences of which defendants were probably innocent, and relying on the judge's discretion as to sentence (*Quick*; *Sullivan*; *Hennessy*). The prevailing attitude prior to 1991 was that the special verdict was the 'psychiatric equivalent of a life sentence' (Dell, *Wanted: An Insanity Defence that can be Used* [1983]). This was, clearly, an extremely unsatisfactory state of affairs that required reform.

The 1991 reforms

The position described above was modified by the Criminal Procedure (Insanity and Unfitness to Plead) Act 1991. The Act made a number of changes but, most significantly, substituted a new s.5 into the Criminal Procedure (Insanity) Act 1964. The new section allowed the judge considerable discretion with regard to disposal on a special verdict being returned. That section has since been replaced by another version of s.5 following the enactment of the Domestic Violence, Crime and Victims Act 2004. Now, following a special verdict, the judge may make either:

- a Hospital Order, with or without restrictions;

- a Supervision Order; or

- absolute Discharge. This is particularly useful where the offence is trivial and/or the offender does not require treatment.

Nevertheless, neither the 1991 Act nor the 2004 Act tackle the definition of insanity, and so the stigma of being labelled 'insane' remains.

The special verdict and murder

For those defendants charged with murder the position is unchanged; D found not guilty of murder by reason of insanity must be hospitalised indefinitely. Of course, the vast majority of defendants charged with murder plead diminished responsibility instead. One advantage of doing so is that if D is hospitalised, following conviction for manslaughter, he is entitled to be discharged by a Mental Health Review Tribunal once it is satisfied that he is no longer mentally disordered. But, if D is hospitalised following a special verdict, then his release is entirely at the discretion of the Home Secretary. On the other hand, the trial judge may impose a term of imprisonment following a manslaughter conviction, and potentially this could be a life sentence.

Procedure

Often D does not specifically raise the defence of insanity, but places the state of his mind in issue by raising another defence such as automatism. The question whether such a defence, or a denial of *mens rea*, really amounts to the defence of insanity is a question of law to be decided by the judge on the basis of medical evidence. Whether D, or his medical witnesses, would call it insanity or not is irrelevant.

Importance of medical evidence

If the judge decides the evidence does support the defence, then it should be left to the jury to determine whether D was insane. S.1 of the 1991 Act provides that a jury shall not return a special verdict except on the written or oral evidence of two or more registered medical practitioners, at least one of whom being approved as having special expertise in the field of medical disorder.

The jury must act upon the evidence before them. If this points towards D being insane, but they nevertheless convict, then such a conviction may be overturned on the ground that no reasonable jury could have reached such a verdict. But, if there is evidence to the contrary, then a jury verdict will not be quashed simply because there was medical evidence supporting the defence.

Reform

Writing about the M'Naghten Rules, the academic N. Morris commented in 1953:

> As a rigid, precise definition of a defence to a criminal charge they are woolly, semantically confused, psychologically immature nonsense

[but] as a means whereby juries work rough justice in a difficult peripheral area of law and morality they are reasonably satisfactory. ('"Wrong" in the M'Naghten Rules', 16 MLR 435.)

Various criticisms that can be made about the M'Naghten Rules include:

- The word 'insanity' is itself inappropriate in many cases and stigmatising in all of them. The Butler Committee and, more recently, the Law Commission's Criminal Code Bill (1989), at least recommend a change to 'mental disorder' – defined broadly so as to include mental illness, arrested or incomplete development of mind, and psychopathic disorders. This change has also been effected in Canada.

- The defence is based on a legal definition of insanity, not a medical one. 'Disease of the mind' is a meaningless concept to any psychiatrist.

- The over-reliance on the external factor test produces bizarre abnormalities (*Quick*; *Hennessy*). It means that diabetics (sometimes), epileptics and sleepwalkers are legally, but not medically, insane.

- The emphasis on legality in deciding whether D knew his acts were 'wrong' is inappropriate and too narrow.

- There is no irresistible impulse defence.

Summary

- Insanity is subject to the M'Naghten Rules from 1843.

- Everyone is presumed to be sane. With insanity, D must prove all the elements of the defence, on the balance of probabilities.

- The result of a successful defence is the 'special verdict'. Apart from murder cases, which means indefinite hospitalisation, the judge can impose a variety of orders.

- D must be suffering a 'defect of reason'. This means being deprived of the power of reason, not simply failing to use it (*Clarke*).

- The 'defect of reason' must be the result of a 'disease of the mind'. This is a legal, not a medical, term. Whether D has such a disease is a question of law for the judge (*Bratty*).

- In determining whether D had a 'disease of the mind', judges use two tests: whether or not the disease is prone to recur (*Bratty*) and whether it was caused by an internal or external factor (*Quick*; *Sullivan*).

- Thus, epileptics (*Sullivan*) and sleepwalkers (*Burgess*) are insane. Diabetics who fail to take insulin are also insane (*Hennessy*). But diabetics who take too much insulin are not (*Quick*). People who suffer a dissociative state caused by emotional trauma are probably insane (*Rabey*; *Burgess*) – unless the trauma was extraordinary (*T*; *Falconer*).

- If D is suffering a disease of the mind, he must be prevented from knowing the 'nature and quality' of his act or that it was 'wrong'.

- 'Wrong' means legally, as opposed to morally, wrong (*Windle*; *Johnson*).

- There is no irresistible impulse defence.

16   Automatism

Introduction

In *Bratty v Attorney-General for Northern Ireland* (1963), Lord Denning said that 'the requirement that (the act of the accused) should be a voluntary act is essential ... in every criminal case. No act is punishable if it is done involuntarily.' The classic example of this is when A grabs B's hand, in which B happens to be holding a knife, and plunges the knife into C. Although B 'stabbed' C, he is excused liability. Not only does B have no *mens rea*, he also has the defence of automatism. Voluntariness is an essential element of the *actus reus*.

What is 'automatism'?

'Automatism' is a phrase that was brought into the law from the medical world. There it has a very limited meaning, describing the state of unconsciousness suffered by certain epileptics. In law it seems to have two meanings. In *Bratty*, Lord Denning said:

> Automatism ... means an act which is done by the muscles without any control by the mind such as a spasm, a reflex action or a convulsion; or an act done by a person who is not conscious of what he is doing such as an act done whilst suffering from concussion or whilst sleepwalking.

Mental capacity is presumed. Hence, if D wishes to plead automatism, it is necessary for him to place evidence in support of his plea before the court. In *Hill v Baxter* (1958), Devlin J explained the reasoning behind this rule. He pointed out how 'unreasonable' it would be if in every single criminal case the Crown had to prove that D was 'not sleepwalking or not in a trance or black-out'. He concluded that 'such matters ought not to be considered at all until the defence has provided at least *prima facie* evidence' that D's acts were involuntary. The evidence of D himself will rarely be sufficient, unless it is supported by medical or other evidence, because otherwise there is a possibility of the jury being deceived by spurious or fraudulent claims. It is insufficient for D simply to say, 'I had a black-out' because that was 'one of the first refuges of a guilty conscience and a popular excuse', according to Lord Denning in *Bratty* (1963). More recently, in *C* (2007), Moses LJ in the Court of Appeal said that 'it is a crucial principle in cases such as this that D cannot rely on the defence of automatism without providing some evidence of it'.

Examples of automatism

Over the years, the courts have given a number of examples of possible causes of automatism:

- severe blows to the head

- hypnotism

- the administration of anaesthetic

- being attacked by a swarm of bees (the famous *hypothetical* example given in *Hill v Baxter*).

In some cases the courts have been prepared to rule that a 'dissociative state' caused by some extraordinary event may be classed as automatism. In *T* (1990), Miss T pleaded automatism to charges of robbery and assault occasioning actual bodily harm. She had been raped three days earlier. A psychiatrist diagnosed that she was suffering post-traumatic stress disorder, and at the time of the alleged offences had entered a dissociative state. The judge allowed automatism to be left to the jury: 'such an incident could have an appalling effect on any young woman, however well-balanced normally.'

This also represents the law in Australia. In *Falconer* (1991), D shot her husband at point-blank range with a shotgun, killing him instantly. She was charged with murder. In court she testified that he had sexually assaulted her, hit her across the face and taunted her; she had also just been informed that he was facing charges of incest involving their two daughters. D claimed that she could remember nothing until her husband was found dead. She was convicted of murder but, on appeal, a majority of the High Court of Australia held that automatism was available.

However, in *Burgess* (1991) it was held that a dissociative state, if caused by the *ordinary* stresses of life, such as unrequited love, will be classed as insanity. This was also the decision of the Supreme Court of Canada in *Rabey* (1977). *Parks* (1992), another Canadian case, decided that somnambulism was an example of automatism, but that conflicts with the decision of the Court of Appeal in *Burgess*, where it was held that sleepwalking was an example of insanity. All of these cases were discussed fully in Chapter 15.

Comments made by the Court of Appeal in *Narbrough* (2004) seriously undermine the value of *T* (1990) as a precedent. D had been convicted of wounding with intent to do GBH contrary to s.18 OAPA after stabbing V with a Stanley knife. On appeal, he argued that psychiatric evidence that he had been seriously sexually abused as a child had left him suffering post-traumatic stress disorder, with flashbacks, so that he sometimes confused the past and the present. He claimed that, during the attack on V, he had suffered such a flashback and had acted 'like a zombie'. The trial judge declared this evidence to be inadmissible and the Court of Appeal rejected D's appeal. Zucker J said that the defence psychiatrist had not referred 'to any authority or to any research which supports the conclusion that a post-traumatic stress disorder can so affect a person's normal mental processes that his mind is no longer in control of his actions or that he behaves as an automaton. We have no doubt that the evidence . . . was rightly ruled by the judge to be inadmissible.'

Extent of involuntariness required

How unconscious does D have to be before he can be said to be an automaton? There are many possible levels of consciousness. When dealing with something as abstract as 'consciousness', it is more a matter of degree. There is no clear dividing line at which point D becomes an automaton. It seems that the extent of involuntariness required to be established depends on the offence charged. There are two categories.

Crimes of strict liability

D must show that they were exercising no control over their bodily movements whatsoever. If, despite some lack of control, they were still able to appreciate what they were doing and operate their body to a degree, then the defence is not made out. The position has been demonstrated in a series of driving cases. In *Hill v Baxter* (1958), where D claimed to have become unconscious as a result of being overcome by a sudden illness, the Queen's Bench Divisional Court found that the facts showed that D was 'driving', in the sense of controlling the car and directing its movements, and rejected D's plea of automatism. In *Watmore v Jenkins* (1962), the Divisional Court said that only 'a complete destruction of voluntary control . . . could constitute in law automatism'. There had to be some evidence to raise a reasonable doubt that D's bodily movements were 'wholly uncontrolled and uninitiated by any function of conscious will'. In *Isitt* (1978), Lawton LJ said:

> It may well be that, because of panic or stress or alcohol, the appellant's mind was shut to the moral inhibitions which control the lives of most of us. But the fact that his moral inhibitions were not working properly . . . does not mean that the mind was not working at all.

These decisions may be explained on the ground that the automatism must be of such a degree that D cannot be said to have performed the *actus reus* voluntarily. But it seems harsh. D who, though not completely unconscious, retains the merest grasp on his senses, faces conviction. Clause 33 of the Law Commission's Criminal Code Bill (1989) proposes that a lack of control to the extent that D is no longer in effective control of his bodily movements should suffice for the defence. Such a reform is to be welcomed. There is little to be said for a rule of law which criminalises behaviour which D was incapable of preventing.

Crimes of *mens rea*

In this category the degree of automatism is, or should be, much reduced. D should have a good defence provided he was prevented from forming *mens rea*. There is a dearth of English case law on this point. In *T*, above, the crimes with which Miss T had been charged both required *mens rea*. The prosecution had claimed that her opening of a pen-knife blade had required a 'controlled and positive action', that this was a case of partial loss of control only and that, following *Isitt*, automatism was therefore not available. However, the trial judge distinguished *Isitt* and held that T was 'acting as though in a dream' and the defence was available after all.

In *Attorney-General's Reference (No. 2 of 1992)* (1993), another driving case, the Court of Appeal held that a partial loss of control was insufficient to establish the defence, apparently confirming *Watmore v Jenkins* and *Isitt*, above. D, a long-distance lorry driver, had crashed his lorry into a stationary vehicle, killing two people. When charged with causing death by reckless driving, he pleaded that he was suffering from a condition called 'driving without awareness', a trance-like state brought on by the lack of visual stimuli on long motorway journeys. The Court of Appeal held that this did *not* satisfy the defence of automatism. However, the crime with which D was charged required objective *Caldwell* recklessness (now, of course, abolished by *G and R* [2003]) – in other words, D was guilty if he failed to appreciate a risk that would have been obvious to the ordinary prudent individual. Moreover, the reason for failure was immaterial. Hence, the court's ruling that partial loss of control was no defence. Arguably, however, had D been charged with a crime requiring intention or subjective recklessness, he would have been entitled to the defence on the basis that his lack of awareness would have prevented the prosecution from proving *mens rea*.

Self-induced automatism

Where automatism was due to D's consumption of alcohol and/or drugs, then the rules of intoxication apply (*Lipman* [1970]). In other words, D may have a defence to a crime requiring intention, but could be convicted of an offence requiring some lower level of *mens rea*, such as recklessness. This principle should apply whenever automatism is self-induced. For example, a driver who feels drowsy but continues to drive, then falls asleep at the wheel, may still be held liable for a motoring offence should he cause an accident (*Kay v Butterworth* [1945]).

Likewise, a driver who suffers an epileptic fit or hypoglycaemic episode whilst driving and causes an accident may be held liable, despite being in an automatic state at the time of the accident, depending on whether he was aware in advance of the onset of the automatic state. In other words, he is liable if the automatic state can be regarded as self-induced. This was the situation in two recent and very similar cases, *C* (2007) and *Clarke* (2009). In both cases, D was a diabetic who suffered a hypoglycaemic episode whilst driving, lost control of his car, left the road and hit and killed a pedestrian. Both pleaded automatism to charges of causing death by dangerous driving. In *C* the trial judge accepted the plea and ruled that the driver had no case to answer but the Appeal Court disagreed and allowed the Crown's appeal against that ruling on the basis that there was evidence that D was aware of his deteriorating condition before the onset of the hypoglycaemic episode. In *Clarke*, D was convicted after the jury rejected his automatism plea on the basis that it was self-induced and the Court of Appeal upheld his conviction. In the *C* case, Moses LJ summarised the situation as follows:

> Automatism due to a hypoglycaemic attack will not be a defence if the attack might reasonably have been avoided. If the driver ought to have tested his blood glucose level before embarking on his journey, or appreciated the onset of symptoms during the journey, then the fact that he did suffer a hypoglycaemic attack, even if it caused a total loss of control over his limbs at the moment the car left the road, would be no defence.

Reflex actions

A 'reflex action' was one of the examples given by Lord Denning in *Bratty* of an involuntary act. That case did not involve reflex actions; so Lord Denning's view is *obiter*. In *Ryan* (1967), a defence of reflex action was advanced, but the High Court of Australia was unsympathetic. Windeyer J said that there were only two legally recognised categories of involuntary 'act':

- those which were involuntary because 'by no exercise of the will could [D] refrain from doing it', such as convulsions or an epileptic seizure; and

- those which were involuntary 'because he knew not what he was doing', such as the sleepwalker or a person rendered unconscious for some other reason.

However, reflex actions did not bear true analogy to either category. It is not surprising that the Court was unsympathetic in *Ryan*: D had shot a petrol station attendant, V, at point-blank range with a shotgun after V had moved while D was trying to tie him up. He claimed that when V struggled this led to D pulling the trigger involuntarily. The Court, quite rightly, upheld his conviction. However, the case – which is persuasive authority at the most anyway – is not authority for the proposition that reflex actions may never provide a good automatism defence.

Reform

The Law Commission's Criminal Code Bill (1989) provides an interesting definition of 'automatism', one which, if it were ever to be adopted, would change the present law. Clause 33(1) states that 'a person is not guilty of an offence if':

(a) he acts in a state of automatism, that is, his act (i) is a reflex, spasm or convulsion; or (ii) occurs while he is in a condition (whether of sleep, unconsciousness, impaired consciousness or otherwise) depriving him of effective control of his act; and
(b) the act or condition is the result neither of anything done or omitted with the fault required for the offence nor of voluntary intoxication.

The inclusion of 'sleep' as one of the causes of automatism involves a reversal of the Court of Appeal decision in *Burgess* that a sleepwalker is legally 'insane' and a tacit approval of the Supreme Court of Canada's decision in *Parks*.

Clause 33(2) states that 'a person is not guilty of an offence by virtue of an omission to act if':

(a) he is physically incapable of acting in the way required; and
(b) his being so incapable is the result neither of anything done or omitted with the fault required for the offence nor of voluntary intoxication.

Summary

- Automatism is a defence if D's act was involuntary (*Bratty v Attorney-General for Northern Ireland*).

- It includes: spasms, reflex actions or convulsions or situations where D was unconscious through, for example, concussion or hypnotism (*Bratty*). In *Ryan* a 'reflex action' defence was, however, denied.

- Automatism may include dissociative states – but only those caused by an extraordinary event (*T*; *Falconer*). Dissociative states caused by ordinary events are classed as insanity (*Rabey*; *Burgess*).

- Crimes of strict liability require a total destruction of voluntary control (*Hill v Baxter*; *Watmore v Jenkins*; *Isitt*).

- For crimes requiring *mens rea*, automatism that prevents proof of *mens rea* should suffice for a good defence.

- Self-induced automatism through drink and/or drugs is classed as intoxication (*Lipman*).

- Automatism caused by a 'disease of the mind' is classed as insanity – see Chapter 15.

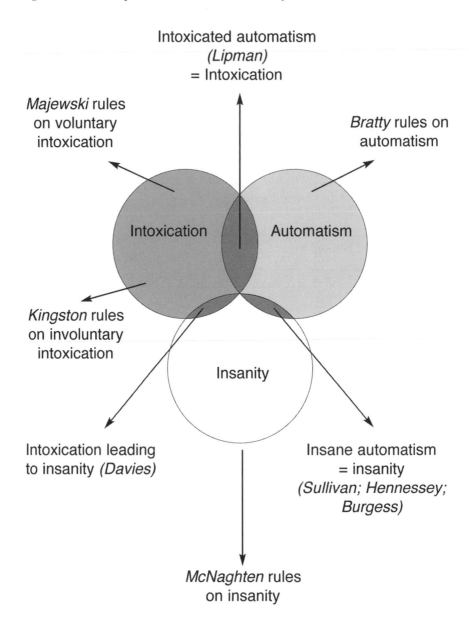

Figure 6 Relationship between intoxication, insanity and automatism

17 Mistake

Introduction

It is a basic principle of English criminal law that D is entitled to be judged against the facts as he honestly supposed them to exist. This is the position even if he is mistaken as to the facts, and even if the mistake was quite unreasonable.

At first glance, this may seem unduly favourable towards an accused. You may think that all the accused has to do is to swear in court that 'I was mistaken at the time your honour. I believed that the victim was going to attack me so I hit him over the head with a glass ashtray.' However, the crucial element in a defence of mistake claim is that the accused must convince a bench of magistrates or a jury of the honesty of his belief. The reality is that the more far-fetched the claim that the accused is making, the less likely it is that a jury will believe that it could have been honestly held at the time of the offence.

General principles

The leading cases are *Morgan and Others* (1976), *Kimber* (1983) and *Williams* (1987). In *Morgan and Others* and *Kimber* the question was whether D was guilty of rape and indecent assault, respectively, if he honestly thought (wrongly as it happens) that the victim was consenting. The House of Lords in *Morgan* held that a genuine, mistaken belief in consent was a good defence, because it denied the *mens rea* in rape (which, at the time, was either knowledge or recklessness that V was not consenting to intercourse). Crucially, the Court stressed that mistake is a good defence even if D's belief is unreasonable, provided that it was honestly held. However, the more unreasonable a belief, the more likely it is that a jury will decide that D was lying and did not really have that belief at all.

Morgan and Others (1976)
Morgan, a senior officer in the RAF, invited three junior officers to his house to have sex with his wife. The other officers were at first incredulous but were persuaded when Morgan told them about his wife's sexual behaviour and provided them with condoms. They also

claimed that Morgan said to expect some resistance, but not to take this seriously as it was simply pretence on his wife's part to stimulate her own excitement. In due course, the officers had sex with Morgan's wife, despite her struggling and screaming for her son to call the police. The officers were convicted of rape and Morgan of aiding and abetting rape, after a jury direction that their belief in consent had to be based on reasonable grounds. The Court of Appeal and the House of Lords actually rejected their appeals (applying the proviso – this means the court thought that a reasonable jury – properly instructed – would also have convicted), on the basis that the whole story was 'a pack of lies'. But Lords Cross, Hailsham and Fraser nevertheless held that the trial judge had misdirected the jury by telling them that the defendants' belief had to be reasonable.

In *Kimber*, the Court of Appeal confirmed that the principles established in *Morgan* were not limited to rape but were of general application to all offences. This is still the case apart from the crime with which the defendants in *Morgan* were actually charged: rape. Section 1(1) of the Sexual Offences Act 2003 states that D is guilty of rape if he has sex with another person (V) who does not consent and D 'does not reasonably believe' that V consents. Thus, in future cases of criminal damage, assault and battery, ABH, GBH, wounding, manslaughter and even murder, D will be able to rely upon *Morgan* and plead not guilty based on a genuine mistake. However, if D is charged with rape and argued that he thought V was consenting to sex, he will be convicted unless his belief is both honest and reasonable. In *Williams*, the Court of Appeal decided that honest mistakes could also be used to support a defence, such as self-defence, as well as to deny proof of *mens rea*. Lord Lane CJ attempted to sum up the role of mistake in criminal law generally, as follows:

The reasonableness or unreasonableness of [D]'s belief is material to the question of whether the belief was held by [D] at all. If the belief was in fact held, its unreasonableness, so far as guilt or innocence is concerned, is neither here nor there. It is irrelevant.

Williams (1987)
Gladstone Williams was charged with assaulting a man called Mason. His defence was that he was preventing M from assaulting and torturing a young man. Williams claimed that he was returning

from work on a bus when he saw Mason repeatedly punching the youth who was struggling and calling for help. Williams was so concerned at this that he got off the bus and approached Mason to ask him what on earth he was doing. Mason replied that he was arresting the youth for mugging an old lady (which was true) and that he was a police officer (which was not true). Williams asked to see Mason's warrant card, which was of course not forthcoming, at which point a struggle broke out between them. As a result of this altercation Mason sustained injuries to his face, loosened teeth and bleeding gums. Williams did not deny punching Mason, but claimed that he did so in order to save the youth from further beatings and torture. The jury was directed that Williams had a defence only if he believed on *reasonable grounds* that Mason was acting unlawfully. The Court of Appeal quashed his conviction.

Intoxicated mistakes

An important exception to the general rule (above) is where D's mistake was caused by voluntary intoxication. A drunken mistake is likely to be honest – but unreasonable. To allow D to rely upon intoxicated mistakes as a general defence would create some alarming loopholes in the law. Thus, for example, D is **not** entitled to rely upon a mistaken belief in either:

- V's consent to sex if charged with rape (or other sexual offence); or

- the need to use force in self-defence,

if, in either of those cases, D's mistaken belief was caused by voluntary intoxication. *Fotheringham* (1988) illustrates the former situation. D, a middle-aged man, had been out drinking with his wife. When they returned home, D went to bed. Finding a woman already in the bed, he assumed that it was his wife and proceeded to have sex with her. In fact, it was the couple's teenage babysitter, who had felt tired and gone to sleep in their bed. He was charged with rape and pleaded not guilty on the basis that he honestly believed that the woman with whom he had sex was, in fact, his wife. (No doubt D's drunken condition hindered his ability to tell the difference between his middle-aged wife and a teenage girl.) The law at the time meant that it was legally impossible for a man to rape his wife because it was assumed that she always consented (this ancient legal rule was abolished by the House of Lords only in *R* [1992]). However, D was convicted and the Court of Appeal upheld the conviction, holding that an intoxicated mistake was no defence in rape, whether the issue was mistaken belief as to consent or, as in this case, mistaken belief as to identity.

Indeed, whenever the offence with which D is charged is one of 'basic intent' – such as assault and battery, wounding, actual and grievous bodily harm, sexual assault and criminal damage – D cannot use evidence of intoxication to support a plea that he made a genuine mistake. The policy of protecting the public that was stressed in the leading intoxication case, *DPP v Majewski* (1977), makes this position inevitable.

On the other hand, D should still be able to rely upon an intoxicated mistake if charged with a specific intent offence. A good example of this situation is *Lipman* (1970), discussed in Chapter 14. You will recall that D, having taken hallucinogenic drugs, genuinely thought that he was being attacked by giant snakes at the centre of the Earth, and ended up suffocating his girlfriend to death. Of course, D was not really being attacked by anything, let alone giant snakes, yet he was able to rely on his intoxicated mistake as a means of denying the intent required for murder (although he was, of course, convicted of manslaughter instead).

Meanwhile, where D relies upon self-defence, the *Williams* principle (above) does not apply where D's mistake was caused by intoxication. In *O'Grady* (1987), D and his friend V had been drinking heavily when they fell asleep in the former's flat. D claimed that he woke up because he thought that V was attacking him. D picked up an ashtray and hit V with it, then went back to sleep. In the morning, V was dead. D was convicted of manslaughter. The Court of Appeal refused to allow D to rely upon his intoxicated mistake about the need to defend himself, and upheld the conviction, distinguishing *Williams* on the ground that that case was not concerned with intoxicated mistakes. Lord Lane CJ stated:

> There are two competing interests. On the one hand the defendant who has only acted according to what he believed to be necessary to protect himself, and on the other hand that of the public and the victim in particular who . . . has been injured or perhaps killed because of the defendant's drunken mistake. Reason recoils from the conclusion that in such circumstances a defendant is entitled to leave the court without a stain on his character.

The Court of Appeal confirmed the *O'Grady* decision in *O'Connor* (1991) and again in *Hatton* (2005). In the latter case, D was on trial for murder, a specific intent offence. The defence suggested that V may have attacked D and that D, in his drunken condition, may have believed that V was attacking him with a sword. The trial judge, however, ruled that a mistaken belief in the need to use force in self-defence, where the mistake was due to intoxication, provided no defence – even to murder. The jury convicted D of murder and the Court of Appeal upheld his conviction. Referring to *O'Grady*, Lord Phillips CJ stated:

> We do not believe that upon a proper application of the law of precedence we can treat the general principle that was the reason for this court's decision [in *O'Grady*] as being mere *obiter dicta* so far as the law of murder is concerned. We are obliged to follow *O'Grady* and to reject [counsel's] contention that the judge should have directed the jury to consider whether the appellant's drunkenness might have led him to make a mistake as to the severity of any attack to which he may have been subjected by [V].

Lord Phillips did acknowledge that academic criticism that had been made of *O'Grady*, but concluded that 'whether or not the law is soundly based must be decided elsewhere' (meaning either the House of Lords or in Parliament).

Hatton (2005)

D and V met one evening, at a nightclub, before returning to D's flat. There, D battered V to death with a sledgehammer. During the evening V, who was a manic depressive, had been behaving 'strangely', falsely representing that he had been an SAS officer, striking martial art poses and exhibiting a hatred of homosexuals. After D's arrest, he claimed to have no recollection of the killing because he had been drinking heavily beforehand (some 20 pints of beer according to his own evidence). However, he did claim to have a 'vague recollection of being involved in an altercation' with V, that V may have thought that D was homosexual and attacked him first and thus D may have been acting in self-defence. A stick belonging to D, which had been fashioned into the shape of a samurai sword and which was found under V's body, provided the basis for D's claim that he may have been attacked by V. The jury rejected the defence and D's murder conviction was upheld.

As it happens, the decisions in *Williams*, *O'Grady* (1987), *O'Connor* (1991) and *Hatton* (2005) have all now been confirmed by Parliament. Section 76(4) and (5) of the Criminal Justice and Immigration Act 2008 (which deals with the use of force for the purposes of self-defence) contains the following provisions:

(4) If D claims to have held a particular belief as regards the existence of any circumstances –

269

(a) the reasonableness or otherwise of that belief is relevant to the question whether D genuinely held it; but

(b) if it is determined that D did genuinely hold it, D is entitled to rely on it for the purposes of subsection (3), whether or not –

(i) it was mistaken, or
(ii) (if it was mistaken) the mistake was a reasonable one to have made.

(5) But subsection (4)(b) does not enable D to rely on any mistaken belief attributable to intoxication that was voluntarily induced.

Summary

- Where D is charged with an offence but denies *mens rea*, an honestly held, but mistaken, belief that prevents the Crown from proving *mens rea* will be a good defence (*Morgan and Others*; *Kimber*).

- The crucial point is that D's mistake must be honest but need not necessarily be reasonable. However, the more unreasonable the belief, the more likely it is that the jury will decide that D was lying.

- Where D pleads self-defence, then an honestly held, but mistaken, belief in the need to use force will be a good defence (*Williams*; s.76(4) Criminal Justice and Immigration Act 2008).

- However, this is not the case where D's mistaken belief in the need to use self-defence was caused by intoxication (*O'Grady*; *O'Connor*; *Hatton*; s.76(5) Criminal Justice and Immigration Act 2008).

- Intoxicated mistakes can be used to deny *mens rea* in the context of specific intent offences such as murder (*Lipman*).

- However, intoxicated mistakes cannot be used to deny *mens rea* in the context of basic intent crimes such as rape (*Fotheringham*).

18   Duress and necessity

Introduction

Imagine you are standing in a queue at your bank. Suddenly, armed robbers burst into the bank, waving guns around and shouting at everyone to get down on the floor and shut up. One of them then comes over to you – it's obviously not your lucky day – and tells you to help them fill their bags with cash. There is a gun pointed at your head. What do you do? Of course, if you don't pass out, you do exactly as you're told. Five minutes later the robbers have gone and it's all over. Or is it? What if the police decide to charge *you* with participating in a robbery? After all, without your help, the robbers might not have succeeded. Well, relax: there is a defence ready and waiting: duress. With duress, D claims that, although they committed the *actus reus* of the offence, with *mens rea*, they did so only because they had no effective choice, being faced with threats of serious injury or death, or with similar threats against others close to them.

Sources of the duress

Duress comes in two types:

- Duress by threats

- Duress of circumstances (sometimes referred to as 'necessity', but in this book necessity will be dealt with separately, at the end of this chapter).

The principles applying are identical in either case of duress.

Duress by threats

Here, D is threatened by another person to commit a criminal offence. For example, D is ordered at gunpoint to drive armed robbers away from the scene of a robbery or they will be shot. Duress by threats is available only if D commits a criminal offence of a type that was nominated by the person making the threat. In *Cole* (1994), moneylenders had pressurised D for money. They had threatened D, his girlfriend and child, and hit him with a baseball bat. Eventually, D robbed two building societies. To a charge of robbery he pleaded duress but the trial judge ruled that the defence was not available. The duressors had not said, 'Go and rob a building society or else.'

Duress of circumstances

Here, the threat does not come from a person but the circumstances in which D finds themself. Duress of circumstances has received official recognition from the appellate courts only in the last 20 years. The first cases all, coincidentally, involved driving offences:

- *Willer* (1986). D was forced to drive his car on the pavement in order to escape a gang of youths who were intent on attacking him and his passenger. The Court of Appeal allowed D's appeal against a conviction of reckless driving, on the basis of duress of circumstances. Watkins LJ said that D was 'wholly driven by force of circumstance into doing what he did and did not drive the car otherwise than under that form of compulsion, i.e. under duress'.

- *Conway* (1988). D again successfully appealed against a conviction of reckless driving. He had driven his car at high speed to escape what he thought were two men intent on attacking his passenger (in fact they were police officers).

- *Martin* (1989). D's conviction of driving while disqualified was quashed. He had driven his car only after his wife became hysterical and threatened to kill herself if D did not drive his stepson to work.

In *Martin*, Brown J said that English law did 'in extreme circumstances recognise a defence of necessity. Most commonly, this defence arises as duress (by threats). Equally, however, it can arise from other objective dangers threatening the accused or others. Arising thus it is conveniently called 'duress of circumstances'. For a time there was a perception that duress of circumstances might be limited to driving offences, but in *Pommell* (1995) – involving a charge of possession of an unlicensed firearm – the Court of Appeal confirmed that the defence was of general application.

The seriousness of the threat

In *Hasan* (2005), the House of Lords made it clear that the threat must be very serious. Lord Bingham said that 'to found a plea of duress the threat relied on must be to cause death or serious injury'. A threat to damage or destroy property is therefore insufficient. In *Lynch* (1975), Lord Simon said, 'The law must draw a line somewhere; and ... the law draws it between threats to property and threats to the person.' Threats to expose D's secret sexual orientation are also insufficient (*Valderrama-Vega* [1985]). However, although there must be a threat of death or serious personal injury, that need not be the sole reason why D committed the offence with which he is charged. In *Valderrama-Vega*, D claimed that he had imported cocaine because of death threats made by a Mafia-type organisation. But he also needed the money because he was heavily in debt to his bank. Furthermore, he had been threatened with having his (secret) homosexuality disclosed. His conviction of drug smuggling was quashed: the jury had been directed he had a defence only if the death threats were the sole reason for acting.

Threats against whom?

As well as threats to D personally, threats to certain other people will also support the defence. In *Hasan* (2005), Lord Bingham stated that 'the threat must be directed against [D] or his immediate family or someone close to him'. Examples include *Martin* (1989), where D's wife had threatened to kill herself unless he drove whilst disqualified; *Willer* (1986) and *Conway* (1988), in both of which D committed driving offences because of threats made to his friends, who were passengers in D's car. In *Wright* (2000), D was allowed the defence (to a charge of drug smuggling) because her boyfriend, Darren, had been threatened with violence. D had actually been convicted after the trial judge directed the jury that duress was available only if a threat was directed at D herself or at a 'member of her immediate family', but the Court of Appeal held that this was too restrictive and allowed the appeal. This was confirmed in *Hasan*.

This question was posed by Professor Sir John Smith in his commentary on *Wright* in the *Criminal Law Review*: Could a fan of Manchester United be reasonably expected to resist a threat to kill the team's star player if he did not participate in a robbery?

Immediacy of the threat

In some of the older cases, the Court of Appeal decided that the threat to D (or other persons) had to be believed by D to be 'imminent', but not necessarily 'immediate'. However, in *Hasan* (2005), the House of Lords rejected this and held that the correct test was that the threat had to be believed by D to be 'immediate' or 'almost immediate'. Lord Bingham said:

It should be made clear to juries that if the retribution threatened against the defendant or his family, or a person for whom he reasonably feels responsible, is not such as he reasonably expects to follow immediately, or almost immediately, on his failure to comply with the threat, there may be little, if any, room for doubt that he could have taken evasive action, whether by going to the police or in some other way, to avoid committing the crime with which he is charged.

273

Escape opportunities and police protection

D will be expected to take advantage of any reasonable opportunity that they have to escape or seek police protection. In *Pommell* (1995), D was found in bed one morning with a loaded gun in his hand. He claimed to have persuaded another man, E, to hand over the gun as E appeared determined to use it and D wanted to prevent that from happening. This had been in the early hours of the morning; D had intended to hand over the gun to the police the next day. However, D was convicted of possessing a prohibited weapon after the trial judge refused to allow the defence of duress of circumstances on the basis of the time delay. The Court of Appeal allowed the appeal and ordered a retrial, at which the defence would be left to the jury. Kennedy LJ accepted that 'in some cases a delay, especially if unexplained' would deny the defence but, in this case, the delay of a few hours was not excessive and in any case D had offered an explanation for the delay (it was the middle of the night).

In *Hudson and Taylor* (1971), the Court of Appeal took a very pragmatic approach to the realities of many duress cases. The Court recognised that, in some cases, the police would be unable to provide effective protection against later reprisals.

> *Hudson and Taylor* (1971)
> Linda Hudson, 17, and Elaine Taylor, 19, were the principal prosecution witnesses at the trial of a man called Jimmy Wright, who had been charged with wounding another man in a Salford pub. Both girls were present in the pub and gave statements to the police. However, at the trial, the girls refused to identify Wright and he was acquitted. In due course, the girls were charged with perjury (lying in court under oath). At the perjury trial, Hudson claimed that a man called Farrell, who had a reputation for violence, had threatened her that if she 'told on Wright in court' she would be cut up. She passed this threat on to Taylor. They were frightened by this and resolved not to identify Wright. This resolve was strengthened when they arrived in court and saw Farrell in the public gallery. The judge at the perjury trial withdrew the defence of duress from the jury because the threat of harm could not be immediately put into effect when they were testifying in the safety of the courtroom. But their perjury convictions were quashed on appeal.

Voluntary exposure to risk of compulsion

D will be denied the defence if they voluntarily place themselves in such a situation that they risk being threatened with violence to commit crime.

This may be because they join a criminal organisation. In *Fitzpatrick* (1977), D pleaded duress to a catalogue of offences including murder, even though he was a voluntary member of the IRA. The trial judge rejected the defence. The Northern Ireland Court of Appeal dismissed the appeal. Lowry LCJ said:

> It would be only too easy for every member of an unlawful conspiracy and for every member of a gang except the leader to obtain an immunity denied to ordinary citizens. Indeed, the better organised the conspiracy and the more brutal its internal discipline, the surer would be the defence of duress for its members. It can hardly be supposed that the common law tolerates such an absurdity.

Sharp (1987) confirmed that this was case in English law. Lord Lane CJ stated:

> Where a person has voluntarily, and with knowledge of its nature, joined a criminal organisation or gang which he knew might bring pressure on him to commit an offence and was an active member when he was put under such pressure, he cannot avail himself of the defence of duress.

Sharp (1987)
David Sharp, along with two men, A and H, had attempted an armed robbery of a sub-post office, which resulted in the death of the sub-postmaster. Sharp claimed that he was only the 'bagman', he was not armed and took part in the second robbery only because he had been threatened with having his head blown off by H if he did not co-operate. The trial judge withdrew the defence, and Sharp was convicted of manslaughter, robbery and attempted robbery. The Court of Appeal upheld the convictions.

This principle has been confirmed in a number of subsequent cases. It is now firmly established that D does not necessarily have to have joined a criminal organisation (as in *Fitzpatrick* or *Sharp*). Voluntarily associating with persons with a reputation for violence (typically by buying unlawful drugs from suppliers) may well be enough to deny the defence. For example, in *Heath* (2000), D was a heroin addict who had become indebted to his dealer. After being threatened with violence if he did not co-operate, he agreed to transport £300,000 of cannabis. However, he was caught and charged with possession of drugs with intent to supply. His duress defence was rejected. The Court of Appeal pointed out that he knew that, by becoming indebted to a drugs supplier, D had put himself in 'a bad position' because 'in the drugs world people collect their debts in one way – by threatening and on occasion inflicting serious violence'.

In *Hasan* (2005), the House of Lords narrowed even further the availability of duress when D has voluntarily associated with violent criminals. Lord Bingham said that the defence would be denied if, when D first associated himself with criminals, he 'knows or *ought reasonably* to know' the risk of being subjected to compulsion by threats of violence. Thus, even if D did not personally realise that he was getting into a situation where violent threats were likely – but he should have realised – the defence of duress will not be available.

Hasan (2005)

Hasan was charged with aggravated burglary contrary to s.10 of the Theft Act 1968. He admitted forcing his way into V's house while armed with a knife and attempting to steal money from a safe. However, he pleaded duress on the basis that he and his family had been threatened with serious violence by a man called Sullivan, who had a reputation as a violent gangster and drug dealer, if he did not co-operate. Hasan and Sullivan knew each other because Hasan worked as a driver for X, a woman who ran an escort agency involving prostitution, and Sullivan and X were in a relationship. The trial judge told the jury that Hasan had no defence if he had voluntarily exposed himself to the risk of threats of violence. The jury rejected the defence and D was convicted. Although the Court of Appeal quashed his conviction, it was reinstated by the House of Lords.

Thus, the defence of duress fails if D knew, or ought to have known, that by joining a criminal organisation he might be subjected to violence. It follows that, if D joins a criminal organisation not known to have a reputation for violence, the defence should still be available. In *Shepherd* (1987), D was a member of a gang of shoplifters. They would enter a shop and one of them would distract the shopkeeper while the rest made off with property, usually boxes of cigarettes. Eventually D was charged with theft and pleaded duress on the basis that, when he tried to leave the gang, one of the others had threatened him and his family with violence unless he continued to participate. The trial judge withdrew the defence from the jury but, on appeal, his conviction was quashed. The question should have been put to the jury of whether D knew of a propensity to violence when he joined the gang.

Hasan was followed in *Ali* (2008), where D was charged with robbery. He had taken a Golf Turbo car on a test drive but then forced the car salesman out of the car at knifepoint before driving off. At his trial, D claimed that he had been threatened with violence by a man called Hussein if he did not commit the robbery. However, his duress defence was rejected on the basis that he had been friends with Hussein, who had a violent reputation, for many years. In the words of the trial judge, D had chosen to join 'very bad company'. Dismissing D's appeal, Dyson LJ stated:

> The core question is whether [D] voluntarily put himself in the position in which he foresaw or ought reasonably to have foreseen the risk of being subjected to any compulsion by threats of violence. As a matter of fact, threats of violence will almost always be made by persons engaged in a criminal activity; but in our judgment it is the risk of being subjected to compulsion by threats of violence that must be foreseen or foreseeable that is relevant, rather than the nature of the activity in which the threatener is engaged.

Should D have resisted the threats?

The defence is not available just because D reacted to a threat; the threat must be one that the ordinary man would not have resisted. In *Graham* (1982), a duress case where D claimed he had been threatened by another man called King into killing D's wife, Lord Lane CJ said:

> The correct approach [is] as follows: (1) Was [D], or may he have been, impelled to act as he did because, as a result of what he reasonably believed [King] had said or done, he had good cause to fear that if he did not so act King would kill him or . . . cause him serious physical injury? (2) If so, have the prosecution made the jury sure that a sober person of reasonable firmness, sharing the characteristics of [D], would not have responded to whatever he reasonably believed King said or did by taking part in the killing? The fact that [D's] will to resist has been eroded by drink or drugs or both is not relevant to this test.

In *Howe* (1987), the House of Lords approved the *Graham* test. The test is carefully framed in such a way to ensure the burden of proof remains on the prosecution at all times (although D must raise evidence of duress). If the jury feel that D *may* have been threatened, and that the 'sober person of reasonable firmness' *might* have responded to it, then they *must* acquit D. Both *Graham* and *Howe* were cases of duress by threats. In *Conway* (1988), the Court of Appeal applied the same test to duress of circumstances.

The first question

The first question is whether D was, or might have been, impelled to act as he did because, as a result of his reasonable belief, he had good cause to fear that if he did not so act, he (or some other person for whom he was responsible) would die or suffer serious physical (and possibly mental) injury. The test concentrates on D's belief. In *Cairns* (1999), the Court of Appeal held that it was not fatal to a plea of duress that there was, in fact, no threat to D of death or serious injury. What was important was that D *reasonably believed* that such a threat existed.

Cairns (1999)

John Cairns was driving home through the Newcastle suburbs around midnight when he was forced to stop by a young man, Anthony Allen, who had been out drinking with a group of friends. Allen spread-eagled himself on Cairns' car bonnet with his face pressed against the windscreen. Cairns decided to drive off, with Allen still on the bonnet, because he thought he was in danger of attack from the rest of what he thought was a gang of drunken youths. The 'gang' had, in fact, been chasing after Cairns' car, shouting and gesturing but claimed later that they just wanted to rescue Allen and not do any harm to Cairns. Unfortunately for Allen, Cairns had to brake in order to drive over a speed bump. Allen fell off in front of the car, and was run over, fracturing his spine and leaving him so badly injured that he faced spending the rest of life in a wheelchair. Cairns was convicted of causing grievous bodily harm with intent; but this conviction was quashed. The trial judge had told the jury that duress was available as a defence only if the threat of danger (or, in the trial judge's words, 'evil in question') was, in fact, real. The Court of Appeal confirmed that it was not necessary for the danger to have existed.

The *Graham/Howe* test does not *just* concentrate on D's subjective view of the threat or circumstances (as the case may be) but also insists that:

- D's belief must have been 'reasonable'. If D *unreasonably* believed that he was being threatened and committed an offence, the defence is unavailable. In *Hasan* (2005), the House of Lords confirmed this point. Lord Bingham stated, 'It is of course essential that [D] should genuinely, i.e. actually, believe in the efficacy of the threat by which he claims to have been compelled. But there is no warrant for relaxing the requirement that the belief must be reasonable as well as genuine.'

- D's belief must have given him 'good cause' to fear death or serious injury. The defence will, therefore, fail if, viewed objectively (that is, in the opinion of the jury), death or serious injury was unlikely.

The second question

This second question is whether a 'sober person of reasonable firmness' – but sharing D's characteristics – would have responded to whatever it was that D reasonably believed would happen to him, by committing a criminal offence. Put another way, the defence is unavailable if the ordinary person, sharing D's characteristics, would have resisted the threats. Relevant characteristics include age, sex and certain other permanent physical and mental attributes which would affect the ability of D to resist pressure and threats. In *Bowen* (1996), the Court of Appeal said that the following characteristics were obviously relevant:

- Age: a young person may not be as robust as a mature one

- Pregnancy: where there was an added fear for the unborn child

- Serious physical disability: as that might inhibit self-protection

- Recognised mental illness or psychiatric condition: such as post-traumatic stress disorder leading to learnt helplessness. Psychiatric evidence might be admissible to show that D was suffering from such condition, provided persons generally suffering them might be more susceptible to pressure and threats. It was not admissible simply to show that in a doctor's opinion D, not suffering from such illness or condition, was especially timid, suggestible or vulnerable to pressure and threats.

Finally, sex might possibly be relevant, although the court thought that many women might consider they had as much moral courage to resist pressure as men.

Bowen (1996)
Cecil Bowen was convicted of five counts of obtaining property by deception. He claimed to have been acting under duress. Two men had accosted him in a pub and told him that he and his family would be petrol-bombed if he did not obtain goods for them. The judge had left duress to the jury but did not mention Bowen's low intelligence (his IQ was only 68). The Court of Appeal dismissed Bowen's appeal. A low IQ, falling short of mental impairment or mental defectiveness, could not be said to be a characteristic that made those who had it less courageous and less able to withstand threats and pressure.

The suggestion in *Bowen* that evidence of post-traumatic stress disorder leading to learnt helplessness could be admitted as a characteristic is interesting, and not particularly easy to reconcile with the earlier decision in *Horne* (1994). There, D was charged with fraud and pleaded duress. He sought to support it with psychological evidence that he was unusually pliable and vulnerable to pressure. The judge refused to consider the evidence. D was convicted, and the Court of Appeal dismissed his appeal.

> Suppose you were on a jury in a case where duress was pleaded following threats of violence. How would you react to the question, 'Would the sober person of reasonable firmness but suffering from learnt helplessness have yielded to the threat?'

Self-induced characteristics

In *Bowen*, the Court of Appeal held that self-imposed characteristics caused by the abuse of alcohol, drugs or sniffing glue, could *not* be relevant. This is consistent with the earlier case of *Flatt* (1996). D was addicted to cocaine and owed his supplier £1,500. The dealer had apparently told him to look after some drugs, and that if he did not, D's mother, grandmother and girlfriend would be shot. Some 17 hours later, the drugs were found in D's flat by the police. He pleaded duress but was convicted of possession of drugs with intent to supply. On appeal, he argued that the judge should have told the jury, in assessing the response of the reasonable person to the threats, to consider his drug addiction. The Court of Appeal held, dismissing the appeal, that self-induced addiction was *not* a relevant characteristic.

The rationale for this exclusion is not absolutely clear. There are two possible explanations. Either self-induced conditions are excluded, generally, as a matter of policy; or D's condition did not affect his ability to resist threats. Clearly the former is a much broader principle. If this is the correct explanation, then there is an interesting contrast to be drawn between *Flatt* and the provocation case of *Morhall* (1996), considered in Chapter 6, where the House of Lords held that an addiction to glue-sniffing was admissible as a characteristic. The answer could be that the courts in provocation cases are prepared to be more generous because that defence leads, if successful, to a manslaughter conviction, whereas a successful plea of duress leads to an acquittal.

The scope of the defence

Duress (either by threats or circumstances or both) has been accepted as a defence to a very wide range of criminal offences including manslaughter (*Evans and Gardiner* [1976], an Australian case) and causing grievous bodily harm with intent (*Cairns* [1999]). Indeed, it seems that duress (both forms) will be accepted as a defence to any crime except murder and attempted murder (and possibly some forms of treason).

Attempted murder

In *Gotts* (1991), D was a 16-year-old who had been threatened with death by his violent father unless he killed his own mother. D tracked his mother down to a refuge and stabbed her, intending to kill her. However, although seriously injured, his mother survived. The trial judge withdrew the defence of duress and D was convicted. The Court of Appeal and the House of Lords (by 3:2) upheld his conviction. Lord Jauncey said that he could 'see no justification in logic, morality or law in affording to an attempted murderer the defence which is withheld from a murderer'. If anything, the opposite was true: because attempted murder requires an intent to kill, whereas murder requires an intent to kill *or* an intent to cause grievous bodily harm, Lord Jauncey said that the 'intent required of an attempted murderer is more evil than that required of a murderer'.

Murder

Duress is no defence to murder. In *Howe* (1987), the House of Lords gave a variety of reasons for withholding the defence from murderers, none of which is *totally* convincing.

- *Reason*: The ordinary person of reasonable fortitude, if asked to take an innocent life, might be expected to sacrifice their own life instead. Lord Hailsham said that he could not 'regard a law as either "just" or "humane" which withdraws the protection of the criminal law from the innocent victim, and casts the cloak of protection on the cowards and the poltroon in the name of a concession to human frailty'. *Response*: Why should the law require heroism? Indeed it doesn't – Lord Lane CJ's test in *Graham* (approved in *Howe*) sets the standard as the 'sober person of reasonable firmness'. If the reasonable man would have killed in the same circumstances, why should D be punished – *with a life sentence for murder* – when they did only what anyone else would have done?

- *Reason*: One who takes the life of an innocent cannot claim they are choosing the lesser of two evils (per Lord Hailsham). *Response*: This may be true if D is threatened; but what if D is told to kill V and that if they do not, a bomb will explode in the middle of a crowded shopping centre? Surely that is the lesser of two evils. The situation where D's family is held hostage and threatened with death if D does not kill a third party is far from uncommon.

- *Reason*: The Law Commission had recommended in 1977 that duress be a defence to murder. That recommendation was unimplemented; that suggested Parliament was happy with the law as it was. *Response*: Parliament might equally be taken to have approved *Lynch* (1975) – which allowed duress for accessories to murder – and was good law until overruled by the House of Lords in *Howe*.

- *Reason*: Hard cases could be dealt with by not prosecuting, or by action of the Parole Board or exercise of the Royal Prerogative of Mercy in ordering D's early release. *Response*: D still faces being branded, in law, as a 'murderer', and a morally innocent person should not have to rely on an administrative decision for their freedom. In *Lynch* (1975), Lord Wilberforce said, 'A law which required innocent victims of terrorist threats to be tried and convicted as murderers, is an unjust law.'

- *Reason*: To recognise the defence would involve overruling *Dudley and Stephens* (1884), a necessity case (see below). According to Lord Griffiths, that decision was based on 'the special sanctity that the law attaches to human life and which denies to a man the right to take an innocent life even at the price of his own or another's life'. *Response*: The *ratio* of *Dudley and Stephens* is not absolutely clear. It *could* be, and usually is, taken to mean that necessity is no defence to murder – but, instead, it *could* be taken to mean that, on the facts of the case, duress was not available.

- *Reason*: Lord Griffiths thought the defence should not be available because it was 'so easy to raise and may be difficult for the prosecution to disprove'. *Response:* This would apply to most defences! It also ignores the fact that in *Howe*, like *Lynch* (1975), the jury had rejected the defence and convicted. Indeed, Lord Hailsham said that, 'juries have been commendably robust' in rejecting the defence in other cases.

- *Reason*: Lord Bridge thought that it was for the legislature to decide the limits of the defence. *Response*: Why? Duress is a common law defence, so the judges should decide its scope. In *Lynch* (1975), Lord Wilberforce said that, 'the House . . . would not discharge its judicial duty if it failed to define the law's attitude to this particular defence in particular circumstances'.

Howe (1987)
Michael Howe, 19, and two other men aged 19 and 20, participated in the torture, assault and strangling of two young male victims at a remote spot on the Derbyshire moors. At their trial on two counts

of murder and one of conspiracy to murder, they pleaded duress, arguing that they feared for their lives if they did not do as directed by a man called Murray, aged 35. M was not only much older than the others but had appeared in court several times before and had convictions for violence. However, they were convicted of all charges, and their appeals failed in the Court of Appeal and House of Lords.

Howe was followed in *Wilson* (2007), where the Court of Appeal confirmed that duress was never a defence to murder, even though D was only 13 years old. Ashlea Wilson and his father Sean murdered Sean's neighbour, V, using a variety of weapons. Ashlea and Sean admitted killing V, but Ashlea pleaded duress, on the basis that Sean had threatened him with violence if he did not participate. This was rejected. Lord Phillips CJ stated:

> There may be grounds for criticising a principle of law that does not afford a 13-year-old boy any defence to a charge of murder on the ground that he was complying with his father's instructions, which he was too frightened to refuse to disobey. But our criminal law holds that a 13-year-old boy is responsible for his actions and the rule that duress provides no defence to a charge of murder applies however susceptible D may be to the duress.

The decision in *Wilson* may be criticised for its refusal to take into account any of D's characteristics, in particular his age. Suppose that V had survived, and Ashlea had been charged with causing GBH with intent. There is a good chance that he would have been acquitted:

- First, duress would have been available (*Cairns* [1999]).

- Second, the *Graham/Bowen* test would have applied. The jury would have been asked to decide (1) whether Ashlea may have been impelled to act as he did because, as a result of what he reasonably believed Sean had said or done, he had good cause to fear that if he did not so act Sean would kill or seriously injure him; (2) whether a sober 13-year-old boy of reasonable firmness might have taken part in the attack.

> Should duress ever be a defence to murder? Should the law not make allowances for the characteristics of the accused in duress cases where murder is alleged?

Reform of duress

In its 2005 Consultation Paper, *A New Homicide Act?*, the Law Commission (LC) suggested that duress should be made available as a partial defence to first-degree murder, reducing liability to second-degree murder (you will recall from Chapter 5 that the LC also recommended that murder be split into first- and second-degree murder). However, by the time of their 2006 Report, *Murder, Manslaughter and Infanticide*, the LC had changed their position and now recommend that duress should be a full defence to both first- and second-degree murder, and attempted murder. This would entail abolishing the principles established by the House of Lords in *Howe* and *Gotts*. It remains to be seen whether the government, and Parliament, will support the LC in their proposals.

Necessity

In *Dudley and Stephens* (1884), D and S had been shipwrecked in the South Atlantic Ocean in a small boat with another man and a cabinboy. After several days without food or water, they decided to kill and eat the boy, who was the weakest of the four. Four days later they were rescued. They pleaded the defence of necessity. However, this was rejected and they were sentenced to death. In the event, Queen Victoria intervened and exercised the 'Royal Prerogative' to spare their lives. To this day, it is not entirely clear what principle of law is established by this case. There are at least three:

1. Necessity does not exist as a defence in English law.
2. Necessity is generally available, but is not a defence to murder.
3. Necessity is generally available, including as a defence to murder, but the defence was not satisfied in the *Dudley and Stephens* case.

In *Re A* (2000), the Court of Appeal (Civil Division) was prepared to accept that necessity is a defence – and that it is a defence to murder – thereby indicating that option (3) above is correct. Brooke LJ stated that 'there are three necessary requirements for the application of the doctrine of necessity':

- the act is needed to avoid inevitable and irreparable evil

- no more should be done than is reasonably necessary for the purpose to be achieved

- the evil inflicted must not be disproportionate to the evil avoided.

This definition is very different from that regarded as the test for duress of circumstances, which requires that D must have acted in order to avoid a perceived threat of immediate death or serious injury and with no reasonable opportunity for escaping from the threat or contacting the authorities. Brooke LJ said, 'In cases of pure necessity the actor's mind is not irresistibly overborne by external pressures. The claim is that his or her conduct was not harmful because on a choice of two evils the choice of avoiding the greater harm was justified.'

Re A (2000)

In August 2000, twin girls (initially known as J and M to protect their identities) were born in St Mary's Hospital in Manchester. Tragically, they were joined together at the abdomen (known as 'conjoined twins') and, if left as they were, doctors predicted that both would die, probably within 3 to 6 months. This was because M's heart was not strong enough to keep her alive and she was relying on J's stronger heart, which was pumping blood around both tiny bodies, to keep her alive too. However, eventually, as the babies grew, J's heart would be incapable of supporting them both. On the other hand, if surgically separated, J was capable of surviving but M would die within a short time.

The twins' parents, both Catholics, refused to give consent for the operation because of a conviction that deliberately ending the life of one baby to save another was wrong. However, Central Manchester NHS Trust applied to the High Court for permission to operate, which was given. On appeal, the Court of Appeal held that, if the doctors operated, knowing that M would inevitably die, they would commit murder ... except that the defence of necessity would be available. The Court therefore gave permission to operate.

Postscript. The parents decided not to appeal to the House of Lords, and the operation – lasting 20 hours – went ahead in November 2000. M died, as expected, within hours. J, whose real name was revealed to be Gracie Attard, finally left St Mary's Hospital in June 2001. One of the surgeons described her as a 'bright, alert and interested child ... mentally ahead for her age ... we expect her to lead a full and normal life'.

Ward LJ was careful not to create too broad a defence. He pointed out that the facts in *Re A* were unique, and listed them as follows:

Lest it be thought that this decision could become authority for wider propositions, such as that a doctor, once he has determined that a patient cannot survive, can kill the patient, it is important to restate the unique circumstances for which this case is authority. They are that it must be impossible to preserve the life of X without bringing about the death of Y, that Y by his or her very continued existence will inevitably bring about the death of X within a short period of time, and that X is capable of living an independent life but Y is incapable under any circumstances of viable independent existence.

It should be noted that *Re A* is a decision of the Court of Appeal (Civil Division), authorising a surgical operation, and not a decision of the Court of Appeal (Criminal Division). Its status as an authority on criminal law is therefore persuasive only.

In *Quayle and Others* (2005), the Court of Appeal dismissed claims that necessity should be available to those charged with drugs offences because they used it not as a recreational drug but for the purposes of relieving painful symptoms of conditions such as multiple sclerosis or physical injuries. Mance LJ said that whatever benefits there might be (real or perceived) for any individual patients, such benefits were regarded by Parliament as outweighed by disbenefits 'of sufficient strength to require a general prohibition in the national interest'. The suggested defence of 'necessitous medical use' on an individual basis was in conflict with the purpose of the drugs legislation (the Misuse of Drugs Act 1971), for two reasons:

1. No such use was permitted under the legislation, even on doctor's prescription, except for medical research trials; and
2. It would involve unqualified individuals prescribing cannabis to themselves as patients or assuming the role of unqualified doctors by obtaining, prescribing and supplying it to other individual 'patients'.

More recently, in *Altham* (2006), the Court of Appeal held that a person who used cannabis for pain relief and who was charged with possessing a controlled drug could not raise a defence of necessity by relying on Article 3 of the European Convention on Human Rights (prohibition of inhuman or degrading treatment or punishment). D had been involved in a road traffic accident some 15 years earlier which left him with both hips dislocated; subsequently, his left hip had to be surgically removed altogether leaving him 'in chronic pain in his lower limbs ever since'. After several pain-relieving strategies, including acupuncture and prescribed antidepressants had failed, D turned to cannabis, which apparently provided the first form of pain relief since his accident. However, he was eventually prosecuted for and convicted of possessing a controlled drug. The Court of Appeal upheld his conviction, relying heavily upon the judgment in *Quayle and Others*.

There is clearly uncertainty regarding necessity as a defence in English criminal law. Which of the following propositions about the decisions in *Quayle and Others* and *Altham* is correct?

- Necessity as a separate defence (different from duress of circumstances) simply does not exist; or

- Necessity as a separate defence does exist, but it was not available on the facts of those cases.

In his commentary in the *Criminal Law Review* on *Quayle and Others*, Professor David Ormerod supports the second proposition. He argues that the case could be regarded as one of 'pure necessity'. He refers to the 'general principles of necessity' identified by Brooke LJ in *Re A* (2000) and adds that:

> Applying those criteria it would come as no surprise if a jury, having heard expert evidence of the genuine nature and severity of pain being avoided, regarded the action of breaking the law as justified. A plea of necessity avoids many of the restrictions which constrain duress of circumstances: there is no requirement of a threat of death or serious injury ... the defence is potentially available to all crimes, even murder, and there is no requirement of immediacy ... Clarification from the House of Lords as to the elements of the defence of necessity, its rationale, and its relationship with duress of circumstances is urgently needed.

Summary

- Duress comes in two types: duress by threats and duress of circumstances. The principles are identical in either case.

- The threat must be to D personally or to D's family members or to other people close to D (*Wright*; *Hasan*).

- The threat must be believed by D to be following 'immediately or almost immediately' (*Hasan*).

- D will be expected to take advantage of any opportunity that he has to escape or seek police protection. If he fails to take it, the defence may fail unless D can put forward some explanation for this (*Pommell*).

- D will be denied the defence if he voluntarily places himself in such a situation that he risks being threatened with violence. This may be because he joins a criminal organisation or gang (*Fitzpatrick*; *Sharp*) or because he associates himself with people known to be violent criminals (*Heath*; *Hasan*; *Ali*). The defence of duress will fail if D knew, or should have known, that there was a risk of being subjected to compulsion by threats of violence (*Hasan*).

- D must have acted because, as a result of what he reasonably believed, he had good cause to fear death or serious physical injury (*Graham*; *Howe*). It is not necessary for D to actually be in danger of death or serious physical injury; it is whether D believed such a threat existed (*Cairns*).

- The prosecution must prove that the 'sober person of reasonable firmness', and sharing some of D's characteristics, would have resisted the threats (*Graham*). Relevant characteristics include age, physical disability and recognised mental illness (*Bowen*). Certain characteristics are never relevant, e.g. low IQ (*Bowen*) and pliability (*Hegarty*; *Horne*).

- Duress is no defence to murder (*Howe*; *Wilson*) or attempted murder (*Gotts*).

- Necessity is a separate defence from either form of duress (*Re A*). It is available when D acts to avoid an 'act of greater evil'.

- Necessity is probably a defence to murder (*Re A*) and most other crimes but 'medical necessity' is not a defence to possession of unlawful drugs (*Quayle and Others*; *Altham*).

19 Self-defence and the prevention of crime

Introduction

While it is accepted that a person may generally defend themselves and their property from attack, the courts and Parliament have always been mindful of minimising the risk of encouraging over-zealous retaliation in such a situation. There is always the danger that the defender may take on the role of attacker. Public policy also dictates that revenge attacks or vigilante-type behaviour must be discouraged at all costs. For this reason, the use of any force in self-defence must always pass the test of reasonableness. In essence, this is a question of fact for the jury, taking into account all the relevant factors in the case.

Force causing damage to property, injury or even death to other persons may be justified if the force was reasonably used in the defence of certain public or private interests. If D is charged with malicious wounding and pleads self-defence, he is arguing that the wounding was justified and, thus, lawful. The use of lawful force is not an offence; an element of the *actus reus* is missing. There are three situations where force can be used:

- Self-defence. This is regulated primarily by the common law, although some of the common law principles have now been codified in s.76 of the Criminal Justice and Immigration Act 2008 (see below).

- Prevention of crime. This is covered by s.3(1) of the Criminal Law Act 1967, which provides that a 'person may use such force as is reasonable in the circumstances in the prevention of crime, or in effecting or assisting in the lawful arrest of offenders or suspected offenders or of persons unlawfully at large'.

- Defence of property. This is partially but not exclusively covered by s.5(2) of the Criminal Damage Act 1971 (see Chapter 13).

This chapter will concentrate on self-defence and the prevention of crime defence. There is the potential for overlap between the two defences. Suppose a married couple are walking home one night when they are confronted by a mugger. If the man uses force to fight and overpower the mugger he is using self-defence in respect of himself as well as using force in order to prevent crime (robbery). For convenience, the rest of this chapter will simply refer to self-defence unless specific reference to the prevention of crime defence is required. Where this happens the defence will be called 'the s.3 defence'.

Where there is evidence of self-defence this must be left to the jury. However, there must be evidence before the court on which a reasonable jury might think it was reasonably possible that D was acting in self-defence. The judge is not required to direct a jury on what appears to the judge to be a fanciful or speculative matter.

Scope of the defence

Self-defence is usually raised to charges of offences against the person, but it is not confined to them. In *Symonds* (1998), a case of 'pedestrian rage', D was convicted of careless driving after the trial judge omitted to direct the jury on the possibility that he had driven his car in self-defence to escape an irate pedestrian. The Court of Appeal acknowledged that there was some difficulty (though more of theory than substance) with deploying self-defence to offences other than those where force is involved, but nevertheless held that the judge should have directed the jury on the defence. The Court's hesitancy about allowing self-defence was justified: on the facts, the more appropriate defence was surely duress of circumstances (see Chapter 18).

Limits on the defence

When D pleads self-defence, the onus is placed on the prosecution to disprove it. The prosecution must prove that:

• the use of *any* force was unnecessary or, if some force was justifiable, that:

• the actual degree of force used was unreasonable.

The necessity of force

The use of any force is not justified if it is not necessary. The test is whether it was necessary *in the circumstances as they appeared to D*. The danger that D apprehends must be sufficiently specific or imminent to justify their actions, and of a nature which could not reasonably be met by more pacific means.

Threats and pre-emptive strikes

It is not necessary for there to be an attack in progress. It is sufficient if D apprehends an attack. In *Beckford* (1988), Lord Griffiths said, 'A man about to be attacked does not have to wait for his assailant to strike the first blow or fire the first shot; circumstances may justify a pre-emptive strike.'

It follows that it will be permissible for D to issue threats of force, even threats of death, if that might prevent an attack upon themselves or prevent a crime from taking place. In *Cousins* (1982), D believed that a contract had been taken out on his life. He armed himself with his nephew's double-barrelled shotgun and paid a visit to the father of the person he thought was behind the contract. D told the father that when he saw his son, 'I'm going to kill him. I'm going to blow his brains out.' D was charged with making threats to kill and relied upon the s.3 defence. The trial judge directed the jury that the defence was unavailable because D's life was not in immediate jeopardy. He was convicted but the Court of Appeal quashed the conviction. Milmo J said, 'It can amount to a lawful excuse for a threat to kill if the threat is made in the prevention of crime or for self-defence, provided it is reasonable in the circumstances to make such a threat.'

In *Rashford* (2005), the Court of Appeal decided that – in principle at least – it was possible to plead self-defence to a charge of murder, even though D admitted that he had gone out looking for revenge. Dyson LJ stated that:

> The mere fact that a defendant goes somewhere in order to exact revenge from the victim does not of itself rule out the possibility that in any violence that ensues self-defence is necessarily not available as a defence. It must depend on the circumstances. It is common ground that a person only acts in self-defence if in all the circumstances he honestly believes that it is necessary for him to defend himself and if the amount of force that he uses is reasonable.

In the event, the Court of Appeal upheld D's murder conviction on the basis that, according to his own testimony, he had not actually been placed in a position where it was necessary to use force at the time when he stabbed V through the heart.

Preparing for an attack

Where D apprehends an attack upon himself, may he make preparations to defend himself, even where that involves breaches of the law? In *Attorney-General's Reference (No. 2 of 1983)* (1984), D's shop had been attacked and damaged by rioters. Fearing further attacks he made petrol bombs. He was charged with possessing an explosive substance contrary to the Explosive Substances Act 1883. He pleaded self-defence and the jury acquitted. The Court of Appeal accepted that this was correct.

Thus, acts preparatory to justifiable acts of self-defence may be justified. Otherwise D, caught up in a police shootout, who picks up a gun lying on the ground and uses it to shoot one of the criminals, would have a defence to murder – but not to being in possession of a firearm without a certificate contrary to the Firearms Act 1968!

Is there a duty to retreat?

The leading case in this area concerns a violent incident at a house party in Essex. In *Bird* (1985), D was convicted of malicious wounding after the trial judge directed the jury that D must have demonstrated by her actions that she did not want to fight. The Court of Appeal, allowing the appeal, made it clear that this direction 'placed too great an obligation' on D. In particular, it was going too far to say that it was 'necessary' for her to demonstrate a reluctance to fight.

Bird (1985)
Debbie Bird was celebrating her seventeenth birthday at a house in Harlow when a former boyfriend of hers, M, turned up with a new girlfriend. Bird and M began arguing and, eventually, she poured a glass of Pernod over him. M slapped her and Bird lunged at him with her hand, which still contained the glass. The glass broke in his face and gouged his eye out. Exactly why Bird lunged at him was disputed, but the defence claimed that M was holding her against a wall and had threatened to hit her if she did not shut up, and she had struck out in the 'agony of the moment', not realising that she was holding the glass. The Court of Appeal quashed her conviction of wounding.

The reasonableness of force

The general principle is that only such force may be used as is reasonable in the circumstances. This is a question for the jury (*Cousins* [1982]). However, although the question of what is reasonable force is to be judged by the jury, it is critical that they put themselves in the circumstances which D supposed (whether reasonably or not) to exist. The jury should be reminded not to disregard the state of mind of D altogether. This recognises that the force will commonly be used in a moment of crisis. In the Privy Council case of *Palmer* (1971), Lord Morris said that:

> A person defending himself cannot weigh to a nicety the exact measure of his . . . defensive action. If a jury thought that in a moment of unexpected anguish a person attacked had only done what he honestly and instinctively thought was necessary, that would be most potent evidence that only reasonable defensive action had been taken.

The Court of Appeal has affirmed this passage. In *Whyte* (1987), Lord Lane CJ said that 'in most cases . . . the jury should be reminded that [D]'s state of mind, that is his view of the danger threatening him at the time of the incident, is material. The test of reasonableness is not . . . a purely objective test.'

Then in *Scarlett* (1993), Beldam LJ inadvertently created the impression that the reasonableness test was purely subjective instead. D had been convicted of constructive manslaughter, based on the unlawful act of battery. The prosecution had alleged that D, a landlord, had used excessive force in evicting a drunk from his pub in Halifax. The Court of Appeal quashed his conviction because of a misdirection. Beldam LJ took the opportunity to attempt to clarify the law. He began by stating that a jury ought not to convict 'unless they are satisfied that the degree of force used was plainly more than was called for by the circumstances as he believed them to be'. That much is perfectly consistent with *Palmer*.

Regrettably, Beldam LJ then said that the jury ought not to convict 'provided he believed the circumstances called for the degree of force used . . . even if his belief was unreasonable'. This suggestion, that the defence was based on D's subjective belief, was seized on by the defendant in *Owino* (1996). D had been convicted of assault after repeatedly punching his wife in the face. He claimed that she had 'gone for him' and he had simply used force in order to restrain her. The jury thought that, whatever his wife had done, D had used excessive force and convicted. D appealed, arguing that *Scarlett* allowed him a defence if he believed (reasonably or not) the amount of force used was reasonable. The Court of Appeal rejected D's appeal. Collins J confirmed that the test was neither purely objective nor purely subjective. He said:

> In the context of an issue of self-defence . . . then clearly a person would not be guilty of an assault unless the force used was excessive; and in judging whether the force used was excessive, the jury had to take account of the circumstances as [D] believed them to be.

In *Martin* (2002), the Court of Appeal was asked whether psychiatric evidence that caused D to perceive much greater danger than the average person was relevant when a jury was deciding on the issue of reasonable force. The Court held that it was *not* relevant.

Martin (2002)
Tony Martin lived alone at Bleak House Farm in Norfolk. One night in August 1999, two men, Brendan Fearon, aged 30, and Freddie Barras, aged 16, broke into Martin's farmhouse. He was

awakened by the break-in and, armed with a pump-action shotgun, went downstairs to investigate. He found the intruders and, from a position either on or near the bottom of the stairs (there was a dispute about exactly where he was standing), fired the shotgun three times. Fearon was hit in the legs and Barras in the back and legs. Although Fearon escaped, Barras died shortly afterwards. Martin was convicted of murdering Barras and wounding Fearon. His defence at trial, self-defence, was rejected. He appealed on a number of grounds, one of which was that psychiatric evidence had emerged after the trial to the effect that, at the time of the shootings, he suffered from a paranoid personality disorder with recurrent bouts of depression. This meant that he may have genuinely (but mistakenly) thought he was in an extremely dangerous situation on the night in question. The Court rejected his appeal on the basis of self-defence, for the reasons given above, but did quash the murder conviction (substituting one of manslaughter) on the basis that the evidence would instead have supported a plea of diminished responsibility at his trial.

In *Canns* (2005), the Court of Appeal followed *Martin* (2002) in holding that, when deciding whether D had used reasonable force in self-defence, it was not appropriate to take into account whether D was suffering from some psychiatric condition (in his case, paranoid schizophrenia, which may have produced delusional beliefs that he was about to be attacked), except in 'exceptional circumstances which would make the evidence especially probative'. The Court held that, generally speaking, it was for the jury, considering all the circumstances – but *not* evidence of D's psychiatric condition – to set the standards of reasonableness of force. The Court approved the words of the trial judge, who had directed the jury that 'it cannot be right that the more psychotic a defendant may be the greater his chances of acquittal, because of his genuine delusions'.

Should excessive force causing death reduce murder to manslaughter?

Currently, if the jury conclude that D used more force than was reasonable in self-defence and death results, then he is guilty of murder. That is, excessive self-defence is no defence at all. In *Palmer* (1971), Lord Morris said, 'If the prosecution have shown that what was done was not done in self-defence then that issue is eliminated from the case ... The defence of self-defence either succeeds so as to result in an acquittal or it is disproved in which case as a defence it is rejected.'

This was confirmed by the House of Lords in *Clegg* (1995). D's murder conviction was upheld by the Northern Ireland Court of Appeal on the basis that he had used a 'grossly excessive and disproportionate' amount of force. On further appeal, the House of Lords found that, as the danger had passed when D fired the fatal shot, there was no necessity to use force at all, excessive or otherwise. Nevertheless, Lord Lloyd rejected the proposition that excessive force used in self-defence should reduce liability from murder to manslaughter.

Clegg (1995)
Lee Clegg, a soldier of the Parachute Regiment, was on duty at a checkpoint in Belfast one night. A car approached Clegg's section at speed with its headlights full on. Somebody shouted to stop the car. Clegg fired three shots through the windscreen as the car approached, and a fourth at the car as it passed. This last shot hit a female passenger, Karen Reilly, in the back, and killed her. Forensic evidence showed that, when the last shot was fired, the car would already have been ten yards away. On trial for murder, Clegg pleaded self-defence. He was convicted after the trial judge found that this last shot could not have been fired in self-defence because, once the car had passed, Clegg was no longer in any danger. His conviction was upheld.

However, it has been argued that excessive force in self-defence should, like provocation and diminished responsibility, reduce murder to manslaughter. In *Attorney-General's Reference (No. 1 of 1975)* (1977), Viscount Dilhorne said, 'It may be that a strong case can be made for an alteration of the law to enable a verdict of manslaughter to be returned where the use of some force was justifiable [but excessive force was used] but that is a matter for legislation and not for judicial decision.'

Over 30 years later, it looks as if this legislation is finally about to arrive. You will recall from looking at the reform proposals for voluntary manslaughter in Chapter 5 that the proposed new defence of loss of self-control in the Coroners & Justice Bill will allow a partial defence to murder where D killed in response to 'fear of serious violence' against D or some other identified person, provided that a person of D's sex and age, with a 'normal degree of tolerance and self-restraint' and in the circumstances of D, might have reacted in the same or in a similar way. If successful, the new defence will result in a conviction for manslaughter. In the future, this new defence may allow some defendants who use excessive force and kill, to at least avoid a murder conviction.

The Criminal Justice & Immigration Act 2008

Section 76 of the 2008 Act codifies some (but not all) of the above principles. The section applies to both the common law defence and the s.3 defence (s.76(2)). Section 76(3) states that 'The question whether the degree of force used by D was reasonable in the circumstances is to be decided by reference to the circumstances as D believed them to be.' Section 76(4) and (5), which deal with the mistaken use of force in self-defence, have already been examined in Chapter 17. Section 76(6) states that 'The degree of force used by D is not to be regarded as having been reasonable in the circumstances as D believed them to be if it was disproportionate in those circumstances.'

Section 76(7) states that 'In deciding the question mentioned in subsection (3) the following considerations are to be taken into account (so far as relevant in the circumstances of the case) – (a) that a person acting for a legitimate purpose may not be able to weigh to a nicety the exact measure of any necessary action; and (b) that evidence of a person's having only done what the person honestly and instinctively thought was necessary for a legitimate purpose constitutes strong evidence that only reasonable action was taken by that person for that purpose.'

You may note that the wording of the section closely repeats the words used by the courts in some of the above cases. In particular, s.76(7) is very closely based on the words of Lord Morris in *Palmer* (1971). Indeed, s.76(9) states that 'This section is intended to clarify the operation of the existing defences mentioned in subsection (2)', but without apparently changing anything. This begs the question, 'Why did Parliament bother?'

Summary

- Force may be used to protect oneself or another person or to prevent a crime from being committed.

- There must be evidence of self-defence. If there is evidence, then the issue must be left to the jury (*Cousins*). The burden of proof is on the prosecution to show either that it was not necessary to use any force at all, or that the amount of force in fact used was unreasonable.

- Self-defence will normally be pleaded to as a defence to assaults and murder. However, it is not restricted to these crimes (*Symonds*).

- D does not have to wait to be attacked, he may make a pre-emptive strike (*Beckford*).

- A desire for revenge is not necessarily inconsistent with a plea of self-defence, provided that, at the relevant time, D honestly believed it was necessary to defend himself (*Rashford*).

- D may also issue warnings and threats against perceived attackers (*Cousins*).

- There is no requirement of spontaneity. D may arm himself in preparation for a perceived attack on himself and not be guilty of firearms or explosives offences (*Attorney-General's Reference (No. 2 of 1983)*).

- There is no obligation on D to retreat or to demonstrate an unwillingness to fight (*Bird*).

- Whether force used was reasonable is a question for the jury. They must assess that question by putting themselves in the position that D genuinely believed to exist (*Palmer*; *Whyte*; *Scarlett*; *Owino*). However, evidence of a psychiatric condition that caused D to perceive much greater danger is not relevant (*Martin*; *Canns*).

- Excessive force in self-defence that causes death does not reduce liability for murder to manslaughter (*Palmer*; *Clegg*).

Questions on Part 5 Defences

1 Discuss whether the law relating to intoxication is satisfactory.

(OCR 2007)

2 'Insane and non-insane automatism are similar defences involving mental abnormality. It is vital that the distinction between them is fully understood since they produce very different consequences for a defendant who relies on one or other of them.'

Critically evaluate the truth of the above statement.

(OCR 2006)

3 Discuss the extent to which a person who commits an offence because they have been forced to do so against their will may have a defence of either duress or necessity.

(OCR 2005)

4 Mark calls into a pub on his way home from work. There he consumes several pints of strong beer. He is joined at the bar by Trevor who is well known for

his aggressive nature. Trevor is rude to Mark, suggesting that Mark doesn't know how to hold his drink. Mark reacts angrily by shouting at Trevor and pushing him in the chest. Trevor raises his arms in a gesture of innocence but Mark thinks Trevor is about to hit him so he punches Trevor in the face causing Trevor's nose to bleed. Trevor then grabs Mark's arm so Mark takes his beer glass and thrusts it into Trevor's face cutting Trevor's cheek.

Discuss Mark's criminal liability including any defences that may be available to him.

(OCR 2005)

5 'The justifiable use of force in self-defence depends entirely upon the circumstances in which it is used. Factors such as mistake and intoxication may also be relevant.'

Critically consider the truth of the above statement.

(OCR 2006)

Part 6

General principles 2

20 Participation

Introduction

Many crimes are committed by defendants working alone. But a great number are committed with the help or assistance of possibly just one, or possibly a large number, of other people. These people could be locksmiths, getaway drivers, lookouts . . . the range of situations where other people – known as 'accomplices' or 'accessories' or, sometimes, 'secondary offenders' (the terms are more or less interchangeable) – may participate in a criminal offence is infinitely variable. A slightly different situation occurs where two or more defendants work as a team; this is known as a 'joint enterprise', although many of the legal principles are the same in both situations. How has the law responded to the difficulties posed by the many and varied roles played by accomplices?

Principals and secondary parties

The person who directly and immediately causes the *actus reus* of the offence is the 'perpetrator' or 'principal', while those who assist or contribute to the *actus reus* are 'secondary parties', or 'accessories'. The law for indictable offences (including murder, manslaughter, rape, etc.) is set out in s.8 of the Accessories and Abettors Act 1861, as amended. This provides that 'Whosoever shall aid, abet, counsel or procure the commission of any indictable offence . . . is liable to be tried, indicted and punished as a principal offender.' S.44 of the Magistrates' Court Act 1980 provides the same for summary offences (including assault and battery).

The significance of this provision lies in the discretion given to a judge to sentence the accomplice according to the degree of blame for which he or she deserves to be punished. For example, villains who make a living from organised crime are notoriously difficult to convict. They may provide the money and brains behind criminal operations but rarely expose themselves to the risk of being caught. Often, a so-called 'Mr Big' will use a combination of cunning and intimidation to ensure that it is a 'fall-guy' who takes the blame should any planned crime go wrong. However, when the opportunity does actually arise to convict such a villain it is essential that a judge has the power to sentence them accordingly for their part in counselling the offences. It is for this reason that such an accessory may receive a sentence which is greater than that given to the actual principal offender.

Innocent agency

Where the perpetrator of the *actus reus* of a crime is an 'innocent agent', meaning someone without *mens rea*, or someone who is not guilty because of a defence such as infancy or insanity, then the person most closely connected with the agent is the principal. So if D, an adult, employs his 8-year-old son to break into houses and steal, the child is an innocent agent, and the father liable (for burglary) as a principal.

There may be more than one principal

Just because two or more parties are involved, it does not mean one has to be the principal and the other their accessory. They may be both principals, provided that each of them has *mens rea* and together they carry out the *actus reus*. Suppose two friends agree to burgle a house together, or two brothers gang up on their abusive father and beat him up (as in *Pearson* [1992] – see Chapter 6). This is known as a 'joint enterprise', and will be dealt with later on.

What if the principal lacks *mens rea*, or has a defence?

The accessory may nevertheless be liable here: the presence of the *actus reus* is crucial. In the following cases, the accessory was held liable even though the principal offender was not liable. In *Bourne* (1952), D forced his wife, E, on two occasions to commit buggery with the family dog. D's conviction of aiding and abetting the offence was upheld, even though E could not be convicted, had she been tried, because of his duress. The *actus reus* of buggery had been committed.

In *Cogan and Leak* (1976), D terrorised his wife into having sex with E. E's conviction for rape was quashed but D's rape conviction was upheld. The Court of Appeal thought it irrelevant that E may not have had the *mens rea* for rape (apparently, E believed that D's wife was consenting) and D's conviction was upheld on the basis that he had procured the *actus reus* of rape. Lawton LJ said that 'the act of sexual intercourse without the wife's consent was the *actus reus*; it had been procured by [D] who had the appropriate *mens rea*, namely his intention that [E] should have sexual intercourse with her without her consent'.

However, if there is no *actus reus* at all then D cannot be liable for participating in whatever it was that the other person, E was doing. In *Thornton v Mitchell* (1940), a bus driver, E, was reversing his bus relying on the signals of his conductor, D. Two pedestrians behind the bus were run over. E was cleared of driving a motor vehicle without due care and attention – as he *had* driven the bus with due care and attention – but D was nevertheless convicted of aiding and abetting the offence. The Divisional Court quashed D's conviction: there was simply no *actus reus* to aid or abet.

Actus reus of secondary parties

Generally

An accessory will be charged with aiding, abetting, counselling or procuring the particular offence, and is liable if it can be proved that he participated in any one or more of the four ways. The Court of Appeal has held that the words should simply bear their ordinary meaning. In *Attorney-General's Reference (No. 1 of 1975)* (1977), Lord Widgery CJ said:

> We approach s.8 of the 1861 Act on the basis that the words should be given their ordinary meaning, if possible. We approach the section on the basis also that if four ordinary words are employed here – aid, abet, counsel or procure – the probability is that there is a difference between each of those four words and the other three, because, if there were no such difference, then Parliament would be wasting time in using four words where two or three would do.

There is considerable overlap between them and it is quite possible for D to participate in several different ways.

Does there have to be a 'meeting of minds'?

Yes and no. For D to abet or counsel another person, it seems that there must be some common understanding between them. For aiding and procuring, D may participate without the other even knowing what D is doing, or even against the other's wishes – especially where procuring is concerned. In *Attorney-General's Reference (No. 1 of 1975)* (1977), D surreptitiously added alcohol to E's drink for a joke. When E drove home he was arrested and charged with drink-driving and D was charged with procuring the offence. D's addition of alcohol to E's drink was the direct cause of the offence, and would, the Court of Appeal thought, amount to procuring. Lord Widgery CJ said:

> It may ... be difficult to think of a case of aiding, abetting or counselling when the parties have not met and have not discussed in some respects the terms of the offence which they have in mind. But we do not see why a similar principle should apply to procuring ... To procure means to produce by endeavour. You procure a thing by setting out to see that it happens and taking the appropriate steps to produce that happening.

What about a causal connection?

Again, yes and no. It is essential in procuring. In *Attorney-General's Reference (No. 1 of 1975)* (1977), the Court of Appeal held that 'you cannot procure an offence unless there is a causal link between what you do and the commission of the offence'. However, for aiding, abetting and counselling there is no requirement of a *strong* causal connection. In *Calhaem* (1985), the leading counselling case, Parker LJ said that there was 'no implication in the word itself that there should be any causal connection between the counselling and the offence'. The only 'connection' required was that 'the actual offence must have been committed and committed by the person counselled' and did not happen accidentally.

> *Calhaem* (1985)
> Kathleen Calhaem was so infatuated with Shirley Rendell's boy-friend that she hired a hitman, a private detective called Zajac, to carry out her murder. Zajac apparently changed his mind about the killing but nevertheless went to Rendell's house armed with a hammer, knife and a loaded shotgun wrapped in a parcel intending to make it look like he had at least tried to do the killing. However, once at the house, something made him go 'berserk' and he hit Rendell several times with the hammer and then stabbed her in the neck. He pleaded guilty to murder and Calhaem was convicted of counselling. On appeal, she argued that the causal connection between her instigation of the crime and the killing was broken when Zajac decided to kill Rendell of his own accord. However, the conviction was upheld.

'Aiding'

Aiding refers to the provision of help or assistance, either before or during the commission by the principal of the *actus reus*. A good example is *Bainbridge* (1960), where D supplied equipment that was subsequently used in a bank robbery. Other common examples of aiding include D driving E to the scene of the crime, or where D acts as a lookout while E commits an offence (e.g. burglary).

'Abetting'

For abetting, the threshold of involvement is very low. The Court of Appeal in *Giannetto* (1996) stated that 'any involvement from mere encouragement upwards would suffice' for conviction of abetting. The Court commented that if E was to say to D, 'I am going to kill your wife', then if D patted him on the back, nodded, or said, 'Oh goody', then that would make D liable for abetting 'because he is encouraging the murder'.

Mere presence at the scene of the crime

Is it possible for D's presence at the scene of a crime to amount to abetting? In *Coney and Others* (1882), an illegal, bare-knuckle fight was held in a makeshift ring by the road between Ascot and Maidenhead. A large crowd gathered to watch. Many of the crowd were seen to be actively encouraging the fighters. The three defendants, who were in the crowd but were simply watching, were convicted of abetting assault – but the conviction was quashed on appeal. The jury had been directed that persons watching an illegal fight were guilty by virtue of their mere presence. Hawkins J laid down the following propositions:

- Encouragement may be intentional (e.g. by expressions, gestures or actions intended to signify approval) or unintentional (e.g. by misinterpreted words, or gestures, or by silence). However, only intentional encouragement amounts to aiding and abetting.

- Generally speaking, it is not criminal to stand by, to be a mere passive spectator of a crime; some active steps by word or action are required. However, there is an exception if a person was 'voluntarily and purposely present' at the scene of a crime and offered no opposition or did not even express dissent. This might, under some circumstances, 'afford cogent evidence' upon which conviction for aiding and abetting would be justified.

From this, and other cases, the following requirements can be identified before secondary liability can be imposed on spectators for their presence at the scene of a crime:

- D must have intended to encourage the principal; and

- D's presence must have actually encouraged the principal.

In *Coney and Others*, the convictions were quashed because the first requirement was missing. A similar result occurred in *Clarkson and Others* (1971). An 18-year-old girl, Elke von Groen, had been subjected to a brutal gang-rape at a British Army barracks in West Germany. Although Clarkson and others were present in the room, there was no evidence that they had done anything – such as hold the girl down, or shout encouragement – other than just watch. Their convictions of rape were quashed. Megaw LJ stated that it was not enough 'that the presence of the accused person has, in fact, given encouragement. It must be proved that he intended to give encouragement; that he *wilfully* encouraged.'

Meanwhile, in *Allan* (1965), the second requirement was missing. D was present – but totally passive – at an affray. Apparently, he had a secret intention to join in to help his 'side' if need be. The Court of Appeal quashed his conviction for abetting the others. Although he *was* present, it seems clear that the affray would have taken place anyway – so there was no encouragement *in fact*. This decision must be correct: upholding the trial court's decision would have been tantamount to convicting Allan for his thoughts alone.

An example of a successful conviction, because both elements were established, occurred in *Wilcox v Jeffrey* (1951). An American saxophonist, Coleman Hawkins, appeared at a concert in London, despite a legal prohibition on him being employed in the UK. Herbert Wilcox, the proprietor of a magazine, *Jazz Illustrated*, had attended the concert and then written a 'most laudatory' review in his magazine. The Divisional Court upheld his conviction for abetting Hawkins' illegal employment. Wilcox's presence in the audience was intended to encourage, and did in fact encourage.

Figure 7 The elements needed for a conviction of aiding and abetting

Case	Encouragement in fact?	Intention to encourage?	Guilty of aiding and abetting?
Coney & Others	Yes	No	No
Clarkson & Others	Yes	No	No
Allan	No	Yes	No
Wilcox v Jeffrey	Yes	Yes	Yes

Aiding and abetting by omission

If D has knowledge of the actions of E, plus the duty or right to control them, but deliberately chooses not to, then he may be guilty of aiding or abetting by omission. In *Tuck v Robson* (1970), Lord Parker CJ asked the rhetorical question, whether 'inaction, passive tolerance, can amount to assistance so as to make the accused guilty of aiding and abetting' – and answered it in the affirmative. D, a pub landlord, with the authority to remove persons from the pub, tolerated after-hours drinking. He was convicted of aiding and abetting breaches of the Licensing Act.

The same principle was used in *Webster* (2006). E, who had been drinking all day, drove D's car erratically and at high speed before losing control, leaving the road and crashing in a field. V, a rear-seat passenger, was thrown out of the car and killed. E pleaded guilty to causing V's death by dangerous driving and D was convicted of abetting him by allowing him to drive his car when E was obviously drunk. The Court of Appeal held that the crucial issue was whether D had an opportunity to intervene once he realised (because of the speed at which he was going) that E was driving dangerously. (D's conviction was subsequently quashed because of a misdirection concerning *mens rea* – see below.)

'Counselling'

In *Calhaem* (1985), Parker LJ said that 'we should give to the word "counsel" its ordinary meaning, which is . . . advise, solicit, or something of that sort . . .'. The recent case of *Luffman* (2008) provides a good example. D was convicted of counselling murder on the basis that she had asked E to murder her ex-husband, agreed to pay him £30,000 to do it, and then pestered him to carry out the killing as quickly as possible, until he eventually did so.

'Procuring'

Traditionally it was thought that 'to procure means to produce by endeavour' (*Attorney-General's Reference (No. 1 of 1975)* (1977), *per* Lord Widgery CJ). However, in *Milward* (1994), D, a farmer, instructed an employee to drive a tractor on public roads. The tractor was poorly maintained and a trailer became detached, hit a car and killed a passenger. D was convicted of procuring the offence of causing death by reckless driving. Yet D certainly did not 'endeavour' to produce the passenger's death. All that seems to be required now is a causal connection between D's act and the principal's commission of the offence.

Mens rea of secondary parties

The accessory must:

• Have *intended* to assist, encourage, etc., the commission of the offence; and

• Have *knowledge* of the circumstances which constituted the offence.

Intention

D must have intended to participate in the commission of the offence. Any motives or desires that D may have had are, of course, irrelevant. It is therefore no defence that D is utterly indifferent as to whether the principal commits the offence or not. In *National Coal Board v Gamble* (1959), a colliery weighbridge operator, H, allowed a lorry driver to leave the colliery and drive onto a public road even though the lorry was overweight. The Coal Board was found guilty (vicariously, that is, by assuming responsibility for the actions of its employee) of aiding and abetting the offence of driving an overloaded lorry on the public roads. It was no defence that H was indifferent to the commission of the offence.

This gives accessorial liability a very wide scope. The problem was discussed in *Gillick v West Norfolk and Wisbech* AHA (1986), a civil case. G was seeking a declaration that it would be unlawful for a GP to give contraceptive advice to a girl under 16, because this would amount to aiding and abetting the girl's boyfriend to have unlawful sexual intercourse. The House of Lords thought that the GP would not be acting illegally, provided what they did was 'necessary' for the girl's physical, mental and emotional health. Lord Scarman said that the '*bona fide* exercise by a doctor of his clinical judgment must be a complete negation of the guilty mind which is an essential ingredient of the criminal offence of aiding, abetting the commission of unlawful sexual intercourse'.

Does this decision mean that motive is relevant in criminal law?

What difference is there between a gun salesman, interested only in cash, and a GP, interested only in the best interests of a 15-year-old girl?

Of course, *Gillick* is a civil case and anything said therein is not binding on courts dealing with criminal cases. However, Lord Scarman's statement received the approval of Lord Hutton in the criminal case of *English* (1999) – see below.

Knowledge of the circumstances

D must have knowledge of the circumstances that constitute the offence. In *Johnson v Youden and Others* (1950), Lord Goddard CJ said:

> Before a person can be convicted of aiding and abetting the commission of an offence, he must at least know the essential matters which constitute that offence. He need not actually know that an offence has been committed, because he may not know that the facts constitute an offence and ignorance of the law is no defence.

This principle was applied in *Webster* (2006), the facts of which were given above. The Court of Appeal allowed D's appeal because the judge had invited the jury to consider whether D knew, or ought to have realised, that E was drunk. The Court of Appeal decided that the reference to what D 'ought to have realised' posed an objective standard instead of a purely subjective standard for D's *mens rea*.

The 'essential matters' will be the circumstances and consequences of the *actus reus*. If D is not aware of these he cannot be liable. In *Ferguson v Weaving* (1951), D was the landlady of a large pub. One night, customers were found drinking after time, an offence under s.4 of the Licensing Act 1921. Crucially, there was no evidence that D actually knew that her customers were drinking after hours. A charge of counselling and procuring the customers' offences was dismissed and the Divisional Court confirmed that decision.

Extent of knowledge required: the contemplation principle

> Suppose D supplies E with a screwdriver – what else (if anything) should D need to know before he can be held liable as an accessory to burglary if the screwdriver is subsequently used in order to break into a house? Suppose D and E are on a joint enterprise to commit burglary. D knows that E is armed with a screwdriver. If they are disturbed and E uses the screwdriver to kill the householder, with intent, does this make D guilty of murder?

Secondary parties

If D is accused of aiding, abetting, etc., then there must be proof that he was aware that a crime of a particular type may be committed. D does not need to know the exact details, but he must be aware of more than that some illegality is planned. In *Bainbridge* (1960), D had purchased some oxygen-cutting equipment for E, which E used six weeks later in breaking into the Midland Bank at Stoke Newington, north London. The equipment was left behind and it was subsequently traced back to D. He was convicted of aiding and abetting burglary, and the Court of Criminal Appeal dismissed his appeal. Lord Parker CJ laid down the following propositions:

- D need not have knowledge of 'the precise crime' or 'the particular crime'

- However, D must know 'the type of crime that was in fact committed'

- But it is not enough that D merely knows that 'some illegal venture is intended'.

Applying these principles, it was sufficient that D knew the equipment was going to be used for stealing money from a bank. It was not necessary that he knew in advance that it was going to be the Midland Bank, or the date on which the raid was to take place. But it would not suffice for a conviction if he simply knew that the equipment was going to be used to dispose of stolen property.

In *DPP for Northern Ireland v Maxwell* (1978), D was a member of the UVF, a Protestant terrorist organisation. One night, he guided other members of the UVF to a Catholic pub, where one of them threw a bomb.

D was convicted of doing an act with intent to cause an explosion and possession of a bomb. He appealed on the basis that he was unaware of the precise nature of the attack, but the House of Lords upheld his conviction. The Lords took the opportunity to confirm – and extend – the *Bainbridge* principle. Both Lord Fraser and Lord Scarman said that D was guilty if he knew that any one of a 'range' of crimes might be committed. This extends *Bainbridge*, which referred only to crimes of certain 'type'. Lord Scarman said (emphasis added):

> A man will not be convicted of aiding and abetting any offence his principal may commit, but only one which is within his contemplation. He may have in contemplation only one offence, *or several; and the several which he contemplates he may see as alternatives.* An accessory who leaves it to his principal to choose is liable, provided always the choice is made from *the range of offences* from which the accessory contemplates the choice will be made.

Joint enterprise

The slight difference here is that D and E are already committed to carrying out one crime, typically robbery or burglary. The question is whether D can be held liable for another crime, typically murder, that is in fact committed, usually because things do not go according to plan. What is required is proof that D participated in the joint enterprise with foresight of that other crime. Indeed, D is liable for *all* crimes committed by E as a result of carrying out the joint enterprise, *provided* that they were contemplated, in advance, by D. In *English* (1999), Lord Hutton said:

> Where two parties embark on a joint enterprise to commit a crime and one party foresees that, in the course of the enterprise, the other party may commit, with the requisite *mens rea*, an act constituting another crime, the former is liable for that crime if committed by the latter in the course of the enterprise.

The requirements for liability are as follows:

- D must have foresight that E may commit another crime

- D must foresee that E will have the requisite *mens rea* at the time of committing it

- The crime foreseen must be committed in the course of the enterprise.

English (1999)

Philip English and a man called Weddle agreed to attack a police officer with wooden posts. However, in the course of the attack, W produced a knife with which he killed the officer. English said that he did not know that W was armed with the knife. The judge nevertheless directed the jury to convict English of murder if they believed that he knew that W might cause really serious injury with the wooden post. The House of Lords quashed English's conviction on the basis that Weddle's use of the knife had not been contemplated, and amounted to a departure from the scope of the joint enterprise.

Rahman and Others (2008) involved a joint enterprise to attack V, which actually resulted in V's murder by E. The House of Lords was asked whether, in such a case, D could be held liable if he had contemplated that E might attack V with the *intent to do GBH*, whereas E had actually attacked V with the *intent to kill*. The Law Lords answered this question 'Yes'. This must be correct – in *English*, the House of Lords had ruled that, generally speaking, it was sufficient that D contemplated that E might commit murder, i.e. kill with malice aforethought. The distinction suggested by the appellant in *Rahman* would have introduced a very fine factual distinction which would only complicate the law.

Justification of the contemplation principle

In *English* (1999) it was argued that the different standards of liability for imposition of murder liability on the members of the joint enterprise, where one of the members kills, was anomalous. The law is as follows:

- The perpetrator (the person who actually does the killing) must be proven to have malice aforethought

- The other members of a joint enterprise need only foresee that the principal *might* commit murder.

Lord Steyn took a forthright view. He said that 'the answer to this supposed anomaly ... is to be found in practical and policy considerations'. He specifically referred to 'the utility of the accessory principle' and how it would be 'gravely undermined' if the law required proof of intention on the part of all members of the enterprise. The reasons for this stance are twofold.

1. The *difficulty in establishing proof of intention.* Lord Steyn thought that it would 'almost invariably be impossible for a jury to say that the

secondary party wanted death to be caused or that he regarded it as virtually certain'.

2. *The desirability of controlling gangs.* Lord Steyn said that the criminal law had to deal 'justly but effectively with those who join with others in criminal enterprises'. He stated that 'joint criminal enterprises only too readily escalate into the commission of greater offences. In order to deal with this important social problem the accessory principle . . . cannot be . . . relaxed'.

The contemplation principle and weapons

In *Anderson and Morris* (1966), Lord Parker CJ said that if one member of a joint enterprise 'departed completely' from what had been agreed, 'suddenly formed an intent to kill' and acted upon it, then to hold the other members liable even for manslaughter was 'something which would revolt the conscience of people today'. This was approved in *English* (1999). The unforeseen use of the knife by Weddle took the killing outside the scope of the joint enterprise. This was the case even though English had participated in a joint enterprise involving the use of a weapon (wooden posts). The House of Lords nevertheless decided that, because Weddle had produced a completely different weapon (a knife), the killing fell outside the scope of the joint enterprise and English was not liable for murder.

Several joint enterprise cases involving murder have looked at this issue – where the use of one particular weapon was contemplated by D but another, different weapon was actually used by E in order to kill V. The question is, does the use of a different weapon always take the killing outside of the scope of the joint enterprise, allowing D to avoid liability for murder? The answer is 'No'. In *English* (1999), Lord Hutton said (emphasis added):

> If the weapon used by [E] is *different to, but as dangerous as*, the weapon which [D] contemplated he might use, [D] should not escape liability for murder because of the difference in the weapon; for example, if he foresaw that [E] might use a gun to kill and the latter used a knife to kill, or *vice versa*.

Similarly, in *Rahman and Others* (2008), Lord Bingham noted that 'it is clear that some weapons are more dangerous than others and have the potential to cause more serious injury, as a sawn-off shotgun is more dangerous than a child's catapult'. Ultimately, it is a question of fact for the jury whether one weapon is more dangerous than another.

The 'fundamentally different' rule

Another way of looking at the liability of the members of a joint enterprise is to use the 'fundamentally' or 'radically' different rule. It involves asking whether E committed an act which was 'fundamentally' or 'radically' different from what D had contemplated in advance. If so, then D is not liable for that act. A good example of this rule is provided by *Rafferty* (2007). D, E and F jointly attacked V on a beach in South Wales. While the attack continued, D left the scene with V's debit card and tried unsuccessfully to withdraw cash from his bank account. In D's absence, V was dragged across the beach by E and F, stripped naked, taken some distance into the sea and drowned. All three defendants were convicted of murder but, on appeal, D's conviction was quashed. D had participated in a joint enterprise involving the crimes of assault (by kicking and punching) and robbery. The deliberate drowning of V by E and F was of a 'fundamentally different' nature from those crimes and therefore D was not liable for murder.

Joint enterprise and murder: summary

This is, inevitably, quite a complex area of law, as it always involves two (or sometimes more) defendants, whose *mens rea* is often different. You may find helpful this summary of the various legal principles provided by Lord Brown in *Rahman and Others* (2008):

> If D realises that E may kill or intentionally inflict serious injury, but nevertheless continues to participate with E in the venture, that will amount to a sufficient mental element for D to be guilty of murder if E, with the requisite intent, kills in the course of the venture unless (i) E suddenly produces and uses a weapon of which D knows nothing and which is more lethal than any weapon which D contemplates that E or any other participant may be carrying and (ii) for that reason E's act is to be regarded as fundamentally different from anything foreseen by D.

Withdrawal

An accessory, or a member of a joint enterprise, may withdraw, and escape liability for the full offence, subject to certain conditions being met. These conditions appear to be identical in either case. However, a crucial distinction must be drawn between, on the one hand, pre-planned criminal activity and, on the other, spontaneous criminal behaviour.

Pre-planned criminal activity

In this situation, the fundamental principle is that mere repentance without action is not enough. Specifically, D will need to satisfy two conditions:

- They must communicate their withdrawal to E

- They must (depending on how advanced the crime is) take active steps to prevent it.

Communication

In *Becerra and Cooper* (1975), a joint enterprise case, Roskill LJ said that there must be 'timely communication' by the person wishing to terminate their involvement in the enterprise. Roskill LJ said that:

> What is 'timely communication' must be determined by the facts of each case but where practicable and reasonable it ought to be such communication, verbal or otherwise, that will serve unequivocal notice upon the other party to the common unlawful cause that if he proceeds upon it he does so without the further aid and assistance of those who withdraw.

Becerra and Cooper (1975)
Becerra and Cooper were in the middle of the burglary of an old woman in Swansea when they were disturbed by a neighbour, a Mr Lewis. B shouted, 'Come on, let's go', climbed out of the window and ran off. There was a struggle and C, who had the knife, stabbed Lewis four times, once in the heart. C then escaped through the window. B and C were convicted of murder. B appealed, *inter alia*, on the ground that by the time C stabbed Lewis he had withdrawn from the common enterprise. The Court of Appeal upheld the convictions. Roskill LJ was clearly unimpressed with B's argument: he said that something 'vastly different and vastly more effective' was required for withdrawal than shouting 'Let's go'.

Thus in *Whitefield* (1984), where D had tipped off a burglar that his neighbours' flat was unoccupied, but subsequently informed the man of his wanting no more to do with it, his withdrawal was effective. However, in *Rook* (1993), where D had been heavily involved in the planning stage of a contract killing, his failure to tell anyone of his decision to withdraw meant that his disappearance before the killing took place was insufficient.

Spontaneous criminal activity

In *Mitchell and King* (1999), the Court of Appeal held that communication of withdrawal from a joint enterprise was a necessary condition only for cases of *pre-planned* criminal activity, as in *Rook*, above. This was not the case where the criminal behaviour was *spontaneous*, as in this case, where an argument quickly developed into a fight outside a fast-food takeaway. In such cases, it was possible to withdraw merely by walking away.

This principle has been confirmed in two subsequent 'spontaneous' joint enterprise cases, both culminating in murder. However, in neither case was D successful in avoiding liability. This was because, although it is possible to withdraw merely by walking away, the defendants had not even done that. In *O'Flaherty and Others* (2004), D was involved in an outbreak of spontaneous violence on the streets of Luton involving rival groups who had just left a concert by So Solid Crew. After a few minutes, V was stabbed to death. D was convicted using joint enterprise principles. The Court of Appeal rejected his argument that he had withdrawn by the time of the stabbing, as CCTV footage placed him in the same street at the crucial time. Similarly, in *Mitchell* (2008), violence had erupted spontaneously outside a pub in Bradford, culminating in V being stamped to death. Again, D was convicted using joint enterprise principles, and again the Court of Appeal rejected her argument that she had withdrawn by the time of the killing on the basis that she was still present at the scene of the killing.

Victims as accessories

The mere fact that D is also a victim does not protect them from accessorial liability. Suppose D, a masochist, allows E, a sadist, to wound him for sexual gratification, then D should be liable for aiding and abetting E's unlawful assault.

Occasionally a statute may protect a particular class or type of person, for example, a child, so that they may not be convicted. In *Tyrrell* (1894), D, a 14-year-old girl, was convicted of aiding and abetting her father to have incest *with her*, contrary to s.5 of the Criminal Law Amendment Act 1885 (since repealed). Her conviction was quashed. The Court of Criminal Appeal thought it impossible that an Act designed to protect young girls could have been intended to punish them instead.

Reform

In May 2007, the Law Commission (LC) published a Report, *Participation in Crime* (Law Com No. 305), in which they made a number of proposals for reforming secondary liability and joint enterprise. The report includes the following proposals (amongst others):

- The abolition of the offences of aiding, abetting, counselling and procuring, under s.8 of the Accessories and Abettors Act 1861 and s.44 of the Magistrates' Courts Act 1980.

- The creation of a new secondary liability offence of 'assisting or encouraging' the commission of an offence. 'Encouraging' would be defined as including (but not limited to) emboldening, threatening or pressurising someone else to commit an offence.

- The new offence could be committed by omission, if D failed to take 'reasonable steps' to discharge a duty.

- For liability under the new offence, D must intend that the 'conduct element' of the substantive offence be committed.

- The principle of 'innocent agency' should be retained.

- Joint enterprise should be retained, but the *mens rea* required should be modified. The LC suggest that, for liability as part of a 'joint criminal venture', D should either intend that E should, or believe that E would or might, commit the 'conduct element' of the 'principal offence'. However, even if D had the required intent or belief, he would not be liable if E's conduct 'fell outside the scope of the joint venture'.

- D should be able to withdraw and therefore 'escape liability as a secondary party if he or she is able to demonstrate that he or she had negated the effect of his or her acts of assistance, encouragement or agreement before the principal offence was committed'.

- There should be a defence available if D acted for the purpose of 'preventing the commission' of an offence or 'to prevent or limit the occurrence of harm', provided in either case that it was 'reasonable' to act as D did in the circumstances.

- The exemption for victims (the *Tyrrell* principle) should be retained. This would apply where D assisted or encouraged an offence which existed in order to protect a 'particular category' of persons and D fell within that category.

In July 2008, the government published a Report entitled *Murder, Manslaughter and Infanticide: Proposals for reform of the law*. In the Report the government makes some proposals of its own for reform of secondary liability and joint enterprise – but only in the context of murder. The government proposes the creation of two new statutory offences:

1. Assisting and encouraging murder.
2. Assisting and encouraging manslaughter.

Both offences require E to kill V with assistance or encouragement from D, with D's intent being to assist or encourage E to kill or cause serious injury. The difference between the offences would be determined by E's liability. Offence (1) would apply if E actually committed murder, whereas offence (2) would apply if E committed only (involuntary) manslaughter.

The government also proposes placing the present law of joint enterprise involving murder onto a statutory basis. The government's proposed draft offence, 'murder in the context of a joint criminal venture', essentially codifies the principles set out in cases such as *English* (1999) and *Rahman and Others* (2008), above. It would be committed if E committed murder in the context of a 'joint criminal venture', and D foresaw that, either:

- a person *might* be killed by one of the other participants (not necessarily E) acting with intent to kill or cause serious injury; or

- serious injury *might* be caused to a person by one of the other participants (not necessarily E) acting with intent to cause such injury and E's criminal act was within the 'scope of the venture'.

E's criminal act would be within the 'scope of the venture' if it did not 'go far beyond' that which was planned, or agreed to, or foreseen, by D. Furthermore, D would not escape liability merely because at the time of the murder he was 'absent'. This is designed to place the decision in *Rook* (1993) on a statutory basis.

Summary

- An accomplice is anyone who aids, abets, counsels or procures the principal offender to commit a criminal offence. The words bear their ordinary meaning (*Attorney-General's Reference (No. 1 of 1975)*).

- A joint enterprise occurs where two defendants embark on a criminal venture together (*Pearson*).

- Accessories are liable to be 'tried, indicted and punished' as a principal offender.

- Accessories may be liable even if the principal offender is not guilty for some reason – provided the principal performed the required *actus reus* (*Bourne*; *Cogan and Leak*; *Thornton v Mitchell*).

- Mere presence at the scene of a crime does not, generally speaking, amount to abetting (*Coney and Others*). There must be encouragement in fact and an intention to encourage (*Wilcox v Jeffrey*). If only one or other of these is present, there is no liability (*Clarkson and Others*; *Allan*).

- The accessory must have intended to aid, abet, etc., the commission of the offence (*National Coal Board v Gamble*) and have knowledge of the circumstances which constitute the offence (*Johnson v Youden and Others*).

- D does not need to know the exact details of the offence but he must be aware of more than that some illegality is planned (*Bainbridge*; *DPP for Northern Ireland v Maxwell*).

- In joint enterprise cases, D is liable for all crimes committed by E within the scope of the joint enterprise (*English*). This includes all offences that D contemplated that E might commit. However, D must foresee that the other would have the required *mens rea*, as well as the *actus reus* (*English*). D's awareness of E being armed – and, if so, with what weapon – may be a crucial factor in establishing what crimes D contemplated (*Rahman & Others*).

- Under the 'fundamentally' or 'radically' different rule of joint enterprise, if D contemplates that E may commit a certain crime, but E actually commits a fundamentally or radically different crime, then D is not liable for that crime (*Rafferty*; *Rahman and Others*).

- An accessory, or a member of a joint enterprise, may withdraw, and escape liability for the full offence. If the criminal venture was pre-planned, then D must, at the least, communicate their unequivocal withdrawal (*Becerra and Cooper*; *Rook*).

- If the criminal venture was spontaneous, then D simply walking away might suffice for a withdrawal (*Mitchell and King*). But a failure to even walk away will result in D being held liable (*O'Flaherty and Others*; *Mitchell*).

- Victims cannot be guilty of offences under statutes designed for their own protection (*Tyrrell*).

21 Attempts

Introduction

If D poisons his mother's drink, fully intending to kill her so that he can inherit under her Will, but she drops dead from a heart attack by some freak coincidence before drinking it, should D escape liability because he failed to kill her? If D bursts into a post office with a sawn-off shotgun, terrifies the staff and customers, but leaves empty-handed because one of the staff reacted quickly enough to press the alarm, should he escape liability because he failed to steal anything? Of course, both defendants are not liable for murder or robbery respectively, as they did not complete the crime. But they would almost certainly be guilty of an attempt. Indeed, the first illustration is taken from the facts of *White* (1910), where D tried to kill his own mother with potassium cyanide, only for her to die of natural causes. However, D was found guilty of attempted murder.

The law relating to attempts perfectly illustrates that element of criminal liability which addresses the significance of *mens rea* or the guilty mind. Clearly, in the above examples, the accused is intent upon committing an offence but fails in the attempt. It would be ludicrous to regard their actions as innocent. They deserve to be sentenced for their actions just as much as they would had their attempted crime been successful. After all, they intended to commit a criminal offence. However, a person cannot be convicted for harbouring evil thoughts by themselves.

Attempt (alongside conspiracy and the new offences of encouraging and assisting crime, which will be examined in the next chapter) is an example of an 'inchoate' offence. The term 'inchoate' refers to the situation where a person has done something which can be regarded as a preparatory criminal act with the intention that a substantive offence (such as murder or robbery) should be carried out. Apart from the moral justification of punishing a person who intends to commit criminal activity, there is a practical reason for the existence of these crimes. After all, it is the duty of the police to prevent crime as well as to detect it. It would do little for the protection of the public were the police always required to wait until a substantive offence had actually been committed before being able to make an arrest. For example, if an informant reveals that a gang is planning a robbery, it makes sense for the police to pre-empt the danger to the public that could accompany such a venture. Provided there is good evidence that an agreement to commit the robbery has been entered into, the police may arrest and charge those concerned with the offence of conspiracy.

The *actus reus* of attempts

Section 1(1) of the Criminal Attempts Act 1981 provides that 'If, with intent to commit an offence to which this section applies, a person does an act which is more than merely preparatory to the commission of the offence, he is guilty of attempting to commit the offence.' Although the judge must decide whether there is evidence on which a jury could find that there has been such an act, the test of whether D's acts have gone beyond the merely preparatory stage is essentially a question of fact for the jury (s.4(3) of the 1981 Act). If the judge decides there is no such evidence, he or she must direct them to acquit; otherwise the question must be left to the jury, even if the judge feels the only possible answer is guilty.

'More than merely preparatory'

When is D guilty of an attempt? When they have gone beyond the 'merely preparatory' stage. But when is that? Consider the following scenario: Ken discovers that his girlfriend is seeing another man (F). Ken decides to do something about it. He decides to kill this love rival. But at which point does he become liable for attempted murder?

- He buys a shotgun.

- He shortens the barrel.

- He loads it.

- He leaves his house, wearing overalls and a crash helmet with the visor down, carrying a bag containing the loaded gun.

- He approaches F's car as F drops his daughter off at school.

- He opens the car door and gets in.

- He says he wants to 'sort things out'.

- He takes the shotgun from the bag.

- He points it at F, and says, 'You are not going to like this'.

At this point F was able to grab the end of the gun, throw it out of the window and escape. These are the facts of *Jones* (1990), who was convicted of attempted murder, the Court of Appeal upholding his conviction. Taylor LJ said that obtaining the gun, shortening the barrel, loading the gun, and disguising himself were clearly preparatory acts but – once Jones had got into the car and pointed the loaded gun – then there was sufficient evidence of an attempt, to leave to the jury.

The common law offence of attempt was abolished by the Criminal Attempts Act 1981. The 1981 Act is a codifying Act. This means that the 'natural meaning' of the statutory words must be considered first but, if any provision is 'of doubtful import', then previous cases may be referred to. They are not binding, but are persuasive. At common law, there was a variety of tests used by the courts to determine whether D had done an act which could be described as 'an attempt' to commit an offence.

The 'Proximity' or 'Last Act' test

The Law Commission thought that the most suitable of these tests was the 'Proximity' or 'Last Act' test. In *Eagleton* (1855), it was said that 'acts remotely leading towards the commission of the offence are not to be considered as attempts to commit it, but acts immediately connected with it are. In this case, no other act on the part of the defendant would have been required. It was the last act ... and therefore it ought to be considered as an attempt.' This test was applied in *Robinson* (1915). D, a jeweller, insured his stock against theft. He then concealed it around his shop, tied himself up and called for help. He told the police that he had been attacked and his safe robbed. However, his scheme was discovered. Although D confessed, his conviction for attempting to obtain £1,200 from his insurers by false pretences was quashed. He still had to approach the insurers for a claim form, fill it in, submit it, etc. His acts were not 'immediately connected' with the substantive offence.

The Law Commission's support for this test was surprising. First, the expression 'immediately connected' could be interpreted very narrowly, as *Robinson* shows. Second, the Proximity test looked *backwards* from the commission of the full offence, to see if D's acts were close to that. The 'more than merely preparatory' test looks *forward* from the point of preparatory acts to see whether D's acts have gone beyond that stage.

The 'Rubicon' test

Obviously the Law Commission's views on what test the courts should use was not binding, and in *Widdowson* (1986), the Court of Appeal adopted a different common law test, the 'Rubicon' test as proposed by Lord Diplock in *Stonehouse* (1978). He stated that there was an attempt only where D had 'crossed the Rubicon'. (*Note*: The Rubicon is a river in northern Italy, the crossing of which by Julius Caesar and his army in

49 BC led to inevitable civil war. 'Crossing the Rubicon' therefore means to pass the point of no return.) In *Widdowson*, D wished to obtain a van on hire purchase but, realising that his application would be rejected, filled in the form under a false identity. The Court of Appeal quashed his conviction of attempting to obtain services by deception. The acts he had done were too remote from the substantive offence. Too many acts remained unperformed; in particular he had not actually submitted the form to the hire purchase company. He had not yet 'crossed the Rubicon'.

The 'series of acts' test

In *Boyle and Boyle* (1986), the Court of Appeal referred to another pre-1981 Act test: the 'series of acts' test, put forward by the 19th-century judge and writer Sir James Stephen, according to whom 'an attempt to commit a crime is an act done with intent to commit that crime, and forming part of a series of acts which would constitute its actual commission if it were not interrupted'. In *Boyle and Boyle*, the defendants were convicted of attempted burglary, having been found by a policeman standing near a door, the lock and one hinge of which were broken. The Court of Appeal upheld this conviction.

'Embarking upon the crime'

This divergence of approaches after the 1981 Act was clearly unsatisfactory. However, progress was made in *Gullefer* (1990). D had placed an £18 bet on a greyhound race at Romford Stadium. Seeing that his dog was losing, he climbed onto the track in front of the dogs, waving his arms and attempting to distract them, in an effort to get the stewards to declare 'no race', in which case he would get his stake back. His conviction of attempted theft was quashed; his act was merely preparatory. He still had to go to the bookmakers and demand his money back. Lord Lane CJ recognised that the problem with Stephen's test was that it did not specify when the 'series of acts' begins. Further, acts which were obviously merely preparatory could be described as part of a 'series'. Instead, he said:

> The words of the Act seek to steer a midway course. [A crime] begins when the merely preparatory acts have come to an end and [D] embarks upon the crime proper. When that is will depend, of course, upon the facts in any particular case.

In *Jones* (1990), above, Taylor LJ agreed with Lord Lane CJ, adding that the correct approach was to 'look first at the natural meaning of the statutory words, not to turn back to earlier case law and seek to fit some previous test to the words of the section'. In the light of the more expansive approach signalled by *Gullefer* and *Jones*, the decision in *Campbell* (1991) is surprisingly narrow. D was arrested by police when, armed with an imitation gun, he approached to within a yard of a post office door. His conviction for attempted robbery was quashed: the Court of Appeal thought that there was no evidence on which a jury could 'properly and safely' have concluded that his acts were more than merely preparatory. It seems that the police should have waited until D had entered the post office, or even approached the counter.

'Trying to commit the crime'

In *Geddes* (1996), the Court of Appeal offered another formulation for identifying the threshold. A member of school staff discovered D lurking in the boys' toilet. He ran off, leaving behind a rucksack, in which was found various items including string, sealing tape and a knife. He was charged with attempted false imprisonment of a person unknown. The judge ruled that there was evidence of an attempt and the jury convicted. On appeal, the conviction was quashed. There was serious doubt about whether he had gone beyond the mere preparation stage. He had not even tried to make contact with any pupils. The Court of Appeal postulated the following questions:

- Had the accused moved from planning or preparation to execution or implementation?

- Had the accused done an act showing that he was actually trying to commit the full offence or had he got only as far as getting ready, or putting himself in a position, or equipping himself, to do so?

In *Tosti* (1997), the Court of Appeal followed the *Geddes* approach. D and his co-accused, White, had provided themselves with oxy-acetylene equipment, driven to a barn which they planned to burgle, concealed the equipment in a hedge, approached the door and examined the padlock. They then became aware that they were being watched and ran off. The Court of Appeal upheld their convictions of attempted burglary. The conviction seems right: the men were clearly 'actually trying to commit the full offence' of burglary by examining a padlock.

More than merely preparatory: conclusion

When D might be said to be 'embarked on the crime proper' (*Gullefer* (1990)) or when he was 'actually trying to commit the full offence' (*Geddes* (1996)), he has committed an act that is 'more than merely preparatory' and is guilty of an attempt.

The *mens rea* of attempt

Intention

A key element of attempt is D's intention. It must be proven that D intended to commit the *actus reus* of the substantive offence. In *Whybrow* (1951), the Court of Appeal held that, although on a charge of murder, an intention to cause GBH would suffice for liability; where attempted murder was alleged, nothing less than an intent to kill would do: 'the intent becomes the principal ingredient of the crime'.

In *Mohan* (1975), the Court of Appeal defined 'intent' as 'a decision to bring about, insofar as it lies within [D]'s power, the commission of the offence which it is alleged [D] attempted to commit, no matter whether [D] desired that consequence of his act or not'. 'Intent' clearly includes D's purpose. If D is *trying* to do something, then it does not matter whether he views his chances of success as remote, or even just possible. In *Walker and Hayles* (1990), the Court of Appeal applied the *Nedrick* (1986) direction (see Chapter 5) on oblique intent in the common law to 'intent' in s.1 of the 1981 Act.

Conditional intent

Attempted theft and burglary cases have caused difficulties when it comes to framing the indictment. The problem is that most burglars, pickpockets, etc. are opportunists who do not have something particular in mind to steal. Two cases from the 1970s illustrated the problem:

- *Easom* (1971) – D had been observed rummaging in a handbag in a cinema but did not take anything from it. The Court of Appeal quashed his conviction of stealing the handbag, purse, notebook, tissues, cosmetics and pen. The Court declined to substitute a conviction of attempted theft of those articles.

- *Husseyn* (1977) – D and another man had been observed loitering near the back of a van. As police approached they ran off. The Court of Appeal quashed D's conviction of attempting to steal the sub-aqua equipment that was in a holdall in the van.

The convictions in *Easom* and *Husseyn* were quashed because the defendants had not been charged correctly. With hindsight, it was wrong to suggest that Easom wanted to steal some tissues, or cosmetics. Clearly, he was looking to steal any money that might have been in the handbag. The same is true in *Husseyn* – here, D wanted to steal anything valuable that might have been in the holdall; he was not interested in the sub-aqua equipment that was actually in the van. In *Attorney-General's Reference*

(Nos. 1 and 2 of 1979) (1979), the Court of Appeal identified the solution to this problem. In cases like this, D should be charged with attempting to steal 'some or all of the contents' of the handbag, holdall, pocket, etc.

The relevance of recklessness

Although intention is the key element in attempts, recklessness may have a role to play in some cases. Consider the crime of aggravated arson contrary to s.1(2) and (3) of the Criminal Damage Act 1971 (discussed in Chapter 13). The *actus reus* of the substantive offence is committed if D destroys or damages property by fire. The *mens rea* is that D was at least reckless whether property be destroyed or damaged, and also that D was at least reckless whether life be endangered.

To be held liable for attempted aggravated arson, it must be proved that D intended to commit the *actus reus*; that is, destroy or damage property by fire. But is it also necessary to prove that D intended to endanger life? The answer is 'No', because that is not part of the *actus reus*. In *Attorney-General's Reference (No. 3 of 1992)* (1994), the Court of Appeal held that, if D is charged with attempted aggravated arson, then the prosecution simply has to prove that he *intended* to destroy or damage property by fire, being *reckless* whether life be endangered. D had thrown a petrol bomb towards a car containing four men but it missed and smashed harmlessly into a wall. The trial judge ruled that it had to be shown that D intended both to damage property *and* to endanger life. The Court of Appeal held that this was wrong.

Excluded offences

S.1(4) of the Criminal Attempts Act 1981 excludes attempts to commit the following:

- conspiracy

- aiding, abetting, counselling or procuring the commission of an offence (except where this amounts to a substantive offence, e.g. complicity in another's suicide).

Section 1(1) also implicitly excludes other attempts. There must be 'an act', so it is impossible to attempt to commit a crime by omission (e.g. D cannot be convicted of attempting to murder V by omission). Where a crime cannot be committed intentionally (such as involuntary manslaughter), it is impossible to attempt it. Furthermore, because diminished responsibility and provocation are no defence to attempted murder, there is therefore no offence of 'attempted manslaughter'.

Impossibility

If a crime is impossible to commit, obviously no one can be convicted of *committing* it. However, it does not automatically follow that no one can be convicted of *attempting* to commit it. (The situation we are looking at here is different from the situation where D attempts to commit what is not in fact a crime, even if they think that it is. Here there is no offence. Thus, in *Taaffe* [1983], which was considered in Chapter 1, D would not have been guilty of 'attempting to import currency' either – there is simply no such offence.)

There may, therefore, be liability for an attempt where D attempts to commit the substantive crime but fails because it was:

- *Physically impossible* (e.g. D attempts to steal from V's pocket, but, unknown to D, the pocket is in fact empty; or D attempts to murder V who, unknown to him, died that morning; or

- *Legally impossible* (D attempts to damage property belonging to another, when the property actually belongs to D himself).

At common law, there was no liability if the crime attempted was physically or legally impossible. Section 1(2) of the Criminal Attempts Act 1981 abolished that loophole. The subsection provides that 'a person may be guilty of attempting to commit an offence to which this section applies even though the facts are such that the commission of the offence is impossible'. However, despite the clear wording of the statutory provision, in *Anderton v Ryan* (1985), the House of Lords decided that the 1981 Act had not been intended to affect the situation of impossibility. Bernadette Ryan bought a video recorder, which she thought was stolen (it wasn't). Later, she confessed to police officers who were investigating a burglary at her home, 'I may as well be honest, it was a stolen one.' Her conviction of attempting to handle a stolen video recorder was quashed on the basis that the video recorder was not actually stolen. Lord Roskill said that there could be no liability for 'doing innocent acts'.

This decision was overruled less than a year later. In *Shivpuri* (1987), Lord Bridge said:

The concept of 'objective innocence' is incapable of sensible application in relation to the law of criminal attempts. The reason for this is that any attempt to commit an offence which involves 'an act which is more than merely preparatory to the commission of the offence' but which for any reason fails, so that in the event no offence is committed, must *ex hypothesi*, from the point of view of the criminal law be 'objectively innocent'. What turns what would otherwise ... be an innocent act into a crime is the intent of the actor to commit an offence.

Shivpuri (1987)

Pyare Shivpuri, on a visit to India, was approached by a man who offered to pay him £1,000 if, on his return to England, he would receive a suitcase, which a courier would deliver to him containing drugs. S would then receive instructions as to how he was to distribute the drugs. The suitcase was duly delivered to him. S then received instructions to go to Southall station to deliver some of the drugs. However, he was arrested outside the station. A package containing a powdered substance was found in his bag. At his flat, he produced the suitcase and more packages of the same powdered substance. S, believing the powder to be either heroin or cannabis, fully confessed to receiving and distributing illegally imported drugs. Subsequently, the powder was scientifically analysed and found to be snuff or some similar harmless vegetable matter. S was convicted of attempting to be knowingly concerned in dealing in prohibited drugs, and the House of Lords dismissed his appeal.

Shivpuri was followed in *Jones* (2007), in which D was convicted of attempting to incite a child under 13 to engage in sexual activity, contrary to s.8 of the Sexual Offences Act 2003. On the facts, the offence was impossible, as the 'child' whom he thought he was inciting was actually an undercover policewoman. The Court of Appeal, however, held that he had rightly been convicted of attempting to commit this impossible offence.

Jones (2007)

D wrote graffiti on the walls of train and station toilets seeking girls aged 8 to 13 for sex in return for payment and requesting contact via his mobile phone. A journalist saw one of the messages and contacted the police who began an operation using an undercover policewoman pretending to be a 12-year-old girl called 'Amy'. D sent several texts to 'Amy' in which he tried to persuade her to engage in sexual activity. Eventually, 'Amy' and D agreed to meet at a Burger King in Brighton, where he was arrested. At his trial, D pointed out that, as 'Amy' didn't exist, he had not intended to incite any actual person under the age of 13. The judge rejected the submission. D changed his plea to guilty and appealed, but the Court of Appeal upheld his conviction.

It has been argued that, in cases like *Shivpuri* and *Jones*, D is being punished solely for his criminal intention. However, this overlooks the fact that, for an attempt, there must be a 'more than merely preparatory' act. Furthermore, defendants like Shivpuri and Jones who intend to smuggle drugs or who intend to have sex with young girls (and are prepared to act on their intentions) are dangerous people; their prosecution and conviction is in the public interest. In many cases, the 'objectively innocent' nature of the acts means that the attempt will not come to light. But, in those cases where it does, D should not escape punishment.

Reform

In September 2007 the Law Commission (LC) published a Consultation Paper, *Conspiracy and Attempts* (Paper No. 183), in which they recommended the following (amongst other things):

- The present offence of attempt should be abolished and replaced with two new offences.
  - First, a new attempt offence, limited to the situation where D reaches the last acts needed to commit the substantive offence.
  - Second, a new offence of 'criminal preparation'.

- Both new offences would require proof of intention to commit the substantive offence (murder, robbery, etc.). Intention could, as at present, be either direct or oblique intent. Conditional intent would continue to suffice.

- Both new offences would carry the same (maximum) penalty as the substantive offence.

- It should be possible to commit either of the new offences by omission.

The LC is trying to resurrect the 'Last Act' test as set out in *Eagleton* (1855), which will significantly narrow the scope of the offence of attempt. It would not be possible, for example, to say that D in *Jones* (1990) would definitely be guilty of attempted murder under the proposed new attempt offence. In pointing the shotgun at V, he had gone beyond the 'merely preparatory' stage, but had he reached the 'last act' stage? However, if not, D could instead be convicted of 'preparing to commit murder'.

The LC describe the proposed new 'criminal preparation' offence as meaning acts which could be regarded (as attempt is at present) as part of the execution of D's intention to commit the substantive offence. Thus, D will still have to go beyond the 'merely preparatory' stage. The LC give some examples of situations where D might incur liability for criminal preparation. One is the situation where D is caught examining or interfering with a door, window or lock. At present, such facts might support a conviction for attempted burglary (see *Boyle and Boyle* [1986] and *Tosti* [1997], above) but under the LC's proposals, this would become the offence of 'preparing to commit burglary'.

The primary motivation for the proposals is the need to address the reluctance of the Court of Appeal in some cases to accept that D has committed an 'attempt', as presently understood. The LC is confident that, in cases such as *Campbell* (1990) and *Geddes* (1996), discussed above, the courts would be more willing to convict the defendants of 'preparing to commit robbery' and 'preparing to commit false imprisonment', respectively, instead.

The proposal to allow for the new attempt/criminal preparation offences to be committed by omission is interesting and, it is submitted, welcome. For example, under the present law, it is possible to commit murder by omission (see *Gibbins and Proctor* [1918], discussed in Chapter 2), but it is not possible to commit attempted murder by omission. Yet if there is sufficient evidence that D is trying to kill V by starving them to death (but has not succeeded), surely D deserves to be punished for this?

Summary

- D is guilty of attempting an offence if he does an act which is 'more than merely preparatory' to the commission of that offence, under s.1(1) of the Criminal Attempts Act 1981.

- The Act replaced the common law crime of attempt. The Act does not give any definition of when the 'more than merely preparatory' stage is reached – it is left entirely to the courts. However, the Law Commission recommended the old 'Proximity' or 'Last Act' test established in *Eagleton, Robinson*, be used.

- Cases decided just after the Act used the 'Rubicon' test established in *Stonehouse* instead (*Widdowson*). Then courts began to use another old test, the 'series of acts' test (*Boyle and Boyle*).

- Since then the courts have developed new tests. One test is whether D has 'embarked on the crime proper' (*Gullefer*). Another is whether D was 'actually trying to commit the full offence' (*Geddes*; *Tosti*).

- Intent is 'the principal ingredient' of attempt (*Whybrow*).

- A conditional intent will suffice (*Attorney-General's Reference (Nos. 1 and 2 of 1979)*).

- Recklessness has a role in attempt (*Attorney-General's Reference [No. 3 of 1992]*).

- Legal or physical impossibility is no defence (*Shivpuri*; *Jones*).

22   Conspiracy, and encouraging or assisting crime

A   Conspiracy

Introduction

Section 1(1) of the Criminal Law Act 1977, as amended, provides that

> *if a person agrees with any other person or persons that a course of conduct shall be pursued which, if the agreement is carried out in accordance with their intentions . . . will necessarily amount to or involve the commission of any offence or offences by one or more of the parties to the agreement, he is guilty of conspiracy.*

Where two or more people have agreed to commit a crime then there may be liability for a conspiracy. Gathering enough evidence to prove that the parties had agreed to commit a crime can present problems for the police but, where evidence is available, conspiracy is a valuable weapon for prosecuting those involved in large-scale organised crime. Typical cases involve prosecutions for conspiring to smuggle drugs (*Siracusa* [1989]) or conspiring to launder stolen money (*Saik* [2006]).

The *actus reus* of conspiracy

'Agreement'
The offence is complete as soon as there is an agreement to commit a criminal offence (*Saik* (2006)). However, the agreement continues until the substantive offence is performed, abandoned or frustrated (*DPP v Doot* [1973]). Thus, further parties may join a subsisting conspiracy at any time until then. There is certainly no requirement that the substantive offence be committed (*Saik*). Indeed, the whole point of the offence of conspiracy is to allow for the prosecution and conviction of those who agree to commit a crime, even if they do not actually succeed in committing it.

'The parties'

There must be at least two parties. It is essential that there is a common purpose or design, and that each alleged conspirator has communicated with at least one, but not necessarily all, of the others.

Excluded parties: s.2 Criminal Law Act 1977

The 'intended victim' of an offence cannot be guilty of conspiring to commit it (s.2(1)). For example, D, a 13-year-old girl, agrees to have sex with E, an older man. D could not be convicted of conspiring to commit the offence of sexual activity with a child, contrary to s.9 of the Sexual Offences Act 2003, because she would be the 'intended victim' of the offence. Section 2(2) – as amended by the Civil Partnership Act 2004 – further provides that D is not guilty of conspiracy if the only other person with whom D makes an agreement is:

(a)   D's spouse or civil partner;

(b)   a person under the age of criminal responsibility (presently 10 years of age); or

(c)   the 'intended victim'.

The exclusion in s.2(2)(a) is controversial, because it means that, if Mr and Mrs X agree to kill their neighbour, no crime has been committed. But if the couple were unmarried and reached exactly the same agreement, this would be conspiracy to murder, a very serious offence. The exclusion in s.2(2)(c) is also controversial as it means that E (the older man in the above example) would also escape liability for conspiracy, even though he has agreed to have sex with a 13-year-old girl. The Law Commission has recently proposed to abolish both of these exclusions (see below).

The *mens rea* of statutory conspiracy

The parties must:

- *agree that a course of conduct shall be pursued* which,

- if the agreement is carried out *in accordance with their intentions* will necessarily amount to or involve the commission of any offence or offences by one or more of the parties to the agreement.

Agreement on a 'course of conduct'

This is not limited to the physical acts, but includes the consequences of those acts too. It is necessary to establish exactly what consequences were agreed upon. If D and E agree that E will kneecap V, this is a conspiracy to wound or cause GBH – it does not metamorphose into a conspiracy to murder if D actually does the kneecapping and V happens to die.

'In accordance with their intentions . . .'

Conspiracy requires that those who are party to the agreement intend to do the substantive offence (*Saik* (2006)). But does this mean that, if D and E agree to commit a crime but D, secretly, has no intention of seeing it through, there will be no conspiracy? In *Anderson* (1986), the House of Lords decided that the answer to this question was 'No'. D had been convicted of conspiracy to effect the escape of a prisoner from Lewes prison. D stood to receive £20,000 for his part in the escape, which was to purchase and supply equipment, transport and accommodation. D's appeal – that he had no intention of seeing the plan put into effect – was rejected. Lord Bridge said that the *mens rea* of conspiracy was 'established if, and only if, it is shown that the accused, when he entered into the agreement, intended to play some part in the agreed course of conduct in furtherance of the criminal purpose'.

Lord Bridge was concerned to see that a 'perfectly respectable citizen' who went along with a conspiracy 'with the purpose of frustrating and exposing the objective of the other parties' should not be liable, and thought he was doing so. In fact, he may have achieved quite the opposite.

Suppose that D is a criminal mastermind. According to Lord Bridge, he is not guilty of conspiracy if he never intended to 'play some part'. On the other hand, an undercover policeman could well be guilty of conspiracy if he intended to play an active role in order to remain undetected and/or to gather evidence. This led the Court of Appeal to undertake a damage-limitation exercise in *Siracusa* (1989). O'Connor LJ said that 'the intention to participate in the furtherance of the criminal purpose is also established by his failure to stop the unlawful activity'. This deals with the problem of the mastermind, although it still requires that he fails to prevent someone else doing something.

As for the undercover policeman, he appears liable for conspiracy precisely because he does intend to 'play some part'. In *Yip Chiu-Cheung* (1994), the Privy Council used this positively in order to uphold a conviction. D had conspired with E, an undercover US drug enforcement officer, to smuggle heroin from Hong Kong to Australia. The judge directed the jury that, if they found that E intended to export the heroin from Hong Kong, he was in law a co-conspirator and, hence, they could convict D of conspiring with him. They convicted and the Privy Council upheld D's conviction: the mere fact that E would not have been prosecuted were he to export the drugs did not mean he did not intend to do it. D and E had conspired to commit the offence.

333

'If the agreement is carried out . . .'

In *Jackson* (1985), D and E agreed with V that they would shoot him in the leg if V, who was then on trial, was convicted of burglary, in order to encourage the court to sentence him more leniently! They were convicted of conspiracy to pervert the course of justice. The Court of Appeal upheld their convictions, dismissing their argument that there was no conspiracy because V may have been acquitted. Although their agreement was 'conditional', there was nevertheless an agreement. In *Saik* (2006), Lord Nicholls gave another example of a 'conditional' agreement. A conspiracy 'to rob a bank tomorrow if the coast is clear when the conspirators reach the bank is not, by reason of this qualification, any less a conspiracy to rob'. In the same case, Lord Brown offered a different example: 'If two men agree to burgle a house, but only if it is unoccupied or not alarmed, they are clearly guilty of conspiracy to burgle.'

Impossibility

At common law, impossibility was a defence (except where it was down to D's choice of method being inadequate). However, the Criminal Law Act 1977 abolished that defence. Hence, D and E could be convicted of a conspiracy to murder a particular politician on the basis of an agreement even if – unknown to them – the politician in question had died in his sleep the previous night.

Reform of conspiracy

In September 2007 the Law Commission (LC) published a Consultation Paper, *Conspiracy and Attempts* (Paper No. 183), in which they recommended the following (amongst other things):

- Abolition of the spousal immunity in s.2(2)(a) of the Criminal Law Act 1977, which the LC describes as 'anomalous and anachronistic'.

- Abolition of the exemptions in s.2(1) and s.2(2)(c) of the 1977 Act for the 'intended victim' and for those who conspire with the 'intended victim'. But the LC also recommends the creation of a specific statutory defence for victims charged with conspiracy based on their 'protected' status.

Summary

- Conspiracy is governed by the Criminal Law Act 1977.

- It requires an agreement between at least two parties. As soon as the agreement is reached, the offence has been committed (*Saik*).

- Certain parties are excluded. The 'intended victim' of an offence cannot conspire to commit it (s.2(1)). There is also no conspiracy where D agrees with his or her spouse, civil partner, a child under the age of criminal responsibility or the 'intended victim' (s.2(2)).

- The parties must agree on a 'course of conduct' that will necessarily amount to the commission of an offence by one of them. However, there is no requirement that any offence actually be committed (*Saik*).

- There may still be a conspiracy even if one party has no intention of seeing it through – provided they intended 'to play some part' (*Anderson*). Playing a part has been taken to include failing to stop the conspiracy (*Siracusa*).

- It is no defence for D to conspire with an undercover police officer – there was still an agreement to commit an offence (*Yip Chiu-Cheung*).

- There is a conspiracy even if the agreement is conditional on some future event or circumstance (*Jackson*; *Saik*).

- Impossibility is no defence.

B   Encouraging or assisting crime

Background

At common law it was an offence to 'incite' someone to commit any offence. This was committed if D encouraged or persuaded someone else to commit an offence, whether or not that offence actually took place. However, the general offence of incitement was abolished by s.59 of the Serious Crime Act 2007 and three new offences of encouraging or assisting crime have been created instead (see below). However, various specific incitement offences survive, including:

- Soliciting murder (s.4, Offences Against the Person Act 1861). In *Abu Hamza* (2006), D, the Imam of Finsbury Park mosque in north London, was convicted of six counts of this offence.

- Incitement to commit certain sexual acts outside the United Kingdom, contrary to the Sexual Offences (Conspiracy and Incitement) Act 1996.

- Inciting a child under 13 to engage in sexual activity, contrary to s.8 of the Sexual Offences Act 2003. In *Jones* (2007), discussed in Chapter 21, D was convicted of attempting to commit this offence.

Liability under the Serious Crime Act 2007

Sections 44–46 of the Serious Crime Act 2007 create three new offences of doing an act 'capable of encouraging or assisting' crime. The new offences came into force in October 2008 and, as yet, there is no case law to demonstrate how the Act will operate in practice. The new offences require the doing of an act 'capable of encouraging or assisting' the commission of:

- an offence, *with intent* to encourage or assist (s.44)

- an offence, *believing* it will be committed and *believing* that the act will encourage or assist (s.45)

- one or more offences, *believing* that one or more of them will be committed and *believing* that the act will encourage or assist (s.46).

The *actus reus* of ss.44 and 45 is identical: they both require D to do 'an act capable of encouraging or assisting the commission of an offence'. The *mens rea* requirements are different, however. Section 44(1) states that D must *intend* to encourage or assist commission of the offence, while s.44(2) adds that D is not to be taken to have the necessary intent 'merely because such encouragement or assistance was a foreseeable consequence of his act'. Section 45 states that D must *believe* that the offence will be committed and that his act will encourage or assist its commission. To illustrate the operation of these provisions, imagine that one night D drives E to a house which E plans to burgle. Here, D's act (driving the car to the house) is clearly 'capable' of assisting burglary, but is D liable under s.44 or s.45? This will depend on D's *mens rea* (if any). For example:

- If D and E and friends and have planned the whole thing in advance, then D is probably liable under s.44 – he *intends* to assist E.

- If D is sure that E is going to burgle the house, perhaps because D knows that E has committed several burglaries before, but drives E to the house anyway, then D is probably liable under s.45 – he *believes* that burglary will be committed.

- If D is a taxi driver and does not think, or even suspect, that E plans a burglary then he has no *mens rea* and is not liable under either s.44 or s.45.

The *actus reus* of s.46 is slightly broader; it requires that D 'does an act capable of encouraging or assisting the commission of one or more of a number of offences'. The *mens rea* of s.46 is that D *believes* that one or more of those offences will be committed (but has no belief as to which); and that D *believes* that his act will encourage or assist the commission of one or more of them. An example of a situation where s.46 might apply is where D lends a knife to E believing that E will use it to commit either wounding or robbery (but D is unsure which).

Sections 45 and 46 both refer to D's 'belief', but this word is not defined anywhere in the 2007 Act. Ormerod and Furston, *Serious Crime Act 2007: The Part 2 offences* [2009] Crim LR 389, suggest that belief 'constitutes a state of subjective awareness short of knowledge, but greater than mere suspicion'.

A key provision in the 2007 Act is s.49. This states that D may be liable for an offence under ss.44–46 'whether or not any offence capable of being encouraged or assisted by his act is committed'. Thus, if D provides E with a gun to be used in a bank robbery, then D is liable under s.44 or s.45, depending on D's *mens rea*, regardless of whether the robbery goes ahead or not. D commits the s.44 or s.45 offence as soon as he hands over the gun. Of course, if the robbery did go ahead, then D could also be convicted, under secondary liability principles, of aiding the offence (see Chapter 20). There is therefore a potential overlap between the Accessories and Abettors Act 1861 and the Serious Crime Act 2007.

Another provision to note is s.47(8). This states that references in the Act to the doing of 'an act' are to be taken to include (a) 'a failure to act', (b) 'the continuation of an act that has already begun' and (c) 'an attempt to do an act'. Thus, s.47(8)(a) means that the offences in ss.44–46 can all be committed by omission. For example, suppose that D is a cleaner with the keys to an office block. One night she deliberately fails to lock the back door to the building after she finishes her shift so that E can slip into the building to burgle it. D could be convicted under s.44 of intentionally *failing* to do an act (locking the back door), which is capable of assisting the commission of an offence (burglary). As noted above, D would be liable whether or not E actually committed the burglary.

Section 47(8)(c) makes it clear that an attempt to do an act capable of assisting or encouraging the commission of an offence will attract liability. Thus, for example, in the scenario given earlier (where D drives E to a house which E plans to burgle), it appears that D will be liable even if on the way the car breaks down, or they are involved in a car crash, or simply get lost, so that they never reach their destination. In each situation, D has probably not done an act which is 'capable' of assisting E to commit burglary, but he has attempted to do so.

Defences of 'acting reasonably'

Section 50(1) and (2) provide defences to anyone charged under ss.44–46 where they can prove that they:

- knew certain circumstances existed; or

- reasonably believed certain circumstances to exist,

provided, in either case, that they can also prove that it was 'reasonable' to act as they did in those circumstances (whether the actual circumstances or those that D reasonably believed to exist). In determining the latter point – whether it was 'reasonable' for D to act as he did – s.50(3) lists three factors to be considered: the seriousness of the anticipated offence(s); any purpose for which D claims to have been acting, or any authority by which D claims to have been acting. Note that the burden of proof is on D, albeit on the balance of probabilities. Without the benefit of case law it is a matter of speculation when (if at all) these defences might operate. One possible scenario involves D, a shopkeeper, who sells tools to E, believing that E is going to use the tools to commit a burglary. D might face liability under s.45 unless he can prove that it was 'reasonable' to act as he did in the circumstances that he believed to exist.

Defence for victims

Section 51 provides a defence, in certain circumstances, for victims. If D is accused of intentionally doing an act capable of encouraging or assisting E to commit an offence, but that offence exists for 'the protection of a particular category of persons', and D falls within the 'protected category', then D has a defence. Thus, where D, a 13-year-old girl, sends a text message to E, an older man, suggesting that they have sex, D would appear not to be guilty under s.44 of intentionally doing an act which is capable of encouraging E to commit an offence (specifically, sexual activity with a child, contrary to s.9 of the Sexual Offences Act 2003). The 2003 Act is designed to protect people like D, so it would be paradoxical to convict her in those circumstances.

Evaluation of the Serious Crime Act provisions

The provisions described above have been heavily criticised by several academics. For example, Ormerod and Furston, *Serious Crime Act 2007: The Part 2 offences* [2009] Crim LR 389, describe the new legislation as containing 'some of the worst criminal provisions to fall from Parliament in recent years ... These are offences of breathtaking scope and complexity. They constitute both an interpretative nightmare and a prosecutor's dream.'

Summary

- Sections 44–46 of the Serious Crime Act 2007 create three new offences of doing an act 'capable of encouraging or assisting' the commission of one (or more) offences.

- In addition to doing the act, s.44 requires that D intends to encourage or assist the substantive offence.

- Sections 45 and 46 require that D believes that his act will encourage or assist the substantive offence(s).

- In all cases, it is immaterial whether or not the substantive offence is committed (s.49).

- Doing 'an act' includes failing to do an act (s.47(8)(a)). Thus, D can commit the ss.44–46 offences by omission.

- Doing 'an act' also includes attempting to do an act (s.47(8)(c)).

- There are defences of acting 'reasonably' (s.50). D bears the burden of proof, on the balance of probabilities.

- There is a defence for victims, if the substantive offence exists for 'the protection of a particular category of persons', and D falls within the 'protected category' (s.51).

- Incitement has been abolished (s.59) but specific incitement offences, such as soliciting murder, survive.

Questions on Part 6 General principles 2

I   'Criminal intentions do not always produce a completed substantive offence. Nevertheless, it is both just and essential for the protection of society that those who intend to carry out criminal acts are subject to prosecution in the same way as those who actually succeed in committing crimes.'

Consider whether you agree with this statement using examples from the current law on attempts.

(OCR 2005)

2   Sandra and Vincent have lived together for five years. One day Vincent suddenly tells Sandra that he is leaving her to start a new relationship with Wendy with whom he has been having an affair. Sandra is shocked and distressed and goes to see her friend Ursula. Ursula never trusted Vincent and also knows Wendy very well.
    Ursula suggests to Sandra that she should take revenge by killing Vincent, who is now living in Wendy's flat. They then agree that, if Sandra can obtain a gun, Ursula will trick Wendy into letting her have a key to the flat. The plan goes ahead and Ursula gives Sandra the spare key which she has obtained from

Wendy. In the meantime, Sandra has bought a pistol and some ammunition from Rudi. Unknown to her, the ammunition contains only blank imitation rounds.

One evening Ursula invites Wendy out for a meal so that Vincent will be alone in the flat. Sandra goes round to the flat, lets herself in with the key given to her by Ursula and confronts Vincent. After a brief argument Sandra produces the pistol from her handbag and fires it at Vincent while he has his back turned. Hearing the loud click, Vincent turns round and says, 'What was that?' By this time, Sandra has hastily thrust the pistol back in her bag and Vincent doesn't even see it.

Discuss the criminal liability, if any, of Sandra, Ursula and Rudi.

(OCR 2003)

Part 7

Studying criminal law

23 Criminal law in context

Introduction

Criminal law does not exist in isolation and any student of criminal law soon realises that it is but one of many branches of law that govern the complex relationships that exist in a modern society. That very complexity is, these days, forcing most practising lawyers to specialise in one or two branches of law. Many specialise in criminal law. The era of the small firm of family solicitors, made up of one or two partners, dealing with every type of legal problem is rapidly disappearing.

Even so, for many the mention of the words 'the law' does still immediately conjure up selective images of the police, criminals, jury trials and judges sentencing villains to terms of imprisonment. The truth is that law touches almost every aspect of our daily lives in one way or another. It imposes duties upon parents to make sure that their children are properly maintained and educated; it imposes duties upon employers to make sure that their employees enjoy a safe working environment; it imposes duties upon motorists to tax and insure their vehicles. All of these potentially carry criminal sanctions should the duties be broken.

'The law', however, casts its net far wider than this. There are laws governing the making of Wills, the buying and selling of houses, the formation of contracts, marriage and divorce, the relationships between neighbours, the rights of citizens of the European Union, the licensing of goods and services, etc. The list is virtually endless and reflects the complicated social, economic and political nature of a democracy in the twenty-first century. Any study of criminal law is bound to recognise this wider context since criminal offences cover almost every aspect of social conduct.

Having studied the earlier chapters in this book, the reader will be aware of some of the major offences, the main defences and the general principles underlying criminal liability. However, it would be a mistake to assume that you are now a complete expert in criminal law. There exist many related issues that it is not possible to address in a work of this length, as well as numerous offences that have not even been mentioned. Nevertheless, it is hoped that attention will have been drawn to some of the factors which contribute to the continuing development of criminal law and which have shaped the evolution of these general principles and offences as they exist today. Let us now consider some of these factors.

Morality

It is traditionally accepted that there must normally be some moral foundation or justification for branding an individual as 'criminal'. 'Morality' is an elusive concept. It is often regarded as a matter for the individual conscience. In many ways this represents the acknowledgement of the ideal concept of freedom of individual thought. Criminal law, however, must pay attention to the needs of society as a whole, which may sometimes conflict with the right of the individual to behave exclusively according to his or her own moral code.

Consider the following scenario:

> Helen chooses to drive into a city centre to work rather than to take public transport, although doing so would alleviate problems of congestion and pollution. One of her reasons for using her car is so she can give a lift in secret to her lover George. Helen has told her husband Barry that she takes the car so that she can listen to her favourite music on the way to work. During their journey to work, a bulb has failed and they are now driving a vehicle with a defective brake light.

In this scenario, some would regard an individual's decision to drive to work as being anti-social whereas others would defend the right of a car owner to drive to work as a basic freedom. Others may focus on other aspects of Helen's conduct. She is apparently intent on committing adultery and, at the very least, being deceitful to her husband about it. You could imagine many arguments and points of view about the morality of these features of her behaviour. Can we properly rush to a moral judgment about this aspect of her activities without knowing about the full circumstances surrounding Helen's married life? Is it our business anyway?

On the other hand, ironically, Helen is technically committing a criminal offence by driving a car with a defective brake light. Few would regard the failure of a light bulb as an event deserving moral blame, let alone one that can be said to justify the imposition of criminal liability. Sometimes the interests of an individual and the rest of society are potentially in conflict with one another, just as the elements of law and morality in the two situations might appear difficult to fully reconcile. These two conflicting interests are balanced in our society by the mechanisms of the State. The Crown Prosecution Service, representing the State in the name of the Crown, brings criminal prosecutions.

Law and morality are often represented as two overlapping spheres of influence. On certain issues the way an individual behaves is acknowledged as being entirely up to their own individual conscience. On other issues the criminal law actually imposes liability where there appears to be doubtful moral justification for doing so.

Figure 8 The relationship between law and morality

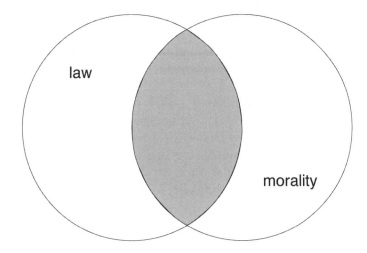

There is, however, a very large area where the two concepts of law and morality appear to happily coincide. A good example is the crime of murder. Few would argue that a murderer does not deserve to be punished for intentionally taking the life of another.

There can be little doubt that a system of criminal law which lacked any basis in morality would have little credibility and would soon lose its authority. For this reason alone Parliament and the judiciary must pay some heed to the influence of moral values.

Many offences involve issues of morality. In theft, one of the key rules for the jury is to assess whether the conduct of an accused is dishonest. A discussion of this issue can be found in the Court of Appeal decision in *Ghosh* (1982) – see page 182.

---

1 What moral and legal arguments surround the topic of euthanasia?
2 Should we implement a 'Good Samaritan' law to encourage people to give assistance to victims of an emergency situation? (Chapter 2)
3 Was the fourteen-year-old defendant in Elliott v C morally to blame for setting fire to the shed? (Chapter 3)
4 What moral blame attaches to someone who attempts the impossible but fails? (Chapter 21)
5 Do you agree that criminal law should confine itself to the minimum rules necessary for the protection of society from harm, or should it intervene to promote higher standards of social behaviour generally?

Policy issues

It is important to remember that the tension at the centre of many issues in criminal law is the critical balance to be achieved between the interests and freedom of the individual and the wider interest of society at large to enjoy protection from the harmful acts or omissions of the individual. Inevitably the development of criminal law is affected by a variety of policy issues. These range from social and political to economic and philosophical. Examples of the influence of policy can be seen in aspects of legislation and the common law alike.

However, the implementation of policy is a complex process. Any government is duty bound by convention at least to consult interested parties when proposing major change in the criminal law. Parliamentary procedures must be observed. There may be influential reports and consultation papers to consider such as those produced by the Law Commission or following a judicial or public enquiry. Full and proper consultation fulfils a valuable function in a democracy by, at the very least, giving the illusion that the views of interested groups are being taken into account and, at its best, informing an open debate prior to proposing new law. Governments are also influenced by events and political factors. In recent years the Protection from Harassment Act 1997 provides a good example of this (see Chapter 8) as do a number of changes that have occurred in sentencing policy in the field of criminal justice.

Equally, there are many examples of the way that the appeal courts have acknowledged the importance of policy issues when considering landmark judgements. The Privy Council in *Gammon* (1985) listed a whole number of policy factors that would assist judges when justifying the imposition of strict liability (see Chapter 4). The House of Lords in *Brown and Others* (1993) weighed up the arguments surrounding the freedom of the individual to consent to being the victim of an assault (see Chapter 9). It is worth reading these judgments to appreciate the way in which the judiciary has adopted views about the function of the public interest in determining criminal liability. It has often been questioned whether it is the role of the judges to act in this manner. After all, they are not democratically elected and hold office by way of appointment and cannot easily be removed from office. Students should always be prepared to debate the arguments that surround 'public policy', as interpreted by the judges, and recognise that decisions involving such issues are frequently open to challenge.

Criminal justice

Criminal law, like all branches of law, must also be susceptible to rational and logical analysis. Should Parliament or the courts create or develop rules which appear to be capricious, then the law would rapidly fall into disrepute. For this reason the lawyer must be able to analyse the basis of liability in crime according to proven logical principles. Much of this is to do with the need to avoid any miscarriage of justice by following a due process of law. Many rules exist to protect the individual against a wrongful conviction, and the appeals system is designed to ensure that any mistakes in the administration of justice may be corrected.

Just as importantly, the student must always remember that sentencing theory and practice exist to complement the law. A finding of guilt means that the sentencing powers of the appropriate court are invoked. You will recall from studying the machinery of justice in the English legal system that, for the vast majority of offences, magistrates or judges exercise their discretion in choosing the suitable sentence. There are few mandatory sentences that automatically apply. The mandatory life sentence for murder is an obvious exception and partly explains why English law has sought to maintain a clear distinction between the definitions of the offences of murder and manslaughter. Of course, the role of the sentencer in nearly all other situations is to choose the appropriate sentence after taking into consideration his or her powers and the circumstances of the case. It should not be forgotten that policy in sentencing has been altered over the years as a result of legislation, particularly the Criminal Justice Act 1991. In addition, judges in the Crown Court must also pay attention to Court of Appeal 'guideline' judgments in this capacity. In recent years these have tended to recognise the needs of the individual victim of a crime as well as the wider interests of society at large.

The relationship between criminal liability and the choice of the appropriate sentence is a significant one. For example, it helps to explain the partial defences of diminished responsibility and provocation which allow a judge to exercise discretion following a murder charge. Here, the accused has put forward a successful mitigation and has been convicted of voluntary manslaughter in circumstances which may vary enormously. The use of discretion in sentencing enables a notion of justice in its natural sense to be incorporated into a technically proper finding of guilt.

Finally, it should be remembered that, in some circumstances, sentences cannot be justified in terms of fairness or natural justice. Strict liability cases have provided examples of technical convictions occurring where it is not easy to attribute blame or fault. (See for example, *Storkwain* in Chapter 4). We have seen that it may be difficult to say that a defendant in such cases is truly 'blameworthy' or at fault. The only real justification for imposing a sentence (usually a fine) is therefore one based upon the protection of society.

Conclusion

The modules of study for the AS level in law are in part designed to prepare students for the in-depth study of a particular branch of substantive law such as criminal law. Hopefully, it is not difficult to recognise the relevance of legislation and the common law as central features of the evolution of the principles and rules that comprise criminal law. As has been emphasised above, it is equally important to recognise and understand the wider context within which you are studying these rules and principles of liability in crime. Curriculum 2000 placed a new emphasis on this relationship with the specification as a whole, and sought to build the specific knowledge acquired in the A2 module upon the foundation that you gained during your AS-level studies.

All boards include marks for analytical content in marking essay questions. This is nothing new and has been happening for years. What is different, however, is that the new A2 specifications (for the full A-level award) must include a clear element of synoptic assessment relating criminal law to the wider context of the English legal system. (See Chapter 25).

24 Sources of law

Introduction

All A-level law students are required to develop a knowledge and understanding of sources of law as part of the study of the general principles underlying English law as a whole. English law does not grow on trees, neither was it handed to Moses on top of a mountain. It is derived from Acts of Parliament (statute law) and from the decisions of judges in decided cases (common law). Students of this book will have already read, in each chapter, countless references to case decisions and to Acts of Parliament. When reading about a particular branch of law, such as criminal law, the significance of these major sources of law becomes apparent. These are the *primary sources* of law. Writers and lawyers, including judges, must take them as the starting point for what the law actually is. Most of the things that you have read in this book are merely the informed interpretations that the authors of this book have placed upon these primary sources. Consequently, most of the views put forward in this book are merely a *secondary source* of reference.

Textbooks as secondary sources

One of the benefits of text books as secondary sources is that they provide a summary version of the very complex and detailed wording that typifies many case law judgments and Acts of Parliament. However, any such summary or interpretation does carry with it the risk that it may no longer be completely accurate and will certainly not be comprehensive. Accuracy is so vital in law that it is essential that law students are encouraged to read at least some samples of primary sources in order to begin to develop an understanding of their importance. One reason for this is that the original source often contains the purest logical statement of the appropriate law.

It follows that the study of primary sources is important. This is not necessarily an easy task since most A-level students probably do not have easy access to them. The increasing availability of the internet, however, is allowing free access to important judgments in the House of Lords and Court of Appeal as well as to Acts of Parliament. A list of useful legal websites is contained in an Appendix at the end of this book.

Primary sources

Case law

If you have already studied the general principles underlying the working of the English legal system, you will be aware of the significance of reported cases and how a system of precedent incorporates them into what is known as the common law. Whole areas of criminal law are still based upon these common law case decisions. The offence of murder is an obvious example. The definition originates in a seventeenth-century statement of the then Lord Chief Justice, Coke. However, this common law definition has been relatively recently developed by the House of Lords decision in *Woollin* [1998] 3 WLR 382.

As stated earlier, however, the courts are constantly being required to interpret existing statutory provisions and the student must be aware of this. Therefore, case law is also important when interpreting and evolving the meaning and application of legislation. This is particularly true of criminal law. For example, the House of Lords ruled in *Burstow* [1997] 3 WLR 534 that serious psychiatric injury caused by silent phone calls can amount to grievous bodily harm for the purposes of s.18 of the Offences Against the Person Act 1861. Recently, in October 2003, the House of Lords effectively abolished the concept of *Caldwell* recklessness in *G and R* [2003] 3 WLR 1060. The Crown Court has acknowledged in *Dica* [2004] EWCA Crim 1103, [2004] QB 1257 that the transmission of the AIDS virus during sexual intercourse amounted to at least maliciously inflicting grievous bodily harm under s.20 of the Offences Against the Person Act 1861. Here the accused had neither informed his partners that he was HIV positive nor taken any contraceptive measure that would have prevented infection.

Statute law

Statute law, in the form of legislation is increasingly important in all branches of law and criminal law is no exception. There have been many new criminal offences that have been created in recent years. However, successive governments appear to have been rather reluctant to implement changes in the more serious offences. This is odd since there have been many proposals for the reform and even codification of the criminal law over the past twenty years. There has been a Draft Criminal Code Bill in existence since 1985 but it has never been implemented.

Most of these proposals for the reform of the criminal law are the work of the Law Commission, a permanent body whose rationale is to research, consult and make recommendations to Parliament on reforming the existing law. In 1993 the Law Commission published a Report, *Offences Against the Person and General Principles*, containing a further Criminal Law Bill. At the time of writing there is little indication that the Offences

Against the Person Bill put forward by the government in 1998 in response (www.homeoffice.gov.uk/documents/cons-1998-violence-reforming-law) will become law in the immediate future. Another area that is ripe for Parliamentary reform is the law relating to involuntary manslaughter which has been subject to much criticism in its present form. The Law Commission has proposed detailed changes in its Report No. 237 (1996) *Legislating the Criminal Code – Involuntary Manslaughter*. These proposals formed the basis of the synoptic papers originally produced by OCR for examination in 2002/2003. They are very good examples of the role of the Law Commission as it exists to reform and improve the existing law. What is far less predictable is whether any government has the time and the will to introduce these proposals into its legislative programme and present them to Parliament for its consideration. Very often desirable, long-term reform is postponed indefinitely in the interests of short-term political expediency. Publications from the Law Commission can be viewed online at their website (www.lawcom.gov.uk/) and downloaded if necessary.

Synoptic assessment based on source materials

The fourth and final unit of the OCR A-level comprises a Criminal Law Special Study Paper. This unit is based on pre-released materials. A special study booklet is sent out to centres at the beginning of the course which provides a starting point for study of the topics set. Each booklet contains source material, such as extracts from judgments or Acts of Parliament or academic articles on a specific area(s) of criminal law. In this way the source material will indicate the area(s) of substantive law which will be tested. It is possible to annotate or highlight this booklet but it cannot be taken into the examination room. Candidates will be issued with an identical unseen copy in the examination. Candidates are expected to demonstrate understanding of the area(s) of law and the development of law and to use legal methods and reasoning to analyse legal material, to select appropriate legal rules and apply these in order to draw conclusions.

Candidates will be expected to draw together knowledge of legal processes and/or legal issues and make connections between these and the substantive criminal law therefore applying knowledge and understanding acquired over the two years of study. This unit is concerned only with the law applicable in England and Wales. Candidates will be required to support their knowledge by citation of relevant leading cases and the main provisions of relevant statutes.

While candidates are encouraged to be aware of the changing nature of law, they are **not** required to be familiar with innovations coming into effect in the **twelve** months immediately preceding the examination.

The theme for the Special Study Paper from January 2010 will be **non-fatal offences against the person** and aspects of the defence of **consent**.

This theme will last for only twelve months, as will any future themes. The time allowed for the paper remains unchanged at 1 ½ hours. There is no longer a discrete first question from the AS content, traditionally aspects of reform, legislation, statutory interpretation or judicial precedent. The demand nevertheless remains the same, so that students will be able to produce more depth in their answers to the three remaining questions.

It is, therefore, vital that you familiarise yourself thoroughly with the relevant published source material and that you consider the surrounding issues that you could fairly expect to see examined on the question paper. A point to note is that the structure of the Special Study Paper remains the same. Question 1 will normally address a significant development in the law in question, here duress and necessity, normally by reference to a particular case referred to in the Special Study booklet. Question 2 is a broader question, worth more marks, which asks for a critical evaluation of one of the main issues of significance arising from the law addressed by the Special Study materials. The final question, Question 3 is usually a three- or four-part skills-based question. Candidates are presented with short hypothetical scenarios based upon the Special Study theme and are expected to demonstrate identification and application skills in order to arrive at a conclusion either about the potential criminal liability of the characters in the scenarios or whether or not a particular defence may be available to them.

OCR materials for the Criminal Law Special Study Paper G154 (for examination from January 2010), with authors' commentary

(Reproduced by kind permission of OCR.)

Module G154 Criminal Law

SPECIAL STUDY MATERIAL

Source materials

Source 1

Extracts from the Offences Against the Person Act 1861

Commentary
NB Although candidates do have the benefit of seeing these definitions reproduced in the exam, it is essential that they have previously familiarised themselves with both the statutory definitions below and the common law definitions of assault and battery so that a good understanding of these is developed in advance.

Candidates should also re-read Chapters 8 and 9 on non-fatal offences against the person and consent.

Section 18 Shooting or attempting to shoot, or wounding, with intent to do grievous bodily harm, or to resist apprehension

Whosoever shall unlawfully and maliciously by any means whatsoever wound or cause grievous bodily harm to any person with intent to do some grievous bodily harm to any person, or with intent to resist or prevent the lawful apprehension or detainer of any person, shall be guilty of felony, and being convicted thereof shall be liable to be kept in penal servitude for life.

Commentary
The key feature of the s.18 offence is that the accused intended to cause serious harm. An intention to cause a lesser degree of harm or recklessness as to whether serious harm is caused is insufficient.

Section 20 Inflicting bodily injury, with or without weapon

Whosoever shall unlawfully and maliciously wound or inflict any grievous bodily harm upon any other person, either with or without any weapon or instrument, shall be guilty of a misdemeanour, and being convicted thereof shall be liable to be kept in penal servitude [for not more than five years].

Commentary
Since *Cunningham 1957*, the term 'maliciously' has been interpreted in the context of the Offences Against the Person Act 1861 as meaning 'recklessly' in the subjective sense. In other words, the accused must be conscientiously aware of the risk posed by his conduct but decide to go ahead anyway and take that risk.

Section 47 Assault occasioning bodily harm

Whosoever shall be convicted upon an indictment of any assault occasioning actual bodily harm shall be liable ... to be kept in penal servitude [for not more than five years].

Commentary
It is often observed that there is little logic in providing the same maximum sentence, five years, for both s.20 and s.47 offences when Parliament apparently intended s.20 to be the more serious. In practice, judges do discriminate by applying the relevant guidelines from the Sentencing Council

and Court of Appeal. Magistrates are constrained by the maximum 12 month sentence which they can impose for s.47 offences.

Interestingly, if a s.47 offence is being tried in the Crown Court it is not possible for a jury to acquit the defendant of the s.47 offence and convict him instead of a lesser assault battery offence. This is because assault and battery is a summary only offence and outside the jurisdiction of the Crown Court.

Extract from the Criminal Justice Act 1988

Section 39 Common assault

Common assault and battery shall be summary offences and a person guilty of either of them shall be liable to a fine not exceeding level 5 on the standard scale, to imprisonment for a term not exceeding six months.

Commentary
Note that s.39 is a procedural provision and does not provide a definition of assault and battery whose meanings are still defined in common law.

Source 2

Extract adapted from the judgment in *Collins v Wilcock* [1984] 1 WLR 1172 by Robert Goff LJ

We are here primarily concerned with battery. The fundamental principle, plain and incontestable, is that every person's body is inviolate. It has long been established that any touching of another person, however slight, might amount to a battery. The effect is that everybody is protected not only against physical injury but against any form of physical molestation.

But so widely drawn a principle must inevitably be subject to some exceptions. For example, . . . people may be subjected to the lawful exercise of the power of arrest; and reasonable force may be used in self-defence . . . Generally speaking, consent is a defence to battery; and most of the physical contacts of everyday life are not battery because they are impliedly consented to . . . Among such forms of conduct long held to be acceptable is touching a person for the purpose of engaging his attention . . . A police officer may wish to engage a man's attention . . . to question him. But if . . . his use of physical contact in the face of non-cooperation persists beyond generally accepted standards of conduct, his action will become unlawful; and if a police officer restrains a man, for example by gripping his arm or his shoulder, then his action will also be unlawful, unless he is lawfully exercising his powers of arrest.

... the respondent took hold of the appellant by the left arm to restrain her. She was not proceeding to her arrest ... her action constituted a battery ... and was therefore unlawful. ... the appeal must be allowed ...

Commentary

Assault and battery have never been defined by statute. Therefore it is important to study previous judgments in decided cases in order to arrive at a definition. In this context candidates should also look again at other cases, such as *Logdon, Light, Martin, Fagan, Lamb, Tuberville v Savage, Smith v Superintendent of Woking Police Station, Wilson v Pringle, Ireland*, etc. Note also that consent in this context may be implied frequently in everyday situations. Know the answers to the following questions:

Q. What is the *mens rea* of assault and battery?

Q. Can there be an assault without a battery? Explain.

Q. Can there be a battery without an assault? Explain.

Q. What degree of harm is sufficient to satisfy a battery?

Q. What particular conduct constituted a battery in the above case?

Source 3

Extract adapted from the judgment in *R v Ireland, R v Burstow* [1997] 4 All ER 225 House of Lords by Lord Steyn

Harassment of women by repeated silent telephone calls, accompanied on occasions by heavy breathing, is apparently a significant social problem. That the criminal law should be able to deal with this problem, and so far as is practicable, afford effective protection to victims is self-evident.

It is to the provisions of the Offences against the Person Act 1861 that one must turn to examine whether our law provides effective criminal sanctions for this type of case.

An ingredient of each of the offences is 'bodily harm' to a person. In respect of each section the threshold question is therefore whether a psychiatric illness, as testified to by a psychiatrist, can amount to 'bodily harm'. If ... the answer to the question is yes, it will be necessary to consider whether the persistent silent caller, who terrifies his victim and causes her to suffer a psychiatric illness, can be criminally liable ...

The correct approach is simply to consider whether the words of the 1861 Act considered in the light of contemporary knowledge cover a recognisable psychiatric injury ...

The proposition that the Victorian legislator, when enacting ss.18, 20 and 47 of the 1861 Act, would not have had in mind psychiatric illness is no doubt correct. Psychiatry was in its infancy. But the subjective intention of the draftsman is immaterial. The only relevant inquiry is as to the sense of the words in the context in which they are used.

[Accordingly] 'bodily harm' must be interpreted so as to include recognisable psychiatric illness.

[In] *Burstow* . . . counsel laid stress on the difference between 'causing' grievous bodily harm in s.18 and 'inflicting' grievous bodily harm in s.20 [and] submitted that it is inherent in the word 'inflict' that there must be a direct or indirect application of force to the body . . .

. . . The question is whether as a matter of current usage the contextual interpretation of 'inflict' can embrace the idea of one person inflicting psychiatric injury on another. One can without straining the language in any way answer . . . in the affirmative . . .

. . . It is now necessary to consider whether the making of silent telephone calls causing psychiatric injury is capable of constituting an assault under s.47 . . .

It is necessary to consider the two forms which an assault may take. The first is battery, which involves the unlawful application of force . . . The second form of assault is an act causing the victim to apprehend an immediate application of force upon her . . .

The proposition that a gesture may amount to an assault, but that words can never suffice, is unrealistic and indefensible . . . There is no reason why something said should be incapable of causing an apprehension of immediate personal violence . . . I would, therefore, reject the proposition that an assault can never be committed by words.

That brings me to the critical question whether a silent caller may be guilty of an assault. The answer to this question seems to me to be 'yes, depending on the facts'. It depends on questions of fact within the province of the jury. After all, there is no reason why a telephone caller who says to a woman in a menacing way, 'I will be at your door in a minute or two' may not be guilty of an assault if he causes his victim to apprehend immediate personal violence. Take now the case of the silent caller. He intends by his silence to cause fear and so he is understood. The victim . . . may fear the *possibility* of immediate personal violence. As a matter of law the caller may be guilty of an assault, whether he is or not will depend on the circumstance and in particular on the impact of the caller's potentially menacing call or calls on the victim. Such a prosecution case under s.47 may be fit to leave to the jury. I conclude that an assault may be committed in the particular factual circumstances which I have envisaged. For this reason I reject the submission that as a matter of law a silent telephone caller cannot ever be guilty of an offence under s.47.

Commentary

Ireland and *Burstow* represent significant developments in the law relating to non-fatal offences against the person. In the light of these decisions do you think the following could amount to an offence?

(a) Sending a series of blank text messages on a mobile phone?
(b) Sending a threatening email?
(c) Directing a laser beam into someone's eyes?

Source 4

Extract adapted from the judgment in *JCC (a minor) v Eisenhower* [1983] 3 All ER 230 QBD by Robert Goff LJ

In my judgment, that conclusion (of the magistrates) was not in accordance with the law. It is not enough that there has been a rupturing of blood vessels internally for there to be a wound under the statute because it is impossible for a court to conclude from that evidence alone whether or not there has been any break in the continuity of the whole skin. There may have simply been internal bleeding of some kind or another, the cause of which is not established. Furthermore, even if there had been a break in some internal skin, there may not have been a break in the whole skin.

In these circumstances, the evidence is not enough, in my judgment, to establish a wound within the statute. In my judgment, the magistrates erred in their conclusion on the evidence before them.

Commentary

Note that, although the s.20 offence is often referred to as 'wounding', it can also be committed where serious harm (GBH) is committed 'maliciously', that is accompanied by subjective recklessness as the relevant accompanying state of mind. Candidates have frequently suggested that s.20 cannot apply unless there is a 'wound' and this is clearly untrue. On the other hand, a wound cannot consist of a mere graze or scratch, since these do not satisfy the definition given above in *Eisenhower*.

Q. Does a wounding occur when someone pierces a victim's skin with a fine needle without drawing blood?

Q. If a person is pushed and their knee is cut open when they fall, does this amount to a wound?

Source 5

Extracts adapted from *Criminal Law* by Michael Jefferson, 8th edition, 2007, Pearson Publishing, pp. 552–3 and 556

For many years there has been debate as to the width of the word 'inflict' under s.20 [Offences Against the Person Act 1861]. These issues were raised in *Ireland; Burstow* ([1997] 4 All ER 225) . . . The first issue was whether or not s.20 required an assault (in the sense of a battery). The authorities were divided. Lord Steyn stated that s.20 does not require an assault on the basis that, if it did, words would have to be read into s.20 ('inflict *by assault* any grievous bodily harm') whereas s.20 'works perfectly satisfactorily without any such implication'.

There is a problem arising from *[R v]* Wilson (Clarence) [1984] AC 242 HL. Lord Roskill apparently believed that 'inflict' required the direct application of force to the victim or the doing of an act which directly resulted in force being applied to the victim's body. What is said is *dictum.* On this approach, to take an old example, if one dug a pit for the victim to fall into, one would be guilty under s.20 because, although one has not directly applied force to the victim, one has done an act which directly resulted in force being applied. One will have caused GBH within s.18 because 'cause' does not require the direct application of force. On the facts of *Martin* ([1881] 8 QBD 54) . . . the accused would be guilty of the more serious offence, s.18, and guilty of the less serious offence, s.20, for the same reason, but one is not guilty in the poisoning example because no force is used. The result is absurd. It could have been avoided by having the same verb in ss.18 and 20 or by the House of Lords in *Wilson* deciding that 'cause' and 'inflict' covered the same ground. The House of Lords took the point further: not just did 'inflict' require direct application force, but so did assault occasioning actual bodily harm and common assault. Therefore, a person could be guilty of the most serious non-fatal assault but not of the lesser assaults! It is about time that the meaning of 'inflict' was settled.

Another issue was whether s.20 required the direct or indirect application of force. The Lords (in *Ireland, Burstow*) held that no direct physical violence was necessary. Lord Steyn said:

> The problem is one of construction. The question is whether as a matter of current usage the contextual interpretation of 'inflict' can embrace the idea of one person inflicting psychiatric injury on another. One can without straining the language in any way answer that question in the affirmative. I am not saying that the words 'cause' and 'inflict' are exactly synonymous. They are not. What I am saying is that in the contextof the Act of 1861 one can nowadays quite naturally speak of inflicting psychiatric injury.

. . . Lord Steyn thought that it would be 'absurd' if 'cause' and 'inflict' were of different width. This interpretation was consistent with the hierarchy of non-fatal offences . . .

In both ss.18 and 20 the mental element is stated to be 'maliciously'. Section 18 requires proof of a further state of mind 'with intent to do some grievous bodily harm'. Coleridge CJ said in *Martin* that 'maliciously' did not mean spitefully. It normally means in a statute 'intentionally or recklessly'. Negligence is insufficient. Yet one can be guilty of a more serious offence, manslaughter by gross negligence . . .

Because s.18 is expressed in terms of 'cause GBH with intent to do GBH', the Court of Appeal in *Mowatt* ([1968] 1 QB 421) opined that the term 'maliciously' was superfluous. The thinking is that if one intends GBH, one must foresee GBH as a probable or possible outcome. If, however, the indictment is based upon GBH with intent to resist arrest, 'maliciously' is not superfluous . . .

Criminal law should work in practice. Clarkson and Keating 'Codification: Offences against the person under the draft Criminal Code' (1986) 50 JCL 405 at 415, wrote, 'Each of the non-fatal offences against the person is, to varying degrees, confused and uncertain . . . in relation to each other, they are incoherent and fail to represent a hierarchy of seriousness.

'. . . It is possible to substitute all the terms in the sections and thereby produce an authoritative modern version of the crimes which gets rid of all the difficult and case-encrusted phraseology. The definition of concepts such as "wound", "cause", "inflict", "actual bodily harm" and "grievous bodily harm" have to be gathered from the cases. The OAPA was a consolidation statute with no attempt made to grade the offences or fit them together . . . it is easy to see why modern judges find difficulty fitting modern methods into the 1861 statute.'

Commentary
Ireland represents a significant development in the law relating to non-fatal offences against the person. For a further explanation of 'psychiatric injury', remember to look at *Chan-Fook* and *Dhaliwal* in Chapter 8. Equally, *Burstow* is significant in recognising that mere silence can amount to an assault which may 'occasion' actual bodily harm and, by extension, inflict or cause grievous bodily harm depending upon the degree of harm suffered by the victim.

Q. To what extent do these cases suggest that 'modern judges find difficulty fitting modern methods into the 1861 statute', as suggested by the extract in Source 5?

Q. Is the 1861 Offences Against the Person Act outdated and in need of reform or is it still workable in the modern world?

Q. What differences are there, if any, between the words 'inflict' and 'cause'?

Source 6

Extract adapted from 'Consent: public policy or legal moralism?' by Susan Nash, *New Law Journal*, 15 March 1996

In *R v Wilson* ([1996] 2 Cr App R 241) the Court of Appeal held that consensual activity between a husband and wife in the privacy of the matrimonial home was not a proper matter for a criminal prosecution. The defendant had been charged with assault occasioning actual bodily harm contrary to s.47 of the Offences Against the Person Act 1861. The 'activity' involved the defendant burning his initials onto his wife's right buttock with a hot knife because 'she had wanted his name on her body'. This decision rekindles the debate regarding the extent to which the criminal law should be concerned with the consensual activities of adults in private. In *R v Brown* ([1994] 1 AC 2112) the House of Lords upheld convictions under ss.20 and 47 of the Offences Against the Person Act notwithstanding that the victims had given their consent. This decision has been described as 'unprincipled and incoherent'.

The trial judge in *Wilson* had ruled that consent was no defence to an assault occasioning actual bodily harm. In arriving at this conclusion he stated that he felt bound by ... *R v Brown*. The Court of Appeal considered it misdirection for the judge to say these cases constrained him to rule that consent was no defence.

The majority of the House of Lords in *Brown* held that it was not in the public interest that a person should wound or cause actual bodily harm to another for no good reason. Thus, in the absence of a good reason the victim's consent would not amount to a defence to a charge under s.47 or s.20 of the 1861 Act.

The defendants had taken part in consensual acts of violence for the purpose of sexual gratification which had resulted in varying degrees of injury. The court was of the opinion that the satisfying of sado-masochistic desires could not be classed as a good reason and dismissed the appeals. Lord Templeman considered that in some circumstances the accused would be entitled to an acquittal although the activity resulted in the infliction of some injury.

'Surgery involves intentional violence resulting in actual or sometimes serious bodily harm but surgery is a lawful activity. Other activities carried on with consent by or on behalf of the injured person have been accepted as lawful notwithstanding that they involve actual bodily harm or may cause serious harm. Ritual circumcision, tattooing, ear-piercing and violent sports including boxing are lawful activities.' This reference to tattooing has now assumed significance. Lords Templeman and Jauncy referred to it as being an activity which, if carried out with the consent of an adult, did not involve an offence under s.47. Wilson had been engaged in an activity which in principle was no more dangerous than professional tattooing. Thus, the Court of Appeal was of the opinion that it was not in the public interest that his activities should amount to criminal behaviour.

The Court of Appeal has now declared that *Brown* is not authority for the proposition that consent is no defence to a charge under s.47 of the 1861 Act *in all circumstances* where actual bodily harm is deliberately inflicted upon a person. Public policy and public interest considerations will become increasingly important in deciding whether it is appropriate to criminalise consensual activity, giving rise to even greater uncertainty in the area.

Commentary

Whilst it is fairly safe to say that consent is a defence to common assault (see *Lamb 1967*), it was also thought until 1993 that, with certain exceptions such as surgery and physical contact sports such as football and rugby, it was against public policy to recognise that consent could be a defence to more serious offences against the person including actual bodily harm (see *Attorney-General's Reference No. 6 of 1980*). In that case the Court of Appeal stated that 'it is not in the public interest that people should try to cause or should cause each other actual bodily harm for no good reason'. Make sure that you know the activities which are recognised as exceptions to the rule that consent may not be given to any injury which exceeds a common assault. In other words what amounts to 'a good reason' according to the courts.

Make sure that you understand the issues surrounding the issue of a genuine or real consent such as age, knowledge and understanding and fraud.

Q. On what basis did the House of Lords in *Brown 1993* decide that the acts of a group of adult males, which resulted in convictions for actual bodily harm and unlawful wounding, were performed 'for no good reason' even though the acts were allegedly performed for the purposes of pleasure and entertainment and in private?

Q. What distinction was drawn between the activities in *Wilson 1996* and those that were declared unlawful in *Brown*?

Q. Do you think that the decision in *Brown* may have been different had the defendants been a group of heterosexual men and women?

Potential questions based on the Criminal Law Special Study Paper G154 OCR (to be examined from January 2010)

Note: The weighting of marks for this paper is different because it carries a synoptic element and is also designed to assess the evaluative and analytical skills which students are developing during the A2 study. In addition, proportionately less credit is given for merely demonstrating knowledge of the topic which is the subject of the stimulus material provided. Candidates have had the benefit of considering this during their study and their understanding of the issues arising is more important on this paper.

Time allowed: 1 hour 30 minutes

You are reminded of the importance of including relevant materials from all areas of your course, where appropriate, including knowledge gained from your study of the English Legal System.

Answer **ALL** Questions

1   Assess the significance of the case of *Collins v Wilcock* [1984] 1 WLR
    1172 (Source 2 Special Study materials) to the law of common assault.
                                                                    [16]

2   Clarkson and Keating 'Codification: Offences against the person under
    the draft Criminal Code' (1986) 50 JCL 405 at 415, wrote, 'Each of the
    non-fatal offences against the person is, to varying degrees, confused and
    uncertain — in relation to each other, they are incoherent and fail to
    represent a hierarchy of seriousness.' (Source 5 Special Study materials)

    Discuss how accurately the statement reflects the current position in
    this area of law.
                                                                    [34]

3   Discuss what offences may have been committed and consider whether
    or not the defence of consent would be available in the situations below.

    (a) Lily is playing hockey when a member of the opposing team, Sandra,
        hits the ball hard against Lily's ankle breaking a bone.
                                                                    [10]
    (b) As Lily is rolling in agony on the ground Sandra raises her hockey
        stick in the air and hits Lily in the face, breaking her nose.
                                                                    [10]
    (c) Lily is admitted to hospital for surgery on her ankle where she is
        given an anaesthetic by Dr Feelwell. Unfortunately, too much
        anaesthetic is given and Lily is left paralysed.
                                                                    [10]

Total marks for the paper: [80]

For suggested answers see pp. 422–425.

25 OCR New specification materials

OXFORD CAMBRIDGE AND RSA EXAMINATIONS
Advanced GCE
LAW [G153QP]
Criminal Law

Specimen Paper 2 hours
Each candidate must be given:
(1) one copy of this question paper, [G153QP];
(2) one 8 page Answer Book.
Item (2) is sent with the stationery parcel.

TIME 2 hours

INSTRUCTIONS TO CANDIDATES

Complete the front page of the Answer Book as directed.

Answer **three** questions, **one** from Section A, **one** from Section B and **one** from Section C.

Read each question carefully and make sure you know what you have to do before starting your answer.

Write the numbers of the questions you answer on the front of your Answer Book.

INFORMATION FOR CANDIDATES

The maximum mark for this paper is **120**.

Quality of Written Communication (QWC). Candidates are reminded of the need to write in continuous prose where appropriate. You will be assessed on your written communication and your use of appropriate legal terminology.

Answer **three** questions.
One from Section A, **one** from Section B and **one** from Section C.

SECTION A

Answer only **one** question from this section.

1 Strict liability offences are an exception to the general rule that the prosecution has the burden of proving that a person accused of a crime possesses the relevant guilty mind.

Discuss, in the light of the above statement, whether you agree that the creation of strict liability offences can ever be justified.

[50]

2 Discuss whether the rules governing insanity as a defence in criminal law are in a satisfactory condition.

[50]

3 Consider whether the current law relating to attempted crimes strikes the right balance between protecting society and convicting only those who deserve to be punished.

[50]

SECTION B

Answer only **one** question from this section.

4 Victoria is the wife and assistant of a knife-throwing expert, Carl, who both work for a circus. Carl is renowned for his hot temper and has recently been off work suffering from depression. Their act consists of Victoria being strapped to a board whilst Carl throws twenty knives all around her from a distance of five metres to within as little as ten centimetres of her body. They have being doing this for many years without a single mishap and Carl regards his technique as perfect. One evening, just before their act begins, Victoria tells Carl that she is having an affair with the lion tamer, Wayne. Carl is shocked and enraged but immediately the fanfare strikes up for the start of their act and Carl and Victoria enter the ring to start their performance. The third knife Carl throws goes straight into Victoria's heart, killing her instantly.

Discuss Carl's liability for Victoria's death.

[50]

5 Carol and Diana decide to go out 'clubbing' for the night. They meet at Carol's house and begin the evening by drinking half a bottle of vodka. They then go out and have some more drinks in a pub and they each take an ecstasy tablet which Diana has brought with her. As they are leaving the pub, Carol takes a leather jacket from the back of a chair, mistaking it for her own very similar jacket which she has, in fact, left at home. By the time that they arrive at the club, both girls are suffering from hallucinations. When the doorman, Barry, asks them for identity, Diana, who thinks Barry is an alien who wants to transport her to another planet, pokes him in the eye with her finger and then hits him over the head with her umbrella, knocking him unconscious.

Consider the offences that Carol and Diana may have committed and whether they may have any defences available to them.

[50]

6 Emma hires Fred, a qualified electrician, to rewire her house. She is unhappy when she notices sparks coming from the switches as she turns some lights on or off. Emma complains to Fred who returns to do some checks. He assures her that everything is in order and perfectly safe. The next morning, Emma goes to take a shower in the bathroom. When she turns on the shower control, she receives an electric shock that causes her to fall and bang her head, knocking her unconscious. Fortunately, her friend, Gita, arrives almost immediately and discovers Emma. Gita calls an ambulance and Emma is rushed to hospital. While Emma is still critically ill she develops an infection.

Hugh, a junior doctor employed by the hospital, fails to read Emma's medical notes properly. The notes clearly show that Emma is allergic to penicillin. Hugh gives Emma penicillin to treat the infection. As a result of her allergy Emma dies.

Discuss the liability of Fred and Hugh for Emma's death.

[50]

SECTION C

Answer only **one** question from this section.

7 John enters a supermarket intending to steal some food. He is in the shop when he notices that the door to the manager's office is open. He goes inside hoping to find something of value. There is no one present but, as he is about to leave, he notices a wallet lying on the manager's desk. John picks the wallet up and takes a £20 note out of it. The manager, Sue, sees him leaving the office and shouts at him. John pushes Sue aside and runs out of the store.

Evaluate the accuracy of **each** of the four statements A, B, C and D individually, as they apply to the facts in the above scenario.
Statement A: John is guilty of burglary under s.9(1)(a) Theft Act 1968.
Statement B: John is guilty of theft under s.1 Theft Act 1968.
Statement C: John is guilty of robbery under s.8 Theft Act 1968.
Statement D: John is guilty of burglary under s.9(1)(b) Theft Act 1968.

[20]

8 Wayne is the captain of the Northport United football team. During an important match against their local rivals, Wayne is involved in a clash of heads in an incident with an opposing player, Andrew. Wayne receives a nasty bruise above his left eye and is badly concussed. Wayne insists on continuing after treatment with a cold sponge but is obviously still in a very dazed condition. A few minutes later Wayne jumps wildly into a foul tackle on Andrew. Andrew is carried off in agony and X-rays later reveal that he has a broken ankle.

Evaluate the accuracy of **each** of the four statements A, B, C and D individually, as they apply to the facts in the above scenario.

Statement A: Andrew is liable for ABH s.47 OAPA 1861 for the bruise suffered by Wayne.

Statement B: Wayne is liable for GBH s.18 OAPA 1861 for the broken ankle sustained by Andrew.

Statement C: Andrew has a defence of consent for any charge brought by Wayne.

Statement D: Wayne has a defence of automatism for any charge brought by Andrew.

[20]

OXFORD CAMBRIDGE AND RSA EXAMINATIONS
Advanced GCE
LAW [Q153MS]
Criminal Law

Specimen Mark Scheme

SECTION A

1 Strict liability offences are an exception to the general rule that the prosecution has the burden of proving that a person accused of a crime possesses the relevant guilty mind.

Discuss, in the light of the above statement, whether you agree that the creation of strict liability offences can ever be justified.

A Level 5 answer is likely to include a number of the following points. These points are neither prescriptive nor exhaustive. Credit should be given for any other relevant points. Candidates can be rewarded for either breadth or depth of knowledge.

Assessment Objective 1: 25 marks

Define the concept of strict liability by reference to the lack of requirement of *mens rea*.

Demonstrate knowledge of the relevant principles relating to strict liability.

Explain the emphasis given to the common law presumption of *mens rea* e.g. *Sweet v Parsley, B v DPP*.

Explain the statutory nature of strict liability offences.

Explain the significance of statutory interpretation in this context.

Recognise the summary nature of strict liability offences.

Provide examples of strict liability offences – road traffic, licensing, food safety, pollution, etc.

Elaborate the examples by reference to appropriate cases, e.g. *Sherras v De Rutzen, Alphacell, Smedleys v Breed, James & Son v Smee*, etc.

Refer to the distinction between 'absolute' and 'strict' liability.

Give examples of 'no-negligence'/'due diligence' defences.

Refer to some of the social benefits claimed or injustices caused, e.g. the regulatory nature or administrative convenience or the possible injustice of imposition of liability without fault, e.g. 'spiking' of drinks or 'planting' of drugs, e.g. *Warner, Gammon, Storkwain, Lim Chin Aik*, etc.

Assessment Objective 2: 20 marks

Discuss the potential unfairness of such offences by a consideration of some of the potential injustices arising from a willingness to dispense with proof of a 'guilty mind':

Too much inconsistent use of discretion used by prosecuting agencies (more parliamentary guidance as to fault element preferable?) / conviction of the morally innocent is never justifiable / public respect for the criminal law is potentially undermined by dubious prosecutions / room for the development of criminal responsibility based on negligence?

Discuss some of the following 'benefits':

Protection of society from harmful acts/the 'quasi-criminal' nature of strict liability offences creates little stigma/regulatory nature, promotes high standards of care in socially important activities/practical effectiveness i.e. too many polluted rivers, too many drunk drivers as it is/administrative convenience, difficulty of establishing *mens rea* in many such cases removed, etc.

Assessment Objective 3: 5 marks

A Level 4 response is likely to present relevant material in a well-planned and logical sequence, with clearly defined structure and communicate clearly and accurately with confident use of appropriate terminology and demonstrate few, if any, errors of grammar, punctuation and spelling.

Total marks [50]

2   Discuss whether the rules governing insanity as a defence in criminal law are in a satisfactory condition.

A Level 5 answer is likely to include a number of the following points. These points are neither prescriptive nor exhaustive. Credit should be given for any other relevant points. Candidates can be rewarded for either breadth or depth of knowledge.

Assessment Objective 1: 25 marks

Define the essential elements of the defence of insanity: the M'Naghten rules.

Explain that insanity is also a legal definition which has been broadened to cover the operation of the mind in all its aspects: *Sullivan, Bratty v A-G for NI*, etc., the policy of controlling dangerous offenders.

Explain that DR is also a special and partial defence to a charge of murder only **but** sanity is a general defence to all crimes, identifying that 'abnormality of mind' means what the jury would term 'abnormal': *Byrne s.2 Homicide Act 1957*.

Explain that insanity may be raised by the prosecution or judge as well as the defence.

Explain the relationship between insanity and automatism and the danger of diabetics, epileptics etc., falling within the terms of the definition of insanity: *Quick, Hennessey*, etc.

Explain the widened powers of disposition given to the court by the Criminal Procedure (Insanity and Unfitness to Plead) Act 1991 upon a finding of 'not guilty owing to insanity' noting that on a murder charge hospitalisation will ensue.

Explain the relative frequency of pleas of DR compared with the rarity of insanity pleas.

Assessment Objective 2: 20 marks

Discuss the definition of insanity and criticise the antiquity and operation of the plea of insanity despite the mitigating effect of the 1991 Act.

Discuss the reluctance of courts to recognise automatism as a complete defence if it could mean releasing potentially dangerous people back into society.

Discuss the unavailability of insanity to the psychopath, with the availability of a plea of DR to a psychopath charged with murder: *Byrne*.

Discuss the problems posed for jurors faced with technical psychiatric terminology.

Discuss the fact that the defences are effectively established or rebutted by medical experts rather than being decided upon by jurors: doctors should not be delivering opinions on legal or moral responsibility which are essentially jury issues.

Discuss the social stigma that can attach to an epileptic etc. from a finding of 'not guilty owing to insanity'.

Discuss the potential for jury confusion and misapplication owing to emotional considerations, sympathy or crude 'gut reaction', e.g. Peter Sutcliffe, the 'Yorkshire Ripper', where psychiatric evidence was unanimous in agreeing he was a paranoid schizophrenic yet he was convicted of murder.

Discuss proposals for reform, e.g. Butler Committee 1975 and Law Commission Draft Criminal Code.

Assessment Objective 3: 5 marks

A Level 4 response is likely to present relevant material in a well-planned and logical sequence, with clearly defined structure and communicate clearly and accurately with confident use of appropriate terminology and demonstrate few, if any, errors of grammar, punctuation and spelling.

Total marks [50]

3   Consider whether the current law relating to attempted crimes strikes the right balance between protecting society and convicting only those who deserve to be punished.

A Level 5 answer is likely to include a number of the following points. These points are neither prescriptive nor exhaustive. Credit should be given for any other relevant points. Candidates can be rewarded for either breadth or depth of knowledge.

Assessment Objective 1: 25 marks

Refer to the 1981 Criminal Attempts Act so as to define the *actus reus* and *mens rea* of the offence.

Recognise importance of establishing at what point a criminal intention can be said to have progressed to the stage of an attempt: *Geddes*, etc.

Cite relevant cases that provide principles applying the meaning of 'more than merely preparatory'; these may include: *Widdowson, Gullefer, Campbell, Jones, Geddes* and *Tosti and White*, etc.

Recognise that aspects of attempting the impossible may very well refer to the practical and theoretical absence of an *actus reus* of any sort unless defined by the accused's belief and refer to ss.1(2) and (3) as well as *Haughton v Smith, Anderton v Ryan* and *Shivpuri*.

Demonstrate an awareness of the Law Commission's report which preceded the Criminal Attempts Act and describe some of the questions considered by the Report, e.g. the desirability of striking a balance between the protection of the public from the social danger caused by the contemplation of crime and the individual freedom to think or even fantasise.

Assessment Objective 2: 20 marks

Consider the rationale of criminalising attempts.

Consider the principle that a person ought not to be punished for merely contemplating the commission of offence.

Consider some reference to 'proximity', 'equivocality' or 'last act' principles which may very well demonstrate the candidate's true understanding of the topic; older relevant cases discussed might include *Robinson, Stonehouse*, etc.

Consider whether the decision in *Gullefer* reflects the wish expressed by the Law Commission that the point at which a course of conduct amounts to an offence is a matter of fact for the jury in each case using principles of common sense and that the older common law principles would not normally need to be considered in order for a jury to come to a conclusion about this.

Consider the difficulties in defining at what precise point if any an attempt can be said to have occurred, e.g. the problems in *Gullefer* and *Jones*.

Refer to the House of Lords' confusion over attempting the impossible in *Anderton v Ryan* and *Shivpuri*.

Consider, for example, any possible alternatives, e.g. the US model of 'substantial steps . . . strongly corroborative of the actor's criminal purpose'.

Consider whether it should be necessary, e.g. in a case of attempted murder, that the accused need go as far as pointing a gun at his/her intended victim etc. Would this limit the power of the police to intervene?

Assessment Objective 3: 5 marks

A Level 4 response is likely to present relevant material in a well-planned and logical sequence, with clearly defined structure and communicate clearly and accurately with confident use of appropriate terminology and demonstrate few, if any, errors of grammar, punctuation and spelling.

Total marks [50]

SECTION B

4   Victoria is the wife and assistant of a knife-throwing expert, Carl, who both work for a circus. Carl is renowned for his hot temper and has recently been off work suffering from depression. Their act consists of Victoria being

strapped to a board whilst Carl throws twenty knives all around her from a distance of five metres to within as little as ten centimetres of her body. They have being doing this for many years without a single mishap and Carl regards his technique as perfect. One evening, just before their act begins, Victoria tells Carl that she is having an affair with the lion tamer, Wayne. Carl is shocked and enraged but immediately the fanfare strikes up for the start of their act and Carl and Victoria enter the ring to start their performance. The third knife Carl throws goes straight into Victoria's heart, killing her instantly.

Discuss Carl's liability for Victoria's death.

A Level 5 answer is likely to include a number of the following points. These points are neither prescriptive nor exhaustive. Credit should be given for any other relevant points. Candidates can be rewarded for either breadth or depth of knowledge.

Assessment Objective 1: 25 marks
Define the elements of the offence of murder recognising it as a common law offence.

Define the defence of provocation under s.3 Homicide Act 1957.

Demonstrate knowledge of the subjective and objective elements of s.3 by reference to relevant cases such as: *Duffy, Ibrams and Gregory, Thornton, Humphreys* and *Smith (Morgan James), Weller.*

Define the defence of diminished responsibility by reference to s.2 Homicide Act 1957.

Demonstrate knowledge of the elements of diminished responsibility and its interpretation: *Byrne, Ahluwalia.*

Explain the offence of reckless manslaughter by reference to *Pike, Lidar and Cunningham.*

Assessment Objective 2: 20 marks
Discuss the potential murder charge against Carl by way of direct intent and causing death.

Consider whether Carl may successfully plead provocation by applying the law to the facts: Was he provoked by Victoria's words?

Was there a sudden and temporary loss of control or a 'cooling off period'? (3rd knife?) Can his hot-tempered personality or history of depression be brought into consideration under the objective 'reasonable man' (ordinary person) test as a 'characteristic'? *Smith (Morgan James), Weller, Holley, Mohammed, Karimi and James.*

Argue to a conclusion.

Discuss whether his history of depression may suffice for a defence of diminished responsibility: *Ahluwalia.*

Discuss whether Carl's actions were not intentional but reckless: the evidence of years without mishap would tend to suggest the act was intentional but not necessarily so.

Assessment Objective 3: 5 marks
A Level 4 response is likely to present relevant material in a well-planned and logical sequence, with clearly defined structure and communicate clearly and accurately with

confident use of appropriate terminology and demonstrate few, if any, errors of grammar, punctuation and spelling.

Total marks [50]

5   Carol and Diana decide to go out 'clubbing' for the night. They meet at Carol's house and begin the evening by drinking half a bottle of vodka. They then go out and have some more drinks in a pub and they each take an ecstasy tablet which Diana has brought with her. As they are leaving the pub, Carol takes a leather jacket from the back of a chair, mistaking it for her own very similar jacket which she has, in fact, left at home. By the time that they arrive at the club, both girls are suffering from hallucinations. When the doorman, Barry, asks them for identity, Diana, who thinks Barry is an alien who wants to transport her to another planet, pokes him in the eye with her finger and then hits him over the head with her umbrella, knocking him unconscious.

Consider the offences that Carol and Diana may have committed and whether they may have any defences available to them.

A Level 5 answer is likely to include a number of the following points. These points are neither prescriptive nor exhaustive. Credit should be given for any other relevant points. Candidates can be rewarded for either breadth or depth of knowledge.

Assessment Objective 1: 25 marks
   Define theft s.1 Theft Act 1968.
   Explain the 'partial dishonesty' defence in s.2(1)(a) Theft Act.
   Explain the defence of voluntary intoxication by reference to the *Majewski* rules, *Lipman* and the distinction between crimes of specific and basic intent.
   Define assault occasioning actual bodily harm by reference to s.47 Offences Against the Person Act 1861 and *Miller*.
   Define 'grievous bodily harm' by reference to s.18 and s.20: *Smith*, *Saunders*.

Assessment Objective 2: 20 marks
   Consider whether Carol has committed theft of the leather jacket by applying either s.2(1)(a) Theft Act or the rules on self-induced intoxication.
   Consider Diana's assault on Barry and conclude that the application of the *Majewski* rules will not provide a defence to the ABH charge for the poke in the eye since it is a crime of basic intent and even if she is charged with s.18 for knocking Barry unconscious and if the prosecution cannot prove that she formed the *mens rea* she will still be convicted of a s.20 offence by applying the 'fall back' formula.

Assessment Objective 3: 5 marks
A Level 4 response is likely to present relevant material in a well-planned and logical sequence, with clearly defined structure and communicate clearly and accurately with confident use of appropriate terminology and demonstrate few, if any, errors of grammar, punctuation and spelling.

Total marks [50]

6 Emma hires Fred, a qualified electrician, to rewire her house. She is unhappy when she notices sparks coming from the switches as she turns some lights on or off. Emma complains to Fred who returns to do some checks. He assures her that everything is in order and perfectly safe. The next morning, Emma goes to take a shower in the bathroom. When she turns on the shower control, she receives an electric shock that causes her to fall and bang her head, knocking her unconscious. Fortunately, her friend, Gita, arrives almost immediately and discovers Emma. Gita calls an ambulance and Emma is rushed to hospital. While Emma is still critically ill she develops an infection.

Hugh, a junior doctor employed by the hospital, fails to read Emma's medical notes properly. The notes clearly show that Emma is allergic to penicillin. Hugh gives Emma penicillin to treat the infection. As a result of her allergy Emma dies.

Discuss the liability of Fred and Hugh for Emma's death.

A Level 5 answer is likely to include a number of the following points. These points are neither prescriptive nor exhaustive. Credit should be given for any other relevant points. Candidates can be rewarded for either breadth or depth of knowledge.

Assessment Objective 1: 25 marks

Define gross negligence manslaughter by reference to *Adamako*:
- duty of care;
- breach of duty;
- risk of death;
- conduct so far below that which is regarded as reasonable as to amount to a crime.

Refer to 'duty' situations:
- contractual: *Pittwood, Holloway*;
- professional: *Adamako, Holloway*.

Outline the principles of causation, factual and legal: *White, Pagett*.

Describe the law relating to intervening acts by third parties and, in particular, medical negligence: *Smith, Jordan, Cheshire*.

Assessment Objective 2: 20 marks

Discuss the fact that Fred owes Emma a duty of care under both contract and his professional qualifications.

Recognise that the duty owed is that of a qualified electrician rather than a handyman or 'neighbour'.

Conclude that there was a breach of duty involving a risk of death and that a jury may well consider that Fred is potentially liable for Emma's manslaughter if they think his conduct has fallen so far below the standards of a qualified electrician to warrant such a finding: *Holloway, Adamako*.

Discuss whether Fred may be relieved of liability by the negligent actions of Hugh.

Apply the relevant rules of causation in *Smith, Jordan* and *Cheshire*.

Identify a potential duty of care owed by Hugh to Emma and apply the principles laid down by *Adamako* as outlined above.

Argue to a reasoned conclusion.

Assessment Objective 3: 5 marks

A Level 4 response is likely to present relevant material in a well-planned and logical sequence, with clearly defined structure and communicate clearly and accurately with confident use of appropriate terminology and demonstrate few, if any, errors of grammar, punctuation and spelling.

Total marks [50]

SECTION C

7   John enters a supermarket intending to steal some food. He is in the shop when he notices that the door to the manager's office is open. He goes inside hoping to find something of value. There is no one present but, as he is about to leave, he notices a wallet lying on the manager's desk. John picks the wallet up and takes a £20 note out of it. The manager, Sue, sees him leaving the office and shouts at him. John pushes Sue aside and runs out of the store

Evaluate the accuracy of each of the four statements A, B, C and D individually, as they apply to the facts in the above scenario.

A Level 5 answer is likely to include a number of the following points. These points are neither prescriptive nor exhaustive. Credit should be given for any other relevant points. Candidates can be rewarded for either breadth or depth of knowledge.

Assessment Objective 2
Statement A: John is guilty of burglary under s.9(1)(a) Theft Act 1968.

Identify that John enters the supermarket as a trespasser because he is exceeding the permission granted to shoppers to enter the supermarket: *Jones and Smith*.

Identify that John has the intention to steal when he enters the supermarket and is guilty at that point of entry of a s.9(1)(a) burglary even if he steals nothing.

John is also potentially guilty of a s.9(1)(a) burglary when he enters the manager's office as a trespasser with a conditional intent to steal anything of value: *A-G.s Ref Nos. 1 and 2 of 1979.*

Conclude that John is guilty of s.9(1)(a) burglary.

Statement B: John is guilty under s.1 Theft Act 1968.

Identify that John probably does not commit theft when he picks up the wallet as there is no apparent intention to permanently deprive the owner of it s.6 Theft Act 1968.

Identify that in any event John is clearly guilty of the full offence of theft when he takes the £20 note: s.1 Theft Act 1968. He is clearly dishonest and cannot argue that it has been abandoned by the rightful owner and cannot claim to be an 'honest finder' in these circumstances.

Conclude that John is guilty of the full offence of theft.

Statement C: John is guilty of robbery under s.8 Theft Act 1968.

Identify that robbery is defined in s.8 Theft Act 1968 as the use of force or the threat of force in order to steal. Identify that when he pushes Sue aside, John is clearly using force.

Identify that the force must be immediately before or at the time of stealing.

Identify that theft may be viewed as a continuing offence: *Hale, Lockley.*

Conclude that John is almost certainly guilty of robbery.

Statement D: John is guilty of burglary under s.9(1)(b) Theft Act 1968.

Identify that a person commits a s.9(1)(b) burglary when, having entered as a trespasser, he goes on to steal.

Reason that, although John may try to argue he is a lawful visitor to the supermarket and not yet a trespasser as his intention to commit theft is a secret one, he certainly enters a 'part of a building' as a trespasser when he enters the manager's office: *Walkington.*

Conclude that when he steals the £20 note he is guilty of a s.9(1)(b) burglary offence.

Total marks [20]

8   Wayne is the captain of the Northport United football team. During an important match against their local rivals, Wayne is involved in a clash of heads in an incident with an opposing player, Andrew. Wayne receives a nasty bruise above his left eye and is badly concussed. Wayne insists on continuing after treatment with a cold sponge but is obviously still in a very dazed condition. A few minutes later Wayne jumps wildly into a foul tackle on Andrew. Andrew is carried off in agony and X-rays later reveal that he has a broken ankle.

Evaluate the accuracy of each of the four statements A, B, C and D individually, as they apply to the facts in the above scenario.

A Level 5 answer is likely to include a number of the following points. These points are neither prescriptive nor exhaustive. Credit should be given for any other relevant points. Candidates can be rewarded for either breadth or depth of knowledge.

Assessment Objective 2
Statement A: Andrew is liable for ABH s.47 OAPA 1861 for the bruise suffered by Wayne.

Reason that a bruise may amount to an assault occasioning actual bodily harm contrary to s.47 Offences Against the Person Act 1861.

Consider whether it satisfies the test of interfering with the health and comfort of the victim: *Miller.*

Consider whether Andrew has caused the injury either recklessly or intentionally.

Conclude that, in either case, Andrew may be liable as s.47 may be committed on proof of at least subjective recklessness in the *Cunningham* sense.

Statement B: Wayne is liable for GBH s.18 OAPA 1861 for the broken ankle sustained by Andrew.

Reason that a broken ankle may amount to 'serious harm' and could be charged under either s.18 or s.20 Offences Against the Person Act 1861.

Consider the possibility that Wayne has caused the injury either recklessly or intentionally.

Conclude that if it is 'reckless' it satisfies the definition in s.20 of maliciously inflicting serious harm. If it is intentional then Wayne may be liable for a s.18 offence.

Statement C: Andrew has a defence of consent for any charge brought by Wayne.

Reason that consent may be available as a defence.

Explain that physical contact sports are an exception to the rule that consent is not available to harm above the level of common assault: *A-G's Ref No.6 1980*.

Consider that Andrew will only be liable if he caused Wayne's injuries outside the rules of the sport, either intentionally or recklessly.

Conclude that Andrew has a potential defence of consent.

Statement D: Wayne has a defence of automatism for any charge brought by Andrew.

Reason that automatism may be available as a defence for Wayne.

Explain that automatism is a defence for acts done by the muscles with no control by the mind.

Identify that the blow to the head is an external factor.

Conclude that Wayne has a potential defence of automatism if his acts were as a result of his concussion and not intentional or reckless: *Bratty*.

Total marks [20]

OXFORD CAMBRIDGE AND RSA EXAMINATIONS
Advanced GCE
LAW [G154QP]
Criminal Law Special Study

Specimen Paper 1 hour 30 minutes

TIME 1 hour 30 minutes

INSTRUCTIONS TO CANDIDATES
Answer **all** questions.
Read each question carefully and make sure you know what you have to do before starting your answer.

Write the numbers of the questions you answer on the front of your Answer Book.

You are reminded of the importance of including relevant knowledge from **all** areas of your course, where appropriate, including the English Legal System.

INFORMATION FOR CANDIDATES

The special study materials have provided a starting point for study of the topics set. Each booklet contains source material which indicates the area(s) of substantive law to be tested. You are expected to demonstrate understanding of the area(s) of law and the development of law and to use legal methods and reasoning to analyse legal material, to select appropriate legal rules and apply these in order to draw conclusions.

The maximum mark for this paper is **80**.

Quality of Written Communication (QWC)

Candidates are reminded of the need to write in continuous prose where appropriate. You will be assessed on your written communication and your use of appropriate legal terminology.

1   Discuss the extent to which the precedent in *Re A (Conjoined Twins)* (Source 10, page 6, and Source 11, page 7, Special Study Materials) represents a development of the law on necessity.

[**12**]

2   Lord Hailsham in *Howe* explains the defence of duress by saying that 'in such circumstances a reasonable man of average courage is entitled to embrace as a matter of choice the alternative which a reasonable man could regard as the lesser of two evils' (Source 2, page 2, lines 7–9, Special Study Materials).

Consider the extent to which the development of the restrictions on the use of duress really allow 'a reasonable man of average courage' to exercise such a choice.

[**29**]

3   Mara, Ian and Claire are all students of Christine's in the law school where Christine works as a lecturer. Consider whether or not Christine would have a defence of duress available in each of the following situations:
   (a) Mara, who has failed EU law, comes to Christine's room with a gun and threatens to kill Christine unless Christine goes directly to the EU lecturer's room and kills her with the knife that Mara gives her. Christine goes to the room, enters and attempts to kill the lecturer but she quickly holds a large book up in front of her preventing the knife from touching her.

[**10**]

(b) Ian comes to Christine's room and threatens that unless Christine immediately steals volumes of law reports for Ian from the research library that he will reveal to the Dean of School that Christine is having an affair with one of the third-year students. Christine steals the law reports for Ian.

[10]

(c) Claire, who has failed all her first-year modules, phones Christine from Spain during the vacation after hearing her results and threatens Christine that unless Christine burns down the law school she will kill her when she returns from Spain. Christine does set fire to the law school.

[10]
QWC [9]

OXFORD CAMBRIDGE AND RSA EXAMINATIONS
Advanced GCE
LAW [G154MS]
Criminal Law Special Study
Specimen Mark Scheme

The mark scheme must be read in conjunction with the Advanced GCE Law Assessment Grid. When using the mark scheme the points made are merely those which a well prepared candidate would be likely to make. The cases cited in the scheme are not prescriptive and credit must be given for any relevant examples given. Similarly, candidates who make unexpected points, perhaps approaching the question from an unusual point of view, must be credited with all that is relevant.

Candidates can score in the top bands without citing all the points suggested in the scheme.

I   Discuss the extent to which the precedent in *Re A (Conjoined Twins)* (Source 10, page 6, and Source 11, page 7, Special Study Materials) represents a development of the law on necessity.

[12]

A Level 5 answer is likely to include a number of the following points. These points are neither prescriptive nor exhaustive. Credit should be given for any other relevant points. Candidates can be rewarded for either breadth or depth of knowledge.

Assessment Objective 2
Define the principle arising from the case.

Link to any leading case e.g. *R v Dudley and Stephens, Kitson.*

Consider how the case confirms the existing definition of necessity: necessity is a defence based on justification – the avoidance of a worse evil.

Necessity is a defence generally unavailable in criminal law and certainly not for murder.

Discuss how the case represents a development: CA decided that there were extreme situations where there could be a right to choose that one innocent person could die to save the life of another.

The application of the defence depends on three requirements:
- act needed to avoid a worse evil;
- no more is done than is necessary for the purpose to be achieved;
- in all the circumstances the evil inflicted is not disproportionate to the evil avoided.

Identify that the decision was by the Court of Appeal (Civil Division) so is not binding on the Criminal Division.

Assessment Objective 3
Marks are awarded holistically at the end of the paper.

[9 in total]

2   Lord Hailsham in *Howe* explains the defence of duress by saying that 'in such circumstances a reasonable man of average courage is entitled to embrace as a matter of choice the alternative which a reasonable man could regard as the lesser of two evils'. (Source 2, page 2, lines 7–9, Special Study Materials).

Consider the extent to which the development of the restrictions on the use of duress really allow 'a reasonable man of average courage' to exercise such a choice.

[29]

A Level 5 answer is likely to include a number of the following points. These points are neither prescriptive nor exhaustive. Credit should be given for any other relevant points. Candidates can be rewarded for either breadth or depth of knowledge.

Assessment Objective 1
Define the defence of duress and the two-part test in *Graham*:
- defendant's will was overborne by threat of imminent violence to self or close family so defendant was impelled to act as he did;
- court is satisfied that a sober person of reasonable firmness would have been similarly affected by the threats and would have reacted in the same way.

Explain that the defendant escapes liability as a result of a successful defence having provided an acceptable excuse for his behaviour.

Identify offences where the defence will be available and those where it will not, e.g.:
- generally available;
- but not available to murder or secondary participation in murder: *Howe*;
- nor to attempted murder: *Gotts* – though it would be available to s.18 GBH.

Identify some obvious limitations, e.g.

- not available if self-induced: *Shepherd*;
- not available if a means of escape exists: *Hudson and Taylor*;
- not available if the threat is not immediate: *Abdul-Hussain, Hasan*;
- not available if there is no connection between the threat and the offence committed: *Cole*.

Assessment Objective 2

Discuss some of the criticisms that can be made of the limitations, e.g.:

- there can be circumstances where even a person of reasonable fortitude submits to threats, however repugnant what they are forced to do;
- the effect of *Howe* may be to legally force a person into being a hero;
- while a person may put his/her own life at risk to save someone else (s)he may not feel capable of applying the same test to his family;
- there is an inconsistency with the defence of provocation.

Denying the defence to attempted murder but accepting it for s.18 is anomalous since the harm suffered in the former might actually be less than that in the latter.

Consider the fairness of denying the defence if the threat is not immediate or if the person trying to use the defence has voluntarily associated with the person making it, since the impact on the person claiming the defence may still be very real.

Consider the effect of self-induced defence (arguably limiting the restrictive nature of the defence) and compare with *Bowen*, restrictive because IQ not relevant.

Consider that the Law Commission has in any case suggested reforming the defence.

Assessment Objective 3

Marks are awarded holistically at the end of the paper.

[9 in total]

3 Mara, Ian and Claire are all students of Christine's in the law school where Christine works as a lecturer. Consider whether or not Christine would have a defence of duress available in each of the following situations:
   (a) Mara, who has failed EU law, comes to Christine's room with a gun and threatens to kill Christine unless Christine goes directly to the EU lecturer's room and kills her with the knife that Mara gives her. Christine goes to the room, enters and attempts to kill the lecturer but she quickly holds a large book up in front of her preventing the knife from touching her.

[10]

   (b) Ian comes to Christine's room and threatens that unless Christine immediately steals volumes of law reports for Ian from the research library that he will reveal to the Dean of School that Christine is having an affair with one of the third-year students. Christine steals the law reports for Ian.

[10]

(c) Claire, who has failed all her first-year modules, phones Christine from Spain during the vacation after hearing her results and threatens Christine that unless Christine burns down the law school she will kill her when she returns from Spain. Christine does set fire to the law school.

[10]

Candidates will not be credited for repeating information given in previous answers, but may refer to that knowledge in order to apply it appropriately.

A Level 5 answer is likely to include a number of the following points. These points are neither prescriptive nor exhaustive. Credit should be given for any other relevant points. Candidates can be rewarded for either breadth or depth of knowledge.

Assessment Objective 1

Define duress.
Use any relevant cases in illustration.

Assessment Objective 2

3(a)

Apply the two-part test from *Graham*.
Consider that the threat in this case is one of death or serious harm to Christine.
Consider also that on this basis the threat is one that is likely to produce the same response Christine's in persons of reasonable fortitude.
Consider the rule in *Howe* that the defence is unavailable to a charge of murder and nor is it available to attempted murder: *Gotts*.
Conclude on this basis that the defence would fail.

3(b)

Apply the two-part test from *Graham*.
Consider that the threat here is not one of immediate violence towards Christine although it may produce the same response in a person of reasonable fortitude.
Identify the similarity with *Valderrama-Vega*.
Consider that even the argument that Christine might suffer psychological harm would fail as it did in *Valderrama-Vega*.

3(c)

Apply the two-part test from *Graham*.
Consider that the threat is serious and may produce a similar effect in a person of reasonable fortitude.
Identify the similarity with *R v Hudson and Taylor* and conclude that Christine would have had ample opportunity to take alternative action to seek protection.
Consider also whether the threat can be seen as immediate: *Abdul-Hussain*.
Conclude that the defence is not available.

Assessment Objective 3

Marks are awarded holistically for the whole paper.

[9 in total]

A Level 4 response is likely to present material in a well-planned and logical sequence, with a clearly defined structure and communicate clearly and accurately with confident use of appropriate terminology and demonstrate few, if any, errors of grammar, punctuation and spelling.

26 Objective questions

The new OCR specification for examination from January 2008 contains a new **Section C** with questions in a different format from those previously seen. These are objective in nature and require students to adopt a different approach to their answering technique. There is a choice of one from two questions which consist of a short scenario focusing on any topic or combination of offences and defences from any part of the specification.

These questions are not 'multiple choice' in nature but have been variously described as objective questions or 'dilemma' questions. Students are required to respond to a variety of propositions (rather than in question format) and decide whether the various propositions are true or not. In doing so students will obviously rely upon their knowledge and understanding but are essentially being assessed upon their analytical and application skills in order to argue to a short reasoned conclusion. Thus they are neither essay-style Section A answers nor even the more in-depth answers that would be expected to the traditional 'problem-style' question in Section B. It follows therefore that neither detailed citation nor lengthy paragraphs in continuous prose are required in order to gain full marks. Examples of the types of questions are provided below and the suggested answer to Question 1 is provided immediately below it. The suggested answers to Questions 2–6 appear in a separate 'Section C – Suggested Answers' section on pp. 426–434. The length of the scenarios in the actual examinations may be a little shorter but these examples are indicative of the type of scenarios and propositions that are likely to occur. Also included is an example of a diagrammatic 'dilemma board' for Question 1 showing how this type of technique could be applied using a blank template or interactive whiteboard.

Question 1

John enters a supermarket intending to steal some food. He is in the shop when he notices that the door to the manager's office is open. He goes inside hoping to find something of value. There is no one present but, as he is about to leave, he notices a wallet lying on the manager's desk. John picks the wallet up and takes a £20 note out of it. The manager, Sue, sees him leaving the office and shouts at him. John pushes Sue aside and runs out of the store.

Evaluate the accuracy of **each** of the four statements A, B, C and D individually, as they apply to the facts in the above scenario.

Statement A: John is guilty of burglary under s.9(1)(a) Theft Act 1968.
Statement B: John is guilty of theft under s.1 Theft Act 1968.
Statement C: John is guilty of robbery under s.8 Theft Act 1968.
Statement D: John is guilty of burglary under s.9(1)(b) Theft Act 1968.

[20 marks]

Suggested answer

In the case of Statement A: John is guilty of burglary under s.9(1)(a) Theft Act 1968.

- Identify that John enters the supermarket as a trespasser because he is exceeding the permission granted to shoppers to enter the supermarket (*Jones and Smith*).

- John has the intention to steal when he enters the supermarket and is guilty at that point of entry of a s.9(1)(a) burglary even if he steals nothing.

- John is also potentially guilty of a s.9(1) (a) burglary when he enters the manager's office as a trespasser with a conditional intent to steal anything of value (*A-G's Ref Nos. 1 & 2 of 1979*).

- Conclude that John is guilty of s.9(1) (a) burglary.

In the case of statement B: John is guilty of theft under s.1 Theft Act 1968.

- Identify that John probably does not commit theft when he picks up the wallet as there is no apparent intention to permanently deprive the owner of it (s.6 Theft Act 1968).

- Identify that in any event John is clearly guilty of the full offence of theft when he takes the £20 note (s.1 Theft Act 1968). He is clearly dishonest and cannot argue that it has been abandoned by the rightful owner and cannot claim to be an 'honest finder' in these circumstances.

- Conclude that John is guilty of the full offence of theft.

In the case of statement C: John is guilty of robbery under s.8 Theft Act 1968.

- Identify that robbery is defined in s.8 Theft Act 1968 as the use of force or the threat of force in order to steal.

SECTION C

I   In the Dilemma Board below consider the accuracy of **each** of the four statements A, B, C and D as they apply to the facts in the central scenario.

[20 marks]

Answer

A	B
John is guilty of burglary under s.9(1)(a) Theft Act 1968.	John is guilty of theft under s.1 Theft Act 1968.

John enters a supermarket to steal some food. He is in the shop when he notices that the door to the manager's office is open. He goes inside hoping to find something of value. There is no one present but, as he is about to leave, he notices a wallet lying on the manager's desk. John picks the wallet up and takes a £20 note out of it. The manager, Sue, sees him leaving the office and shouts at him. John pushes Sue aside and runs out of the store.

C	D
John is guilty of robbery under s.8 Theft Act 1968	John is guilty of burglary under s.9(1)(b) Theft Act 1968.

SECTION C

Answer

I   In the Dilemma Board below consider the accuracy of **each** of the four statements A, B, C and D as they apply to the facts in the central scenario.   [20 marks]

Central scenario

John enters a supermarket to steal some food. He is in the shop when he notices that the door to the manager's office is open. He goes inside hoping to find something of value. There is no one present but, as he is about to leave, he notices a wallet lying on the manager's desk. John picks the wallet up and takes a £20 note out of it. The manager, Sue, sees him leaving the office and shouts at him. John pushes Sue aside and runs out of the store.

A

John enters the supermarket as a trespasser because he is exceeding the permission granted to shoppers to enter (Jones & Smith).

John has the intention to steal when he enters the supermarket and is guilty of a s.9(1)(a) burglary even if he steals nothing.

He is potentially guilty of a s.9(1)(a) burglary when he enters the manager's office as a trespasser with a conditional intent to steal anything of value (A-G'a Ref Nos. 1 & 2 of 1979).

B

John does not commit theft when he picks up the wallet. He is dishonestly appropriating it but with no intent to permanently deprive the owner of it.

In any event John is clearly guilty of the full offence of theft when he takes the £20 note.

C

Robbery is defined in s.8 Theft Act 1968 as the use of force or the threat of force in order to steal.

As only the threat of force is enough for robbery any slight force in order to steal is sufficient.

When he pushes Sue aside John is clearly using force.

As theft may be viewed as a 'continuing offence' (Hale, Lockley) John is guilty of robbery.

D

John commits a s.9(1)(b) burglary when 'having entered as a trespasser' he goes on to steal.

Although John may argue he is not yet a trespasser as his intention to steal is a secret one he certainly enters a 'part of a building' as trespasser when he enters the manager's office (Walkington).

He steals the £20 note and is guilty of a s.9(1)(b) burglary offence.

Conclusion boxes:

John is guilty of theft under s.1 Theft Act 1968.

John is guilty of burglary under s.9(1)(a) Theft Act 1968.

John is guilty of burglary under s.9(1)(b) Theft Act 1968.

John is guilty of robbery under s.8 Theft Act 1968

385

- Identify that as only the threat of force is enough for robbery any slight force in order to steal is sufficient.

- Identify that when he 'pushes Sue aside' John is clearly using force.

- Identify that the force must be 'immediately before or at the time of stealing'.

- Identify that theft may be viewed as a 'continuing offence' (*Hale, Lockley*).

- Conclude that John is almost certainly guilty of robbery.

In the case of statement D: John is guilty of burglary under s.9(1)(b) Theft Act 1968.

- Identify that a person commits a s.9(1)(b) burglary when 'having entered as a trespasser' he goes on to steal.

- Reason that although John may try to argue he is not yet a trespasser in the supermarket as his intention to steal is a secret one he certainly enters a 'part of a building' as trespasser when he enters the manager's office (*Walkington*).

- Conclude that when he steals the £20 note he is guilty of a s.9(1)(b) burglary offence.

Alternatively exercises can be constructed for these questions for teaching and learning or revision aids in the form of a true 'Dilemma Board' – see pp. 384–385.

Question 2

Wayne is the captain of the Northport United football team. During an important match against their local rivals, Wayne is involved in a clash of heads in an incident with an opposing player, Andrew. Wayne receives a nasty bruise above his left eye and is badly concussed. Wayne insists on continuing after treatment with a cold sponge but is obviously still in a very dazed condition. A few minutes later Wayne jumps wildly into a foul tackle on Andrew. Andrew is carried off in agony and x-rays later reveal that he has a broken ankle.

Evaluate the accuracy of **each** of the four statements A, B, C and D individually, as they apply to the facts in the above scenario.

Statement A: Andrew is liable for occasioning actual bodily harm to Wayne.

Statement B: Wayne is liable for intentionally causing the broken ankle sustained by Andrew.

Statement C: Andrew has a defence of consent for any charge brought by Wayne.

Statement D: Wayne has a defence of automatism for any charge brought by Andrew.

[20 marks]

Question 3

Adrian's wife owes Brian £10. Brian sees Adrian in the street and threatens to beat him up unless he gives him £10. Adrian hands over the money. Brian enters a shopping mall. He tries to snatch a bag from a shopper, Carol, but she resists and it falls to the ground. Brian runs off. He goes into a supermarket and takes a bottle of whisky from the shelf and puts it in his pocket. Dan, another shopper, sees him but Brian pushes Barry away and leaves without paying. He is getting into his car outside when a security guard, Elvis, approaches him. Brian drives his car at Elvis who jumps out of the way and Brian drives off.

Evaluate the accuracy of **each** of the four statements A, B, C and D individually, as they apply to the facts in the above scenario.

Statement A: Brian is liable for robbery when he forces Adrian to hand him £10.

Statement B: Brian is liable for robbery when he snatches at Carol's bag.

Statement C: Brian is liable for robbery in the supermarket.

Statement D: Brian is guilty of robbery when he drives his car at Elvis.

[20 marks]

Question 4

Angelo, is having an affair with Beyonce, owes Colin money and is a member of a drugs gang run by Desmond. Colin tells Angelo that unless he repays the debt he will reveal his criminal activities to the police. Angelo robs a shop to pay the debt. Desmond e-mails Angelo from Italy and orders Angelo to beat up Ethan, an addict who owes Desmond money, or Angelo will be killed. Angelo goes to Ethan's flat and beats him up. As he is leaving in his car he sees Capone, a member of Desmond's gang, sitting in the car behind. Desmond drives across a pedestrianised precinct to escape. When he gets home, Beyonce says she will harm Angelo's child unless he kills his wife within the next week. Angelo puts poisons in his wife's drink.

Evaluate the accuracy of **each** of the four statements A, B, C and D individually, as they apply to the facts in the above scenario.

Statement A: Angelo is able to successfully plead the defence of duress if charged with robbery.

Statement B: Angelo is able to successfully plead the defence of duress to the assault on Ethan.

Statement C: Angelo is able to successfully plead the defence of duress of circumstances to a potential charge of dangerous driving.

Statement D: Angelo is able to successfully plead the defence of duress to a charge of murder or attempted murder of his wife.

[20 marks]

Question 5

Erica has been in a steady relationship with Bob for several months. He has often hit her and Erica feels trapped and depressed. Her doctor has been giving her medication to treat her depression. One day during an argument Bob calls her 'a useless pathetic item'. Bob falls asleep in his chair. Erica goes to her bedroom where she drinks several glasses of whisky in an hour. She goes back downstairs and when she sees Bob asleep she suddenly picks up a heavy ashtray and smashes it over Bob's head killing him instantly.

Evaluate the accuracy of **each** of the four statements A, B, C, and D individually, as they apply to the facts in the above scenario.

Statement A: Erica can be charged with murder.

Statement B: Erica may successfully plead intoxication as a defence.

Statement C: Erica cannot plead provocation as a defence.

Statement D: Erica will be successful if she pleads the defence of diminished responsibility.

[20 marks]

Question 6

Valentino escapes from prison. He tries to force open the door to a caravan in the hope of finding something of value but gives up when he sees a policeman, Ahmed, approaching. Valentino takes a gun from his pocket, aims it at Ahmed and squeezes the trigger forgetting that the gun is unloaded. He runs off and goes into a bank intending to threaten the assistant, Shirley, with a gun to force her to hand over money but changes his mind when he sees a security guard. Outside he picks up a wallet lying on the ground but throws it away when he discovers it is empty.

Evaluate the accuracy of **each** of the four statements A, B, C, and D individually, as they apply to the facts in the above scenario.

Statement A: Valentino is liable for attempted burglary when he tries to break into the caravan.

Statement B: Valentino is liable for attempted murder when he squeezes the trigger.

Statement C: Valentino is liable for attempted robbery when he enters the bank.

Statement D: Valentino is liable for attempted theft when he picks up the wallet.

[20 marks]

For suggested answers to questions 2–6 see pp. 426–434.

27   Key skills

Introduction

Whether students are used to thinking about them or not, certain key skills have always underpinned learning and build upon the basic skills that have already been acquired in the early years of education. They are certainly nothing to be afraid of. On the contrary, key skills provide an opportunity for the first time for students to acquire recognition for these skills. Key skills are in fact the means through which learning takes place and which, in a rapidly changing world, must be updated throughout life. What is new is that a key skills qualification, valued by employers and higher education institutions, is now available at Levels 2, 3 (and probably 4). This chapter is intended to provide some general advice and guidance to students and teachers and also points out some specific suggestions about how evidence for the key skills qualification can be produced on the A-level Law specification. (Specification, remember, is the new term for syllabus – see the Introduction to this book.)

Key skills to be assessed

The 'Main' key skills at Level 3

- C3 Communication

- N3 Application of number

- IT3 Information technology

The 'Wider' key skills at Level 3

- WO3 Working with others

- LP3 Improving own learning and performance

- PS3 Problem solving

At present the wider key skills do not form part of the qualification for the purposes of assessment but they are nevertheless seen as integral to post-16 education and training, and the Government has made it clear that these wider skills must be developed and promoted. Consequently, all new specifications have 'signposted' these wider skills.

In order to enable as many students as possible to achieve a key skills qualification, developing and assessing these skills is designed to be a straightforward task. Examples of the 'keys to attainment' may be essays, oral presentations or information displays using technology or graphical interpretation.

To achieve the new qualification, students must pass internal (e.g. portfolio and coursework) and external (set assignments, tests) components of assessment. Extra information, support and guidance concerning assessment is available on two websites:

• www.qca.org.uk/keyskills/newunits/htm and

• www.dfee.gov.uk/qualify/key.htm where case studies and exemplars of students' work to specified standards are available.

Although key skills underpin all learning, they are not actually embedded in each specification. Rather, key skills should be the subject of a separate qualification with opportunities for producing relevant evidence 'signposted' within each specification. In this way, it is hoped that undue artificiality and repetition in key skills assessments will be avoided or minimised. The rest of this chapter deals with the variety of opportunities that exist for students and teachers for the compilation of such evidence within the Law specifications concerning criminal law.

Opportunities for evidencing key skills

Communication (C3)

C3.1a: Contribute to a group discussion about a complex topic

• What is the moral significance of assessing a person's guilty mind? (Chapter 1)

• How have the courts developed an approach to the coincidence of *actus reus* and *mens rea* and what is the significance of these terms? (Chapter 1)

• When and why is it possible to justify imposing criminal liability upon a person who simply fails to act? (Chapter 2)

• Why is there a need for two tests to assess 'recklessness'? (Chapters 3, 7, 8 and 13)

- How can strict liability offences be justified? (Chapter 4)

- Why is there a need to distinguish between different forms of homicide? (Chapter 5)

- How should the offence of involuntary manslaughter be reformed? (Chapter 7)

- Is the law on assaults satisfactory? (Chapter 8)

- What might be the impact of the Human Rights Act 1998? (Chapter 9)

- Is the law relating to dishonesty and appropriation in a satisfactory state? (Chapter 10)

- How can the decision in *Elliott v C* be justified? (Chapters 3 and 13)

- How does the law address the problems of conduct whilst intoxicated? (Chapter 14)

- Should the law on insanity be reformed? (Chapter 15)

- Justify the limitations on the availability of duress as a defence? (Chapter 18)

- Is the law relating to participation in crime fair? (Chapter 20)

- Why is there a need for inchoate offences? (Chapters 21 and 22)

C3.1b: Make a presentation about a complex subject using at least one image to illustrate complex points

- Describe the principles of causation using a flow chart to illustrate this. (Chapter 2)

- Illustrate the distinctions between subjective and objective recklessness by means of a diagram. (Chapter 3)

- By means of a flow chart, illustrate the historical development of the law on foresight of consequences as a means of assessing the concept of intention. (Chapter 5)

- Produce a diagrammatic analysis of the offence of homicide. (Chapters 5, 6 and 7)

- Demonstrate the operation of the defence of intoxication using a chart. (Chapter 14)

- Compare and contrast the defences of insanity and automatism by means of a flow chart or diagram. (Chapters 15 and 16)

- Illustrate the availability of the various general defences. (Chapters 14–19)

- Produce a chart showing how liability for participation in crime may be analysed. (Chapter 20)

- Using a diagram, illustrate the classification of inchoate offences. (Chapters 21 and 22)

C3.2: Read and synthesise information from two extended documents that deal with a complex subject. One of these documents should include at least one image

- Access to an extended document should not be a problem – a case report or legal article ought to be readily available to most students either in hard copy or via the internet (a list of useful legal websites appears in an Appendix at the end of this book). Interesting and relevant cases among many would be *Woollin* (Chapter 5), *Brown* (Chapter 9) or *Pommell* (Chapter 18).

- In addition, there are many examples of Law Commission reports (e.g. 237 on Corporate Manslaughter), draft bills and recent legislation available on the internet. The *Times*, *Independent* and *Guardian* newspapers all carry dedicated law reports and features.

- Other sources are legal journals such as the *New Law Journal*, published weekly, and the *Criminal Law Review*, published monthly. Access to these may be more limited, but many colleges and some libraries take these publications. Graphs, tables or illustrations are often contained in these publications.

C3.3: Write two different types of documents about complex subjects. One piece of writing should be an extended document and include at least one image

- There are ample opportunities to produce this element of evidence. Extended essays on almost any criminal law topic should satisfy the first criterion, e.g. on the concept of dishonesty in theft.

- Draft an advice on legal liability based on a scenario arising from homicide using a scattergram to illustrate the various issues involved.

Information technology (IT3)

IT 3.1: Plan and use different sources to search for and select information required for two different purposes

- A number of opportunities exist. Students can research the internet (in some cases through in-house intranet systems) and commercially available CD ROMs for Acts of Parliament, law reports, legal databases, Home Office Reports, etc. (See Appendix at the end of the book.)

IT 3.2: Explore, develop and exchange information and derive new information to meet two different purposes

- Design a mini-project involving the creation of a database of cases and statutes in criminal law using one field to contain a key word to identify the main topic of the case or related statute. You could work as a team on this so that a large number of cases can be entered. This could be used for:

- fellow students to access a set of cases on a topic by entering a query

- the production of a law magazine

- e-mailing a list of cases on a particular topic in response to requests by other students.

IT 3.3: Present information from different sources for two different purposes and audiences. Your work must include at least one example of images and one example of numbers

- Create a report and presentation for members of staff, describing how you compiled your database. Illustrate how the system works and how it is possible to incorporate some of the results into a law magazine. Show a table of cases requested and construct a chart to show how many times they were requested.

- Create a series of supplementary related references and/or questions arising from the issues addressed by the cases.

- Create a presentation to explain the current criticisms surrounding involuntary manslaughter, using graphical representations of the various issues.

- Extend into synoptic topics by presenting a review of the various proposals for reform of involuntary manslaughter put forward by the Law Commission.

Working with others (WO3)

The evidence for this area of skill needs to be produced in at least two substantial activities that each includes tasks for WO3.1, WO3.2 and WO3.3 respectively. You need to show that you can work in a group and in one-to-one situations. The aspects of activity for which you are required to supply evidence are:

WO3.1: Plan a group activity, agreeing objectives, responsibilities and working arrangements.

WO3.2: Work towards achieving the agreed objectives, seeking to establish and maintain co-operative working relationships in meeting individual responsibilities.

WO3.3: Review the activity with others against the agreed objectives and agree ways of enhancing collaborative work.

Suggested activities

This is an opportunity to combine one or more aspects of the machinery of justice and criminal procedure so as to incorporate them synoptically into the specification. Aspects of procedure and sentencing are particularly appropriate for this purpose.

1 Organise a moot, debate or role play based on a given scenario (e.g. a problem question from the examples given at the end of chapters in the book). The stages could be:

- meet as a group and agree upon the chosen scenario

- create an action plan to:

  - organise the breakdown of tasks

  - agree pairings or groupings to undertake the various tasks to include the following:
    research of different aspects of the legal problem;

    obtain case/statute details and references and research them;
    prepare a report and presentation;
    plan meetings or appoint a chair responsible for co-ordinating the work;
    agree deadlines and methods of communication, e.g. e-mail;
    monitor progress and working relationships;
    review progress and goals;
    review and change action plans where necessary.

- hold the moot/debate inviting others to attend or preside

- arrange a post-moot discussion group to review and provide feedback on the exercise and make conclusions and recommendations for improvement.

2 Make a presentation as a small group, to the class as a whole, on a given topic of general interest from the specification. For example, whether the defence of duress should be extended from its current limitations or whether the current law on consent to assaults amounts to an undue restriction on individual freedom. The stages could be:

- meet as a group and organise the distribution of tasks

- create OHPs or a 'Powerpoint' presentation

- agree on the allocation of tasks and responsibilities for research, oral presentation, etc.

- agree on deadlines and methods of co-ordination and communication

- invite others to attend the presentation

- arrange a post-presentation discussion group to review and provide feedback on the exercise and make conclusions and recommendations for improvement or produce a questionnaire to elicit staff and student perceptions of the exercise.

Improving own learning and performance (LP3)

An increasingly important aspect of improvement is that students are involved in planning, managing and reviewing their own learning. To provide evidence of improvement you need two examples of study-based learning, two examples of activity-based learning and one example of using learning from at least two different contexts to meet the demands of a new situation. For this assessment it is important that you arrange to meet a tutor who will support you in providing the necessary evidence. An action plan could be drawn up to include the following steps:

LP3.1: Agree targets and plan how these will be met using support from tutors.

LP3.2: Use your plan, seeking and using feedback and support from relevant sources to help meet your targets using different ways of learning to meet new demands.

LP3.3: Review your progress in meeting targets, establishing evidence of achievements and agree action for improving performance using support from appropriate people.

Suggested activity

You can monitor your progress in several ways, but each should include appropriate feedback, recording of achievement and setting of targets:

- through essay writing and solving hypothetical situations as homework assignments;

- through timed essays;

- through set tests;

- through oral and practical contribution to group activities;

- by attending court and writing an appropriate report;

- by attending student law conferences;

- by improving literacy and ICT skills.

Problem solving (PS3)

For this skill you need to undertake an activity which involves identifying, solving and validating the proposed solution to a complex problem. You can easily find a problem scenario from criminal law – most of the problem questions at the end of the Parts, and in the Additional Questions Chapter, would be suitable. Identifying, analysing and suggesting a solution to legal problems is a central feature of this specification. However, you cannot properly implement the solution since the scenarios presented are hypothetical in nature, not real cases which will be taken to court. Accordingly your evidence here will be limited to PS3.1 and PS3.2.

PS3.1: Recognise, explore and analyse the problem and agree how to show success in solving it.

PS3.2: Plan and compare at least two options that could be used for solving the problem and justify the option chosen.

Suggested activity

Choose a complex problem question and research it in detail – for example, question 2 at the end of Chapter 7. Compile your answer to the problem, and review the work done. Consider any practical alternative solutions. In such an instance, it may again be possible to incorporate a synoptic element by considering the various sentencing alternatives that might be appropriate in such a scenario.

Conclusion

Remember that the total portfolio of evidence you produce for your key skills qualification will not normally be drawn exclusively from the study of law. Indeed, a study of A-level law will provide very limited opportunity to display evidence of N3: Application of Number, other than in a highly artificial context. It is therefore important that you develop a strategy with your tutors which will enable you to gather appropriate evidence from all your AS and A2 studies. It should be clear that law provides many opportunities to compile the necessary evidence for the key skills addressed above.

28   Legal resources on the internet

General awareness sites
Excellent starting points for free and subscription services
www.venables.co.uk
www.the-lawyer.co.uk
www.lawzone.co.uk
www.bailii.org

Legislation
Acts of Parliament   www.hmso.gov.uk/acts
Statutory Instruments   www.hmso.gov.uk/stat
Parliamentary Bills, etc.   www.parliament.the-stationery-office.co.uk
The Law Commission   www.lawcom.gov.uk
More Government information   www.coi.gov.uk
www.criminal-justice-system.gov.uk

Case law
House of Lords decisions   www.parliament.the-stationery-office.co.uk
The Court Service   www.courtservice.gov.uk
Criminal Cases Review Commission   www.ccrc.gov.uk
Casetrack   www.casetrack.com
The Lord Chancellor's Department   www.open.gov.uk/lcd
The Times   www.the-times.co.uk
General   www.lawreports.co.uk

Professional bodies
www.lawsociety.org.uk
www.barcouncil.org.uk
www.ilex.org.uk

Academic websites
www.cardiff.ac.uk
www.law.warwick.ac.uk
www.newcastle.co.uk

European law sites
www.europa.eu.int
www.europa.eu.int/celex
www.europa.eu.int/eur-lex/en/index.html
www.europarl.eu.int/dors/oeil/en
www.curia.eu.int
www.eurotext.ulst.ac.uk

Magazines/journals, etc.
www.lawgazette.co.uk
www.butterworths.co.uk
www.smlawpub.co.uk

29   Answers guide

A. END OF PART QUESTIONS

Part 1 General principles 1 (p. 64)

Question 1

- Define the concept of strict liability by reference to the lack of requirement of *mens rea*.

- Emphasise the common law presumption of *mens rea*, e.g. *Sweet v Parsley*; *B v DPP*.

- Identify the statutory nature of strict liability offences and realise the significance of statutory interpretation in this context.

- Recognise the summary nature of most strict liability offences.

- Provide examples of strict liability offences – road traffic, licensing, food safety, pollution, etc. and elaborate the examples by reference to appropriate cases, e.g. *Sherras v De Rutzen*; *Alphacell*; *Smedleys v Breed*; *James & Son v Smee*, etc.

- Discuss the potential unfairness of such offences by a consideration of some of the potential injustices arising from a willingness to dispense with proof of a 'guilty mind' (*Callow v Tillstone*).

- Discuss whether there is too much inconsistent use of discretion used by prosecuting agencies (more Parliamentary guidance as to fault element preferable?)/conviction of the morally innocent is never justifiable/public respect for the criminal law is potentially undermined by dubious prosecutions/room for the development of criminal responsibility based on negligence.

- Refer to some of the social benefits claimed or injustices caused, e.g. the regulatory nature or administrative convenience or the possible injustice of imposition of liability without fault e.g. 'spiking' of drinks or 'planting' of drugs, e.g. *Warner*; *Gammon*; *Storkwain*; *Lim Chin Aik*, etc.

- Discuss some of the following 'benefits': protection of society from harmful acts/the 'quasi-criminal' nature of strict liability offences creates little stigma/regulatory nature promotes high standards of care in socially important activities/practical effectiveness, i.e. too many polluted rivers, too many drunk drivers as it is/administrative convenience, difficulty of establishing *mens rea* in many such cases removed, etc.

Question 2

- Recognise that the vast majority of true crimes involve prohibited conduct, e.g. an act in unlawful killing, an appropriation in theft, etc. but identify that some offences may be brought about by omission, e.g. gross negligence manslaughter.

- Describe 'duty' situations that may arise from: statute, public office, common law, close relationship, voluntary assumption of care, creation of a dangerous situation, etc.

- Cite relevant examples to illustrate some of the above, e.g. *Children and Young Persons Act 1933*; *Gibbins v Proctor*; *Dytham*; *Pittwood*; *Stone v Dobinson*; *Miller*; *Khan and Khan*.

- Refer to the issues arising in the *Bland* case.

- Consider the difficulties in defining the extent of these duties.

- Criticise the strict liability context of many omissions in the Road Traffic Acts.

- Comment upon the relationship between legal and moral codes of behaviour in this context.

- Examine the uncertainty over prescribing or defining when a 'caring duty' ought to be imposed.

- Discuss the desirability of imposing standards of 'good practice' on the holders of public office.

- Analyse the difference between a mere breach of duty and a failure to intervene.

- Make reference to the issues in *Bland*, e.g. can a 'carer' be released from their duty?

- Analyse the principles concerning coincidence and prior fault discussed in *Miller*; *Fagan*, etc.

- Suggest whether the criminal law strikes an appropriate balance in this regard or whether it may be desirable to adopt a more prescriptive approach, c.f. Netherlands/France.

Question 3

- Define strict liability and refer to the way the judiciary approaches strict liability offences including the presumption of *mens rea* (*Sweet v Parsley*).

- Describe the concept of regulatory offences and the guidelines outlined for the imposition of strict liability in *Sherras v De Rutzen*; *Gammon*; *Alphacell* etc.

- Explain that the word 'using' without reference to *mens rea* has been interpreted strictly (*James v Smee*).

- Define the liability of accessories for strict liability offences (*Johnson v Youden*; *Callow v Tillstone*).

- Refer to the personal and vicarious liability principles concerning 'permitting' the use of the jetski (*Tesco v Natrass*; *Vane v Yiannopoulos*).

- Consider that Hugh physically uses the jetski and the *actus reus* is present and could be guilty if this is a strict liability offence.

- Identify whether this is a strict liability offence applying the principles outlined in *Sweet v Parsley*; *Gammon*; *James & Son v Smee*, etc.

- Conclude that, although it may be unfair, Hugh appears to be guilty of an offence; if *Sherras v De Rutzen* were to be followed there would be no liability.

- Evaluate Crapp's liability identifying that Crapp would not be liable as an accessory to the 'using' of the jetski if Hugh has committed no offence since there would be no principal offence to aid and abet.

- Consider that Crapp may be liable as an accessory if Hugh has committed a strict liability offence (*Johnson v Youden*) but he lacks the *mens rea* necessary as an accessory even if he is negligent (*Callow v Tillstone*).

- Discuss whether Sharp or Jetskis Are Us Ltd may be liable on the similar basis and identify that Crapp, Sharp and Jetskis Are Us Ltd may all have 'permitted' the use of the jetski by Hugh but that the word 'permit' appears to require an element of *mens rea* (*James & Son v Smee*) which appears to be lacking in each case.

Part 2 Homicide (p. 131)

Question 1

- Define murder – *Coke*'s definition as amended – the unlawful killing of a human being under the Queen's Peace with malice aforethought.

- Explain the phrase 'malice aforethought' – an intention to kill or to do serious harm.

- Explain that a person may possess direct intent but that they may also be liable for consequences which are not necessarily their main aim, purpose or desire.

- Explain oblique/indirect intention – (*Moloney*; *Woollin*, etc.).

- Explain and illustrate the principles of causation (*White*; *Pagett*; *Cheshire*; *novus actus interveniens*).

- Discuss whether Dipak possesses sufficient *mens rea* (malice aforethought) for murder.

- Discuss whether he possesses direct intent as he intended a crash to occur but was 'hoping' he would only scare Sarev.

- Discuss whether Dipak has oblique intent by questioning whether he foresees death or serious harm resulting as a virtually certain consequence of his actions towards Sarev by applying the *Woollin* principles and the evidence from which such a conclusion may be drawn.

- Question whether Dipak's actions are the factual and legal cause of death or whether there has been a break in the chain of causation caused by the negligence of John and Carol.

- Consider that Ron's van is the ultimate cause of death and whether that may break the chain.

- Discuss possible liability for the attempted murder of Sarev if Dipak has done an act which is 'more than merely preparatory' to the commission of the substantive offence (*Jones*, etc.) and there is a possibility that there was a break in the chain of causation. BUT then:

- Question whether Dipak has sufficient *mens rea* for the attempted murder of Sarev – only an intention to kill will suffice (*Whybrow*).

Question 2

- Define murder, *Coke*'s amended definition.

- Explain the concept of direct intention (*Mohan*).

- Define diminished responsibility s.2 Homicide Act 1957 and interpretation (*Byrne*; *Tandy*; *Gittens*; *Atkinson*; *Dietschmann*).

- Define provocation s.3 Homicide Act 1957 and the relevant interpretation in cases such as *Duffy*; *Thornton*; *Camplin*; *Luc Thiet Thuan*; *Smith (Morgan James)*; *Weller*; *Rowland*; *Holley*; *Mohammed*, including a statement of the subjective and objective features of the defence.

- Explain the dichotomy over the 'objective' reasonable man test as applied to the gravity of the provocation to the defendant and the defendant's powers of self-control.

- Define intoxication by explaining the *Majewski* rules.

- Identify that this would be a murder charge and recognise this as an example of direct intention (*Mohan*).

- Discuss the potential relevance of alcoholism as a factor capable of establishing the defence of diminished responsibility s.2 Homicide Act 1957 (*Tandy*; *Dietschmann*).

- Apply the evidence that Andy has been receiving treatment from his doctor but consider the decisions in *Tandy* and *Dietschmann*.

- Identify the potential relevance of provocation s.3 Homicide Act 1957.

- Identify that words may be evidence of provocative conduct.

- Apply the evidence of Andy's loss of self-control as 'sudden and temporary' (*Duffy*).

- Discuss the relevance of alcoholism as a potential characteristic to be attributed to the 'reasonable' man in these circumstances (*Camplin*; *Smith (Morgan James)*; *Weller*; *Holley*, etc.).

- Consider an analogy with 'battered woman syndrome'.

- Conclude that the jury may well decide that neither defence is available to Andy in these circumstances.

- Apply the *Majewski* rules on intoxication, identifying that Andy may have been prevented from forming an intention to kill or do serious harm to Barbara.

- Recognise that murder is a crime of specific intent and that, if he is successful with an intoxication plea, he will be convicted of manslaughter applying the 'fall back' principle.

Question 3

- Define involuntary manslaughter as a form of unlawful homicide which has not been caused with intent.

- Explain the different types of manslaughter as unlawful act/constructive; gross negligence and, probably, reckless manslaughter.

- Describe corporate manslaughter.

- Define unlawful act manslaughter by reference to the relevant cases (*Lowe*; *Dalby*; *Cato*; *Church*; *Newbury and Jones*; *Lamb*; *Ariobeke*; *Goodfellow*; *Mitchell*; *Watson*; *Slingsby*, etc.).

- Define gross negligence manslaughter by reference to *Adamako*; *Donoghue v Stevenson*; *Bateman*; *Andrews*; *Stone and Dobinson*; *Litchfield*; *Singh*; *Khan*; *Wacker; Misra and Sriravastra*, etc.

- Explain the existence of reckless manslaughter by reference to *Cunningham*; *Pike*; *Goodfellow*; *Lidar*, etc.

- State the current law relating to corporate manslaughter.

- Refer to the Law Commission's proposals for reform and the government's draft Bill.

- Assess the advantages and disadvantages of the offence having been developed entirely through common law decisions.

- Assess the breadth of conduct potentially covered by the offence from blameworthy killing bordering on murder to the boundary with accidental death.

- Assess the criticism that the present law has been described as a 'rag bag' of offences.

- Assess the existing law of unlawful act manslaughter, in particular the objective test for 'dangerousness' of the unlawful act which may result in a conviction for manslaughter where a defendant has not foreseen even the risk of harm (*Newbury and Jones*).

- Assess the existing law of gross negligence manslaughter, in particular the circularity of the *Adamako* test.

- Assess whether Professor Smith, among others, is correct to assert that subjective reckless manslaughter must surely still exist.

- Assess the unsatisfactory state of corporate manslaughter and the very few successful decisions as a result of having to identify senior company officials as the 'mind' of the organisation (*Tesco v Nattrass*).

- Assess the Law Commission's proposals for offences of 'reckless killing', 'killing by gross carelessness' and 'corporate killing' and the government's response.

- Assess the government's draft bill for reforming corporate manslaughter.

Question 4

- Define the offence of murder recognising that it is a common law offence and identify the concept of intention in criminal law as an aspect of *mens rea*; dismissing motive as irrelevant (*Steane*).

- Recognise the development of intention through the common law (*Mohan*; *Hyam*; *Moloney*; *Woollin* etc.) and refer to different aspects of intention – direct/oblique; distinguish between intention and foresight of consequences (*Moloney*).

- Appreciate the fact that foresight of intention is not the same as intention but may be used in conjunction with s.8 Criminal Justice Act 1967 – evidence from which intention may be inferred by the jury.

- Refer to and explain an alternative manslaughter charge – presumably constructive manslaughter based on a dangerous act of criminal damage or even subjective recklessness (*Lidar*).

- Recognise the causation issues and state the main principles emerging from *White*; *Smith*; *Pagett*; *Jordan*; *Blaue*; *Cheshire*, etc.

- Apply the principles of murder, oblique intention and causation to the facts discussing the significance of the 'fifty'/'fifteen' confusion.

- Conclude that whether or not Clive would be convicted of murder is a question of fact for the jury in the light of the evidence having been directed as to the law by the judge and that a jury may or may not find that the required intention has been established.

- The alternative may be an unlawful act or subjective reckless manslaughter conviction.

Part 3 Offences against the person (p. 167)
Question 1

- Refer to the defence of consent when applied to offences against the person.

- Recognise the limitations imposed upon the availability of consent, e.g. not available to a charge of homicide – euthanasia is not recognised in the UK, aiding and abetting a suicide is an offence.

- Mention that consent to minor assaults in the course of everyday life is generally implied although mere touching or the non-consensual cutting of hair may nevertheless amount to a battery (*Collins v Wilcock*; *Thomas*; *Smith*).

- Refer to policy decisions restricting the availability of consent as a defence, e.g. not to prize-fighting with bare fists (*Coney*), nor to agreeing to settle differences by means of a fight or duel (*A-G's Reference No.6 of 1980*), nor to sado-masochistic activities deemed to be against the public interest (*Brown*).

- Indicate with appropriate citation that a true consent may excuse what would otherwise be an assault, e.g.
  - surgery, injections, tattooing, body piercing for cosmetic purposes, etc. (*Corbett v Corbett*; *Wilson*);
  - physical contact sports (*Billinghurst*; *Barnes*);
  - sexual relations (*Donovan*; *Brown*; *Slingsby*);
  - rough horseplay (*Jones*);
  - lawful parental chastisement.

- Fraud negatives consent to an assault only if V was deceived as to the identity of the person concerned or the nature of the act performed (*Linekar*; *Richardson*; *Tabassum*; *Dica*; *Cuerrier*).

- Honest mistaken belief in consent is a defence (*Morgan*).

- Evaluate policy that allows consent as an effective defence to a charge of injury sustained in the course of properly conducted sport or games but recognises that an assault may be prosecuted should a participant exceed what is allowable within the rules of that sport or game.

- Distinguish between deliberate and accidental harm inflicted in physical contact sports: deliberate harm is the essence of boxing but unacceptable in a variety of ball sports such as football, rugby or hockey (*Billinghurst*; *Barnes*).

- Comment upon the social utility of surgical treatment as a justification for the defence whether or not the patient is conscious and capable of giving consent.

- Evaluate the reasons for the decisions given in *Brown* and *Wilson*.

- Evaluate when and why it is appropriate for the law to interfere with individual freedom of choice on the grounds of public interest.

- Evaluate whether the judges are in the better position to proceed on a case-by-case basis rather than Parliament attempting to lay down general principles in this regard. Discuss whether euthanasia should be made lawful.

Question 2

- Define assault and battery at common law and refer to charging under s.39 CJA 1988 and identify that the spilling of John's drink is accidental – no liability without *mens rea*.

- John pouring his drink over Mike's head – probably both assault and battery at common law.

- Define assault occasioning actual bodily harm under S47 OAP 1861 (*Miller*; *Chan Fook*, etc.)

- Define criminal damage s.1 Criminal Damage Act 1971 – 'damage or destroy' (*Hardman*; *Roe v Kingerlee*) probable criminal damage to Mike's shirt.

- Refer to the use of reasonable force in self-defence or the prevention of crime – Criminal law Act 1977 – and state the principles which apply to the defence of consent and recognise that agreeing to settle differences by means of a fight is against public policy and consent is not available (*A-G's Ref No.6 of 1980*).

- Define s.18 and s.20 OAP 1861 GBH and malicious wounding. John's punch amounts to GBH with intent.

- Contrast transferred malice with transferred intent in relation to the smashed window, (attempted GBH with intent is a possible charge for Mike) – s.1 Criminal Damage Act 1981, and dismiss it (*Latimer*; *Pembliton*).

- Apply the *Majewski* rules to the various offences, distinguishing between specific and basic intent (*Cunningham* recklessness and 'fall back' for the assaults and *Caldwell* for the criminal damage).

Question 3

The relevant law

- Define assault at common law.

- Define assault occasioning actual bodily harm s.47 Offences Against the Person Act 1861 (*Miller; Chan Fook; Ireland*).

- Define unlawful wounding/grievous bodily harm ss. 20 and 18 OAP Act (*Eisenhower; J v C (a minor)*).

- Define criminal damage – Criminal Damage Act 1971.

- Explain the principles of the defence of consent at common law (*Donovan; Brown; Wilson*).

- Define automatism (*Bratty*).

- Explain the principles of the use of force in self-defence.

Application to problem

- Identify the branding as a potential ABH by Mark but apply *Wilson* to argue the probable defence of consent provided that Kate's consent was real and not induced by threats.

- Identify a potential s.47/20 offence when Kate lashes out.

- Identify potential criminal damage to Mark's glasses.

- Consider whether Kate would be able to plead automatism to the above and conclude that she probably could.

- Identify the potential s.47 assault by Mark when he punches her and causes her nose to bleed.

- Consider whether the phone calls amount to ABH (*Chan Fook; Ireland; Constanza*).

- Identify assault in the pub when Mark raises his fist and criminal damage when Kate damages Mark's mobile phone.

Part 4 Offences against property (p. 216)

Question 1

Students should outline the law relating to the following issues:

• Define theft s.1 Theft Act 1968.

• Define the relevant elements of theft in more detail:.
  – dishonesty s.2;
  – appropriation s.3;
  – property s.4;
  – belonging to another s.5;
  – intention to permanently deprive s.6.

• Discuss whether Fred has committed theft of the £10 paid to him by mistake – he has clearly appropriated it but was arguably not dishonest at the time of the original appropriation; however, s.3(1) says that a person who comes by property innocently may nevertheless later appropriate it. When Fred discovers he has been overpaid and dishonestly decides to keep it by spending it he arguably commits theft applying the *Ghosh* test.

• Identify that appropriation may be a continuing act in these circumstances (*Atakpu and Abrahams*) so problems of coincidence of dishonesty can be resolved.

• Discuss that, in any event, s.5(4) covers property acquired by mistake by stating that it still belongs to another where D is under an obligation to restore it to the rightful owner (*R v Gilks*).

• Discuss whether Fred commits theft of the whisky: he clearly appropriates property when he places the whisky in his pocket instead of the shopping trolley (*Morris*; *McPherson*); however, his forgetfulness may arguably mean he is not dishonest.

• Discuss that, in any event s.5(4) will still apply when he realises he has the whisky and decides to keep it.

• Discuss whether picking the apples constitutes theft, applying s.4. The apples are clearly capable of being property belonging to another (s.4(2)) and are not growing wild (s.4(3)) if in a cultivated residential garden.

• Dismiss a potential burglary since Fred does not enter a building or part of a building in order to steal the apples.

• Identify that John is also guilty of theft as John has sufficient control and possession of the apples to satisfy the definition of belonging to another (s.5). A thief can steal from a thief.

- Discuss insanity under the M'Naghten Rules regarding Fred's forgetfulness – probably not according to *Clarke* but it is likely to negate any dishonesty.

Question 2

- Identify and define theft and its elements (sections 1–6 Theft Act 1968).

- Identify and define burglary and its elements (s.9 (i) (a) and (b) Theft Act 1968).

- Identify and define attempt and attempting the impossible (Criminal Attempts Act/*Shivpuri*).

- Identify and define robbery and its elements (s.8 Theft Act 1968).

- Identify and define assault and battery at common law and s.47 Offences against Property Act 1861.

- Identify and define intoxication as a defence and refer to the *Majewski* principles.

- Consider Hugh's liability and identify some or all of the following offences:
  - does he commit burglary when he enters the shed belonging to his father?
  - consider 9 (i) (b) if he formed the intention to steal only after entry.
  - is the shed a building?
  - has he entered his father's premises as a trespasser (*Jones* and *Smith*)?
  - was the bike abandoned? The courts are reluctant to infer this.
  - did he intend to permanently deprive? Was he dishonest? (*Ghosh*, etc.)

- Consider Keith's liability and identify some or all of the following offences:
  - can a conditional intent to steal from the jacket amount to theft?
  - is it an attempted theft notwithstanding the impossibility element?
  - is he guilty of theft when he places items inside his coat? (*Morris*; *Gomez*; *McPherson*)
  - whether s.9 (i) (a) or (b) depends upon his state of mind when entering.
  - assault relevant to a possible robbery charge. Was the force used in order to steal?
  - likely to be a s.47 Offences against Property Act charge since there is bruising, recklessness in the subjective sense will suffice (*Savage*; *Parmenter*).

- Consider intoxication as a defence. Did the intoxication prevent the formation of the necessary *mens rea*? If so, it would be a defence to the theft-related offences but not to the assault or criminal damage offences which are crimes of basic intent.

Question 3

The relevant law

• Define theft, Theft Act 1968.

• Refer to appropriation s.3 and *McPherson; Morris; Gomez; Hinks* as regards the items in the shop and show knowledge and understanding of the assumption of rights of the owner.

• Refer to s.2 (1)(c) Theft Act with regard to dishonesty and *Small*.

• Explain s.6 Theft Act with regard to 'borrowing' of the bike.

• Define burglary s.9 (1) (a) Theft Act 1969.

• Explain the term 'vessel' as developed by the Theft Act and cases.

Application to problem

• Apply the relevant law to the facts of the scenario.

• Consider the placing of the whisky in the coat pocket as a dishonest appropriation (*McPherson*).

• Consider the switching of the labels accompanied by a dishonest intention to be an appropriation and completed theft at that point since Graham has assumed 'one of the rights of the owner' by switching the price labels (*Morris*).

• Argue that when Graham takes the bike he may lack an intention to permanently deprive in the literal sense but that he is likely to be caught by s.6 (1) as it probably amounts to 'a person appropriating property belonging to another without meaning the other permanently to lose the thing itself is nevertheless to be regarded as having the intention of permanently depriving the other of it if his intention is to treat the thing as his own to dispose of regardless of the other's rights' when he abandons it at the end of his road.

• His only defence might be that he honestly believed the true owner could not be found by taking reasonable steps, but this is unlikely to be believed in the circumstances (*Small*).

• Identify that the boarding of the canal longboat is a burglary s.9 (1)(a) Theft Act as well as theft as it is clear that a boat which can be a home is capable of being a 'vessel' that is inhabited within s.9(4) and he 'enters' with the intention to steal.

Part 5 Defences (p. 297)

Question 1

- Explain that intoxication is only ever relevant as a defence if it actually prevents the formation of the *mens rea*.

- Explain the distinction between voluntary and involuntary intoxication and illustrate the relevant principles involved in involuntary intoxication by citation of appropriate case law, e.g. *Hardie*; *A-G's Ref (No.1) of 1975*; *Bailey*; *Allen*; *Kingston*.

- Explain the way the courts have distinguished between crimes of specific and basic intent in voluntary intoxication and illustrate this distinction by reference to *Beard*; *Majewski* and selected appropriate offences.

- Refer to the relationship of intoxication and other defences such as mistake, insanity and diminished responsibility by reference to relevant case law (*O'Grady*; *Fotheringham*; *Jaggard v Dickinson*; *Gannon*; *O'Connor*; *Tandy*; *Egan*).

- Describe the 'Dutch Courage' principle by reference to *Gallagher*.

- Discuss the public policy reasons for adopting a pragmatic rather than a principled approach.

- Discuss the fact that liability for voluntary intoxication is based upon the foresight of a general risk rather than foreseeing the specific risk of committing the particular offence in question.

- Discuss the fact that the presumption of recklessness implicit in the *Majewski* rules for crimes of basic intent seems to conflict with s.8 Criminal Justice Act 1967.

- Discuss the justification for separating the *actus reus* from the *mens rea* since the recklessness in becoming intoxicated precedes the commission of the offence.

- Discuss the inconsistencies that occur when there is no lesser offence of basic intent upon which to 'fall back', e.g. theft or the inchoate offences.

- Discuss the harsh effect of the decision in *Kingston*, which does not allow a defence of involuntary intoxication if the effect is merely to disinhibit the accused.

- Discuss the social concern surrounding 'binge' drinking and the correlation between violent crime, criminal damage and intoxication.

- Discuss the Law Commission proposals and the need, or otherwise, for reform.

Question 2

- Define automatism by reference to *Bratty v A-G for N.I.*

- Explain that it is a loss of control by the 'mind' over the movements of the muscles and provides a complete defence as it more than merely negates the *mens rea*.

- Recognise that it may be a complete defence to any crime including crimes of strict liability, providing that there has been a complete loss of control (*Broome v Perkins*).

- Demonstrate knowledge of the 'external factor' theory (*Quick* etc.).

- Provide examples of automatism by reference to cases (*Charlson*; *Quick*; *R v T*; *Wholley*; *Hill v Baxter*).

- Define insanity by reference to the M'Naghten rules.

- Illustrate the definition of insanity by citing relevant cases (*Kemp*; *Quick*; *Sullivan*; *Burgess*, etc.).

- Demonstrate good understanding of the effect of the defence and refer to the 'special verdict' and the provisions of the Criminal Procedure (Insanity and Unfitness to Plead) Act 1991.

- Evaluate the distinction between non-insane automatism and insanity.

- Comment upon the reasons given by the courts for restricting the availability of the defence of automatism since its recognition in *Charlson*. *Charlson* and similar cases would now fall within the M'Naghten rules as his tumour would be an 'internal factor' and is behaviour which 'manifests itself in violence and is prone to recur' (*Kemp*; *Bratty*).

- Evaluate the consequences of the policy by considering examples of these restrictions on automatism in cases (*Bratty*; *Sullivan*; *Burgess*; *Hennessey*; *Broome v Perkins*, etc.).

- Comment that the view of a diabetic in similar circumstances to *Quick* would probably be regarded as a condition that was self-induced and the defence may be available only to a crime of specific intent if at all.

- Consider that the courts thus have the power to deal appropriately with such behaviour under the Criminal Procedure (Insanity and Unfitness to Plead) Act 1991.

Question 3

- Define accurately one or more of the defences by reference to relevant cases.

- Realise that duress in any of its forms is a recognition that an accused may be entitled to be asked to be excused liability on the basis of their will being overborne in the face of an external threat as a result of which they felt compelled to commit the alleged offence.

- Demonstrate knowledge of the relevant principles relating to duress, necessity and/or duress of circumstances.

- Refer to subjective/objective aspects of the defences (*Graham*; *Martin*; *Bowen*; *Emery*) the nature of the threat (*Valderrama Vega*), the requirement of imminence (*Hudson and Taylor*; *Abdul–Hussein*).

- State the limited availability of the defences – not available in answer to a charge of murder etc. (*Lynch*; *Howe*; *Gotts*).

- Recognise the apparent denial of necessity as a defence until the emergence of duress of circumstance (*Dudley and Stephens*; *Buckoke*; *Conway*; *Willer*; *Martin*; *Pommell*, etc.).

- Refer to the impact of *Shayler*; *Re: A*.

- Appreciate duress denied if criminal associations voluntarily joined (*Fitzpatrick*; *Sharp*; *Shepherd*).

- Discuss the type of threat; ought it to be confined to self and immediate family? Why? (*Smith*; *Wright*; *Shayler*; *Hasan*).

- Discuss whether threats other than death or serious harm be allowable.

- Discuss the policy arguments for not allowing duress as a defence to murder etc., the anti-terrorism element of policy, Hailsham in *Howe*, etc.

- Comment on which characteristics (frailty, cowardice, submissiveness, low IQ) ought to be taken into account? c.f. provocation etc.

- Discuss the moral arguments that can be applied to duress, necessity and duress of circumstances concerning the degree of resistance to be expected from an individual under threat.

- Discuss whether there is hypocrisy in claiming this higher moral ground.

- Discuss whether the proposals suggested by the Law Commission and the law as developed by recent cases are becoming more favourable to an accused in terms of the subjective element.

- Discuss the development by the Court of Appeal of the defence of duress of circumstance.

- Discuss whether or not the limitations are justified, based on the preceding arguments.

- Criticise that it is still apparently available to a s.18 OAP Act 1861 GBH charge.

Question 4

- Define assault and battery and refer to s.39 Criminal Justice Act 1988.

- Define s.47 Offences Against the Person Act 1861: assault occasioning actual bodily harm.

- Define s.20 Offences Against the Person Act 1861: wounding (*Eisenhower*).

- Explain the defence of intoxication and the *Majewski* rules.

- Define self-defence (Criminal Law Act 1967).

- Refer to mistake and intoxicated mistaken use of force in self-defence (*Williams*; *O'Grady*; *Fotheringham*).

- Identify assault and battery when Mark pushes Trevor (ignoring provocation as irrelevant to the charge).

- Identify s.47 when Mark punches Trevor causing his nose to bleed (*Miller*; *Chan Fook* [not a wound]).

- Identify s.20 when Mark thrusts the glass in Trevor's face (*Eisenhower*).

- Apply the *Majewski* rules by arguing that intoxication may be a factor for all the above offences which appear to have indeed been committed

417

intentionally but that Mark will nevertheless have no defence as his intoxication was self-induced.

- Argue that even if he was incapable of forming the specific intent required these are all potentially basic intent offences to which voluntary intoxication is no defence.

- Consider that the honest mistaken use of force in self-defence may be a defence provided that the force used is reasonable but that is of no use to Mark if the mistake is an intoxicated one (*O'Grady*; *Fotheringham*).

Question 5

- Refer to both the common law and s.3 Criminal Law Act 1967 and their potential overlap.

- Explain that self-defence is a common law defence.

- Explain that the Criminal Law Act refers to the prevention of crime.

- Explain that self-defence is normally available to murder and assaults but that it is also available to other crimes.

- Note that, once raised, the burden of proof is on the prosecution to show that the defence fails.

- State the basic elements of the defence:.
  – the use of some force must be necessary in the circumstances as they appear to D;
  – the actual degree of force used must be reasonable.

- Recognise that the issue of reasonableness depends upon the circumstances of each case and is a question for the jury (*Palmer*).

- Recognise that the above involves the jury placing themselves in the circumstances that D believed to exist (*Palmer*; *Owino*).

- Explain that there is no duty to retreat or demonstrate a willingness to fight only as a last resort (*Bird*).

- Recognise that the use of excessive force in self-defence does not reduce liability for murder to manslaughter (*Palmer*; *Clegg*).

- Explain the mistaken use of force in self-defence (*Gladstone Williams*).

- Explain the effect of intoxication on the defence (*O'Grady*).

- Credit reference to the proposals regarding the excessive use of force in murder cases in the Law Commission Paper 2003.

- Consider whether it seems sensible that D does not have to wait to be attacked and may use a pre-emptive strike (*Beckford*).

- Comment that threats may be justifiably made against prospective attackers and that D may even go so far as to arm himself against the fear of an attack in certain circumstances and not necessarily be committing an offence (*Cousins*; *A-G's Ref No.2 of 1983*).

- Consider whether the use of excessive force in a murder case should result in a partial defence and a conviction for manslaughter instead as proposed by the Law Commission's Consultation Paper *Partial Defences to Murder 2003*.

- Consider whether an individual's characteristics, e.g. paranoia, ought logically to be taken into account to logically mirror 'characteristics' principles in provocation.

- Comment that cases such as Tony Martin, where the defence was not allowed, and many others too, have caused public disquiet.

- Consider the substitution of a qualification in favour of householders confronted by burglars, i.e. that the force used should not be 'grossly disproportionate', such as put forward by Patrick Mercer MP.

- Consider whether it is fair to expect a vulnerable person under perceived serious threat, e.g. from a robber, to use 'reasonable force' and no more.

- Comment on the public policy reasons for circumscribing this defence, e.g. no wish to promote 'vigilante'-type behaviour or the carrying of weapons of self-defence in public etc.

- Consider whether the availability of the mistaken use of force while intoxicated should be based upon whether the mistake was one which D could honestly have made while sober (*O'Connor*; *Gannon*).

Part 6 General principles 2 (p. 339)

Participation

Question 1

- Refer to the Criminal Attempts Act 1981 so as to define the *actus reus* and *mens rea* of the offence.

- Recognise the importance of establishing at what point a criminal intention can be said to have progressed to the stage of an attempt (*Gullefer*, etc.).

- Cite relevant cases that provide principles applying the meaning of 'more than merely preparatory'; these may include: (*Widdowson*; *Geddes*; *Campbell*; *Jones*; *Tosti and White*, etc.).

- Recognise that aspects of attempting the impossible may very well refer to the practical and theoretical absence of an *actus reus* of any sort unless defined by the accused's belief and refer to ss.1(2) and (3) as well as *Haughton v Smith*; *Anderton v Ryan* and *Shivpuri*.

- Demonstrate an awareness of the Law Commission's Report, which preceded the Criminal Attempts Act and describe some of the questions considered by the report, e.g. the desirability of striking a balance between the protection of the public from the social danger caused by the contemplation of crime, and the individual freedom to think or even fantasise.

- Consider the potential progress of criminality through attempt.

- Analyse the rationale of criminalising attempts.

- Discuss the principle that a person ought not to be punished for merely contemplating the commission of offence.

- Consider, perhaps, some reference to 'proximity', 'equivocality' or 'last act' principles which may very well demonstrate the candidate's true understanding of the topic. Older relevant cases discussed might include *Robinson*; *Stonehouse*, etc.

- Observe that *Gullefer* reflects the wish expressed by the Law Commission that the point at which a course of conduct amounts to an offence is a matter of fact for the jury in each case using principles of common sense and that the older common law principles would not normally need to be considered in order for a jury to come to a conclusion about this.

- Examine the difficulties in defining at what precise point, if any, an attempt can be said to have occurred, e.g. the problems in *Gullefer* and *Jones*.

- Refer to the House of Lords' confusion over attempting the impossible in *Anderton v Ryan* and *Shivpuri*.

- Credit, for example, any possible reference to alternatives, e.g. the US model of 'substantial steps ... strongly corroborative of the actor's criminal purpose'.

● Consider whether it should be necessary, e.g. in a case of attempted murder, that the accused need go as far as pointing a gun at his/her intended victim etc. Would this limit the power of the police to intervene (*Campbell*)?

Question 2

The relevant law

● Define the offence of murder by reference to the common law.

● State the law relating to incitement, conspiracy and attempt.

● Define incitement, encouraging another to commit a criminal offence (*RRB v Applin*) and the law relating to impossibility.

● Define conspiracy Criminal Law Act 1977 and the law relating to impossibility s.1(1)(b) and *Bolton*.

● Define attempt Criminal Attempts Act 1981 as an act that is 'more than merely preparatory' to the commission of the intended substantive offence.

● Describe the *mens rea* for the above offences.

● Define participation by reference to the Accessories and Abettors Act 1861.

Application to problem

● Ursula is liable for inciting Sandra to murder Vincent notwithstanding the impossibility (*Fitzmaurice*) when she suggests that she kills him with the intention that the offence is carried out.

● Ursula and Sandra are liable for conspiracy to murder notwithstanding the impossibility Criminal Law Act 1977 when they agree upon the course of conduct that will result in Vincent's murder with the intention to carry it out.

● Sandra should be liable for the attempted murder of Vincent, certainly when she squeezes the trigger, as she has done an act more than merely preparatory to the commission of murder with the intention to kill Vincent (*Jones*).

● Impossibility is no defence Criminal Attempts Act 1981 and *Shivpuri*.

- Ursula should also be liable as an accessory to attempted murder upon completion of the attempt by Sandra as she has aided and counselled the offence.

- Rudi would possibly be liable for aiding the offence provided he knew it was one of a range of offences which Sandra might commit (*Bainbridge*; *Maxwell*). Can Rudi be liable if he knows the ammunition is only blank rounds?

B. SUGGESTED ANSWERS TO SPECIAL STUDY QUESTIONS G154 on p. 362.

Question 1

- Briefly outline the facts of the case: this was an appeal against a conviction for assaulting a police officer. The woman PC had taken hold of the appellant's arm in order to give her a caution, but not to arrest her.

- Define the principle from the case: the merest touching of another person without consent, however slight, may amount to a battery.

- Recognise the exception that 'most of the physical contacts of everyday life are not battery because they are impliedly consented to' (see Source 2).

- Link to any leading case on battery (*Thomas*; *DPP v Smith* [2006]).

- Consider how this contributes to the law on battery. It distinguishes *Donnelly v Jackman* [1970] 1 All ER 987, [1970] 1 WLR 562, where it was said that if a PC taps, even repeatedly, on another person's shoulder he commits no wrong for he is under a duty to prevent and investigate crime; and so his seeking further, in the exercise of that duty, to engage a man's attention in order to speak to him may in the circumstances be regarded as acceptable.

- Assess the significance of *Collins v Wilcock* in confirming the basic principle that any slight touching may amount to a battery but that 'nobody can complain of the jostling which is inevitable from his presence in, for example, a supermarket, an underground station or a busy street; nor can a person who attends a party complain if his hand is seized in friendship, or even if his back is (within reason) slapped'.

- Conclude that there is a general rule that the low level of harm incurred in the application of a battery may be expressly or even impliedly consented to but may otherwise be unlawful.

Question 2

- Refer to the offences defined in Source 1.

- Discuss the major criticisms of the offences made in the 1993 and 1998 Law Commission Reports:
  - complicated, obscure and old-fashioned language difficult for juries to understand, e.g. occasioning, inflict, actual bodily harm, grievous, malicious, etc.;
  - complicated and technical structure (a huge Act with many sections and offences);
  - complete unintelligibility to the layman.

- Discuss the fact that the boundaries between the offences in terms of the level of injury are very vague even when applying CPS charging standards and this may lead to inconsistent charging.

- Discuss the idea that 'wounding' is a superfluous offence; it is either actual bodily harm or serious harm.

- Consider the criticism that the *mens rea* may not adequately justify conviction through the *actus reus*, e.g. a person who foresees slight injury may still be convicted of s.20 – inflicting serious harm.

- Discuss the potential sentencing conflict where s.47 and the more serious s.20 both attract a maximum five-year sentence.

- Discuss the draft Offences Against the Person Bill 1998 and the new offences proposed: assault; intentional or reckless injury; reckless serious injury; intentional serious injury.

- Discuss the way in which the courts have creatively developed and adapted the old existing law:
  - recognising psychiatric injury (*Chan-Fook*; *Ireland*; *Burstow*; *Constanza*);
  - recognising sexually transmissible diseases (*Dica*; *Feston*; *Konzani*).

Question 3

In the case of (a):

- Identify that the broken ankle may amount to either actual bodily harm (s.47) or, more seriously, grievous bodily harm (s.20).

- Recognise that, although consent is not normally available as a defence to a charge of either s.47 or s.18, there are exceptions to the general rule.

- Identify the fact that Sandra and Lily are participating in a contact sport and this falls within one of the exceptions (*Billinghurst*; *Barnes*).

- Conclude that Sandra is unlikely to be liable for any offence.

In the case of (b):

- Discuss the level and nature of harm suffered by Lily.

- Consider a potential s.18 offence of causing grievous bodily harm with intent.

- Reason that there appears to be clear evidence that by hitting Lily in the face with a hockey stick Sandra intended to cause serious harm to Lily (*Saunders*).

- Discuss whether a defence of consent could apply.

- Reason that Sandra is clearly going beyond the rules of the game of hockey and is liable to be convicted of a s.18 offence (*Barnes*).

In the case of (c):

- Identify that surgery would normally involve intentional wounding/ serious harm by the surgeon contrary to s.18.

- Recognise that, although consent is not normally available as a defence to a charge of either wounding or serious harm contrary to s.18, there are exceptions to the general rule.

- Identify that surgery is regarded as being for the benefit of patients and consent is normally a valid defence unless obtained by fraud or negligence.

- Discuss whether Dr Feelwell's negligence would mean that Sandra cannot be held liable for Lily becoming paralysed.

- Conclude that Dr Feelwell's negligence, although not completely independent of Sandra's initial assault, may well be so potent and overwhelming a factor as to consign Sandra's contribution to the mere history of the case (*Cheshire*).

- Discuss the fact that, although negligent and liable in civil law, there is unlikely to be sufficient *mens rea* for criminal liability.

- Conclude that there may be no criminal liability for this injury.

30 Suggested answers to OCR Section C Objective questions

Question 2 suggested answer

Statement A: Andrew is liable for occasioning actual bodily harm to Wayne.

- Identify that a bruise may amount to an assault occasioning actual bodily harm contrary to s.47 Offences Against the Person Act 1947.

- Consider whether it satisfies the test of 'interfering with the health and comfort of the victim' (*Miller*).

- Concussion may amount to 'serious harm' and a s.20 or s.18 charge.

- Consider whether Andrew has caused the injury either recklessly or intentionally.

- Conclude that, in either case, Andrew may be liable as s.47 and s.20 may be committed on proof of at least subjective recklessness in the *Cunningham* sense.

Statement B: Wayne is liable for intentionally causing the broken ankle sustained by Andrew.

- Identify that a broken ankle may amount to 'serious harm' and could be charged under either s.18 or s.20 Offences Against the Person Act 1947.

- Consider the possibility that Wayne has caused the injury either recklessly or intentionally.

- Conclude that if it is 'reckless' it satisfies the definition in s.20 of 'maliciously' inflicting serious harm. If it is intentional then Wayne may be liable for a s.18 offence.

Statement C: Andrew has a defence of consent for any charge brought by Wayne.

- Identify that consent may be available as a defence for any charge brought by Wayne.

- Explain that physical contact sports are an exception to the rule that consent is not available to harm above the level of common assault (*A-G's Ref No.6 1980*).

- Consider that Andrew will be liable only if he caused Wayne's injuries 'outside the rules of the sport' either intentionally or recklessly.

- Conclude that Andrew has a potential defence of consent.

Statement D: Wayne has a defence of automatism for any charge brought by Andrew.

- Identify that automatism may be available as a defence for Wayne.

- Explain that automatism is a defence for acts done by the muscles with no control by the mind.

- Conclude that Wayne has a potential defence of automatism if his acts were as a result of his concussion and not intentional or reckless (*Bratty*).

Question 3 suggested answer

Statement A: Brian is liable for robbery when he forces Adrian to hand him £10.

- Reason that the offence of robbery involves the use or threat of force in order to steal.

- Reason that 'steal' requires the completion of the offence of theft.

- Reason that Barry may honestly believe that he has the legal right to demand that Adrian repay the debt owed by his wife.

- Reason that no theft may in fact have occurred.

- Conclude that if there is no theft there can be no robbery.

Statement B: Brian is liable for robbery when he snatches at Carol's bag.

- Reason that the offence of robbery involves the use or threat of force in order to steal.

- Reason that theft requires an appropriation of property belonging to another.

- Reason that the merest touching of another's property has been held to amount to an appropriation.

- Reason that the word 'force' includes the slightest touch, nudge or tugging of a bag in someone's grasp even if the property is not taken.

- Conclude that Brian commits robbery here.

Statement C: Brian is liable for robbery in the supermarket.

- Reason that 'steal' requires the completion of the offence of theft.

- Reason that a theft occurs when Brian places the whisky in his coat since he is committing an unauthorised act to which the supermarket does not consent.

- Reason that leaving the shop without paying is conclusive evidence of his dishonest intention to permanently deprive.

- Reason that pushing Dan satisfies the element of force and since appropriation may be a continuing act he uses that force in order to steal and the force need not be used only against the owner of the property.

- Conclude that Brian is guilty of robbery.

Statement D: Brian is guilty of robbery when he drives his car at Elvis.

- Reason that the offence of robbery involves the use or threat of force in order to steal.

- Reason that 'steal' requires the completion of the offence of theft.

- Reason that an appropriation may be a continuing act and that therefore theft may be a continuing offence.

- Reason that driving the car at Elvis amounts to a threat of force.

- Consider that, as a question of fact, the theft of the whisky may already have been completed by this time.

- Conclude that robbery may or may not have occurred but Brian is at least guilty of theft.

Question 4 suggested answer

Statement A: Angelo is able to successfully plead the defence of duress if charged with robbery.

- Reason that the defence of duress is available when the threats made are threats of death or serious harm, and this is not the case.

- Reason that a threat to reveal criminal associations will not be sufficient to constitute the threat.

- Reason that duress by threats is available only where the crime committed has been nominated by the threatener.

- Reason that Colin has not nominated any type of criminal offence to be committed by Angelo.

- Conclude that duress is definitely unavailable as a defence to the robbery.

Statement B: Angelo is able to successfully plead the defence of duress to the assault on Ethan.

- Reason that the defence of duress is available when the threats made are threats of death or serious harm and this is present.

- Reason that the crime to be committed has been nominated by Desmond.

- Reason that the threat must be imminent and that this may or may not be the case as Desmond is in Italy, but other gang members in England may be able to carry out the threat.

- Conclude that duress is not available because Angelo has voluntarily associated himself with a criminal organisation.

Statement C: Angelo is able to successfully plead the defence of duress of circumstances to a potential charge of dangerous driving.

- Reason that the defence of duress of circumstances is available to a motoring offence when the threats made are threats of death or serious harm.

- Reason that the threat must be such that they overbear Angelo's will and would be sufficient to cause a reasonable person to succumb to them.

- Reason that the threat may no longer be real as he has carried out the assault on Ethan.

- Conclude that duress of circumstances may or may not be available.

Statement D: Angelo is able to successfully plead the defence of duress to a charge of murder or attempted murder of his wife.

- Reason that the defence of duress is available when the threats made are threats of death or serious harm.

- Reason that the threat to harm a close family member is potentially sufficient and capable of being carried out.

- Reason that policy dictates that there is sufficient time to inform the police of the threat.

- Reason that, after all, duress is never allowed as a defence to murder or attempted murder.

- Conclude that whether Angelo's wife dies or not, the defence is not available to him.

Question 5 suggested answer

Statement A: Erica can be charged with murder.

- Reason that a person is liable for murder where they cause the death of a reasonable creature in being with 'malice aforethought', an intention to do or cause at least serious harm.

- Reason that Erica intended to cause at least serious harm to Bob because she smashes a heavy object onto his head.

- Identify that this is clearly a case of direct intent to cause at least serious harm.

- Conclude that she is liable to face a murder charge.

Statement B: Erica may successfully plead intoxication as a defence.

- Reason that there is evidence of intoxication as Erica has consumed several glasses of whisky and it may have prevented the formation of the *mens rea*.

- Reason that murder is a specific intent offence and that intoxication may reduce a murder conviction to manslaughter since it may allow a partial defence to a specific intent offence applying the 'fall back' position under the *Majewski* rules.

- Point out that if Erica formed the intent to kill prior to becoming intoxicated then the defence will not be available (*A-G for N.I. v Gallagher*).

- Conclude that Erica may have the defence of intoxication but the evidence suggests she still formed the intention to do at least serious harm.

Statement C: Erica cannot plead provocation as a defence.

- Reason that provocation is a special and partial defence to a murder charge resulting in a conviction for voluntary manslaughter if successfully pleaded.

- Reason that there is evidence of provocation in the final insult and previous cumulative history of provocation by Bob.

- Identify the fact that Erica has waited before she hits Bob and this could undermine her claim that her loss of control is sudden and temporary (*Thornton*; *Ahluwalia*).

- Refer to 'battered woman syndrome' (BWS) and reason that previous similar cases have been unsuccessful because there has been evidence of a 'cooling-off period'.

- Recognise that a mental characteristic such as 'depression' or 'BWS' affecting the power of self-control is apparently no longer applicable as a relevant characteristic when applying the 'reasonable man' test which affects the power of self-control rather than the gravity of the provocation to the accused (*Holley*).

• Conclude that a provocation defence may or may not be available.

Statement D: Erica will be successful if she pleads the defence of diminished responsibility.

• Reason that diminished responsibility is a special and partial defence to a murder charge resulting in a conviction for voluntary manslaughter if successfully pleaded.

• Reason that when charged with murder diminished responsibility requires an abnormality of mind that substantially impairs one's responsibility for one's actions.

• Reason that 'battered woman syndrome' has now been recognised as a genuine psychiatric condition and constitutes 'abnormality of the mind'.

• Reason that Erica needs medical evidence to support this defence and she appears to have this.

• Conclude that she may be able to use diminished responsibility as a defence.

Question 6 suggested answer

Statement A: Valentino is liable for attempted burglary when he tries to break into the caravan.

• Reason that an attempt may be charged where the intended substantive offence is not completed.

• Reason that trying to force open the caravan door appears to be an act that is arguably 'more than merely preparatory' to the intended offence.

• Reason that Valentino appears to have the required intention to commit the intended offence.

• Reason that a burglary must involve entry into a 'building or part of a building'.

• Reason that a caravan may be an inhabited vehicle.

• Conclude that it may therefore amount to an attempted burglary.

Statement B: Valentino is liable for attempted murder when he squeezes the trigger.

- Reason that an attempt may be charged where the intended substantive offence is not completed.

- Reason that the *actus reus* of attempted murder appears to be satisfied since Valentino has not only pointed the gun but has gone as far as squeezing the trigger.

- Reason that this amounts to an act that is therefore capable of being more than merely preparatory to the commission of an intended offence.

- Reason that even though the commission of the intended offence is factually impossible (the gun is not loaded) Valentino could nevertheless be convicted of attempting the impossible.

- Recognise, however, that only an intention to kill is sufficient for a charge of attempted murder.

- Conclude that Valentino may be convicted of attempted murder if he intended to kill Ahmed.

Statement C: Valentino is liable for attempted robbery when he enters the bank.

- Reason that an attempt may be charged where the intended substantive offence is not completed.

- Reason that Valentino has the required intention to commit a theft accompanied by threats of force in order to steal and therefore to commit robbery when he enters the shop.

- Reason, however, that he has probably not done an act that is 'more than merely preparatory to the commission of the intended substantive offence'. Reason, therefore, that he has not yet 'embarked upon the crime proper'.

- Conclude that he is therefore not guilty of attempted robbery.

Statement D: Valentino is liable for attempted theft when he picks up the wallet.

- Reason that a dishonest appropriation has occurred when Valentino picks up the wallet since it is property belonging to another and at that moment he has a dishonest intention to permanently deprive the owner of either the wallet or the contents or both.

- Reason that Valentino is attempting the factually impossible with regard to the contents but still has a conditional intention and this is enough.

- Reason that there may be a completed theft of the wallet if he had the accompanying intention to permanently deprive when he appropriated.

- Reason that he may be liable for an attempted theft of the contents even though there were none to steal.

Glossary

ABH
Actual Bodily Harm. The offence of assault occasioning actual bodily harm is found in s.47 of OAPA.

Actus reus
Latin expression, meaning all the elements of a criminal offence not including the *mens rea*. Depending on the particular crime, this could include the defendant's conduct (e.g. in theft, D must appropriate property), and/or the consequences of D's act (e.g. in murder and manslaughter, D must cause the death of another human being), and/or the circumstances at the time (e.g. in theft, the property must belong to someone else).

Aiding and abetting
To assist in a criminal offence. Aiding refers to providing help at any time (e.g. supplying equipment, acting as lookout, driving a getaway car); abetting refers to encouragement provided at the time of the offence.

Assault
To cause another person to believe that they are about to suffer immediate bodily contact.

Attorney-General's Reference
A case will be referred to the Court of Appeal (Criminal Division) by the Attorney-General (the government's main legal adviser) when he believes that a Crown Court judge misapplied the law resulting in an acquittal. The acquittal may not be reversed but it gives the judges of the Court of Appeal an opportunity to correct any mistakes for the benefit of Crown Court judges in future cases.

Basic intent offence
Describes any one of the group of criminal offences (e.g. manslaughter, assault) to which intoxication is not a defence.

Battery
The application of unlawful force to another person.

Butler Committee
A Committee set up in the 1970s to report on mentally abnormal offenders.

BWS
Battered Woman Syndrome. A recognised (since 1994)

mental disease, affecting victims of sustained domestic abuse (physical and psychological). Relevance in criminal law terms as (a) an abnormality of mind for the purposes of diminished responsibility; (b) a characteristic for the purposes of the objective question in provocation.

CJA   Criminal Justice Act.

Causation/chain of causation

The link between a defendant's conduct and a consequence. Most often discussed in murder/manslaughter cases, where the issue is whether D caused the victim's death.

Consent   General defence, whereby the victim expressly or impliedly (that is, by conduct) agrees to the risk of injury.

Counselling   Encouraging someone to commit a criminal offence.

Court for Crown Cases Reserved

A forerunner of the Court of Appeal, this court no longer exists.

Court of Criminal Appeal/Court of Appeal (Criminal Division)

Prior to 1967 there were two English appeal courts, the Court of Appeal (which dealt with civil matters) and the Court of Criminal Appeal. In 1967 the two courts were amalgamated into the modern Court of Appeal, albeit divided into the Civil Division and Criminal Division.

Criminal Code Bill (1989)

The Law Commission's proposal to place all of English criminal law (general principles, offences and defences) into one legislative document. The Bill is attached to the end of the Commission's Report, *A Criminal Code for England and Wales* (Law Commission Report No.177). Although similar reforms have taken place in Canada and New Zealand, in England the Code Bill remains in draft form, with no legal status. This is mainly due to the lack of political will necessary to push such a major reform through Parliament.

Criminal Law Bill (1993)

The Law Commission's less ambitious proposal to place the non-fatal offences and certain general defences on a statutory basis. It was attached to the end of the Commission's Report *Legislating the Criminal Code: Offences Against the Person and General Principles* (Law Commission Report No.218). This Bill also remains in draft form, with no legal status.

Criminal Law Revision Committee (CLRC)	An English law reform body, comprising mainly judges and leading academics, specialising in criminal law. Not to be confused with the Criminal Cases Review Commission (CCRC), established in 1995.
Cunningham recklessness	See: Recklessness.
Defendant	A person charged with a criminal offence (the accused).
Divisional Court	The Divisional Court of the Queen's Bench Division of the High Court hears appeals from magistrates' courts brought by either the Crown (appealing against acquittals) or the defence (appealing against convictions). These appeals are known as 'appeals by way of case stated' and involve questions on points of law only.
DPP	The Director of Public Prosecutions is the head of the Crown Prosecution Service.
Duty of care	A legal responsibility placed upon the defendant to act in a particular set of circumstances.
GBH	Grievous Bodily Harm. The offence of inflicting grievous bodily harm is found in s.20 of OAPA, and that of causing grievous bodily harm with intent is found in s.18 OAPA.
Ghosh test	The test for establishing dishonesty in crimes such as theft, making off, obtaining property or obtaining services by deception.
Intention	One type of *mens rea*. Comes in two forms: direct intent (meaning desire) and oblique intent (meaning the situation where D foresees a consequence as virtually certain to occur, whether s/he desires it or not).
Joint enterprise	The situation where two or more persons embark upon a criminal operation (typically burglary) together.
Law Commission	An English law reform body, established in 1965, whose job it is to review all aspects of law (not just criminal law) and, where it feels that reform is required, produce reports, including draft legislation. For the purposes of this book, its most interesting reports are *A Criminal Code for England and Wales* in 1989 (Law Commission Report No.177), which included the draft Criminal Code Bill, and *Legislating the Criminal Code: Offences*

437

Against the Person and General Principles in 1993 (Law Commission Report No. 218), which included the draft Criminal Law Bill.

M'Naghten Rules A set of 'rules' established by the judges of the House of Lords in 1843 to deal with cases where a defendant pleads not guilty by reason of insanity. Although technically not of the same legal status as a judicial decision, they have been regarded as legally binding for over 150 years.

Majewski Rules The legal principles covering the intoxication defence.

Manslaughter The unlawful, but unintentional, killing of another human being.

Mens rea The mental element of any criminal offence. Includes intention, recklessness, dishonesty, gross negligence. Most offences satisfied with one of these but some require two (e.g. theft requires a dishonest intention) while others require none at all (crimes of strict liability).

Model Penal Code This is literally a 'model' for a comprehensive, criminal code, produced by the American Law Institute. It contains statements of general principles, definitions of offences and defences. The 50 US states are free to choose whether to adopt all or some of the Code into legislation as they feel appropriate.

Murder The unlawful, and intentional, killing of another human being.

Novus actus Latin expression, dealing with causation, and referring to any external and independent event, sufficient to break the chain of causation that would otherwise exist connecting D's conduct with a particular consequence.

Obiter Statements made by judges in court that are 'by the way'. They do not form part of the ratio, and are not therefore legally binding, but may be highly persuasive, on judges deciding future cases.

Oblique intent A state of mind where D appreciates that his conduct is virtually certain to lead to a particular conclusion (whether or not that conclusion was desired).

OAPA 1861 The Offences Against the Person Act 1861.

Privy Council   The final appeal court for those Commonwealth coun-
                      tries that wish to use it. Over time, many of the larger
                      Commonwealth countries (including Australia, Canada
                      and South Africa) have dropped the Privy Council, but
                      it is still used by New Zealand and Singapore, among
                      others. Its decisions are not binding but, because the
                      Court comprises the same judges as the House of Lords,
                      are highly persuasive on English courts.

Procuring   To take steps to enable someone else to commit a
                      criminal offence.

Ratio   The legally binding part of any court judgment.

Recklessness   One type of *mens rea*. It requires D to have foreseen the
                      risk of some prohibited consequence occurring, but
                      went ahead and took that risk anyway. Sometimes
                      referred to as Cunningham recklessness or subjective
                      recklessness. Applies to arson, criminal damage, non-
                      fatal offences against the person and involuntary man-
                      slaughter.

Specific intent offence   Describes any one of the group of criminal offences (e.g.
                      murder, theft) to which intoxication is a defence.

Strict liability Describes all offences where D may be convicted on
                      proof of *actus reus* alone – *mens rea* not required.

Subjective recklessness   See: Recklessness.

Index